MORAL CLAIMS IN WORLD AFFAIRS

MORAL CLAIMS IN WORLD AFFAIRS

EDITED BY RALPH PETTMAN

CROOM HELM LONDON

©1979 Ralph Pettman
Croom Helm Ltd, 2-10 St John's Road, London SW11

British Library Cataloguing in Publication Data

Moral claims in world affairs
1. International relations – Moral and
religious aspects
I. Pettman, Ralph
172'.4   JX1308

ISBN 0-85664-731-4

Printed in Great Britain by
Biddles Ltd, Guildford, Surrey

CONTENTS

PREFACE

Establishing national needs and the policies that flow from them as
not only contingent or expedient (often, indeed, *despite* questions of
contingency or expediency) but also 'right' and 'due', is meant to lend
them a special and pervasive force. Statesmen alert their audiences in
this way to the fact that whatever the claims being made, they pertain
to more than reflex or merely reasoned matters, but moral ones as well.
They signal an emphatic commitment, a state of enhanced resolve.
Whatever is claimed merits close consideration, since it will carry more
than its ordinary load of the values that any deed or decision affirms or
denies.

For reasons like these practitioners of world affairs are tempted to
invest even their most commonplace behaviour with a sense of moral
sanctity. This tends over time to debase the currency, and negate any
added significance the force of a moral as opposed to an incidental or
instrumental demand might convey. The effect of a sense of righteous-
ness or of unmet obligation comes to be lost; statesmen themselves are
accused of cant or nationalistic self-justification. And yet the practice
persists, and the charge of hypocrisy is vigorously denied.

The rise of the modern nation-state in a system that is 'ungoverned'
in the more familiar sense is one obvious reason for the continued
existence of these rather more fervent overtones to world affairs.
Political sovereignty predisposes ethical sovereignty. The representatives
of countries that compete for predominance or for privileged access to
scarce resources will tend to buttress their behaviour in morally exclusiv-
ist as well as nationalistic terms. Individuals and groups within or without such countries, pressing rival claims to speak on behalf of some or
all of the people, will likewise appeal to standards transcending those
defined by ruling elites. Leaders of weaker states on the one hand,
whether self-established or possessing some more general mandate, will
declaim their moral superiority and thereby seek to compensate for the
frustrations and insecurities inherent in their lack of tangible power.
They will assert their 'due' share of global assets and reserves in the face
of those who monopolise them, and lay 'rightful' claim to idiosyncratic
objectives with a sense of conviction not apparent in their expressions
of 'interest' alone. Stronger states on the other hand will reinforce their
manifest power with declarations of moral intent, and resist any

contentions they find contrary on the implicit or explicit grounds that
such claims remain uninformed by the greater power's own superior
vision of the good world. This vision is never depicted as a purely
private one however. It is usually understood to possess public relevance to the global populace at large.

The following collection of essays is specifically addressed to this
question of partisan cosmopolitanism. Though not a novel ingress it is
a neglected one, and much might be done to elucidate parochial pan-
demics and their relevance for and impact upon the present-day world.
A preliminary attempt might also be made to pass behind the plethora
of competing value systems to delineate the general nature of moral
claims, and their consequences for global equity and order. Here we
perceive the possible emergence of a universal moral realm, based upon
the notion of distributive justice perhaps. To go beyond this would be
to offer some idea of what the substantive dictates of such a realm might
be; suggest the sort of area from which its logical justification might be
drawn; and examine the systemic level at which it is likely to be
achieved. The field is obviously a large and important one, and though
a comprehensive discussion would require more than a single volume,
an attempt has been made to confront some of these central issues in a
coherent and representative way.

Part One outlines a number of the conceptual areas in which contemporary debates proceed. Ralph Pettman attempts in an introductory
fashion to outline something of the scope of the subject and of the
various forays that have been made to rescue a single body of human
ideals from the multitude of possible systems that now prevail. The
tension between the 'statist' and 'class' paradigms of the world
system are indicated as analytically central in this regard. J.D.B. Miller
denies the applicability of ordinary moral considerations to world
affairs, citing group rather than universal ethics as the immediate source
of human behaviour, and 'reasons of state' rather than the brotherhood
of man as the operative principle in global politics. John Vincent
elaborates this basically 'realist' position, highlighting the whole
question of realism versus idealism, the value of equality, and the force
of the doctrine of human rights. He sketches clearly the nature of
dissent about the relevant 'levels' involved (that of the individual, the
state, and the 'society' of states as a whole), while opting for the
second of these levels as the one within which moral claims will be met.
Hedley Bull then addresses the issue of 'human rights' and attempts to
establish what they are, what special questions they raise in the contemporary political arena, and what, in general, we should do about them.

He argues that in terms of world politics the doctrine is a troubled one
and that because *a priori* universal principles of an objective kind do
not exist, ethical expectations derived from the Western experience will
not necessarily find acceptance in the wider world. Hugh Smith
endorses his verdict. The notion of levels is canvassed again, with a
detailed discussion of the single issue of 'justice' (which he places prior
to that of morality in the political realm), and the attempts that have
been made to apply this issue beyond the realm of the nation-state. It is
the state in the end, he argues, that is the most effective distributor of
moral as well as material goods. Arthur Burns resurrects the dichotomy
of 'good' and 'evil' as a necessary complement to the more familiar
ethical distinction between 'justice' and 'injustice', and relates what he
sees as a scriptural theme to the practice of armed collectives. 'Injustice',
he says, 'has its place solely in the dimension of actions and institutions;
but evil belongs also to the dimension of disposition, and indeed has its
source there. . . . Injustice can sometimes be redressed by action, and
free men are under constant obligation to do so. Evil can only be
redeemed.' And to demonstrate the malignant or salutary nature of
contemporary Western beliefs he concentrates upon one theme in
particular: the 'balance of terror' and its contribution to global peace.

Part Two adopts a more concrete perspective. Here moral claims are
considered *in situ*, as they emerge from specific situations that involve
important moral conflicts, and as they are represented in the policies
of two of the Powers. Jan Pettman reviews the complex values that
contend in the African, and particularly the Southern African arena.
The compromising presence of comprador elites, and the manifest
failure of African countries to extricate themselves from external domination and exploitation, has been reflected in the shift, especially
among radical liberation movements, from demands for 'black government' only to demands for social revolution throughout. The widespread ideological reperception required is unlikely to come about,
however, and even more so for those who live under the influence of
the monolithic racist regimes of the south. Claims by African leaders
and their opponents for moral as well as political-economic autonomy
can only be understood in this light. Michael Yahuda selects, in his discussion of China's foreign policy, from a broad range of ethical precepts
lodged therein. The idea he elaborates is that of independence or 'self-
renewal' — a concept, he maintains, which conveys a profound moral
belief, which derives from extended historical experience, and
represents a singular and germane aspect of the Chinese view of a

revised political-economic global order. Though not without its ambiguities and ultimately subordinate, in the Maoist canon at least, to the theory of permanent revolution, China's leaders have sought to edify others, and in particular the inhabitants of the Third World, with this widely disseminated creed. Vendulka Kubálková examines the Soviet concept of morality. She looks, too, at its ideological character, its Marxist heritage, and its fertile 'New Marxist' derivations. An appreciation of the vagaries of ethical philosophy since the Russian Revolution, an acquaintance with the working categories and concepts that have provided the framework and many of the puzzles for Soviet thinkers, the features of the 'moral code' of the party Programme of 1961, are all basic to our comprehension of Soviet belief and behaviour. Contemporary notions like that of 'peaceful coexistence' take on added significance as a result.

It hardly pre-empts what is to follow to say that moral claims are made by diverse actors in global affairs, to multifarious purpose and effect. The self-conscious sense of a supranational system that is said to have characterised the European order of the nineteenth century, or at least, that sense of a shared culture and values displayed by European elites in their dealings with each other, is commonly held to exist no more. Hence the premium often placed upon effective diplomacy. The most strident claims today, however, are those made by representatives of the Third and Fourth Worlds, and these both reinforce and compromise the picture of mankind as one of segmented 'states'. They not only represent the voices of disadvantaged leaders who seek a redistribution of global power, but they help identify an emergent world system of 'horizontal' connections that arches over the considerable expanse of the globe where 'state' is a euphemism for whatever regime is recognised as such by other 'states', irrespective of the social and economic structures the geographic 'boundaries' contain. Reification of the 'state' leads to a definition of the minimal content of a universal morality in terms of common acceptance alone, and fails to accommodate the degree of supra-statal co-operation already necessary to exploit more or less discrete populations, and to protect the living standards of affluent countries and Third World elites. And though claims upon the populations of rich states assume an answer in nation-state form, one should ask by whom such answers are actually received? Who makes 'Third World' claims? And ultimately on whose behalf? The twentieth-century notion of a pluralistic world is one that, beyond a certain as yet ill-defined point, loses its explanatory power. And a complementary structuralist perception of world politics would be the practical basis for a neo-universalist morality built out of a measure of rational utility and of human requirements, rather than the more familiar contemporary dictates of established access, dishonesty and greed.

PART ONE: THEORY

1 MORAL CLAIMS IN WORLD POLITICS

Ralph Pettman

Moral discourse is an integral aspect of any political conversation. The intrinsic character of the moral dimension makes it all the more surprising, then, when we find how little academic attention has been paid to moral claims in world affairs, and this particularly so given the post-behavioural plea for a return to matters of 'value' as well as 'fact',[1] the emergence of the issue of justice in the confrontation rhetoric between the global North and South, and the moves made by American President Carter into the realm of human rights. What *are* the claims, we may ask, made by key actors who dominate the scene, or made on behalf of those who lurk still half-regarded in the wings? Which claims seem justified, and how *are* they justified, and what general criteria for justification might there be? How do such claims conflict and how are they reconciled? What sanctions do they stand on? What lessons from the study of human societies in their diversity, and from the contemplation of the human condition in general, can be brought to bear? Is it really appropriate for statements about world politics to be couched in terms of 'morality' at all?

One can think of many reasons for the lack of attention noted above. There is the tendency, for example, to dismiss moral claims as moralism or as nothing but the rationalisation of interests and desires (a cynical and reductionist stance in this form). There is the problem of establishing standards by which to judge the applicability of a moral system in any particular case.[2] There are, furthermore, the serious meta-ethical problems one encounters in judging the content of a moral system itself, and in establishing what the status of 'right' or 'good' as opposed to 'wrong' or 'evil' propositions might entail.[3] Perhaps, too, there is an insidious sense of irrelevance at work, of man as 'trivial, arrogant, and a little mad'.[4] 'The great world,' Bertrand Russell argued, 'as far as we know it from the philosophy of nature, is neither good nor bad, and is not concerned to make us happy or unhappy. All such philosophies spring from self-importance and are best corrected by a little astronomy.'[5]

There is another more obvious explanation for such neglect. Moral expectations are continually disappointed in the confused realm of practical politics, partly because global dilemmas seem different and often incompatible with those we encounter on an individual plane. 'Power'

and 'morality' tend to be dichotomised as a result, and the former is
placed prior to the latter in understanding global affairs. And yet moral
expectations persist, and continuous attempts are made to close the gap
between the political levels of analysis and to discover in mankind one
moral community — one ethic-bearing whole.

It would accommodate a transatlantic propensity still prevalent
today for clarifying meanings and the complex loan of language, to begin
by asking what the character of moral propositions in general might be,
at least as represented by the debates that have been waged in the West
since the Greeks developed the subject two and a half millennia ago.

The Greek legacy is obviously profound.[6] Socrates and the Sophists
attempted in their own way to press important distinctions between a
subjective and an objective realm, to discriminate between fact and
value, between personal affirmation, social consensus and 'natural'
decree. Prised apart in this way, meta-ethical discussion has been
dominated ever since by attempts either to bridge the gaps these dicho-
tomies represent or to resist such engineering and to drive the splintered
bank-works further apart.

Greek philosophers sought reasons for moral claims other than those
of tradition and use. Some seemed to say much more. Through
thought alone, they argued, men might recover moral precepts satisfying the concerns of both the individual and the community at the
same time. The definitive statement of a set of principles acceptable to
all eluded them, though the idea of such a set has been held before
theorists ever since, and before the 'practical' men that theorists held in
thrall.

It was Plato who helped most to consolidate a lasting vision of a
moral universe not only accessible to human reason but orderly, harmo-
nious and pure.[7] Against Socratic critiques he erected an abstract
intuition of Forms, of ideals inspired by the logic of mathematics that
laid up eternal standards whereby human conduct might be assessed. In
response, Aristotle arrived at a 'naturalistic' doctrine that was not only
more pragmatic and more tolerant of human diversity, but also sought
rather the satisfaction, albeit in a regular and rational way, of human
desires — the happy fulfilment of such personal capacities as naturally
obtain. Though contemporary assessments of what has become a
perennial debate have seen among other things that attempt to disown
it altogether, in one notable case as the unfortunate consequence of
linguistic ambiguity,[8] it would seem that there is ample scope still for
diverse perspectives, neither bound to personal predilections that prove
irrelevant in the social sphere, nor predicated upon a public philosophy

oblivious to private capacity or need.[9]

'Morals' are social products, held out of habit and self-interest to be sure, but motivated also by emphatic urges like love, and a sense of what is right and due. Human beings learn to prefer particular ways of relating to each other, and standards by which to assess their relationships and to endorse or censure what appear to be sociable or anti-social acts, as part of the general educative process whereby they assimilate expectations of how the world is meant to be. On the whole they seem to value the company and support of their more immediate fellows. Human survival depends upon reciprocal assistance, and a communitarian impulse is a (phylogenetically valuable, even perhaps by now a predetermined)[10] means to this end. Whatever the general motive, however, and whatever we may make of their fundamentals, the resultant behavioural preferences differ greatly in detail from group to group, and they change over time in response to changes in the 'culture' or its environment. In an important sense ordinary morality is largely inapplicable at the level of world affairs. Human identification is mostly quite immediate, and on the whole we donate our moral allegiancies to the group to which we feel we primarily belong. The moral codes that such groups practice and defend serve group interests, and moral conflicts are inevitably group conflicts as well.

One important problem in the study of world politics, then, is to determine how far the communitarian impulse does or should extend. What unit of analysis may be considered the most appropriate vehicle for moral claims — the individual, the group, the state (and those transnational institutions that possess at least some state-like characteristics), humankind as a whole, or classes of humankind defined in other than geo-political ways (by 'culture', for example, or by their relationship to the economic and productive forces that might underpin social forms)? 'Appropriate' with respect to what criteria? Given the constant threat of nuclear war or the emergent one of global ecological collapse, the contemporary moral constituency may now be one far removed from the cause of our immediate political concerns, including, it may be argued, the multitudes of those unborn. If a minority holds the power to preserve or destroy the human race as a whole, it may well be enjoined, in principle at least, with obligations to individuals quite remote from it in time and space. Sentiments like these commonly inspire the sort of rhetorical statements that affirm human solidarity.[11] They are rhetorical because global practice reflects competitive values and the radical historical process whereby European patterns have been firmly impressed upon the socio-political configuration of the world.

Are they relevant, however?

I would like to look more closely at what this configuration might be, and its possible consequence for moral claims. There is first, however, the more general question about the impact of present-day knowledge upon social structures, and the properties implicit in the concept of a 'modernised' man. Some brief discussion of these properties is warranted before turning to world affairs as such.

Most people are hard-pressed, it seems, to empathise with those not immediately associated with them. There are good reasons for this, partly to do with questions of scale. In the large societies that contemporary systems of industrial production can now support, we tend to think of ourselves as autonomous and isolate, with duties to carry out and entitlements to affirm.[12] In smaller ones, however, it becomes easier to appreciate the workings of 'effective mutuality'[13] and the reciprocal consequences in what people claim and do. If the criterion for assessing our acts is the 'sociality' of them, then the purely personal and selfish ones are more likely to be repressed in more intimate surroundings and less likely then to operate at cost to our confreres. 'The hunter and gatherer [for example] is lucky: he does not have the choice . . . what for us are virtues are, for him, necessities. We have the choice, and although we insist on intellectually maintaining those same virtues, the discrepancy between them and daily practice becomes increasingly great.'[14]

One key phenomenon here is that termed by Max Weber 'rationalisation'; implicit in present-day modes of managing economies and states is a profound preference for regularised means toward the attainment of preordained ends. 'Indeed, technique transforms ends into means',[15] seemingly independent of what we might otherwise intend. Thus, for example: 'Technical economic analysis is substituted for the older political economy included in which was a major concern with the moral structure of economic activity . . . Politics in turn becomes an arena for contention among rival techniques . . . Purposes drop out of sight and efficiency becomes the central concern.'[16]

Describing the process whereby human beings have become the victims of a technicised economy and a bureaucratic state, rendered, that is, progressively more alienated and anonymous, has become a sociological industry in its own right. These ideas, however, stem in the Westernised world from a deeper critique again. Built into modern science is a pitiless and impassive vision of fate that springs originally from the Greek tragedians and the Ionian world-view. Beside this heritage ran a naive revolt against the medieval scholastic divines that issued in a non-rational faith in the order of things, a faith science has 'never cared to justify or to explain' and one that has remained 'blandly indifferent to its refutation by Hume'.[17] This revolt presupposes as ultimate fact 'an irreducible . . . material, spread throughout space . . . senseless, valueless, purposeless . . . following a fixed routine imposed by external relations which do not spring from the nature of its being'.[18] All of which may have proved enormously productive in understanding physical, chemical and biological events but has had ambiguous consequences for society at large. Whatever instrumental advances now obtain, such a powerful presupposition has generated universalistic truths quite remote from ordinary human experience — a source of liberation and enrichment, but paradoxically one of impoverishment as well. It has sought explicit parallels between social and material affairs, and applied like methodological precepts to both.

Many analysts have now drawn attention to the repressive effects of technological civilisation, and severely qualified the equation intrinsic to the spirit of the age that 'science = reason = all good things'.[19] 'To what lengths will public faith in the wisdom and prowess of the technocracy extend?' Roszak enquires. He answers his own question in very pessimistic terms. 'That faith has already demonstrated itself to be without limit or qualification. How else is one to interpret public compliance . . . with the policy of thermonuclear deterrence? Here is a technological system . . . on which we allow our very survival as a species to depend. It is a reckless commitment, predicated upon a willingness to do genocide which is the moral scandal of the age. Yet we take both the hazard and the ethical obscenity of the matter in our stride . . .'[20]

One may question this diagnosis in whole or in part. It is too pitiless, we reply, in its conception of science as a life-denying force. While closing down some options, technocratic and bureaucratised states may open up others; they are not only the constrained and homogenising agents they might on first glance appear. The pernicious effects of a preference for regularity and expediency is counter-balanced by the fact that many new demands are made upon our sense of responsibility and of judgement, and one should not overlook the sheer number of people such systems can sustain. The balance-of-terror, the cataclysm so graphically poised before contemporary consciousness, presents extreme danger indeed, *and* a range of solemn opportunities as well. The ethical debate about nuclear weapons testifies to this. Scientifically induced eco-crises may well condemn a global host to poverty and despair, but many more are also given the chance to ask

what their lives signify, and in their answers and foreign policies to
define what it means to be humane.

This can be only the most summary of conclusions, but allowing for
the fact that general questions about science and society are very diffuse
indeed, they do provide a much needed perspective upon particular
problems about contemporary political forms and the moral claims
these predispose. While such questions can be pursued no further here,
they permeate all else.

The most common conceptual paradigm in the discipline places primary
stress upon 'states' and 'nation-states'. This has led theorists to discriminate between political and personal ethics, between the moral
burdens of *states*men and those of their less strategically situated
fellows who do not have to secure the welfare of the political whole. It
is not far from a focus on the 'state' to doctrines that positively exalt
its global status, to *realpolitik*, for example, and the notion that the
most moral claims are those that preserve the national interest, however
and by whom this is defined. Such a notion does not necessarily deny
the effect of moral inhibitions upon what statesmen do. Many examples
may be cited of national leaders exercising restraint when 'necessity'
could have justified a round sweep with the flat of the blade. Enlightened self-interest is usually sufficient warning against crude power
politics alone since a completely amoral set of state leaders who disregard all the claims of others might find themselves less powerful
overall as the challenges they face grow apace. *Realpolitik* simply
asserts that successful governments will treat most ethical imperatives
as invalid, and acknowledge no obligation other than that of the
national estate.

Statesmen are nonetheless products of the communities they
represent and might be expected to carry into policy at least some of
the moral injunctions they have been encouraged to observe in
domestic spheres. We might logically suggest a compromise to cover
the ground between personal predilections and the expedients of
raison d'état. This compromise, Martin Wight has argued, seems
'peculiarly related to Western values'[21] (though he arrives at this
conclusion without a single reference to a non-Western system of
values). It assumes (1) 'that moral standards can be upheld without the
heavens falling'; (2) 'that the fabric of social and political life will be
maintained, without accepting the doctrine that to preserve it any
measures are permissible'; and (3) 'that the upholding of moral standards
will in itself tend to strengthen the fabric of political life'.[22] On the

whole, global practice retreats from such moderation. From the 'statist' perspective powerful leaders have often been tempted to present their political claims as uniquely valid and universal decrees. Value habits that depict 'communism' as diabolical and morally contemptible, for example, or 'capitalism' as wholly carnivorous and the soul of human greed, make for a lack of moral restraint. Once antagonists have been cast, cynically or sincerely, as not just different or inferior politically or ideologically, but as the incarnations of the anti-Christ, then 'we' are relieved of the responsibility of moral choice and 'their' assertions can be safely despised.[23] Following Wight, the usual reply under these conditions has been the counsel of prudence, the pointing out that moral principles are not the only guide to those charged with the task of choosing particular policies and that they are not enough when it comes to assessing the outcomes of such policies and their various and often conflicting value costs and consequences.[24]

Much of this debate turns upon the central problem of the 'means-ends' process. The fact that immoral means may be justified in pursuit of some greater good, such as the preservation of the state, was clearly expressed by Niccolo Machiavelli, and he has been used to document the cynics' position ever since. 'A prince', he argued, 'cannot observe all those things which are considered good in men; being often obliged, in order to maintain the state, to act against faith, against charity, against humanity, and against religion . . . he must . . . not deviate from what is good, if possible, but be able to do evil if constrained . . .'[25]

One can point to something much more important in Machiavelli's stance. Implicit in it is a direct attack on one enduring assumption of Western political thought, that of the existence of 'natural law'.[26] Machiavelli himself evaded this tradition, and his neglect was malignant not benign because the morality of the Christian world he saw as simply incompatible for a prince with the sort of secular morality that was necessary to build a secure state. As Isaiah Berlin has argued: 'The notion of Raison d'état entails a conflict of values — those of private and public morality . . . For Machiavelli there is no conflict. Public life has its own rules: to which Christian ethics is a gratuitous obstacle.'[27] There is more to this than the argument that love and goodness cannot be realised in public life, and that generous motives may well be foolish and dangerous when pursued in the context of interstate competition. It goes further than the separation of politics from ethics; 'it is the uncovering of the possibility of more than one ethical system with no criterion common to the systems, whereby a rational choice can be made between them',[28] and not only for princes, perhaps, but as a root condition of human life: 'Why should justice and mercy, humility and *virtu,* happiness and knowledge, glory and liberty, magnificence and sanctity, coincide or indeed be compatible at all?'[29] Why indeed? But deny the notion of an objective and generalised set of human ideals, and a cornerstone of the Western philosophical tradition falls to the ground.

One may see all this as the necessary preface to a desirable alternative, which, given a preference for scepticism and toleration, is the notion of liberal compromise. Monistic certainties breed political extremes but unbridled diversity leads to moderation and away from the definitive resolution of human affairs.

Others have not been content with such anaemic good sense and have sought to rescue something of the original, fundamentalist doctrine and its activist resolve. H.L.A. Hart, for example, posits a modest minimum to 'natural law' based upon the observation that 'most men most of the time' wish to survive, and that '[I]n the absence of this content men, as they are, would have no reason for obeying voluntarily any rules', and using the obedient to coerce the rest would not work.[30] Man's bodily vulnerability, approximate equality, limited altruistic capabilities, restricted access to resources, and qualified understanding and strength of will, enjoin, Hart argues, a 'natural' sanction against intra-specific slaughter, plus a fundamental respect for 'mutual forbearance and compromise' and the *necessity* of a system informed by precepts of this kind. To this he adds 'some minimal form of the institution of property (... not necessarily individual ...) and the distinctive kind of rule which requires respect for it', rules for the transfer, exchange and sale of the products of the division of human labour, 'recognition of promises as a source of obligation', and finally, '*voluntary* cooperation in a *coercive* system' as a protective guarantee against those who join but then seek to subvert the welfare of the whole.[31]

Except for personal sanctity and the propertarian ones the prescriptions given above are *procedural* only. One may seek for more substantive standards of a social or economic kind — minimal levels of health and nutritional wellbeing for example, without which life is not possible let alone enjoyed; and civil and political ones without which the means of material sustenance may never be secured. Thus Barrington Moore adopts as a 'working premise the moral position that human society ought to be organised in such a way as to eliminate useless suffering. . .'[32] There are problems with the notion of 'useless' suffering, since the fact of global 'development' may ultimately depend upon the human costs considered 'useful' or 'necessary' in the pursuit of economic strength or self-reliance. Measures of utility are closely related to those of political interest, and they change over time. Furthermore, though there *are* absolute needs that must be fulfilled for humans to survive, they do not always issue in self-evident standards that generally obtain. We need, in fact, not only a minimalist notion of human sustenance and how it might be obtained, but a maximalist concept of social justice as well.

The minimalist impulse lies behind documents codifying 'natural' or 'human' rights, which like 'natural law' have often been dismissed as value judgements masquerading in absolute metaphysical terms. To mark the twentieth anniversary of the Universal Declaration of Human Rights, UNESCO solicited from member states and others any text with a relationship to or a sense of 'human rights'. The compilers were no doubt predisposed to find common ground, but a significant body of related themes, despite the historical and anthropological diversity, did seem to emerge.[33] It is on the basis of some such empirical demonstration of uniformity that minimalist doctrines of human rights are usually maintained. These rest in turn on a Kantian conviction that man is an end in himself, and does not merit treatment as a means alone.

'Human' or 'natural' rights are a sub-category of moral rights in general, which are moral claims of a particularly important kind. They are considered, at least by their protagonists, to be *justified*. Rights get their peculiar force from the reasons that are advanced to back them up. In particular: 'A human right is a morally justifiable claim made on behalf of all men to the enjoyment and exercise of those basic freedoms, goods, and services which are considered necessary to achieve the human estate . . . Morally justifiable claims, are *proposals* to treat human beings in certain ways.'[34] They are justified in an abstract way by notions of what it means to be a human being; they are argued much more directly by detailing the consequences of meeting them or failing to do so; by describing what can flow from their subversion or disavowal. This way, too, they may issue in policies marginally less arbitrary than would otherwise prevail.

Again, what moral community are we talking about in world politics when we consider rights and the justification of moral claims? In the 'statist' perspective there is no viable world community, no supra-state society that constitutes a separate realm of experience that can offer its own definitions of the global good. 'Power' is vested in national leaders, and though moral stature is a part of this power, power as such generates its own expedient support and determines in considerable part the moral claims that emerge. In support of this position 'statist' theorists

cite the lack of a felt obligation on the part of rich countries to redistribute wealth and to meet the needs of the global poor.[35]

What, however. of those paradigms that do not affirm the 'finality'
of the state, but describe global structures that run across them? What,
for instance, of the neo-Marxist notion of 'class'?[36] Rather than states
competing for 'power', contemporary theories of imperialism, for
example, describe the world in terms of its modes of production,
distribution and exchange, and the social continuities these predispose.
'States' are seen as the conduits of rather deeper currents at work
among human beings, and in particular, as the products of contemporary 'capitalism' and the way this distinctive creature of the 'industrial revolution' has been manifest in world affairs. Though the doctrines
differ in many essential ways, it is generally argued that one effect of
European expansion over 300 years was to secure the exploitative
persistence of merchant capitalism in the colonised areas, at the
expense of the development of autonomous industries and self-sufficient
agricultures. Even after such domains were granted their formal independence, the liaison elites that manned the alluvial political machines
were more committed in their own interests to advancing diverse
metropolitan connections than the life chances of their mass clientele.
European states themselves bear many marks of the historic need for
large protected domestic markets and for political co-operation between
a residual nobility and a dynamic bourgeoisie. It is scarcely surprising,
then, that 'new' states should so profoundly reflect the growing divide
between rich and poor, a divide that has grown more significant in this
century when the costs of a process of globalisation carried on by
Western manufacturers, bankers, traders and armies have been more
clear. Global inequalities have been erected into global socio-economic
structures which are now skewed in fundamental ways. Whatever one
decides about the ultimate benefits to Western Europe of the inflow of
capital from plunder, tribute or unequal exchange, European expansion
obviously wreaked havoc upon the cultural infrastructures of the
societies they contacted or co-opted.[37] The advent of 'classes' on a
world scale has worked to the relative advantage of industrialised
'states', with particular transnationalising consequences for those created
later. In each 'state' case intermediary enclave elites share a world
community (a community in extent though not in the mass; in *breadth*
rather than *depth*) with the populations of the dynamic centres — common
values, agreed rules of concourse, a globally integrated 'bourgeoisie'.

The cultural dimension of such an analysis is critical. The trans-
cultural psychology of profit maximisation[38] has deeply conditioned the

patterns of social interaction apparent today. And peripheral elites are quick to learn that their 'Northern' mentors love to teach: 'For in accepting cultural transmission the Periphery also implicitly validates for the Centre the culture developed in the centre' and creates a 'lasting demand for the latest innovations'.[39] The process is most evident when we consider global patterns of education — the critical part played by the preservation of metropolitan languages and by the installation of a sense of cultural inferiority and alienation in marginalised peoples around the world. Only 'Northern' ways, it is implied, can recreate themselves in a progressive fashion, and these ways the 'South' shall gratefully receive.[40] Moral claims made under circumstances like these are hard pressed to escape terms pre-defined by the 'North', since the 'North' is a powerful publicist in its own cause and 'comprador' elites are committed on the whole to keeping those without most ignorant and afraid.[41] Those who bear the burdens have little voice. They must come to a critical appraisal of the extended cause of their condition before they can speak; but to do that is to become conscious of circumstances specifically designed to assassinate, assimilate, or deceive.

If moral claims do not on the whole issue from the human masses on the periphery and are unlikely to do so, there are certainly more now of those articulate on their behalf. What empirical evidence is there that any of such second-order claims for material wellbeing, or politico-economic liberation, for 'pay-back' or for 'getting out from under', are justified? Here we reach one of the thorniest sections of the 'class' based view. If, for example, we could demonstrate that a transfer of resources had occurred historically from the colonies to the developing 'Northern' world, and continues today, then we could argue that Third World claims for economic redress and the opportunity to attempt something approaching self-reliance service a long-established debt and are justified; we establish a right which has been *earned,* not out of respect for creditors, but out of a justifiable claim for the payment of debts[42] or for self-determination.[43] Proposals for integrated commodity pro-grammes, price indexation, and the democratisation of international financial institutions to improve terms of trade, would be strengthened thereby. If, furthermore, as the 'dependencia' theorists assert, the process of overdevelopment in the global 'North' actually *creates* under-development elsewhere (defined in terms of failing nutritional standards, the loss of a sense of personal competence, and like indices) then the denial of claims for nourishment and autonomy are part of an unde-clared assault on the wellbeing of most of the world. The benefits of

economic growth are co-opted by the rich, and illusory offers of a
share, or outright repression and violence, are used to control the poor
and unemployed. This leads to the conventional Marxist stance that
moral claims are an act of class war, and rather than labour with
bourgeois precepts we must, in this view, condemn the exploiters and
call upon new values that will hasten their demise.

Demonstrating the empirical status of 'dependence' and 'exploitation'
is not a simple task however. 'Exploitation' in particular presents
problems because there is considerable debate about what we should
measure, and because it contains qualitative judgements that are not
easily expressed in quantitative terms. We are asked, primarily, to assess
the degree to which an exchange process is 'unfair'.[44] Empirical details
about terms of trade, tariff discrimination and capital flows are
obviously important. But the question of 'fairness' turns upon competing moral claims for a 'just' world economy, and there is therefore the
prior question of what 'justice' involves in the global context, and what
'justice as fairness' might mean.

We may readily distinguish general and particular, formal and substantive, arithmetical and proportionate, commutative and distributive
forms of 'justice', and there is no reason to take issue with these well
worn categories here. Such forms may be seen to reside in the individual,
state, or cosmopolitan domain.[45] But what, again, of the *class*? If we
accept the objective presence, as historical and contemporary evidence
suggests we should do, of a relatively standardised, urban, global elite
sharing similar values and interests and technocratic assumptions, and
we counterpose the poor and underemployed dwellers on the rural and
city fringes, then a 'political' economy of 'justice' can be given specific
shape and its claims made more clear.[46] In practice, the 'justice-constituency'[47] of the global hinterland cuts across that of the territorial society
or state. To talk as many do in terms of autonomous state regimes
arbitrating domestic disputes is to underrate, and drastically so, the
place of those regimes in a much wider system of social relationships,
and the way such arbitration does not proceed by *in*trinsic criteria alone.
To place present-day state regimes in sole control of 'development' and
'distribution' is to abdicate to the particular and usually self-regarding
interests of global and more particularly 'Third World' elites. To call
for *sacrifices* on the part of affluent states is to confuse a humid
euphemism with the debt-bound obligations that really prevail.[48]

If there is any strength to a claim by or on behalf of a submerged
global proletariat and peasantry we have to assess its formal standing
against that of the more 'satisfied' elites. Here the notion advanced by

John Rawls, which he specifically extends to any human collectivity, might be applied. To be just, Rawls says, is at least to be fair. When confronted by inequalities we should enquire whether they assume general precepts which any social group would have endorsed before it knew just where in the ensuing process of discrimination it would emerge — on the top or on the bottom or somewhere between.[49] How would we structure an ongoing global political economy if antagonists were to allot us our place therein? Contemporary global inequalities, we may safely assume, would rapidly recede (though not disappear) if they were to be measured by such contractual criteria as contribution to the common good, merit, and need. They are not on the whole so measured, except by those in the weakest position to enforce any radical conclusions. But the criteria exist, and they extend a promise of their own. The rejoinder that such promise may never be realised reminds us how difficult it is to sustain truly universalist values in the face of group interests and conflict.

Is 'justice' what we really want in the world anyway? Could we not cause more problems than we solve by our constant appeal to justifiable moral claims? Do we create happiness by alleviating suffering alone? May the tenacious pursuit of developmental self-reliance not jeopardise social freedoms or economic growth already extant? Is there not a need for *order* in world affairs regardless and perhaps even because of the gross discrepancies between global classes and the political discontent explicit or implicit therein? Is justice only to be achieved in a stable and orderly environment; should the latter be prior and preferred?[50] In the obvious sense that an outright end to nuclear coexistence would mean annihilation for us all, this is clearly true. Any disposition less than this, however, will convey and defend the preferred values of one social group rather than another, and we are obliged to consider what distribution of values such a disposition defines. There still exists a widespread bias among students and practitioners of world affairs toward a reified, denatured concept of 'order', and it is no accident perhaps that global elites tend to subscribe to the same idea. 'Order' is of 'primary' or 'elemental' concern, while justice is residual, to catch as catch can.

It is a familiar task to trace the way social struggles became domesticated over the last century or so with the spread of nation-states. We are still less familiar, however, with a picture of the social continuities that crystallised, in most cases after World War II, between the 'old' states and the 'new'. Class struggles, which tended to disappear in the face of rivalry, began to re-emerge again though in a global context this time. Much of the pattern of present world politics has to do with their second sublimation. E.H. Carr wrote before this pattern was apparent, but he demonstrates a perceptive awareness of the fact that conflicts of this kind 'cannot be resolved without real sacrifices, involving in all probability a substantial reduction of consumption by privileged groups and in privileged countries. There may be other obstacles to the establishment of a new international order. But failure to recognise the fundamental character of the conflict and the radical nature of the measures necessary to meet it, is certainly one of them'.[51]

In conclusion it may be worth pointing out that there is the distinct possibility of a deeper malaise again. Behind the moral claims for social justice put forward in the 'first', 'second' and 'third' worlds on behalf of the 'fourth' may lurk psychological motives hardly discerned. Freud once drew attention to the sense of guilt that was, he said, a decisive concomitant of 'civilisation' and grew in equal strength as it did. From his theory of instincts, and his own estimates of growing unease in industrialised societies, he argued that the 'most important problem in the evolution of culture', and the 'price of progress in civilisation' is the 'forfeiting [of] happiness through the heightening of the sense of guilt'.[52] This thesis seems unconvincing, however, given the capacity of the affluent and powerful to ignore the plight of those less well placed than themselves, and to remain unapologetic about it. His one-time colleague, Carl Jung, pushed into a parallel, in some ways more interesting vein. In a letter to Freud, dated 1910, he wrote that '. . . only the wise are ethical from sheer intellectual presumption – the rest of us need the eternal truth of myth . . .'[53] The problem is that 'Northern' man in particular seems to have divested himself of sustaining myths at an alarming rate:

> . . . he has abandoned his animism; his Ptolemaic astronomy that assured his position in the center of the universe; his faith in a hereafter that endowed him with eternal life; his belief in the supreme and infinite worth of his person that assured him a position of isolate dignity in an otherwise meaningless and impersonal world; and even perhaps his faith in a God whose attributes, under the impact of man's rationalistic scrutiny, became ever more abstract until He vanished in the metaphysical concept of the Whole. The shedding of these inestimable illusions may be merely stages in his diminishing stature before he himself vanishes from the scene – lost in the icy fixity of his final state in a posthistoric age.[54]

Presumptive ethics may comfort the wise as Jung assumed, but what of the rest? Can they be made wise in time too, or do they have to generate new myths to steer by, or are there other options, hardly apparent to us now, which will emerge in due course? To contemplate answers to questions like these is to contemplate the purpose of the human enterprise as a whole, which is an aspect of the discipline of world affairs, if not positively trivialised, then at least largely ignored.

Notes

1. D. Easton, 'The New Revolution in Political Science', *American Political Science Review,* vol. 63, no. 4 (Dec. 1969), pp. 1051-61.

2. The *deontologist* (or at least his/her ideal type) will consider moral precepts as radical, cardinal, prime — as imperious objects in their own right. Such a stance tends to see an 'additional component of meaning outside nature. Plato located it in a realm of abstract Forms, Christianity in the will of God, the intuitionists in the direct recognition of the quality of rightness, the moral-sense theorists in the feeling of approbation'. It reveals, that is, those 'prescriptive aspects of moral concepts that are independent of prudential considerations'. Raziel Abelson, 'History of Ethics', *The Encyclopaedia of Philosophy* (The Macmillan Co. & the Free Press, NY, 1967), vol. 3, p. 100. The *teleologist,* on the other hand, will want to consider *consequences* and whether such precepts foster the 'good' things any moral system permits, and inhibits the 'bad' that it forbids. He/she tends to define ' "good" and related concepts in terms of observable criteria, such as fulfilment of natural tendencies (Aristotle), satisfaction of desire (Hobbes and Spinoza), production of pleasure for the greatest number (utilitarianism), conduciveness to historical progress (Spencer and Marx), or efficiency of means to ends (Dewey)'. This reveals 'various ways in which ethical judgement is grounded on the fulfilment of biological and social needs' (loc. cit.). Unless one is merely mouthing moral absolutes any human act will situate a moral proposal in a social context where there are consequences. The separation is an analytic one, which does not in practice obtain.

3. *Value non-cognitivists* argue that moral claims have 'no cognitive status; they cannot be *known* to be either true or false because they *are* not true or false; and they are neither true nor false because they do not affirm or deny that something is the case'. See Felix Oppenheim, *Moral Principles in Political Philosophy* (Random House, NY, 1968), p. 24. Thus they may be sentimental, declaratory, influential, and even decisive, but they are never objective or observable matters of fact. *Value cognitivists,* on the other hand, affirm that 'valuational and moral statements are assertions about objective states of affairs and have, as such, cognitive status; that is, they are, and can be known to be, either true or false'. Oppenheim, *Moral Principles,* p. 21. The 'naturalists' derive such statements from 'true descriptive generalisations', from non-moral propositions of an empirical or teleological sort, or else they simply legislate so as to define moral claims in non-moral ways. The 'intuitionalists', however, agree with the 'naturalists' that 'ethical terms refer to objective characteristics, but interpret them as designating "non-natural" or "simple" properties which cannot be further defined'. Oppenheim, *Moral Principles,* pp. 22-3. While one may agree with the non-cognitivists that behind all moral claims lurk residual meanings that may not be 'factual' in any strict sense, it also seems apparent that, as the 'naturalists' argue, valuing precepts are connected very closely with factual convictions of one sort or another, indeed may well presuppose them. Furthermore, as the 'intuitionalists' seem to say, 'the connections, whatever they may be are not

going to prove to be the philosophically favoured ones of explicit definition and logical derivation'. Arthur Danto, *Mysticism and Morality: oriental thought and moral philosophy* (Basic Books, NY, 1972), p. x. Thus moral judgements demand more than cognitive treatment since they also prescribe and recommend. But neither are they 'mere expressions or evocations of emotion, attitude, or desire', nor are they 'mere commands . . . They claim a certain authority and support; they claim to be backed by reasons which are generally valid, or at least to have certain consensus in their favor'. William Frankena, 'The Concept of Social Justice', in R. Brandt (ed.), *Social Justice* (Prentice-Hall, NJ, 1962), p. 24.

4. B. Russell, 'On Comets', in his *In Praise of Idleness and other essays* (George Allen and Unwin, London, 1948), pp. 224-5.

5. 'What I Believe', in *The Basic Writings of Bertrand Russell* (George Allen and Unwin, London, 1961), p. 371.

6. In isolating common doctrines that occur at different points in time regardless of their immediate environments, common that is with respect to some general pattern of human preoccupations that seems to change only slowly and perhaps does not even change at all, I do not want to underplay the role of novel events and processes in the world or the sort of analysis, reductionist again, that identifies our contemporary predicament with that of the Greeks and overlooks the enormous variety of events that have intervened.

7. Though Plato was by no means the first to do so. This honour he attributed to Pythagoras.

8. This ambiguity may be much more important and productive than we generally realise. George Steiner, in his book *After Babel* (OUP, 1975) suggests that: 'The dialectic of "alternity", the genius of language for planned counter-factuality, are overwhelmingly positive and creative . . . human tongues, with their conspicuous consumption of subjective, future, and optative forms are a decisive evolutionary advantage. Through them we proceed in a substantive illusion of freedom. Man's sensibility endures and transcends the brevity, the haphazard ravages, the physiological programming of individual life because the semantically coded responses of the mind are constantly broader, freer, more inventive than the demands and stimulus of the material fact . . . Metaphysics, religion, ethics, knowledge — all derive from man's will to art, to lies, from his flight before truth, from his negation of truth, said Nietzsche . . . The relevant framework is not one of morality but of survival. At every level, from brute camouflage to poetic vision, the linguistic capacity to conceal, misinform, leave ambiguous, hypothesize, invent is indispensable to the equilibrium of human consciousness and the development of man in society' (pp. 226-8).

9. The scope is not limitless; it has many concrete features. Moral differences, in part at least, reflect disagreements as to fact. It is, as Danto points out, through their factual components and premises that ethical concepts engage our attention, and to comprehend a moral injunction is to know at least how it might be applied (Danto, *Mysticism and Morality*, p. 11). Resolving matters of fact does not ultimately resolve matters of moral meaning. Ethical assertions pertain to social relations and social relations have 'no material existence. We can only "observe" social relations indirectly by interpreting other people's behaviour, and we can only do this if we first invent an artificial code which attaches social meaning to cultural facts'. (E. Leach, *A Runaway World?*, BBC, London, 1968, p. 55). Cracking these codes so they may be understood in terms more familiar to us is an academic trade of its own, and '[w]hatever may be the logical connections between factual and moral propositions . . . there is enough of a tie between them, so that when we reckon in the application conditions of moral beliefs, we have some basis for rational criticism and rational debate in the moral sphere' (Danto, *Mysticism and Morality*, p. 13).

10. Colin Turnbull's work among the Ik of Uganda, and published reports of life in concentration camps, indicate that under extreme conditions of cultural disarray or material privation this capacity is severely distorted or altogether lost. '[H] umanity, as we generally define it, *is* an option', Turnbull argues in 'Human Nature and Primal Man', *Social Research*, vol. 4, no. 3 (Autumn 1973), p. 530.

11. See, for example, Leach's Lament: 'If only we could come to feel that consciousness is not something which makes human beings different and sets them apart but something which connects us all together — both with each other and with everything else' (Leach, *A Runaway World?*, p. 18).

12. Note, however, the monolithic consciousness generated by fascist parties, religious crusades, and by socialist mobilisation regimes as well, perhaps.

13. Turnbull, 'Human Nature and Primal Man', p. 528.

14. Ibid., pp. 529-30.

15. Robert Merton in the Foreword to Jacques Ellul, *The Technological Society* (Cape, London, 1965), p. x.

16. Ibid., p. xi.

17. A.N. Whitehead, *Science and the Modern World* (CUP, 1946), p. 20.

18. Ibid., p. 22.

19. T. Roszak, *Where the Wasteland Ends: politics and transcendence in post-industrial society* (Doubleday and Co., NY, 1972), p. 208.

20. Ibid., p. 58.

21. M. Wight, 'Western Values in International Relations', in H. Butterfield and M. Wight (eds.), *Diplomatic Investigations* (George Allen and Unwin, London, 1966), p. 127.

22. Ibid., pp. 130-31.

23. Thus Morgenthau has attributed what he sees as a general deterioration in moral limitations upon world politics to the growth of 'nationalistic universalism', to the dissolution of the aristocratic society that for three or four hundred years caused Europe, morally at least, to cohere, and to the rise of competitive state systems that construe their moral claims in global terms. Hans Morgenthau, 'The Twilight of International Morality', *Ethics*, vol. 56, no. 2 (January 1948), pp. 88, 94.

24. A. Wolfers, 'Statesmanship and Moral Choice', *World Politics*, vol. 1, no. 2 (1949), p. 192.

25. See *The Prince and the Discourses* (Random House, NY, 1950), pp. 64-6.

26. I. Berlin, 'The Originality of Machiavelli', a paper delivered to the Political Studies Conference, Oxford, 27 March 1963, p. 1. By 'natural law' is meant the notion 'that there is some single principle that not only regulates the course of the sun and the stars, but one that prescribes their proper behaviour to all animate creatures: animals, sub-rational beings of all kinds, follow it by instinct, others attain to consciousness of it and are free to abandon it only at their peril'.

27. Ibid., p. 15.

28. Ibid., p. 17.

29. Loc. cit.

30. H.L.A. Hart, *The Concept of Law* (OUP, 1961), p. 189.

31. Ibid., pp. 190-3.

32. Barrington Moore Jr., *Reflections on the Causes of Human Misery and upon certain proposals to eliminate them* (Allen Lane, London, 1972), p. 5.

33. *Birthright of Man* (UNESCO, 1969); also Jeanne Hersch, 'Is the Declaration of Human Rights a Western Concept?', in H. Kiefer and M. Munitz (eds.), *Ethics and Social Justice* (State University of New York Press, Albany, 1970).

34. Sidney Hook, 'Reflections on Human Rights', in Kiefer and Munitz, *Ethics and Social Justice*, p. 263.

35. See, for example, A. Linklater, 'Moral Agents and International Politics', *International Relations*, vol. 4, no. 3 (May 1973), p. 299.

36. The behavioural preoccupation with the 'system', because of its preference

for scientific methodology, led away from 'value' questions, and hence any discussion of moral claims at all.

37. E. Krippendorff, 'Peace Research and the Industrial Revolution', *Journal of Peace Research*, vol. 10, no. 3 (1973), p. 189. Also, Samir Amin, 'Accumulation and development: a theoretical model', *Review of African Political Economy*, no. 1 (1974), p. 23.

38. A. Mazrui, 'Modernisation and reform in Africa', in J. Bhagwati (ed.), *Economics and World Order* (The Macmillan Co., NY, 1972).

39. J. Galtung, 'A Structural Theory of Imperialism', *Journal of Peace Research*, vol. 8, no. 2 (1971), p. 93.

40. Cogently demonstrated by Abdou Moumouni, *Education in Africa* (Praeger, NY, 1968).

41. See P. Freire, *Pedagogy of the Oppressed* (Penguin, 1972), p. 15. There is an important question closely related to this about the place of university pedagogues and their part in the social definition of what is knowledge – in our own case, whether we teach the 'politics of ruling', or the 'alternative politics of mobilisation and self-management', to use Terry Irving's phrase.

42. M. Cranston, *What Are Human Rights?* (The Bodley Head, London, 1973), p.22; also, Mahbub ul Haq, 'Mr. Polanski's Dilemma', in B. Ward *et al.*, *The Widening Gap: development in the 1970s* (Columbia University Press, NY, 1971) pp. 278-9. Not all transfers create debts. Apart from gifts or displays, for example, consider market ethics: all mature adults are competent to enter contracts, and should expect no redress when they commit themselves to (as they later perceive) their disadvantage. The process referred to in the text is not one of contract, however, but one of exploitation, and the notion of market ethics does not obtain.

43. Implicit, if not explicit, in neo-Marxist analyses of the politico-socio-economic structures of the present global system are prescriptions for both state and collective-state self-reliance. These issue in part from the manifest success of the Yenan model in post-revolutionary China, but also derive directly from radical theoretical analyses of world affairs themselves. The literature is extensive, including the work of the Latin American 'dependencia' theorists (Furtado, Dos Santos, Sunkel, Cardoso, for example) as well as A. Gunder Frank, Samir Amin, Pierre Jalee, Suzanne Bodenheimer and many more. See also, for example, Surendra Patel, 'Collective Self-reliance of Developing Countries', *The Journal of Modern African Studies*, vol. 13, no. 4 (December 1975), pp. 569-83.

44. J. Caporaso, 'Methodological Issues in the Measurement of Inequality, Dependence, and Exploitation', in S. Rosen and J. Kurth (eds.), *Testing Theories of Economic Imperialism* (Lexington Books, Mass., 1974), p. 91.

45. H. Bull, 'Order vs. Justice in International Society', *Political Studies*, vol. 19, no. 3 (September 1971), pp. 272-4.

46. R. Kothari, *Footsteps into the Future: diagnosis of the present world and a design for an alternative* (Orient Longman, 1974), Ch. 3 and particularly pp. 68-74. See also, M. Haq, 'Employment in the 1970's', *International Development Review*, no. 4 (1971), pp. 9-13.

47. A term used by Julius Stone throughout his *Approaches to the Notion of International Justice*, Truman Center Publications, no. 4 (January 1970).

48. Though ethical discourse normally fastens obligations upon individuals, it is not uncommon in world politics for obligations to be placed between groups. Postwar reparations are only one example.

49. J. Rawls, 'Justice as Fairness', *Philosophical Review*, vol. 67 (1958), pp. 164-94; also, W. Runciman, *Relative Deprivation and Social Justice* (Routledge and Kegan Paul, London, 1966). This notion has been seriously challenged by Rawls's fellow philosophers, for example, Alain Zaitchik, 'Just Enough', *Philosophical Quarterly*, vol. 25, no. 101 (October 1975), pp. 340-45; Brian Barry, *The*

liberal theory of justice: a critical examination of the principal doctrines in 'A theory of justice' by John Rawls (Clarendon Press, Oxford, 1973). Enough seems to survive this challenge, however, to give it the credence accorded here.

50. H. Bull, 'Order vs. Justice', p. 277.

51. E.H. Carr, *The Twenty Years' Crisis* (Macmillan, London, 1962), p. 237.

52. S. Freud, *Civilisation and its Discontents* (Hogarth Press, London, 1949), p. 123; see also, H. Marcuse, *Eros and Civilization* (Routledge and Kegan Paul, London, 1956).

53. Quoted in Anthony Storr, 'The Significance of Jung', *Times Literary Supplement,* 25 July 1975.

54. Roderick Seidenberg, *Posthistoric Man: an inquiry* (University of North Carolina Press, Chapel Hill, 1950).

2 MORALITY, INTERESTS AND RATIONALISATION

J.D.B. Miller

Morality is right conduct. It is the way we think we ought to behave, even when we do not observe it. In this paper I shall try to explain why ordinary moral considerations appear to have so little application to world politics, and to answer some questions about the relationship of the sovereign state to morality. To start with, we should keep in mind two considerations.

The first is that no system of morality is fully observed in any society. If it were, there would be no need for courts, police, and the other coercive aspects of the state, because everyone would behave towards other people as they and he thought he should. Systems of morality are only partially observed anywhere. The lack of application of moral considerations to the actions of states has numerous parallels in the domestic life of states; it is not so remarkable as is often made out.

The second is that, while discussion often gives predominance to notions of universal morality (i.e. to any man's conceivable treatment of any other), in practice most people adhere to *group* morality (i.e. a code of conduct based on one's membership of a particular group, with rights and duties flowing from loyalty to that group). From the family onwards, groups give meaning and significance to life, and provide minimum protection and opportunity. To the great mass of mankind, the dichotomy in Western philosophy between the individual and mankind is meaningless: the individual is part of a tribe, clan, sect, family, village, and the like, and this serves as the effective middle term between him and the world at large. The essence of the group is its distinction from outsiders; morality consists primarily of right conduct towards the other members of the group. The kind of violent morality practised by the Mafia and by gangs of outlaws and buccaneers is the extreme case of a general rule: that the group comes first, that it makes its own morality, and that, if others suffer, that is too bad.

We should thus not be surprised if states prescribe their own morality in relation to other states, since the same is done, to a greater or lesser extent, by all the other human groupings of which we have knowledge. Within any complex society, the groups aim at getting what they can for themselves. Their degree of ferocity, and the exclusiveness of their several moralities, will depend on the degree of scarcity in the society, on the cohesiveness of the group itself, and upon the degree of intermixing which has taken place between groups and sections, i.e. upon the success of 'melting-pot' policies, and the widening or narrowing of opportunities to emerge from 'ghetto' conditions of economic and social life. Generally speaking, groups operate so as to maximise advantage but not to pull down the temple about their own ears: they do not challenge the basis on which the society rests, but work within it to secure the most they can, consistent with a relatively peaceful life. The greater the scarcity of opportunities and material goods, the stronger is likely to be the exclusiveness of the moralities practised by groups.

Thus, in any society which goes beyond the simple village or tribe, there will be found not one, but a variety, of moral imperatives and moral orders. The kind of social and moral patchwork represented by the Turkish and Austro-Hungarian Empires before World War I was an extreme but not untypical example of what a modern state is composed of. These states often hang together because to do so is self-evidently better than to have the parts hanging separately, i.e. carrying their differences to the point of open violence. In some such cases, as in Malaysia, basic conflicts are underplayed because it suits the leaders of the groups, as distinct from the rank and file, to maintain a common interest in the preservation of the existing form of the state. In others, e.g. Northern Ireland and Lebanon, the basic conflicts may be contained beneath the surface for long periods but then break loose, in spite of the efforts of formal leaders. In all these instances one can discern, not simply a clash of groups, but also a clash of moralities.[1] One does not need to go to these bitterly divided societies to see a variety of moralities in operation within a single state: the cross-hatching of ethnic, regional and national moralities in the United States is sufficient evidence.

My point is that the assertion of 'reason of state' or 'national interest' as a sufficient basis for morality by the sovereign state is not an isolated or unusual case. One can compare it with the operation of social groups before the state was a central feature of social life, and with the operation of more or less organised groups in societies today. In all these cases the essential element is the assertion of a special morality against a universalist one, whether it is the attempt of the European state in medieval and Renaissance times to evade the morality which the Papacy attempted to impose, or the insistence of certain groups in modern societies that they will not accept the imperatives about drinking, drugs and sex which are present in the laws of the society, or

the determination of Catholics to preserve their own schools in the face
of bitter majority resistance in late nineteenth-century Australia. The
'universalist' morality is in each case a morality serving the interests of
particular people, who may or may not constitute a majority in the
society, but who usually command effective political power. If we think
of each moral code as serving some people's interests more than others',
we shall have a fair picture of the actual state of morality of a society.
Competing moral codes correspond to competing groups, and can be
used to support the perceived interests of the members of each group.
Just as, in the political sphere, the groups achieve compromises and
trade-offs, so in the moral sphere the moralities may be compromised
one with another to produce a vague result referred to as 'the contemporary moral climate'; but if there are attempts forcibly to impose one
group's morality upon another, there will be conflict. This conflict may
reach the levels of violence at times, but it is more likely to be contained conflict which occasionally breaks the surface.

In the case of the sovereign state, the assertion of a separate and
superior morality — 'reason of state' — can be interpreted both
historically and in social terms. Historically the theory of 'reason of
state', given solid form by Machiavelli, was a response by European
rulers to the pretensions to absolute power of the Church. It has its
religio-political sponsor in Luther. I cannot forbear to quote a long
passage from J.N. Figgis, whose works are too little read:

> It is in international politics that Machiavelli has had his greatest
> influence. With territorialism dominant, and the unity, however
> vague, afforded by a single supra-national religious system with a
> recognized code of law, at an end, the relations of States became
> more definitely those of the 'state of nature' than they had been
> since the early days of the Roman Republic. The struggle for
> existence or power became more keen, and less obviously subject
> to any rules than it had ever been before among civilised peoples.
> Now the remarkable point about Machiavelli (and even of his
> adversaries) is what he omits . . . The question at the back of his
> mind was . . . what rules of prudence may be garnered from history
> or contemporary experience to guide us here and now. What dis-
> tinguishes him from his predecessors is his entire discarding of any
> attempt to found a philosophy of right. To speak generally, all
> political speculation in the past few centuries might be described as
> directed to that end. To Machiavelli, however, the questions which
> seemed of such importance to St. Thomas and the innumerable other

writers on the subject of politics, *whatever side they took,* were
beside the mark. He did not consciously omit them; it did not
occur to him to discuss them. The practical end ruled everything,
and, as has been said, 'he is the founder of utilitarian ethics'. It is
remarkable, too, that he expresses the atmosphere of the Italy
of his day. Even a writer definitely hostile to him, like Botero, in his
work *Il Ragion di Stato*, makes very much the same assumptions,
and appeals to the same kind of motives.

What has vanished from Machiavelli is the conception of natural
law. So long as this belief is held, however inadequate may be the
conception as a view of the facts of life, it affords some criterion for
submitting the acts of statesmen to the rule of justice, and some
check on the rule of pure expediency in internal and of force in
external politics. The more law comes to be thought of as merely
positive, the command of a law-giver, the more difficult is it to put
any restraints upon the action of the legislator, and in cases of
monarchical government to avoid a tyranny. So long as ordinary law
is regarded as to some extent merely the explication of law natural,
so long as there is some general conception remaining by which
governments may be judged; so long, in fact, do they rest on a con-
fessedly moral basis. This remains true, however little their ordinary
actions may be justifiable, however much they may in practice over-
step their limits. When, however, natural law and its outcome in
custom are discarded, it is clear that the ruler must be consciously
sovereign in a way he has not been before, and that his relations to
other rulers will also be much freer — especially owing to the confusion of *jus naturale* with *jus gentium* which is at the bottom of
International Law. The despots of Italy were, in fact, in the Greek
sense, tyrants, and Machiavelli did little more than say so. What
gives him his importance is that what was true of the small despots
of Italy was about to become true of the national monarchs of
Europe. To Machiavelli the State, i.e., Italy, is an end in itself. The
restraints of natural law seem mere moonshine to a man of his
positif habit. He substitutes the practical conceptions of *reason of
state* as a ground of all government action, and the *balance of power*
as the goal of all international efforts, in place of the ancient ideals,
inefficient enough but not insignificant, of internal justice and international unity. No one can deny that very largely they have been
ruling in Europe ever since; just as it was only three centuries and a
half after his day that Italy herself reached, under the leadership of
Cavour, the goal which Machiavelli had set before her, by methods

which his typical man of *virtu* would scarcely have disdained.

. . . Social justice had no meaning to him apart from the one great end of the salvation of his country. He had the limited horizon and unlimited influence which always come of narrowing the problem. There is a sense in which it is true that *salus populi* is *suprema lex*; for laws and rules suitable for ordinary times are not always suitable for emergencies . . . Every nation would allow that there are emergencies in which it is the right and duty of a government to proclaim a state of siege and authorise the supersession of the common rules of remedy by the rapid methods of martial law. What Machiavelli did, or rather what his followers have been doing ever since, is to elevate this principle into the normal rule for statesmen's actions. When his books are made into a system they must result in a perpetual suspension of the *habeas corpus* acts of the whole human race. It is not the removal of restraints under extraordinary emergencies that is the fallacy of Machiavelli, it is the erection of this removal into an ordinary and every-day rule of action. Machiavelli's maxims are merely the para-doxes of self-defence . . . It is the transformation of these paradoxes into principles, that has been so dangerous. The net result of his writings has been that, in the long run, Machiavelli's principles have remained, as they ought, as a mere *Deus ex machina* for internal politics, but have become a commonplace in International diplomacy.[2]

Machiavelli's defence, of course, would be that he was no stranger to the idea of right, that he respected it as significant in the lives of individuals, but that it was simply not applicable to dealings between states:

for how we live is so far removed from how we ought to live, that he who abandons what is done for what ought to be done, will rather learn to bring about his own ruin than his preservation. A man who wishes to make a profession of goodness in everything must necessarily come to grief among so many who are not good. There-fore it is necessary for a prince, who wishes to maintain himself, to learn how not to be good, and to use it and not use it according to the necessities of the case.[3]

Machiavelli does not think of this as simply a description of what a *prince* must do to preserve personal power; he also thinks of it in nationalist terms as what a *people* must do in order to 'save the life and preserve the freedom of one's country'.[4] What made Machiavelli's doctrine so readily adaptable to international relations was this nationalist element: to him, the saving of the state was paramount. Figgis is right in saying that Machiavelli disregards the idea of natural law, as it might apply to relations between states or rulers. He does not disregard it as a means of judging personal conduct; his categories here are the normal ones, involving the keeping of promises, the need for just cause when people are killed, and the like. But Machiavelli maintains that these axioms do not apply to inter-state politics (or indeed to internal politics), because in the political realm men's selfishness is boundless; one must not let oneself be sacrificed to it. One's own selfishness can reasonably be given free play in the service of one's state. It is the state, as an end in itself, that ultimately justifies the means which Machiavelli is prepared to see employed.

We do not have to suggest that Machiavelli was the inventor of 'reason of state' in order to recognise that he gave coherent expression to a doctrine which was well in evidence in his own time and has become so much more important in later times. It is useful, however, to keep in mind Figgis's contrast between the natural law doctrine and Machiavelli's, since this is what so many arguments about morality in world politics turn upon. Ultimately, some universal imperative has to be found if the people of one country are to be made to regard the people of other countries as brothers, entitled to the same consideration as themselves. Some form of the 'reason and nature' doctrine must prevail. Otherwise, Machiavelli's view that nationalist expediency is proper will be the norm from which national policies flow, whether they flow in the form of war and conquest or in that of co-operation and regulated competition. Historically, Machiavellianism has proved to be normal for all kinds of state — democratic authoritarian, new, old, capitalist, socialist, poor, rich — with certain variations of time and place.

In terms of individual societies, the state has been able to continue to put Machiavelli's maxims into practice, partly because it can use or threaten force, but also because it can go beyond force in appealing to its citizens. Here we arrive at the social reality behind Machiavelli's doctrine. If we regard the state, not simply as a mutual conspiracy of force and fraud between those who control power, but as a body which provides certain guarantees and opportunities to its citizens — especially in respect of security and prosperity — we shall have a clearer picture of why it can maintain its pretensions of internal and external sovereignty, and why its citizens so often give it loyalty in spite of its manifest injustices. I have gone into this elsewhere,[5] and shall state the point here only briefly. States gain credibility to the extent that they protect their citizens from external attack and internal disturbances and deprivation. 'Their citizens' must, of course, be understood in this context as meaning mainly those citizens who matter, in the sense of being able to organise some effective opposition to a government which does not please them. In a wider sense, however, the state loses its credibility even if it satisfies the generals and politicos but signally fails the mass of the people, as the Tsarist regime did in Russia in its mismanagement of the war and its inability to provide basic needs to workers and peasants. Hobbes and Machiavelli, both realists, fully acknowledged this point: in spite of Hobbes's emphasis upon one's duty to obey the ruler, he regards this duty as nullified if the ruler cannot protect his citizens; and Machiavelli, while recognising that 'a prince who possesses a strong city and does not make himself hated, cannot be assaulted',[6] sees clearly that a prince who is weak and hateful cannot command the allegiance of his subjects.

In modern terms, while the function of security remains significant in enabling a state to command the loyalty of its citizens, the function of provision — of welfare services of various kinds in particular — has increasingly become the mark of a strong state. The more that citizens conceive they have a stake in the country, in the sense of dependence upon the state for jobs and benefits, the more they will adhere to it as the ultimate group to which their loyalty is given and from which they derive their morality towards people of other countries. In brief, if the state provides the rations, it can give the orders.

It is largely in this respect that we can apply Figgis's point that Machiavelli's is a philosophy of emergency, siege and self-defence. From Machiavelli's point of view, the state of emergency was so potent and permanent that it created its own morality towards other states. The modern state operates primarily upon this principle, with the underlying assumption that if its people are not protected against foreigners, not only their independence but also their standard of living will fall. Just as Machiavelli allowed for occasional combinations and alliances with other states, in order that particular advantages might be gained, the modern state enters into these to a considerable extent; but it does not provide the structures thus created with supra-national power, and it insists on its right of individual action when circumstances go against it. Such bodies as NATO, EEC and ASEAN illustrate the point. The state's normal posture is one of either permanent emergency or of the recognition that an emergency may occur at any time. To say this is not to deny the possibility or the existence of co-operation between states, or to suggest that they are all potentially in a state of war. It is simply to assert that states operate as essentially self-regarding entities which submit all questions to the standard of their own advantage as they see it. The norms, rules and associations of international life are fashioned so as to take account of this prime characteristic. If there is an international morality, it is simply that minimum degree of common acceptance which the separate moralities of the individual states will permit. There is no higher morality than reason of state; but states may agree that their reasons coincide for particular purposes and within limited spheres. The fragility of detente between the United States and the Soviet Union is not an exceptional or surprising attribute: it is merely an expression of the fact that the interests and moralities of these two mighty states coincide at only a few (though vital) points. Each, like lesser states, is able to sustain its individual posture because of the conviction of the effective body of its citizens that unless that posture is sustained they will be worse off.

In using the term 'state' as I have used it in the foregoing paragraphs, I run the risk of its seeming that I regard all states as alike or even the same, thus inviting the charge that it is absurd to treat such disparate bodies as Singapore, China, Nigeria and the United States as examples of the same thing. This particular difficulty can never be satisfactorily resolved. The point of underlying importance, in my view, is that states have agreed, for the sake of convenience, to recognise one another's existence, to provide a minimum degree of non-intervention in one another's affairs, and, in particular, to agree that what is done domestically is not normally brought to international account. This still leaves room for enormous differences between states in strength, efficiency and cohesion. What it does, however, is to enable the governments of states (i.e. the actual bodies of persons who decide and execute policy) to try to use effectively the powers which a state is assumed to possess. Some are much better at this than others. In some, a constant regime is maintained; in others, there is a succession of governments, none of which seems able to do what it or anyone else wants. But in all these cases, effective and ineffective, there is a common factor — the freedom of the state machine to fashion whatever system of protection, provision and coercion it regards as suitable for its own people. In this respect all states are alike, although in so many other respects they are not.

Another point of importance is that co-operation between states can go a long way, even though each maintains that it is concerned with national interest when it does co-operate. States may be built up on the

basis of co-operation with others (as in the case of Australia and
Britain); they may have inescapable economic ties of a buyer-seller
nature; they may be linked by a common ideology; they may have
ethnic connections which induce close relations. But their co-operation
(even when institutionalised in formal treaties) is always subject to
demur by either party, because of the fundamental assumption of each
state that it is the final judge of its own interests.

The argument to this stage may be summed up as follows: if we
juxtapose reason of state and natural law, we have two opposing conceptions of international morality, the one stressing the exclusive
character of the people composing the state, and the other stressing
the brotherhood of man at large. The latter is usually regarded as the
more 'moral'. In fact, both express moralities; but one is supported by
force and loyalty, by appeal to potent symbols of patriotism and to the
joint selfish interests of a particular group, while the other has to rest
upon a vaguer sense of common humanity. Both assert 'brotherhood',
but one is narrower in definition than the other. If we ever had a War
of the Worlds, we might find the wider brotherhood made real, in
essentially the same way as the narrower one now is. Short of that outcome, however, we have no warrant for thinking that loyalty to mankind, or to any system of morality based upon common humanity, will
prevail against the morality of the state. The fact that there have always
been some people who wanted the wider morality to prevail is no indication that it will; the weight of experience is firmly on the other side.

This analysis seems to be true of all kinds of states, and to be true in
particular whether states are authoritarian or not. Obviously the basic
Machiavellian approach can often be more easily applied in authoritarian states in which opinion can be more readily manipulated, and
censorship applied over a wide area, than in less disciplined states in
which citizens can become independently aware of what the world is
like. But the attractions of the state are such that governments can
expect them to be heeded, even if they are flawed or misrepresented.
It is a sad conclusion that unjust, corrupt and cruel states successfully
claim the allegiance of the great body of their people, and can, to a
large degree, gain assent to whatever version of morality they care to
apply to international issues; but it is correct.

Against this background, certain further questions may be asked:

(1) Why does the wider morality make so little headway, short of a
   War of the Worlds?
(2) Why, in spite of this little headway, does the sovereign state custom-
   arily borrow the concepts of the wider morality to justify its pursuit

of national interests?

(3) Why does the state, rather than class, colour, or religion, prove the deciding element in the morality pursued in world politics?

(4) Is it true that the notion of a moral order in world politics is essentially Anglo-Saxon (or, as some would say, 'Wilsonian') in character, and does not affect other peoples?

(5) In what sense does the Third World demand for economic 'justice' (as expressed in the demand for a new economic order) alter the framework of contending moral imperatives to which we have been accustomed?

(6) Is there any prospect of agreement on a wider morality than that which states now exercise?

The first question can be answered only in terms of experience, along the lines indicated above. States are, so far, the biggest and most utilitarian groups to which people belong. Because they can exercise force and pressure, both internally and externally, they can be used to procure advantage, through governmental means, by particular groups within a society, and the society can be plausibly represented as a group sufficiently distinct to make its interests appear general. These interests are assumed — rightly — to be pursued in a world of comparative scarcity and insecurity, within which the state provides advantages through such means as tariffs, trade agreements, supervision of investment, currency manipulation, alliances and armed force. In such a situation it is not surprising that a wider morality, which either invites or commands people to treat as equals those who are worse off than themselves, makes so little headway. It is an invitation to be worse off oneself. Whether this is true in the long run or not (and the point is arguable, but in no sense settled), it is not acceptable to most people. The notion that foreigners should be treated as if they mattered as much as oneself and one's fellow citizens is a moral claim which few will accept; the competing claim, that only within one's own state can a reasonable standard be attained and preserved for oneself and one's family, is intrinsically more plausible and is much more acceptable in terms of the morality which effectively applies.

Given such an explanation, how do we explain the fact that wider moral claims are often made for national policies which are clearly selfish, and intended to benefit only a particular state? Everyone knows how each warlike move is presented as a gesture towards peace; how proposals for higher tariffs are said to be good for world trade; how immigration restrictions are intended to benefit potential immigrants;

and the like. The most naked policies of national aggrandisement have habitually been put forward as benefiting everyone.[7] One has only to re-read the nauseous claims by leaders on both sides in World War II to realise how ingrained is the business of saying that what is right for one's own country will be right for everyone else.

This is essentially a matter of the rationalisation of interests. Just as sectional claims are advertised as general in impact within a society, so in the world at large the claims of states are represented as benefiting mankind. In part this is because the natural law tradition of the Western world has shown an obstinate power of survival in rhetoric, but it is mainly because generalised statements enable the impact of specific policies to be disguised. It is more comforting to speaker and listener alike if statements are made in general terms. It fortifies the sense of self-assurance, and throws the onus on the foreigner to appear to be going against what is proper and above all moral. The more general in application appears to be the law which we are obeying or our opponent is breaking, the more moral our behaviour can be made to appear. It was thus quite in character for the Allied Prosecution in the War Crimes Trials in Japan to base its case against the Japanese upon natural law principles which were specifically Western rather than Japanese.[8] We are confronted, as in all cases of rationalisation, by a mixture of levels at which argument, action and justification occur. Although one speaks of 'hypocrisy' in respect of the more flagrant cases of rationalisation, this is often unfair and indeed misleading, since most statesmen appear to be quite sincere in the use of a wider morality to justify what has been, in fact, the outcome of a morality centred upon the interests of their own states. The process is not con-fined to states, or to any particular group of states, though the Western intellectual tradition provides a firm foundation for it.

The third question is somewhat detached from the first two. It asks, not why men neglect their common humanity as the basis of the morality which they obey, but why they choose the state as a basis, rather than other forms of association which go beyond state bound-aries, such as class, colour and religion. The answer is that these trans-national links may provide a basis for loyalties and for the exercise of a somewhat different morality, but that this extension normally occurs under the aegis of the sovereign state and is not allowed to progress beyond the point at which it becomes inconvenient for those who run the state. Pan-Arabism is a source of morality which Arab leaders employ but which they are anxious not to have used against them: one thus sees the kind of alternate co-operation and estrangement which has been so notable between the leaders of Egypt, Jordan, Libya and Syria in recent years. Pan-Africanism provides a morality for use against South Africa and Rhodesia, but those who employ it are careful to see that it does not dictate imperatives for the conduct of one black African state towards another. When Nkrumah tried to turn Pan-Africanism into a movement requiring general obedience by African states to a general African government, he had few supporters. The class situation is not significantly different. Never since the Second International dissolved into national fragments at the outbreak of World War I has it been possible to pretend that a common class interest would motivate the workers of the world (or any significant part of it) to go against the orders of their several governments.

The answer would seem to be that national interests are stronger than those of class, colour, or religion, largely because they are so much more concrete, so much more capable of enforcement, and so much more agreed upon by those who are asked to support them. The sovereign state is a concrete reality of provision and command. It offers both a refuge and a boundary: to disobey it is not only to risk punishment, but to risk exchanging the concrete reality, with all its imperfections, for the untried structures of organisation and morality which may be turned against one in the interest of others. It is significant that, whenever specific proposals for a new economic order are made, they come in forms which will provide benefits within a national framework of which the state machinery is the regulator. No proposal which requires the benefiting states to submit themselves to external decisions about what they will receive is entertained. Even though the common attributes of poverty and underdevelopment are stressed in demands by developing states upon the richer countries, the answer emerges in a national form.[9]

The fact that Third World states so zealously pursue a universalist morality in their efforts to obtain a new economic order (while ensuring that this will operate in essentially inter-state forms) is sufficient answer to the claim that recourse to general moral precepts is confined to Anglo-Saxon countries. There is, however, a special kind of universalist approach which appeals to elements of opinion in Britain, the United States and other English-speaking countries, and which is viewed with distaste by others such as the French. This, as before, is a case of competing moralities which correspond largely to national interests; but it is more a matter of style and tradition than a clear contrast between a narrow and broad morality. Wilson's formulations in the Fourteen Points were extremely broad in statement, and breathed a universalist morality, but they were regarded by the British government as well as the French as primarily representing the interests of the United States. Nonetheless, they appealed to the Gladstonian and Cobdenite tradition amongst British thinkers, and helped to create pressure upon the British government for what eventually became the League of Nations. Something similar occurred in World War II in respect of Roosevelt's Atlantic Charter. Certainly, one can say that a preoccupation with universalist international morality is more marked in the Anglo-Saxon countries; one can also say that elements of this 'Wilsonian' tradition appear in the approaches of former British dependencies, such as India, to international questions. The Indian case is, however, a good example of how general moral claims can act as a cloak for particular national interests. Nehru and his successors used as much of the universalist morality as suited them, and no more.

India offers something of a test for the fifth question, that which asks whether Third World demands for a new economic order change the framework of contending moral imperatives (and of no viable universalist morality) to which we have been accustomed. The Third World claims are made in terms of justice, which is another way of saying that right conduct towards the Third World involves a fairer share of the world's goods and services. In practice, fairer shares would mean that nearly all the countries of the world -- not just the rich ones -- had to contribute to raise the standard of life in India. Any attempt at equality would involve so vast a shareout that the mind boggles at conceiving the machinery which could accomplish it, let alone the united will which would need to lie behind it.

In practice, however, the ideas which lie behind the demand for a new economic order are conceived in nationalist terms, so that solutions are to be achieved in ways which suit individual states. International investment is not to be carried out by a worldwide controlling authority making overall decisions on the basis of need; instead, individual states are to control more effectively the investment made in their territories by multi-national companies. Broadly speaking, the Third World economic demands since the first UNCTAD have been pursued in terms which ensure that the rich states should suffer but that there should be no shareout between the others — except that a Least Developed Country category has been worked out for the receipt of UN aid. To this latter extent, a further step towards a universalist morality has been taken; but the sums involved are small, and the approach does not affect the main problem of economic development on the grand scale, i.e. the problem of how to achieve sufficient productive investment in poor countries to bring them up to a viable standard. Third World economic demands are best viewed as strategy, not morality. They are intended to work simultaneously upon the conscience and sense of security of the rich countries, to the point at which those make concessions which provide benefits for all underdeveloped countries in some measure, and to some in large measure. But the national element remains strong, the universalist element weak.

It is true that some Third World theorists are not prepared to accept the national element in demands for justice; they maintain that the governments which make the demands are so closely linked with Western economic interests (i.e. are 'compradore' in character) that they cannot be said to represent their peoples. It is sometimes argued that if these people were 'truly' represented (i.e. by genuinely revolutionary governments), they would accept genuinely universalist solutions. Put this way, the argument is very like that which Mazzini and other European nationalists of the nineteenth century used against Austrian and Russian imperialism, and that which Lenin and the Bolsheviks used in respect of European labour movements in World War I.[10] Like those two, it can be tested by two questions: (i) what evidence is there that popular movements, left to themselves (i.e. not subject to pressure from the presumed enemy), incline towards universalism in sympthy; and (ii) what evidence is there that, if governments are constructed out of these movements, they will be less inclined to use the weapons of state, and to construct a 'reason of state' morality, than other regimes? The difficulty in answering the questions is that a 'truly revolutionary' government is like the Snark: one hunts it but finds it always beyond reach. All such governments (i.e. all declaring themselves such) have compromised their positions and have made accommodation with capitalist international economics; all have adopted strong local versions of 'reason of state', and have frequently found it more congenial to attack the pretensions of other allegedly revolutionary states than to affirm a wider morality. The matter goes further than economics; it moves into the larger sphere of power politics, as it has with the Soviet Union and China. If we take the revolutionary states which have appeared, rather than those which might be imagined to appear, then nationalist morality can be expected from them as from other sorts of state.

The sixth question will be answered by different people in different ways. A wider morality can variously be said to come from a change of heart, a universal revolution, a canalisation of religious urges, the destruction of the sovereign state, better publicity, and so on:

basically, approaches like these maintain that, if people can be made aware of their common humanity, they will accept both a universal morality and its consequences. I do not believe any of this, although I believe that there are always people to whom the universal impulse is paramount. There are not enough of them, and they normally yield to reason of state when it is applied. To someone who holds the view of international morality expressed in this chapter, the only hope of a wider morality being applied lies in the acceptance of the state as the dominant continuing force in men's lives, rather than in any attempt to supplant it. Such a hope must necessarily be limited and prudential, since the main characteristic of the state is the protection of its own interests and no one else's: this limits the possibilities of wider moral imperatives, and forces one to base any hope of advance upon the state's own view of what is prudential for it to undertake.

The key to such a possible outcome is the same as that which produces relative harmony, and a degree of common morality, in a society in which a number of groups co-exist: the notion that there should be sufficient mutual accommodation to ensure that, on the one hand, no group is entirely shut out from the good things of the society, and, on the other, that the pillars of the temple are not pulled down by groups which want more than the others are willing to provide. In other words, the problem of whether morality can be made wider internationally is much the same as the problem of war. War will be avoided if states are convinced that they will lose by it, or if they believe that in the long run they cannot gain from it. A wider morality in world politics will result, slowly and painfully, from more and more accommodation between competing interests. There are certain practical matters, such as merchant shipping and international communications, in which this kind of accommodation of mutual interests has been achieved, to such a degree that one may sometimes hardly recognise that sovereign states are involved in it. There is, in fact, a superior morality involved in posting a letter to a foreign country than in discussing arms limitation with it, although the process of negotiating arms limitation, with all the threats to survival implicit in the process, is a step on the way to what might in the end prove to be a superior morality.

Notes

1. There may often be nice examples of conflicting moralities within the one group. The IRA, while relying for its support upon Catholics, openly defies important elements in Catholic morality, replacing these by the imperatives of group loyalty.

2. J.N. Figgis, *From Gerson to Grotius* (Cambridge, 1923), pp. 74-7.

3. *The Prince*, Ch. XV. See also the notorious Ch. XVIII.

4. *Discourses*, III, 41.

5. *The Nature of Politics*, Ch. VIII, and in statements about 'state nationalism' in *The Politics of the Third World*, Chs. 1 and 5.

6. *The Prince*, Ch. X.

7. As both a relief from, and a highlight to, contemporary efforts of this kind, I recommend Lord Ivywood's speeches in Ch. II of G.K. Chesterton's *The Flying Inn*.

8. My reference here is to Brendan F. Brown (ed.), *The Natural Law Reader* (New York, 1960), p. 109.

9. This comes out strikingly in the Charter of Economic Rights and Duties of States adopted by the UN General Assembly in December 1974.

10. A neglected book in the examination of these important questions is D.W. Brogan, *The Price of Revolution* (London, 1951).

3 WESTERN CONCEPTIONS OF A UNIVERSAL MORAL ORDER*

R.J. Vincent

Morality, says Bruce Miller, in his account of why it is something that has such a small place in world politics, is about right conduct.[1] In practice, he goes on to say, the content of right conduct is determined by people's group, and especially their state, affiliation, so that the vision of a universal morality depicted in Western philosophy is not matched by the historical record. Part of the concern of this chapter will be to attempt to save the notion of a universal morality from the savaging administered by Professor Miller, and to do this in two ways: firstly, by stressing that universality is something implied by the very idea of morality itself; and secondly, by pointing out the extent to which morality, in its strong form as the good enjoining action as well as in its weak form as rights and duties requiring forbearance and abstention, is something that informs and mobilises international politics. It will be argued that morality is not simply a decoration for a cake made with other ingredients.

The chief object of this chapter is, however, expository rather than argumentative. Part One sets out those moral orders or frameworks that have been held in Western thought to enclose systems of morality, and highlights the particular moral attitudes seemingly characteristic of each system. Part Two looks at some particular moral issues that have been and remain controversial in international politics, and seeks to show the extent to which the controversy derives from a disagreement about the frameworks set out in the first part. The conclusion returns to Professor Miller and the relationship between morality and interests.

A discussion of moral frameworks should perhaps be introduced by reference to that theme in Western thought which denies the possibility of their construction. Thrasymachus' doctrine of 'justice as the interest of the stronger' allows no room for morality that is not taken up by what suits the ruling party.[2] There is not in this conception the material for building any moral framework at all, but only a name for a structure raised up on different principles. Whether this is a theme which has dominated Western thought and practice at the expense of doctrines

---

* An earlier version of this chapter was published in the *British Journal of International Studies*, Vol. 4, No. 1, April 1978.

that have not conceded right to might is a question which this chapter must try to resolve. Meanwhile, it can already be said that even Thrasymachus, by bothering to seek a definition of justice, pays homage to virtue, albeit that of the 'good-natured simpleton'.[3] The conception of justice as the rationalisation of interest does at least accept some form of moral constituency, however inchoate, which insists on a moral defence if not on moral motivation.[4] And this is the beginning of the idea that morality exists as a standard apart from its interpretation from the standpoint of interests. From here it is not such a long step to the positivist position which admits morality to a place in society which might indeed arise from interests but which then forms a body of imperatives which are separate from them and defended against them. But these imperatives, in the positivist account, are special to the society in which they find a place: morality is relative. A particular morality can have, on this view, no truth value, and can lay no claim to universality. This relativist position, which Bernard Williams attacks as 'the anthropologist's heresy' (though he had in mind the now defunct functionalist anthropology of a previous generation), would deny the contention that the 'element of universalization' is integral to any morality.[5] This is a contention which is characteristic of the tradition of natural law: that pattern of thought which is clustered round the view that there are certain moral principles inherent in human nature, which contain thereby the element of universalisation, and which are discoverable by the application of right reason. Morality is now no longer relativist, and the attachment of 'right' to 'reason' asserts that it is a subject which has truth and not mere emotion or opinion as its stock in trade. And if, described in this way, naturalist doctrine has a medieval flavour, it has nevertheless maintained its grip on Western thought, and its contentions are not so unscientific or metaphysical as to place them beyond the attempt at vindication by contemporary biologists.[6]

There is then a range in Western thought about morality from the denial that it has any autonomous existence whatever, to the insistence on its universality based on the ethical capacity of the individual. Marx bestrides this range by agreeing with Thrasymachus that morality is the rationalised interest of the ruling class, at the same time as looking forward to a final stage of communism in which men and nature would be in harmony in a society which conformed with the innate needs of man.[7] It is with the latter (and longer) end of this range that I am concerned in the consideration of moral frameworks and the attitudes they enclose, and what follows will look first at the

state (or rather at the *polis*), and then at the individual, the society of
states, and world society.

Those rights and obligations, goods and ideals that are commonly
thought of as the things that morality is about are qualities that tend
now to be associated with the individual. This was not a dominant
tendency of Greek thought. Plato's own account of justice begins with
the treatment of it as a quality which exists in a whole community.
Socrates says that justice might be easier to make out at that level than
at the level of the individual, and suggests that the growth of justice be
observed in the construction of the state.[8] Aristotle too, thinking of
wholes before parts, has the state prior to the household and the
individual in the order of nature, and the achievement of the good of
the state as the 'greater and more perfect good' than the good of the
individual.[9] This priority of the *polis* as the framework for morality
had consequences for the quality of its principles. In Plato, the discussion of social organisation is concerned with the division of labour and
embraces as a result a principle of interdependence rather than independence. Such rights and duties as follow are attached to services and
functions rather than to individuals.[10] The definition of justice as
'giving to every man his due' pays attention not to some *a priori* individual claim to equal treatment, but to a social measure of worth in the
community. And the position is similar in Aristotle. He does accept the
principle of equality in his account of justice as fairness, and it is this
quality which continues to recommend him to modern writers on
ethics. But in the course of establishing distributive and corrective
justice he finds good reasons to depart from his original principle of
equality, so that desert, or proportion, or appropriateness might each
of them set equality aside.[11] Rights are assigned here to classes of
people according to principles of social order, and there is little hint of
the modern idea of individual rights which are prior to the rules of
society. True, a fair distribution is one in which those who are equal
have equal shares, but the decision about who is equal is made
according to the criterion of equal ability to serve the state.[12]

Outside the *polis*, then, the good life was impossible, for virtue had
a social meaning. This Greek idea of the state as the primary moral
constituency was to reappear with the emergence of the modern state
and to reach its apogee in Hegel.[13] In the meantime, it was a notion
that disappeared with the submergence of the *polis* in the *cosmopolis*
of the Macedonian Empire. And where, in this system, political power
was located at some distance from the daily preoccupations of men, the
speculation of moralists turned from the public to the private domain,

and the virtuous individual replaced the virtuous state.[14] The retreat from the mundane that was involved in this process found its justification in the Christian gospel of individual salvation, and its unworldliness has been a more or less visible characteristic of Christianity ever since. 'When it is considered how short is the span of human life', said Augustine, 'does it really matter to a man whose days are numbered what government he must obey, so long as he is not compelled to act against God or his conscience?'[15] It was the life hereafter that mattered, and in virtue of this and its contemplation no really holy man concerned himself with the political except from his duty to release others from such concern,[16] and no earthly distinction between bond and free, or between rich and poor was of any consequence.[17] There is in this obliviousness to politics and society the material for an attack on Christianity as a 'slave morality',[18] but it was an obliviousness that gave rise to three doctrines about morality that were to have more noble consequences for the Western experience of politics.

How did these doctrines differ from their Greek predecessors? In the first place, men were confronted with a dual loyalty to the city of God and to the city of man where the Greek *polis* had required no such division. Secondly, where Aristotle had ethics as a branch of politics, the Augustinian legacy sharply separated them. And in the third place, Christian moralists, in the debate about ethics as ends or means, placed virtue in the means, the moral action itself if not regardless of ends then at least, in a moral scale, before them.[19]

The worldlessness of Augustine is, however, an extreme doctrine of what has been called 'primitive Christianity'.[20] The great medieval institution of the Church was necessarily worldly, and could not avoid a concern with society and politics. It was Aquinas who provided the theory to accompany this practice in accepting the world as an arena for the present achievement of a Christian civilisation, as well as a mere preparation for the life which was to come. The Aristotelian conception of the state, and the Roman idea of universal law, were channelled into Christian doctrine by Aquinas's use of the natural law of rational creatures. And this enabled him not merely to establish and defend a system of ethics, but also to render politics and society as Christian institutions. This achievement, however, meant a departure from Augustine's individual, and the just ordering of society came back into view. It was not until natural law became natural right that the Christian emphasis on the individual made its full political impact.

The way from natural law to natural right passes from the demise in the Reformation of the medieval notion of a single Christian commonwealth to the eighteenth-century enlistment of Christian doctrine in the service of political principle. The first step was taken by the Reformers in their attack on the Papacy, which, since they accepted the divine character of the Church, depended for its success on an appeal that had no less claim to divinity. They thus reasserted the doctrine of the divine nature of princely rule, and derived from it a right on the part of rulers to control the religion of their subjects.[21] It is not this claim itself that is important for the route we are tracing, but the one to which it gave rise. For once the central façade of medieval unity had been breached, and the right of the prince to religious sovereignty proclaimed, the new problem was for the domestic dissenter to find a basis for reducing princely pretension. And in the wake of the Massacre of Saint Bartholomew, which had destroyed the myth of the prince as protector of all his subjects, the New Testament, in Laski's phrase, was ransacked for texts that might justify rebellion.[22] In this way, the Christian attachment of importance to the individual conscience had its worldly impact: the 'political liberty of the seventeenth and eighteenth centuries was the outcome of the protest against religious intolerance'.[23] And this is the second stage along the route we are following – the secularisation of a religious tradition famously exemplified by Grotius's emancipation of natural law from divine law.[24] From here the way was open for social contract theory, placing the origin of society in an agreement among individuals who had natural rights, and thence to the rights of man, on whose behalf Tom Paine could invoke, in a style that bore no resemblance to the preoccupation with Christian doctrine in the *Vindiciae,* the unity or equality of men as all being of one degree from the Creation. This unity of degree, he says, is a feature of all known religions, not merely of Christianity, and by this observation he takes natural right back to natural law.

Praise or blame for the place of the individual in modern Western political thought has then to be apportioned between Christianity and the tradition of natural law. Both of these were by implication universalist: Christianity in its doctrine of the equality of all in the sight of God, and the law of nature in assigning rights to men as men. But the universe of individuals was not crowned by a universal state. The individual, even at the high-water mark of the doctrine of rights inhering in him in the eighteenth century, looked to his state to protect them. Nor was this simply a position maintained *faute de mieux.* Article III of the Declaration of the Rights of Man and of Citizens declared that the 'Nation is essentially the source of all sovereignty; nor can any individual, or any body of men, be entitled to any authority which is not expressly derived from it'.[25] The importance, then, of the framework of morality based upon the individual has not been that such a framework has provided for the enforcement of morals, but that it has kept alive the idea of a domain that was sacrosanct, beyond the reach of the political world,[26] and also the notion of an ideal pattern for society which lies ahead of man's present condition.[27] It is, perhaps, not a negligible framework for morality that has provided a buttress against totalitarianism, and a reason for progress.

The idea that rights and duties inhere in individuals was important for the birth of the idea of a society of states. The prince, as an individual, was no less bound by natural law than any other individual, and the obligation endured into action taken by him in the name of his realm. By this means, the idea was made possible that the realm itself was the bearer of rights and duties in an inter-state society, and it was the doctrine that international society was populated exclusively by sovereign states that became orthodox in the pages of the positivist international lawyers of the nineteenth century. In the course of this evolution, the status of the individual declined from one of full membership in international society alongside states to that of being a mere object of international law of which states took no legal notice. And with this eclipse, the idea of a morality that was special to the society of states had to find a place between, on the one hand, the position of the naturalists that there was no essential difference between the domestic and international domains – natural law applying in them both, and the position of *raison d'état*, which, in its extreme form, excluded morality with the exclusion of the individual.[28]

This middle course is first marked out by Hobbes: not indeed in his account of the state of nature as a state of war, but in his remark that the state of nature is a less miserable condition as it applies among states than it is in the relations of individuals.[29] If states in a posture of war uphold thereby the industry of their subjects, are less vulnerable to violent attack than are individuals at the same time as being more self-sufficient, and provide by their inequality the possibility of ordering their relations according to the principle that might is right, then there are in virtue of these contingencies the grounds for an international morality that has as its central feature the defence of the sovereign state as the provider of a degree of security in a hostile world. It is to be sure a morality in the weak sense of the word that we distinguished above, and it is, moreover, a morality that in comparison with our domestic expectations about justice is almost uniformly offensive: in its projection of special interests as moral principles; in its disposition to recognise *faits accomplis* as creative of values regardless of previous conceptions of right; and in the welcome it extends to war as a means of changing or policing international society.[30] Nor is this assessment much improved by the observation that, empirically, states have felt the need to act morally, or at least to justify their action in international relations. For in a decentralised system which allows no effective impartial verdict about the justice of any action, self-righteousness generated by a domestic justice constituency may be a greater hazard to international order than a self-interest which denies the force of morality in international affairs.

This is not, however, quite moral bankruptcy. It is true that the criterion of individual morality which leads us to esteem a man who takes into account the interests of another to the extent of preferring them to his own is not the hallmark of international morality.[31] But when the argument is taken a step further to the observation that we should be disposed to criticise (on moral grounds) a state for preferring another's interests to its own, sacrificing thereby the interests of its own citizens, then the idea of a *different* moral order rather than an *inferior* one begins to take shape. If the protection of the interests of individuals or groups is something which in general the state does more effectively than any more inclusive entity, then the interests of the state itself acquire thereby a moral dignity which is not automatically to be despised. 'The fundamental error which has thwarted American foreign policy in thought and action', said Morgenthau in 1950, 'is the antithesis of national interest and moral principles . . . The choice is not between moral principles and the national interest, devoid of moral dignity, but between one set of moral principles, divorced from political reality, and another set of moral principles, derived from political reality.'[32] And because it was not possible to attain a world based on universal moral principles, a foreign policy derived not from such a goal, but from the national interest, was in fact morally superior.

International morality might then be impoverished by being the outcome of a decision to prefer the order established within the state, but the defence of it rests on the assertion that any more ambitious doctrine that neglects the reality of a morally plural world is likely to undermine the international moral order rather than to protect and advance it. The unglamorous doctrine of non-intervention bears witness to the minimal unity of international society, and retains such universal validity as it has (universal that is in international society) by the acknowledgement on the part of states that most moral claims are to be made and met at a place other than in international society.[33] The

framework for morality that is provided by the society of states is thus
hostile to the substantial claims to justice of any individual, group or
class that is not a member of that society, and there is, as Hedley Bull
has said, a 'conspiracy of silence' against them.[34] For this reason, a
group to whose grievance international (or strictly inter-state) society
remains necessarily deaf, must base its appeal on the erosion of international society into a society based on a more inclusive principle which
will then admit new members.[35]

I use the term 'world society' to describe the framework of morality
that encompasses groups of this kind whose claims, not being accommodated by the society of states, are voiced in a tone which is hostile
to it. It is not a wholly accurate term, for the moral order which such
groups would build might stop short of a world society in the sense of
some great society of mankind: their designs might be restricted to a
society of nations, or to a society of states within each member of
which republican government was instituted or the dictatorship of the
proletariat established. A world society properly so-called might be one
in which all human beings owed allegiance to one sovereign, or one in
which a universal cultural pattern prevailed such that no part of the
society could mount a defence against it, and I shall treat presently the
view that a world society in a particular sense already exists. But
between the society that has failed to move far from the society of
states, and those world societies which might exist in virtue of the
global achievement of a single order, there are a number of claims that
surface in world politics because they do not find complete satisfaction
at the state or inter-state level and which have established some form of
non-state moral constituency in which they are considered legitimate:
the claim of an individual to human rights recognised in regional and
global institutions; the claim of a tribe or a cultural group in some
sense to survive the depredations of its host state recognised if nowhere
else by the class of professional anthropologists; the claim of a multi-
national corporation to penetrate the domain of the sovereign state
recognised by those who assert the autonomy of the economic order;
or the claim to recompense of an exploited class now voiced by the
Third World under the title of the 'New International Economic Order'
and recognised in some degree in the developed world.

This last claim arises from a view of world society as something
already established. If the idea of society is conceived not according to
some juridicial formula such as *ubi societas ibi jus est,* but in Marxian
terms as a system of collective productive activity, then it can be argued
that a world society exists and that it takes a form very different from

the account of international society that starts with the state. For in the Marxian view, society is not something enclosed within the state, and while the two might coincide, as in the Greek *polis*, there is no necessary connection between them.[36] The necessary connection is not between society and state, but between system of production and cultural form. And if the capitalist system of production is taken as the key to the evolution of modern world society, then it is possible to render that society in terms of the more powerful capitalist nations grafting their mode of production on the rest of the world, of an international division of labour between manufacturing countries and producers of raw materials, and of the creation of an international hierarchy maintained by a structure of dependence.[37] This is not a pluralist society of states with authority apportioned horizontally, but an imperial society in which authority is allocated vertically. And with the change of perspective, different moral scenery comes into view. In particular, it is when set in this context that the moral claims of an exploited class are at their most persuasive.

Whether or not it represents a liberal following of a radical lead, there is also a non-Marxist account of a world society existing in virtue of transnational relations, and of interdependence established across state frontiers. In view of developments of this kind which mark out a 'world in which national boundaries can no longer be regarded as the outer limits of social cooperation', it has been argued that principles of justice ought to apply globally, and not merely within states set apart by a principle of non-intervention.[38] According to this view, a norm of non-intervention might suffice in a world of more or less self-contained states, but in an interdependent world reliance on such a norm is a moral abdication. By benign or malign neglect, it has the effect of withdrawing an important area of social interaction from moral scrutiny. This is a point of view to which I shall return later: I merely notice it here as a moral framework whose scope is global.

To whatever extent these renderings of world society are a reality in world politics, there is a formula in the Western political tradition which would enable them to be co-opted into a world moral order. The conception originating in Stoic thought of a great society of mankind contained in it, as we have seen, the idea of a universal law applying to both individuals and to any institutions that they formed among themselves — since these too were made up of individuals. It was this doctrine (in addition to the idea of princely obligation) that enabled natural law to be applied to states, and by the same token, it might be applied to any entity beyond them. Indeed, this process would constitute a return to the medieval conception of a *communitas humani generis* rather than being the departure from it that the idea of a society of states itself was. But the observation that natural law is in principle applicable to any kind of society that might be emerging – so that whither the framework thither the morality – is, it might be said, rather a vacuous one. The difficulty with it is the very lack of any kind of established, consensual framework that might enclose a robust morality. There is not *a* framework, but rather competing frameworks built to accompany each vision of world society, some of which as we have seen, assert the reality of world society as a structure of dependence or of interdependence, others of which merely invite us to consider world society from a certain point of view,[39] and still others of which assert the shape which world society ought to take without suggesting that it is yet a reality.[40]

And the idea of world society as constituting a moral framework is not problematical only because of the variety of Western conceptions of it. The more intractable difficulty is that, in being *Western* conceptions, they are inescapably a partial view of the world social whole. Thus, while it is true that, for example, John Rawls's *A Theory of Justice*[41] is a theory framed *sub specie aeternitatis,* applicable in principle at any time and place, to all of humanity (as his critics, but not Rawls himself, have said) or to any part of it, it does in fact arise from a particular philosophic tradition, and has an appeal which is unlikely to be felt outside it.[42]

For these reasons, the harsh conclusion about world society as a moral framework is that, like the one formed by the universe of individuals, it has nurtured some noble ideas but has not yet taken a form concrete enough to uphold them in practice. But this harsh conclusion is not the only one. The moral claims of individuals, or of tribes, or of multinational corporations, or of classes have a reality in world politics, and a more or less well-articulated constituency in which they are recognised, which are not simply to be measured as an inverse proportion of their distance from the sovereign state. And while it may be true that these claims might be stifled as claims before world society the more effectively they are met by the state, the finality of the latter community is a hypothesis denied by their appearance in world politics in the first place.

This discussion of moral frameworks in Western thought might be summarised by the remark that the individual is to the state as the society of states is to world society. The individual framework, and the framework of the state in international society, enclose rights and duties that are prior to society, which social rules must then protect: they assert, as it were, a private domain which is exclusive of public arrangements. The framework of the state, and that of world society, invert this order of priority and take virtue as a public property rather than a private one: the good of society comes before the right of the individual.[43] And this is the point of the proportion sum done to summarise the discussion: on either side of it there is a swing from the right to the good. The distinction between these two qualities is a theme in Western thought most graphically illustrated by the debate between the theorists of natural right and the utilitarians: the peremptory quality of individual claims against the greatest happiness of the greatest number. The long ascendancy of the latter doctrine has been challenged by Rawls's expression of justice as fairness as the priority of the concept of right over that of the good, so that the 'principles of justice . . . specify the boundaries that men's systems of ends must respect'.[44] And this is a blow struck not merely on behalf of natural right against utilitarianism, but against that other long-standing orthodoxy of positivism — since, in Laski's usage, it pits right against rights, expediency being able to establish the latter but not the former.[45] And this is to arrive again at the question of the sources of morality with which this section of the chapter was introduced. I pass now from frameworks to issues.

This section will treat three moral issues that recur in Western thought — realism versus idealism, equality and human rights — with a view to showing that much of the vitality of moral debate in international politics is produced by a contest among the frameworks that have just been described. The choice of these three issues, rather than certain others which have a claim to be treated in a study of this kind — such as the doctrine of just war, or the question of national self-determination, or the moral problems that are raised by the appearance of particular weapons in international politics — is not simply an arbitrary one, but arises from their topicality: not only have they recurred historically, but examples of them are the burning questions of the hour.

The debate between realism and idealism in international relations can be thought of in four dimensions. In the first place, it is a disagreement about the principles that are to direct action in international politics. Thus, in the Melian controversy, the Athenians, having camped on the island of Melos with a superior force, then set out to persuade the Melians that their best course was prudently to accept the Athenian

preponderance and make their island over to Athens without the fight
that would be in the interest of neither party.[46] The Athenians made
no pretence to a right to rule in Melos, but merely invited the Melians
to look circumstances in the face, and to aim with the Athenians only
at what was possible — for the 'question of justice enters only where
the pressure of necessity is equal', and 'the powerful exact what they
can, and the weak grant what they must'. Against this celebration of
the possible by the power with the upper hand, the Melians excused
themselves to the Athenians for wishing things otherwise, and sought
to persuade them to act according to right for this was their true
interest. But if this should fail, the Melians would fight for principle
and trust to good fortune. This course did not profit the Melians, but
their failure did not decide the debate between idealism and realism
in favour of the latter, for the Athenian point about might being
accepted, that of right remained, attached only problematically to it.

The second dimension of the debate between realists and idealists
is close to the first, and involves its contemplation from another angle:
not what principles are to guide action, but the criteria by which we are
to judge actions once they have occurred. A realist might admire a
statesman for his prudence, an idealist for his vision, and so the ranks of
commentators are drawn up in support of Athenians or Melians. In the
history of the study of international relations in the twentieth century
both sides have been heard, the idealists in support of a view of the
subject as a vehicle for international improvement, the realists in
defence of a conception of it as a chronicle of certain dismal regulari-
ties in the human experience, and I shall come presently to their place
in contemporary international politics.

The third dimension of the debate relates to the origin of the rules
that instruct behaviour and provide standards for its judgement, and to
the basis of obligation to them. In this mode it is an argument carried on
between naturalists and positivists, some of which we have already
heard. The naturalists asserted rules of right reason discoverable by the
use of the intellect which applied to men (and human institutions) in
virtue of their very humanity, while the positivists derived rules from
command, custom or treaty and thought of them as sprung from practice rather than precept. Whatever the reasons for the ascendancy of
positivism in the nineteenth century — its appeal to good sense in not
setting rules too far ahead of behaviour, or in observing that different
societies did in fact have different moral regimes — it is a doctrine that
has been challenged in the international relations of the twentieth century. The attention paid to human rights in such instruments as the

United Nations Charter, the Charter of the Nuremberg International
Military Tribunal and the Universal Declaration of Human Rights arose
not from evidence of state practice, but from a conviction about right
conduct regardless of state practice. And there are four different
grounds on which naturalism, to which these developments represent
a return, might be defended as a source of morality. In the first place,
the positivist doctrine that what is thought to be right in any society is
right, might have the effect of raising a protective umbrella over
practices that the philosophers' ordinary man might find morally
offensive: natural law, it might be said, is the ordinary man's informant.
Secondly, the unscientific quality of the naturalist formula for a universal morality — 'principles of conduct discouraged by the use of right
reason' — might be removed by converting it into a logical question
about what is necessary for social life,[47] or into an empirical question:
Are there as a matter of observation certain principles of human conduct which are universal in the sense that no society is to be found that
does not in some degree observe them? A less ambitious form of this
question might ask whether it is true to say that a capacity for ethical
behaviour is an observable characteristic of men everywhere, so that
even if the rules are different, an ethical competence is universal. These
questions take us into the domains of anthropology and biology, and
neither of them seems as inherently unsound as the propositions of
natural law sometimes appeared.

A third defence of natural law relies not on its form but on its function, and this is the essence of d'Entrèves' account of it. His argument
is that whatever might be thought of the particular pronouncements of
natural law at particular times, it is a body of doctrine that has fulfilled
three majestic functions in the Western experience of politics. It has
established a universal basis for law (the Stoics; Rome). It has provided
a rational foundation for ethics (Aquinas). And it has produced a theory
of natural rights (the American and French Revolutions).[48] Rationalism
is a thread that runs through each of these functions, and provides
itself a fourth defence of natural law. A large part of morality might be
conveyed by rendering it as something which requires that good reasons
be given for any action. This is a weak defence because it takes 'right'
away from 'reason', allowing thereby the possibility that positivism
might rule by default, but it does at least provide a protest against
arbitrariness. That the function of naturalism might be reduced to this
shows its worldlessness to be a central weakness, where its worldliness
is the weakness of positivism. Both weaknesses, as we shall see, endure.

The final dimension of the debate between realism and idealism has its appeal for academic international relations intramurally: it is a way of organising a history of thought about the subject, so that the tradition of *raison d'état* is opposed to that of universal morality.[49] The difficulty with this polarisation is that it leaves no room for a middle ground between the schools of thought which is, as a matter of observation, occupied even by those who are commonly considered as belonging uncompromisingly to one group or the other.[50] And it is a difficulty that applies in each of the other dimensions of the polarity. Thus the long and sometimes tedious argument between naturalists and positivists has been seen by an outsider as a local dispute between groups sharing a legalist ideology that is more striking for what unites its brethren than for what divides them.[51] In the matter of how events are to be judged it has been remarked that the debate between idealism and realism as it took place in the subject of international relations in the twentieth century was cloistered within the English-speaking world, and accepted a common framework of moral discourse.[52] And in relation to the principles that are to guide action, the Melians were concerned to show the Athenians that it was on grounds of expediency that a moral principle should be respected, while the Athenians, for their part, after an initial disclaimer about pretending to rights in Melos, defended as a law of nature the principle that might was right.

But it is not as though mere argument can break up these schools of thought, and they survive in each of the four dimensions outlined. In regard to the principles that are to guide foreign policy and by which it is to be judged, the 'realist' Henry Kissinger, working through the traditional agenda of the international politics – the 'structure of peace' – can be divided from his 'idealist' critics who lament his belated awareness of the new agenda of international politics – interdependence, the global crisis, systematic injustice to the Third (or Fourth) Worlds – and his failure fundamentally to take it seriously.[53] On the source of rules, it is possible to separate into positivist and naturalist categories the notion of 'law' as involving *stability of expectations* inherited from the past', and the idea of 'justice' as involving *changing expectations* about what needs to be done in the future'.[54] Law is connected realistically with stability, justice idealistically with chance. Within the discipline of international relations it is still possible to discern a debate 'gently raging'[55] between 'realists' who believe that international relations remains a state of war dominated by the concern for security, and idealists who believe that world politics are becoming more like domestic politics. And just as the realist and idealist dispensations endure in these ways into contemporary thought, so also does the dissatisfaction with the dichotomy and the attempt to transcend it. Thus Falk describes the domains of both law and justice as enclosed in a states-system which it is the purpose of the world order radical massively to subvert in order to achieve that central guidance on whose emergence the survival of the planet might depend.[56] And the defence of this programme is not just an idealist one, but one that depends on a realist demand for the construction of relevant utopias to guide a world that has to escape its present predicament.[57] One of the things that might stand in the way of such constructions is the doctrine of state equality, and it is to this that I now turn.

The idea of the equality of states arrived in international relations via an analogy with domestic politics, drawn first by Hobbes and Pufendorf, but having its clearest expression in the writings of Wolff and his follower Vattel. 'Since by nature all men are equal', said Wolff, 'all nations too are by nature equal the one to the other . . . Just as the tallest man is no more a man than the dwarf, so also a nation, however small, is no less a nation than the greatest nation. Therefore, since the moral equality of men has no relation to the size of their bodies, the moral equality of nations has no relation to the number of men of which they are composed'.[58] Vattel used the same image of giant and dwarf to show that strength and weakness counted for nothing in the attribution of equality to states.[59] States had an absolute equality because they were states, and no factual inequality was considered relevant.

A slightly less ambitious version of this doctrine, according to which states, having an equal capacity for rights, are potentially equal, has been taken as what most writers on international law have meant by the principle of equality.[60] The objection to the principle in this form, or in the stronger absolute form, is that in paying either very little or no attention to the fact of inequality, it was likely to build a system of international law that bore small relation to the actual practice of states. And even the more tentative doctrine of equality — which holds that for certain purposes factual inequalities between states are not to be considered relevant, so that, for example, states are to be thought of as at least equal before the law — has been taken as a spurious application of a nominally democratic principle to the unsuitable environment of international relations.[61] Thus, in regard to the United Nations, it might be argued that the doctrine of one-state-one-vote that follows from the principle of equality gets in the way of the efficient working of the organisation. It does so by preventing the writ of the powerful, on whose support the survival of the organisation depends, from running, and by allowing resolutions to be carried by coalitions of small states of whose acceptance in the international community at large there is little prospect. Against this it can be argued that equality of status for states that are not great powers attaches them to the purposes of the international community, an institution which they might otherwise regard as a systematic denial of their interests.

But if equality of status is all that small powers can be said to have gained in international relations, it is possible to think of the extension of the principle of equality in at least two directions. In the first place, international society might come to admit more respects in which the principle of equality is to apply, so that, in it, the same course for the doctrine might be traced as in domestic politics — extending gradually from the sphere of ethics to that of law, then to religious belief, politics and society, and finally to economics.[62] And secondly, international society might admit institutions other than states as bearers of rights and duties in it, recognising to that extent their equality, and welcoming them into what would then have become a world society.

In contemporary international society there has been little progress in either of these directions, but that more has taken place in the first of them than in the second can be illustrated by reference to the General Assembly's Charter of Economic Rights and Duties of States. As to the first direction the references to equality in the Charter are mainly traditional and procedural, and do not in general constitute substantial demands for economic equality. The fundamentals of international economic relations which it lays down are for the most part a mild enough reiteration of principles already familiar from earlier Assembly resolutions. The rights it asserts are mainly to equal sovereignty for all states over foreign economic activities within their territories, and to equal access to such international economic institutions as exist between states. And equal access means either simply the right to engage in trade, or to join together in associations for the producers of primary products, or to participate in the process of decision-making about world economic matters.

In two senses only does the Charter require something more than mere juridical equality. Thus, in the first place, there is in the idea that the less-developed countries have more rights, while the developed states have more duties — to transfer technology, to give aid and to allow tariff preferences, and generally to take special account of the interests of developing countries — the beginnings of a notion that in international society economic goods must be distributed more evenly.

And secondly, there is in the idea that the states responsible for exploitation and depletion of, or damage to the natural and other resources of other countries, territories or peoples, should make restitution to them and fully compensate them,[63] the beginnings of a notion in international society of a right of redress for economic injury. But while these concepts of distributive justice, and of justice as compensation for injury,[64] do demonstrate a movement away from mere juridical equality, they do not signify the arrival of substantial equality: the former requires only that goods be distributed more evenly (not necessarily equally); the latter requires compensation that might set an historical record straight (but not the current record equal). Even in these weakened senses, and however seriously these principles are taken in the practice of international politics (and to take but two examples, the United States does not accept a target level for development assistance of 0.7 per cent of each industrial country's GNP, nor the notion that commodity prices should be pegged to an index of world inflation), the idea that they should apply in international society as well as in domestic society is itself an important one.

In regard to the second direction in which the principle of equality might be extended involving the admission of institutions beyond the state, there is little evidence in the Charter of any conception of a cosmopolitan justice that applies to men over the heads of governments. The Charter is concerned mainly with states, and refers to entities other than states ('peoples', 'territories') in a language which is used in the Assembly to refer to the remnants of colonialism. For other men and institutions waiting in the wings of international society, and making a case for entry into it on such a basis as, for example, class, the Charter, as a state's Charter, is no comfort at all. And in the practice of the United Nations this represents a retreat from the Universal Declaration of Human Rights, and from the International Convention on Economic, Social and Cultural Rights, in both of which the individual was himself a bearer of economic and social rights and duties.

In the matter of human rights, which is the twentieth century expression[65] for those natural rights which, as we saw in the last section, arose from the importance attached in Western thought to the moral claims of individuals, there are signs of a return in this century to pre-positivist conceptions of the place of the individual in international society. Thus Lauterpacht, in virtue of the recognition of the fundamental rights of the individual in the Charter of the United Nations, and in other international instruments, argues that he has now been constituted a subject of international law whose rights and freedoms states have a duty to observe.[66] The primary difficulty with the assertion of this doctrine as a tenet of positive law agreed between states and largely observed by them, as distinct from a natural law which embodies principles that international society ought to observe but cannot be said yet to have accepted, is the prospect of its enforcement. For while it is true, as Lauterpacht says, that this is a difficulty which attaches to international law in general, and which should not therefore be used to bring down human rights in particular, it can be said that there is more prospect of even the smallest state enforcing its rights than there is of the individual doing so. This is the more true if Article 2(7) of the United Nations Charter — the clause reserving domestic jurisdiction against any intrusion by the international organisation except in the case of the enforcement of peace and security — is taken seriously, as it is by Lauterpacht, and not regarded as an outworn dogma. And in this respect, the practice of the United Nations since Lauterpacht wrote has been to reinforce domestic jurisdiction rather than to give greater recognition to the individual. Thus, the covenants on human rights passed by the United Nations General Assembly in 1966, retreating somewhat from the language of the 1948 Universal Declaration of Human Rights, envisaged only states petitioning the human rights committees provided for in them, so that, there being no direct access for individuals, it was up to a state to take up the cause of an individual within another state.[67] And if states are to be made thus the guardians of human rights within each other's territories, any expectations about their performance in this area have to be measured against their un-promising record in the area with which the Charter was primarily con-cerned — that of the maintenance of peace and security in inter-national relations.

Nevertheless, it is the idea that states do have duties in the area of human rights that has informed the traditional doctrine of humani-tarian intervention, so that if a state by its behaviour outrages the conscience of mankind it should not be entitled to invoke the principle of non-intervention. Thus it is argued that states had not only a right but a duty to intervene in order to protect the Jews against Nazi persecution, and a parallel is drawn and similar conduct urged against apartheid in present-day South Africa. The problem with this doctrine lies not in its identification of the evil to be removed, but in the trust it must place in those who are to act for international society. The moral case for non-intervention even in the face of outrageous conduct within the state stems partly from the lack of such trust, and partly from fear of the consequences of intervention. I shall deal first with the general defence of a principle of non-intervention against any principle of intervention and then with the argument that there are certain special circumstances which should set it aside.[68]

The moral basis for a principle of non-intervention in international society might be said to arise from a criterion familiar from the account of morality among individuals. Just as persons are to be treated as having ends of their own, and are not to be interfered with so long as they do not themselves interfere with the equal rights of others, so, it can be argued, states as 'associations of individuals with their own common interests and aspirations expressed within a common tradition' are entitled to the same treatment.[69] But this is a general criterion for morality that might be applied to groups such as families, or tribes, or classes, or nations, as well as to individuals and states. The particular moral claim of the state to have the principle of non-intervention attached to it rests not on any intrinsic moral superiority on its part compared to these other groups, but on its potential provision of a framework of order within which justice might be achieved. It is to be defended then, on moral grounds, for what it makes possible rather than for what it is, it being hard to see justice provided for except through the agency of order. It is true that, in any instance, this order might play host to injustice, but the general defence of the state as a platform of order does not fall by reference to particular injustice. For the moral defence of the state to fall, and with it the principle of non-intervention, it would have to be shown that its affront to justice was systematic, and not merely possible.

There is a weak and a strong version of the doctrine that the state is a systematic denier of justice. An advocate of the weak version, by referring to such arbitrary patterns of authority as were imposed on Africa by the colonial powers, might reject any moral claims of the state now succeeded to that authority on the grounds that it was in no way an expression of interests and aspirations within a common tradition. Non-intervention here would be a defence of arbitrariness. An advocate of the strong version, by referring to the structure of dependence that was discussed earlier as a description of world society, might reject any moral claims of the state on the grounds that its territorial jurisdiction was over a hollow shell, emptied of any moral content by a pattern of production designed elsewhere. The principle of non-intervention here stands guard over a void, and in the process turns its back on the real subject for moral concern.

Of the advocate of the weaker version of this doctrine, it might be said that his protest is not against the state as such, but against the boundaries in which it is presently confined. If those boundaries were redrawn to coincide with tribal or national boundaries, his protest might be met, and the doctrine of non-intervention restored to moral respectability. Of the advocate of the stronger version of the doctrine, it might be said that while his protest against the moral shortsightedness of the principle of non-intervention is a persuasive one, it is not one that is accompanied by an equally convincing account of a moral order (as distinct from moral claims) that could make up for this lack. This is a question to which I shall return at the conclusion of this chapter, but the point here is that the moral case for non-intervention relies not on the perfection of the state, but on the absence of any substantial competitor for its role as a community within which morals might be enforced.

In this regard, the presumption against the morality of intervention has two aspects. In the first place, there is reason to doubt the impartiality of the state that intervenes in the internal affairs of another, to question the expectation that it can remove with surgical precision the evil that caused the intervention and then withdraw. And while it may be true that the intervention might realise a moral purpose at the same time as securing some other interest, there is no guarantee of such a coincidence. Secondly, even if impartiality could be guaranteed, intervention is likely to be unwelcome simply because it comes from outside, because it is alien to whatever common culture unites the citizens of the target state. The moral purpose of the intervening state, selfless and beyond reproach according to its own ethical lights, might have a different interpretation in the perspective of the target state: impartial perhaps, but within a partial morality. This lack of a coherent and pervasive morality to transcend international frontiers, of a 'justice constituency' in Julius Stone's phrase,[70] which might then not only inform and justify particular acts of intervention, but also make their success a likely outcome, is an important reason for preferring a principle of non-intervention.

But in such cases as the ones I have mentioned — Nazi Germany and South Africa — and in others which might be included in which the charge of genocide has been made, it might be argued, to insist on the purity of the motives of the intervening state, or to draw attention to the lack of a well-developed common morality, is grotesquely out of place. For here, it might be said, the conscience of mankind is outraged, and there is a justice constituency articulate enough to recognise such glaring cases. But if this is so, then not only do the less worthy consequences of any intervention have to be tolerated along with its good effects (so that, for example, a power might aggrandise itself at the expense of a disagreeable neighbour while intervening on purportedly humanitarian grounds), but also the possibility that the intervention might escalate into a full-scale war adding further moral outrages to the one that led to intervention in the first place.

Even in such cases, then, it may not be grotesque to agree with the 'realists' that the inter-state principle of non-intervention is to be preferred, in a moral scale, to a doctrine of humanitarian intervention based on a more inclusive ethic. And though the cases might not always be as pressing, this choice is a classical one that confronts each generation of statesmen. On the contemporary question of detente and human rights for Soviet citizens (and others), President Carter, without going to the lengths of Senator Jackson's assertion that economic concessions to the Soviet Union should be linked with freer Jewish emigration, has declared a commitment to the rights of individuals which distinguishes him from the previous administration. Dr Kissinger's view to the contrary was that making an international issue of something that the Soviet Union regarded as a domestic matter was not only unlikely to succeed, but would also place at risk the structure of peace under construction in areas that did not trouble the Soviet Union domestically. Kissinger's argument for non-intervention was not one that, in his view, surrendered morality to interests, but one that subordinated what was judged to be the lesser moral claim to the greater. There was not perhaps a 'conspiracy of silence' about the rights of Soviet Jews, but these were not to direct the course of relations between the superpowers.

But such a choice need not empty the notion of human rights of any meaning, nor need it indicate the adoption towards them of the scornful attitude of Bentham. The language of human rights, as Maurice Cranston has said, provides some form in which a person can convey that a wrong is being done to him, and that something he ought to have is being denied him.[71] Moral claims that make use of this language are heard in world politics, and their hearing might assist in the building of a transnational justice constituency which might then improve conduct within states by a means more civilised and dependable than intervention.

Involved in each of the issues just dealt with is a disagreement about frameworks for morality. The argument for non-intervention chooses the framework of the society of states, while the case for humanitarian intervention, asserting human rights that states have a duty to observe, derives from the framework of the individual. The argument that the doctrine of the equality of states should apply to economic matters arises within the framework of the society of states, but borrows from the structural dependence model of world society insofar as it asserts a duty on the part of colonialists and neocolonialists to redress past and present injuries. And when the argument for equality is pressed on behalf of individuals — a reasonable outcome of the choice of that framework — it is one that must abandon altogether the 'society of states', and come to grips with the hierarchical account of world society. The debate between realists and idealists, in each of the dimensions discussed, is a disagreement between those who accept the framework of the state, and the society of states, and attempt to work within it, and those making no such concession, who would pull international society towards one or another conception of world society.

This chapter has found more to say in defence of the conventions of diplomacy than its search for a universal morality might have suggested. This is not because of their manifest moral superiority to claims that arise from the hierarchic account of world society, discussed above, or to claims that derive from our common responsibility as travellers on 'spaceship earth', or to any claim that originates outside the society of states, but because they provide a framework of order within which moral claims might be met, and not merely a vocabulary in which they might be articulated. The claim of a peripheral, exploited class in the third or fourth worlds for recompense for injuries received at the hands of central, imperialist powers derives from a hierarchic description of world society, and it might be part of a moral case that is undeniable. The ecologists' case for 'central guidance' might be equally convincing. And there are other claims. But these claims are not matched by a constituency in which they might be met. It may be true that they derive from, in some sense, the reality of world society, but there is no community in which they can be weighed and disposed of. Instead, claims are lodged in the society of states. Their reception there has not been tumultuous, for they present maximalist demands to a society which has been unresponsive to minimalist ones. But the argument here is that there is nowhere else to go: the conventions of international society are accepted because of the absence of any alternative. And this is the difficulty with the assertion that 'the state-centred image of the world has lost its normative relevance because of the rise of global economic interdependence'.[72] It may or may not be true to say that the factual basis for a society of states is being eroded, but this society remains 'normatively relevant' so long as the justice constituency which

exists in virtue of a *sense* of community is more visible within state
frontiers than across them. Indeed, with reference to the notion of a
trans-state hierarchy, it may be that the state-centred image of the
world is to be defended as a normatively relevant means of challenging
it, since it is arguably the state aiming at self-reliance and self-sufficiency
that can detach itself from a structure of dependence. It is in this regard
that the case of China is celebrated.

These words on behalf of the states system and the diplomatic
conventions that sustain it do nothing to save the notion of a universal
morality, and the argument is not yet distinguishable from Bruce Miller's
'rationalised interests'. One way of dignifying international, or strictly
interstate, morality that has been noted more than once in this chapter
is to find in it, with Morgenthau and Kissinger, not merely an alternative moral framework, but a superior one, so that a conception of right
which takes reality into account is to be preferred to one that insists
on certain courses of action regardless of circumstance. The difficulty
with this view is that in making realism the touchstone of what is moral,
or of what is morally superior, it allows the content of morality to be
determined by the convenience of princes, for it is they who, in marking
out the boundaries of political possibility, determine what is realistic.
Rules arrived at in this way might be prudential but never moral except
by accident, since unless conceptions of morality put forward a view
of what is right universally, independent of any particular interest or
convenience, it is a mistake to think of them as moral conceptions at
all.[73] In this sense, universality is implicit in morality, and the expression 'universal morality' is a tautology, albeit a helpful one in unseating
the idea of morality as rationalised interests. In another sense, as was
seen above, universal morality, a universal moral order, is a term that
describes not the nature of moral concepts, but a particular moral order
among others, the framework for morality which encompasses the
globe and has the great society of mankind as its constituency. In
Western thought a principal support for this framework has been
natural law, whose strength in turn derives from its appeal to what by
nature is common to all men as distinct from the artificial obligations
of states which divide them. Rules of right reason which apply to men
as men set a universal standard against which all working moral orders
are measured and their shortcomings noted. The positive side of this
relationship is that at the same time as being an index of failure, natural
law is a wellspring of ideas for international improvement so that, for
example, the moral issues considered in this paper — idealism, equality,
and human rights — each derive from the inspiration of natural law. The

power of natural law is as a source of right, and of interstate morality as a record of what has been achieved. There is no good reason to reduce morality in international politics to the latter.

Notes

1. J.D.B. Miller, 'Morality, Interests and Rationalisation' in this volume.
2. Plato, *The Republic*, Book 1, Ch. III.
3. Ibid., Book 1, Ch. IV.
4. Bruce Miller concedes more than this when he defends statesmen against the charge of hypocrisy, and allows their sincerity in invoking a morality beyond the nation for policies that in fact derive from a national morality.
5. Bernard Williams, *Morality: An Introduction to Ethics* (Harmondsworth, 1973), pp. 34-9. I should draw attention here to a possible confusion between universalisation as application to all members of a particular class (citizens of Rome), and universalisation as application to all members of the human race (citizens of the world). That Williams means the latter and not the (relativist) former is clear from his remark that morality involves internalised norms that 'cannot merely evaporate because one is confronted with human beings in another society', ibid., p. 37.
6. See, e.g., C.H. Waddington, *The Ethical Animal* (London, 1960), *passim*. I return to naturalism vs. positivism in Part II below.
7. For Marx as a moralist in the tradition of natural law, see Paul E. Sigmund, *Natural Law in Political Thought* (Cambridge, Mass., 1971), pp. 165-6. For a trenchant denial of this view, see Allen W. Wood, 'The Marxian critique of Justice', *Philosophy and Public Affairs*, vol. 1, no. 3 (Spring 1972).
8. *The Republic*, Book II, Ch. VI.
9. *The Politics*, Iii; The *Nicomachean Ethics*, Iii.
10. See George H. Sabine, *A History of Political Theory*, 3rd edn (London, 1948), p. 60, who notes the absence in Plato of the modern notion of right.
11. *The Nicomachean Ethics*, Viii and Viv.
12. *The Politics*, IIIxii and IIIxiii.
13. I should add here that while the *polis* might have been the primary moral constituency in Greek thought, it was not the final one. Maurice Cranston begins his discussion of the history of human rights with Antigone's defiance of Creon's edict that her brother Polynices should remain unburied on the battlefield because he had fought traitorously against his own city. See *What are Human Rights?* (London, 1973), pp. 9-10. Antigone's forum is one of conscience not enclosed by the state.
14. Bertrand Russell, *History of Western Philosophy*, 2nd edn (London, 1961), p. 240. I shall return later to the distinction between individual and collectivist ethics.
15. *City of God*, Book V, Ch. 17.
16. Russell, *History of Western Philosophy*, p. 329; Hannah Arendt, *The Human Condition* (Chicago, 1958), p. 60.
17. The worldly consequence of this doctrine was, however, the failure to translate equality for slaves in the early church into an improvement in their civil status, and as Reinhold Niebuhr says, to this day the churches pride themselves on being able to transcend economic and social inequalities within their walls without it following that they should move vigorously against them. *Moral*

Man and Immoral Society (New York, 1948), pp. 77-8.
    18. This is Nietzsche's phrase, but I do not meant it here in his sense. His objection to Christian morality was that its doctrine of equality before God pulled down the worthy to the level of the worthless, and prevented thereby the noble and artistic from 'fashioning man'. Slave morality was the triumph of the worthless. See *Beyond Good and Evil*, trans. Helen Zimmern (Edinburgh and London, 1909), pp. 84, 117, 227-32. The attack on Christian worldlessness that I have in mind in using the phrase 'slave morality' is the one to which I have already drawn attention — that equality stopped at the church door: slave morality as the continued oppression of the humble not their triumph.
    19. Russell, *History of Western Philosophy*, p. 190.
    20. By A.P. d'Entrèves, *Natural Law*, 2nd edn (London, 1970), Ch. 3, on which the following discussion of Aquinas is based.
    21. Harold J. Laski, *A Defence of Liberty Against Tyrants*, (London, 1924), introduction, p. 2.
    22. Ibid., p. 23.
    23. Ibid., p. 27.
    24. *De Jure Belli ad Pacis*, Prolegomena, para. 11.
    25. *The Rights of Man*, Everyman edition, pp. 42-3. And just as Paine shows thus his emancipation from Christian dogma, so in a different way does the tract against which his was a protest. In founding society on human wants, and on interdependence, rather than on individual rights, and in preserving the differences of degree which Paine made a unity, Burke inclined more closely to the Greek account of society than to one that was dependent on a Christian view of the relations of individuals. See *Reflections on The Revolution in France*, in E.J. Payne (ed.), *Burke: Select Works*, vol. II (Oxford, 1898), pp.70-71.
    26. 'The Christian', says Herbert Butterfield, 'is particularly called to carry his thinking outside that framework which a nation or a political party or a social system or an accepted regime or a mundane ideology provides.' *Christianity, Diplomacy and War* (London, 1953), p. 4.
    27. This is a recurring defence of natural law in d'Entrèves, *Natural Law*.
    28. Nor is this a primitive doctrine of old-fashioned 'Machiavellism'. Hans J. Morgenthau, though this is not a view he holds consistently, does declare that 'the reference to a moral rule of conduct requires an individual conscience from which it emanates, and there is no individual conscience from which what we call the international morality of Great Britain or of any other nation could emanate'. *Politics Among Nations*, 4th edn (New York, 1967), p. 240. E.H. Carr's answer to this point of view is that the attribution of personality to the state, so that it might be thought of as subject to moral rules, is a necessary fiction in international society, just as the notion of the corporate responsibility of a joint stock company is a fiction necessary to municipal law. *The Twenty Years' Crisis*, 2nd edn (London, 1946), pp. 148-9.
    29. See *Leviathan*, Ch. XIII, and Hedley Bull, 'Society and Anarchy in International Relations', in Butterfield and Wight, *Diplomatic Investigations*, pp. 45-8.
    30. It is this moral offensiveness, or so it seems to me, that renders somewhat out of place the liking among some English writers for the cosy simile of the club in describing this aspect of international society. Thus Butterfield: 'It was certainly true that, though the international order [after the Treaty of Utrecht] performed its function, aggression was not eliminated, and the nations still often came into conflict with one another. But it was as though the members of the international club were competing for the best armchairs, or the best service at dinner — jockeying one another, shall we say, to obtain the best room in the house . . .' *Christianity, Diplomacy and War*, p. 81.
    31. See Niebuhr, *Moral Man and Immoral Society*, pp. xi-xii.

32. 'The Mainsprings of American Foreign Policy: The National Interest vs. Moral Abstractions', *American Political Science Review*, vol. XLIV, no. 4, (December 1950), pp. 853-4. I return to this argument in Part II, and in the conclusion.

33. I say most rather than all, for the assertion of a principle of non-intervention is itself a moral claim as I shall argue in the next section of the paper.

34. 'Order vs. Justice in International Society', *Political Studies*, vol. XIX, no. 3 (September 1971), p. 275.

35. This is true even though a new entrant, having made a claim of this kind in order to gain admission, might want to revert to the old principles once successful. I have in mind the group that would be a state basing its claim to such status on the principle of national self-determination, but then having become a state, insisting on the principle of state sovereignty to deter further disintegration,

36. See Wood, 'The Marxian Critique of Justice', *Philosophy and Public Affairs* (Spring 1972), pp. 251-5.

37. See Harry Magdoff, 'Imperialism: A Historical Survey', *Monthly Review*, vol. 24, no. 1 (May 1972), pp. 4 and 12.

38. See Charles L. Beitz, 'Justice and International Relations', *Philosophy and Public Affairs*, vol. 4, no. 4 (Summer 1975), p. 374. Though Beitz does not deal with this aspect of it, the argument for world justice to accommodate transnational relations involves a judgement about their importance compared to interstate relations, as well as the mere observation that they exist (or have expanded) and are norm-creating. As Raymond Aron has said, transnational relations have been regulated in all periods by custom, or convention, or by a specific code. The question, as Aron puts it, is one between public and private international law — whether in, for example, contemporary international politics, the heterogeneous inter-state system divides transnational society. *Peace and War* (London, 1966), p. 106.

39. See George Modelski's layer-cake model of it in *Principles of World Politics* (New York, 1972), Ch. 13.

40. One thinks here of the use of the domestic analogy in international relations, asserting that what is required for the establishment of a world political society is the same single sovereign that was established within the state. A modern version of this doctrine asserting the need for a 'central guidance mechanism' is Richard A. Falk, *A Study of Future Worlds* (New York, 1975), Ch. 4.

41. (London, 1972).

42. Rawls says that his aim is to generalise and carry to a higher level of abstraction the familiar theory of the social contract as found in Locke, Rousseau and Kant, *Theory of Justice*. p. 11. It is the difficulty of applying this 'familiar theory' to non-Western societies in which it is not familiar, in my view, that those who argue for the global application of Rawls's principles of justice have failed adequately to confront. Thus Beitz, for example, notices that different principles may be appropriate for different societies, but does not give this the central place in his analysis that it seems to me to require, 'Justice and International Relations', p. 377, note 24.

43. I am not here making the silly point that two of the moral frameworks are for individuals, and the other two are for societies, for morality is a notion that presupposes society. Nobody, as Marx said, seen in his isolation produces values, and nobody, as Hannah Arendt adds, in his isolation cares about them — things, or ideas, or moral ideals 'become values only in their social relationship'. Arendt, *The Human Condition*, p. 165.

44. Rawls, *Theory of Justice*, p. 31.

45. Laski, *A Defence of Liberty Against Tyrants*, p. 27.

46. See *Thucydides,* Jowett's translation (Oxford, 1881), vol. I, pp. 398-407, from which the quotations following are taken.

47. As in H.L.A. Hart's 'minimum content of Natural Law' derived from his truisms about human nature. See *The Concept of Law* (Oxford, 1961), pp. 186-95.

48. These three form the structure of d'Entrèves, *Natural Law.*

49. See Graham Evans, 'Some Problems with a History of Thought in International Relations', *International Relations,* vol. IV, no. 6, November 1974.

50. Thus, for example, E.H. Carr's realism did not prevent him from defending the idea of an international morality.

51. Shklar, *Legalism, passim.*

52. Bull, 'The Theory of International Politics 1919-1969', in Brian Porter (ed.), *The Aberystwyth Papers* (London, 1972), p. 37.

53. See, e.g. Falk, *What's Wrong with Henry Kissinger's Foreign Policy?,* Policy Memo. No. 39, Center of International Studies, Princeton University (July, 1974).

54. Falk, 'The Domains of Law and Justice', *International Journal,* vol. XXXI, no. 1 (Winter 1975-6), p. 5.

55. Stanley Hoffmann, 'Choices' *Foreign Policy*, no. 12 (Fall, 1973), p. 7.

56. Falk, 'The Domains of Law and Justice', pp. 6-9.

57. Falk, *A Study of Future Worlds,* Ch. 1. A decade or so earlier, and in another context (that of the problem of civil war), Falk wrote that 'a contemporary Machiavelli perceiving the novel necessity for a community of mankind, might be dismissed by the best minds as recklessly utopian'. 'The International Law of Internal War', in *Legal Order in a Violent World* (Princeton, 1968), pp. 114-15.

58. Christian Wolff, *Ius Gentium Methodo Scientifica Pertractatum,* 1764, trans. J.H. Drake, 1934, rept. (New York, 1964), Prolegomena, para. 16.

59. E. de Vattel, *The Law of Nations or the Principles of Natural Law,* 1758, trans. Charles E. Fenwick (Washington, 1916), Preface, p. 7a.

60. See E.D. Dickinson, *The Equality of States in International Law* (Cambridge, Mass., 1920), pp. 4-5.

61. J.L. Brierly, *The Law of Nations,* 6th edn, C.H.M. Waldock (ed.) (Oxford, 1963), pp. 132-3.

62. David Thomson, *Equality* (Cambridge, 1949), p. 147.

63. Article 16.

64. And with these concepts we are back to Aristotle. For their relationship with the idea of equality see Hart, *The Concept of Law,* Ch. VIII.

65. See Maurice Cranston, *What are Human Rights?,* p. 1.

66. H. Lauterpacht, *International Law and Human Rights* (London, 1950), pp. 4, 33 and 147-54.

67. As Maurice Cranston says: 'There is indeed something deeply absurd in an arrangement by which something so personal and individual as the rights of man should be settled in committees to which only governments have access; it is a situation worthy of Lewis Carroll.' *What are Human Rights?,* p. 81.

68. The outline of the argument here is borrowed from my *Nonintervention and International Order* (Princeton, 1974), Ch. 9.

69. S.I. Benn and R.S. Peters, *Social Principles and the Democratic State* (London, 1959), pp. 361-2.

70. 'Approaches to the Notion of International Justice', in Richard A. Falk and Cyril E. Black (eds.), *The Future of the International Legal Order,* vol. I, *Trends and Patterns* (Princeton, 1969), pp. 425-6.

71. *What are Human Rights?,* pp. 15-16.

72. Beitz, 'Justice and International Relations', *Philosophy and Public Affairs* (Summer, 1975), p. 383.

73. For an exposition of the logic of moral argument in the context of International Relations, see Hidemi Suganami, 'Why Ought Treaties to be Kept?', forthcoming in the *Year Book of World Affairs.*

4 HUMAN RIGHTS AND WORLD POLITICS

Hedley Bull

My purpose in this essay is to raise three questions:

(1) What are human rights, and what place has been and can be occupied by attempts to recognise or to realise them within international politics?
(2) What are the special issues raised by the debate about human rights at the present time, in the context of the international politics of the 1970s?
(3) What, broadly, should we do about human rights? Are there any human rights, and if there are, what steps can be taken, at what risk to other objectives that may be regarded as desirable, to promote them?

Human Rights

Human rights are rights attaching to human beings as such, rather than to this or that class of human beings. They are thought to be enjoyed by all human beings, to be enjoyed by human beings only and to be enjoyed by them equally. The notion that someone has a right, in my view, generally implies that someone else has a duty, and vice versa (although we may note in passing, without pursuing the issue, that this is sometimes disputed). The notions both of a right and of a duty presuppose the notion of a rule. Thus if there are rights belonging to human beings as such, so also are there duties.

When we say that a man or woman has a right to freedom from arbitrary arrest or to security of employment or to racial equality we mean that he or she should be able to enjoy these things not as a favour bestowed or privilege extended, but as entitlements conferred by a valid rule. When we say that such rights are human rights we mean that persons are entitled to these things by virtue of being human beings, that there is a valid rule which establishes such entitlements for the class of human beings as a whole. Such rules, however, may be of different sorts.

Sometimes what we mean is that there are *moral* rights enjoyed by all human beings: that whether or not human beings are accorded these rights by positive legal instruments, and whether or not they actually enjoy freedom from arbitrary arrest, security of employment or racial equality, they are morally entitled to them. One form of this view is the doctrine of 'natural rights', such as that formulated by Locke and reflected in the American Declaration of Independence, the French Declaration of the Rights of Man and of the Citizen and similar documents. It is possible to embrace a form of natural law position that recognises 'natural rights' without subscribing to the whole package of doctrines which were put forward on the subject by Locke and his school, for example that these 'natural rights' are self-evident (or evident in the light of reason and revelation), that they derive from a pre-contractual state of nature, that they are inalienable, that they include rights of property the protection of which is the proper end of government, and that they provide the basis of a right of revolution. Moreover, it is possible to maintain that there are moral rights attaching to all human beings while at the same time rejecting any belief in 'natural rights' or, more broadly, in natural law at all. Nevertheless, the doctrine that there are human rights in a moral sense, and the doctrine that there are 'natural rights', are hard to separate. For the core of what is meant by those who contend that certain rights are 'natural' is that they are inherent in the nature of human beings, more particularly in their 'rational' nature. And those who hold that there are human rights of a moral kind are generally found to adopt the position not merely that all human beings have these rights, but that these rights are an essential part of men's and women's humanity, that is, of their 'nature'.

Sometimes, however, when we speak of human rights, we are referring to *legal* rights that are incorporated in some system of positive law, domestic or international. Domestic legal instruments, such as constitutions, basic laws or bills of rights, seek to establish merely that certain legal rights are enjoyed by the citizens or subjects of the countries concerned. However, in some cases — for example, the 1949 Basic Law of the German Federal Republic, or the Canadian Bill of Rights of 1960 — they refer to 'human rights', just as the American Declaration of 1776 and the French Declaration of 1789 referred to 'natural rights'. But even where — as in the case, for example, of the British Bill of Rights of 1688 or the United States Bill of Rights of 1791 — no reference is made to rights other than those of citizens of the countries concerned, these may be interpreted as efforts to give local effect to rights believed to be valid for human beings at large. In the case of international legal instruments, which we shall examine below, particularly those which have a universal import, the concern is to establish particular human rights as part of positive international law.[1]

It is important to recognise that neither when we are talking about the moral rights to which human beings as such are entitled, nor when we are referring to legal rights proclaimed in some constitution or international convention are we necessarily talking about rights that are actually implemented and enforced. The fact that rights of freedom of thought are proclaimed in the Constitution of the USSR of 1936 and in the International Covenant on Civil and Political Rights of 1966 is no more evidence that citizens of the Soviet Union actually enjoy rights of that kind than is any belief we may have that since citizens of the Soviet Union are human beings they are morally entitled to them. Alongside human rights in the moral sense and in the legal sense we need to recognise a third category, rights in the *empirical* sense, rights that we know from experience and observation to be observed and implemented. It is worth noting, incidentally, that just as human rights in the first sense fall within the province of moral philosophy, and human rights in the second sense come within the scope of constitutional and international law, human rights in the empirical sense are now the subject of detailed studies that belong to political science or sociology rather than to philosophy or to law, of 'human rights conditions' in various countries. While studies of this sort have long been undertaken by organisations such as Amnesty, the recent American human rights initiatives (dating from before the Carter administration, but much stimulated by it) have had as one of their by-products a burgeoning of highly professional, academic studies of this kind, dealing not with particular violations of human rights, but with the record of countries in relation to a comprehensive array of human rights over a period of time.

Before we leave the subject of the meaning of human rights there is a further matter to which we must allude, because it will dog our path later. Human rights are enjoyed by human beings: but do they enjoy them only individually, or can they also be enjoyed collectively? Our Western conceptions of human rights, like the seventeenth- and eighteenth-century ideas of natural rights from which they derive, are deeply impregnated with the political philosophy of individualism: the rights of which we speak are above all rights possessed by human beings as individuals, and are intended to limit the rights of society or the state. But, of course, even the American Declaration of Independence and the French Declaration of the Rights of Man and of the Citizen refer to the rights of peoples, as well as to those of individuals. Behind the French Revolution stood the Janus-like figure of Rousseau, who spoke not only of men who were born free but also of a general will that was itself a moral person and that expressed the will of all. The German Romantic theory of *Volksgeist* and *Volksrecht* asserted the rights of the nation to unity and liberty but in the same breath asserted the primacy of these rights over those of the individuals of whom the nation was composed. Many of the international declarations and conventions that are taken to convey the content of human rights as they are understood today deal with the rights of groups rather than individuals — nations, racial, ethnic or religious groups, labour organisations and even states. Nor can there be any appeal to the tradition of natural law thinking before the Enlightenment to substantiate the idea that human or natural rights concern only the rights of individuals; this tradition is much concerned with the rights and duties of groups and corporations, so much so that its chronicler Gierke was able to treat it in terms of the history of the right of fellowship, *Das Deutsche Genossenschaftsrecht.* [2]

It is possible to regard the rights of groups as deriving from the rights of individuals, as Locke saw the rights of government as deriving from the consent of the governed, and as J.S. Mill or Woodrow Wilson saw the right of a nation to self-determination as founded upon the rights of individual members of that nation to representative or democratic government. But this is emphatically not how the rights of oppressed nations, states and classes are conceived by some of those who believe that the latter is the core of what is meant by human rights today.

Modern international society has provided — and, I think, continues to provide — a framework of international politics that is basically inhospitable to the idea of human rights, or at least to the idea that they should be internationally recognised and protected. This is most clear if we consider the European states system in its mature period, from the time of Vattel until that of World War I. According to the legal norms which then prevailed states alone were subjects of international law, while individuals and groups other than states were mere objects of it. That is to say, states could enter into agreements that concerned individuals and non-state groups (as they did, for example, in relation to extradition or political asylum or the suppression of piracy) but individuals and non-state groups were not themselves directly the bearers of rights and duties in international law.

International society was a society whose members — or at least whose direct and immediate members — were states; individual persons and groups other than states participated in it only indirectly, through the relationship in which they stood to states. The foundation of this society of states was their mutual recognition of one another's sovereign jurisdiction, and a corollary of this was their acceptance of the obligation

not to interfere in one another's internal affairs. In an international
society of this sort, which treats the maintenance of order among states
as the highest value, the very idea of human or natural rights (like the
idea of human or natural duties) is potentially disruptive. For if human
rights come to assume not merely a moral but a legal form, and if it
comes to be held that one state can interfere within the sovereign
jurisdiction of another to uphold the human rights of its citizens, the
basic rules of the society may be undermined.

It is true that in the nineteenth and early twentieth centuries appeal
was sometimes made to a right of 'humanitarian intervention', for
which one could cite the authority of Grotius and other natural law
thinkers who wrote at a time when the states system had not yet
reached its maturity, and normative conceptions bearing upon international relations were still deeply marked by the legacy of the
Christian republic. Such a right was treated as part of positive international law by many European and American authorities; it was said
to have been exercised, for example, by Britain, France and Russia
when intervening in Turkey on behalf of the Greek insurrection in
1827; by France, authorised by the European Concert and Turkey, in
her intervention in Syria on behalf of the Maronite Christians in 1860;
and by the United States in Cuba in 1898. Leaving aside the question
how far considerations of the protection of human rights actually
motivated these and other purported examples of 'humanitarian intervention', we may note that the latter provide some clue as to the
conditions under which, in a system of legal rules concerned essentially
with the preservation of order among states, a crack may be left in the
door through which some element of concern for the protection of
human rights can creep. One condition is that the state intervening to
uphold human rights should be acting not unilaterally, but with the
agreement of the society of states as a whole, or at least of the great
powers. If intervention to promote human rights proceeds on the basis
of a consensus in favour of it among the society of states as a whole,
then we may imagine that the intervention can take place without
endangering international order. The other condition is that the political entity being intervened against should be a weak state, an entity
whose credentials as a state are uncertain, or — better still — not a state
at all. The promotion of human rights was, of course, a cardinal justification of European expansion and imperial government. The classic
examples of purported 'humanitarian intervention' in the nineteenth
century — the interventions endorsed by the European Concert to
protect the Christian subjects of the Ottoman Empire — met both these

conditions.

The international society that has evolved since 1919 seems at first sight much less inhospitable to recognition and protection of human rights. Beginning with the attempts in the League of Nations period to set standards in such fields as minority rights, forced labour and the responsibilities of Mandatory powers, and rising to a flood in the period of the United Nations, there has been a great development of general treaties, declarations or resolutions of international bodies and adjudications that set standards of human rights in international law. At the centre of this development is the work done or sponsored by the United Nations itself: the provisions of the Charter relating to human rights, the Universal Declaration of Human Rights of 1948; the two Covenants of 1966 – one on Economic, Social and Cultural Rights, the other on Civil and Political Rights; the Convention on the Prevention and Punishment of the Crime of Genocide of 1948; the Declaration on the Granting of Independence to Colonial Countries and Peoples of 1960; and conventions dealing, among other things, with slavery, refugees, stateless persons, women, religious intolerance and racial discrimination. To this one has to add the declarations and conventions of the ILO and UNESCO, the Council of Europe, the Organisation of American States and the Organisation of African Unity.

What is perhaps more impressive than this multiplication of legal or quasi-legal obligations entered into by states with regard to human rights is the evidence that has accumulated that individual persons and groups other than states are now thought to be subjects, and not merely objects, of international law. The Nuremberg and Tokyo international military tribunals witnessed the charging of individual persons with 'war crimes' and 'crimes against the peace'. The machinery developed to implement the European Convention for the Protection of Human Rights and Fundamental Freedoms affords an individual person the right of access to an international court. Non-governmental organisiations now have various kinds of access to international organisations, and enjoy various kinds of international status or recognition as participants in the international political process. Western expositions of international law now often proclaim the arrival of a world society, whose members include individuals and non-state groups, that has replaced the former society of states. Soviet international legal authorities, while they are more conservative in their attitude to the states system, argue that nations are subjects of international law as well as states.

But are these developments evidence of the majestic progress of the prevailing norms of world politics 'from international law to world law', the birth-pangs of a world society or community that is replacing the society of states? We have to note that the legal standing of many of the declarations and resolutions in which standards of human rights are proclaimed, is in dispute. With the important exception of the European Convention, the instruments that have been developed are without effective procedures for implementation and enforcement. There is a great gap between the standards proclaimed and actual 'human rights conditions' in various parts of the world (a gap made more apparent by the great increase that has taken place in our awareness of the latter). It is clear that despite the 'convergence' of values with regard to human rights that one might infer from the proliferation of treaties and declarations (and the arguments for the general similarity of the main principles of human legal systems put forward by C. Wilfred Jenks in *The Common Law of Mankind*) there are divergences of the most fundamental kind as to what these values are.[3] We have to note that human rights standards in international law, for whatever they are worth, rest chiefly on treaties entered into by sovereign states; claims that they express not the consent of states, but 'the general will of the world community', are an aspiration rather than a description of actual trends. Human rights, conceived as legal rather than moral rights, and accompanied by effective procedures for implementation and enforcement, might be expected to gain a firm foothold in a developing world society or cosmopolis. In a society of states, as Kant argued in *Perpetual Peace,* cosmopolitical law can find only a limited expression.[4] The society of states which provides international political life today with its uncertain foundation shows more signs of disintegration than of increasing integration, at all events if we consider it globally rather than regionally; and present contention about human rights, to which I shall now turn, is one of these signs.

There is a certain tendency in the Western countries to believe that human rights are valued and enjoyed only or chiefly in these countries, that the Western countries are the custodians of human rights in the world today, and that the human rights problem is essentially the problem of how the Western countries are to use their influence to bring the Socialist countries and the countries of the Third World into line on this matter. Indeed, one can say — particularly, although not exclusively, with regard to the United States — that the public appeal of human rights as an objective of foreign policy derives in large measure from this belief that the guardianship of human rights in the world as a whole is the special vocation of the Western countries. It helps to restore our flagging conviction of our own virtue, and at the same time enables us to give vent to long-pent-up feelings of frustration and aggression towards our critics in other parts of the world. I think it is perfectly possible that this belief is quite correct, but it does depend on a very particular view of what human rights are, and it neglects to recognise that beliefs about human rights, in one sense or another, are deeply and passionately held in all parts of the world community today.

The Western peoples are inclined to think of human rights principally in terms of the civil and political rights of individuals. They are the countries in which these rights were first achieved (although here one has to recognise that 'Western' is a loose and shifting term, and that the experience of the Anglo-Saxon democracies and France is radically different from that of Germany and again from that of the countries of southern Europe). They correctly believe that they are the countries where these rights are best enjoyed. It is true that since the 1940s they have given increasing attention to economic, social and cultural rights, but they see these rights as a broadening and filling out of civil and political rights previously established. In their experience the civil and political rights were established first; the advances achieved in economic, social and cultural fields took place without serious infringement of civil and political rights, and indeed as a consequence of their exercise. Rights to economic security, to racial equality, or to education are seen as having been established through, and as dependent for their continuance upon, rights of freedom from arbitrary arrest, of freedom of speech and political association.

It is true also that the Western countries recognise not only the rights of individuals but also the collective rights of peoples or nations. The idea of the rights of nations to self-determination is part of the Western moral legacy in terms of which the rest of the world formulates its demands. But an important theme in the Western complex of attitudes to national self-determination (it has to be admitted that there is a counter-theme: here one must set the Founding Fathers, Mazzini and Wilson against Herder and Hegel) is that the right of a nation to become a state is an expression of the right of a people democratically to choose its government.

For the Soviet Union and the socialist countries, or at least for their rulers, human rights are seen primarily in terms of economic, social and cultural rights. They believe that the reality of economic and social security and well being is available to their citizens, and there is truth

in their claim, at least in relation to some of the indices, that their
citizens are better provided for in these respects than those in Western
countries. Civil and political rights that are not built upon economic and
social foundations they regard as the sham of the bourgeois democracies. The Soviet Union and the east European countries apart from
Czechoslovakia have had little experience of civil and political rights as
these are understood in the West, and the economic and social gains that
they believe themselves to have made were achieved through a ruthless
suppression of those whose civil and political rights stood in their way,
which they believe to have been entirely necessary and thoroughly
justified by its results, even if they now acknowledge that excesses took
place in the Stalin era.

It is true that in their domestic constitutions and in the international
undertakings into which they have entered they commit themselves to
the maintenance of civil and political rights. But they do not see
either these, or the economic, social and cultural rights to which they
attach such prominence, as limiting the powers of government. To
preserve the gains of the revolution, and continue its forward march,
what is necessary is that the working class through its agent, the
communist party, should keep a firm grip on the helm of the ship of
state, and to concede individual rights that would be used by the
enemies of the working class to loosen this grip would be a betrayal of
the revolution.

For the countries of the Third World the human rights that are
important are collective rights — of subject peoples to be liberated from
colonialism, subject states from neo-colonialism and subject races from
white domination. National liberation is a moral imperative that does
not presuppose readiness for self-government in a Western sense, or
depend for its validity upon a plebiscitary act of choice. The liberation
of formally independent states from the economic subjection of neo-
colonialism depends not upon standards of minimum welfare or
economic justice applied within poor countries or to the world as a
whole, but on a redistribution of wealth, and along with it a redistribution of power, as between rich states and poor, a 'Charter of the
Economic Rights and Duties of States' in which the rights of individuals
receive no mention, and the duties are imposed only upon the rich
states and the rights conceded only to the poor. Racial equality is
above all a demand for the liberation of coloured peoples from subjection to white rule in southern Africa and elsewhere.

The Third World ideology embraces a great variety of political doctrines and attitudes, and we cannot find within it any uniform hostility

or indifference towards the civil and political or the economic and social rights of individuals. In some Third World countries, and above all in India, the governing elites are deeply affected by a regard for human rights in a Western sense. The common platform of the Third World coalition, however, is that collective rights have priority: without liberation from colonial, neo-colonial and white supremacist domination, the rights of individuals can have no meaning. To those who argue that freedom from colonial rule has led not to an increase but to a decline in respect for civil and political rights, that transfer of wealth from rich countries to poor has merely benefited the rich in the poor countries at the expense of the poor in the rich, or that the economic conditions of blacks in South Africa are the best in the African continent, it can be replied that racial and national dignity represent a more vital human right than any of these things, even if those who have always taken them for granted find this hard to grasp.

It would be wrong to conclude from this very simplified account of the differences in conceptions of human rights which mark the current debate that no common ground exists among them at all. There are certain elementary rules — touching, for example, restrictions on violence, the protection of property and the keeping of promises, and much celebrated by the philosophers — that all societies do in fact endorse.[5] President Carter has been at some pains to show that his policies in this area have been directed not towards bringing other countries to emulate American or Western institutions, but rather towards promoting the observance of what are called 'basic' human rights. Torture, cruel or degrading treatment, and denial of a fair trial are sometimes mentioned as examples of infringements of such 'basic' human rights, and it is true, as United States spokesmen are wont to say, that there is 'nothing parochial' about the insistence that such practices are wrong, however widespread they may be. It is also notable that President Carter has sought to found his policies not upon any uniquely American or Western doctrines about human rights, but on treaties and declarations — the Universal Declaration of Human Rights, the American (that is, the Inter-American) Declaration of the Rights and Duties of Man, the Helsinki Accords — to which the countries he admonishes are parties.

However, these treaties and declarations mask the extent to which the main groups of states in the world are divided on the human rights issue, not merely over the tactics of it or through reluctance to have the bone pointed at themselves but over basic matters of principle. President Carter may have made a correct observation when he said to the UN

General Assembly in April 1977 that 'the basic thrust of human affairs points towards a more universal demand for basic human rights', if by this he meant that the sort of restlessness and turbulence, and striving after new forms of political self-expression that since the eighteenth century have characterised the history of Europe and America, now characterise the world as a whole. But there is no reason to assume that the result of this process will be that other parts of the world will move closer to the social and political practices of the Western countries, rather than further away from them.

The discussion of President Carter's human rights policy has tended to concern only the issues of its cost and its effectiveness. Does the attempt to promote human rights in the Soviet Union involve too high a price in terms of political detente or co-operation in arms control? Does it actually have the effect of advancing the enjoyment of human rights by Soviet citizens, or of retarding it? These questions do not go to the heart of the matter. The basic question that we need to ask is: do human rights of a moral kind exist at all?

In the sense of rights established by some *a priori* moral rule that can be shown to be objectively valid, there are no human rights. Not only is it not self-evident that men are born free and entitled to life, liberty and the pursuit of happiness: these are propositions for which there is no foundation whatever. There is no way of showing that human or any other rights or duties somehow exist objectively in the nature of things rather than in our own attitudes and preferences.

If our conceptions of human rights are rooted not, as the eighteenth-century declarations proclaimed, in the nature of things but only in our own attitudes and preferences this does not mean that our choice of them is capricious or arbitrary. The moral attitudes we take up are the authentic expression of the ways of life we lead, and reflect our own history and character. Because different societies and individuals lead different ways of life and have different histories, disagreement about moral values is a natural and inevitable feature of human life. Theories which impute a natural or objective quality to moral values obscure this fact.

It is true that despite the immense variety of ways of life human beings nevertheless have certain experiences in common as human beings. These common experiences give rise to very widely shared attitudes of support for certain elementary rules of social life, to which reference was made above. It is the absence, or virtual absence, of disagreement about these elementary rules that makes plausible the notion that certain human rights are natural or objective. There is not a natural right to security of the person, or to have one's property respected, or to have contracts honoured, but because *a posteriori* we know these rights to enjoy something like universal support, it is possible for practical purposes to proceed as if they were natural rights.

But such nearly universal attitudes of support relate only to this area of the most elementary or primary rules of social life. They do not obtain in relation to the complex of civil and political, economic, social and cultural rights that are taken to provide the content of human rights today. We know that in China and Central Africa, in Pakistan and Saudi Arabia, it is not merely the case that human rights in the Western sense are not enjoyed; it is also the case that these rights are not regarded as morally valid. The idea that the universal validity of human rights is self-evident in the light of reason is an eighteenth-century illusion, as even President Carter's policy tacitly acknowledges.

It is possible that the area of shared moral attitudes and preferences in world society as a whole will grow. Those who believe that there is occurring at present a process of social and political convergence or homo-genisation, giving rise to a greater uniformity of ways of life, can reason-ably hold also that this is likely to find increasing expression in a conver-gence of attitudes towards the rights that all human beings should be accorded. There is, in President Carter's human rights policy, an implicit cosmopolitanism, a belief that a more homogeneous world culture is developing, or can be encouraged to develop. This may or may not be so: evidence can be adduced that points in both directions. Nor is it easy to say whether such a homogeneous world culture, if it is deve-loping, will lead towards Western conceptions of human rights or away from them. What we can say, however, is that in the absence of any striking new tendency of ways of life to converge, the appeal to a con-ception of human rights that expresses the ways of life simply of our part of the world is not likely to evoke a response elsewhere.

Notes

1. For these and other documents to which reference is made see Ian Brownlie (ed.), *Basic Documents on Human Rights* (Clarendon Press, Oxford, 1971).

2. See Otto von Gierke, *Natural Law and the Theory of Society 1500 to 1800*, trans. E. Barker (Cambridge University Press, 1934).

3. See C. Wilfred Jenks, *The Common Law of Mankind*, 1958.

4. I refer here to Kant's third Definitive Article for a Perpetual Peace: 'The

law of world citizenship shall be limited to the conditions of universal hospitality'.

5. For a perceptive account of these elementary rules, see H.L.A. Hart, *The Concept of Law* (Clarendon Press, Oxford 1961).

5 JUSTICE: NATIONAL, INTERNATIONAL OR GLOBAL?

W.H. Smith

This chapter will look at some of the problems encountered in applying ideas of justice outside the nation-state. Traditionally, political philosophy has dealt with justice in the context of the *polis* or of national societies. This tradition remains important but the intensification of international politics, the development of a global economic system and the shift to thinking in terms of world politics have presented a conceptual challenge in recent decades. Must justice remain bound to the nation-state? What sort of justice is possible between sovereign states? Are we moving toward a notion of justice tied to an emergent world society of which all human beings are members?

Particular attention will be paid to the way that worldwide economic inequalities bear upon questions of justice. Much of the contemporary debate about justice in world politics focuses on this issue: it claims at times not only to be a new item on the agenda of international politics but to have produced a 'new agenda' altogether. How much this reflects the concerns of developed countries and the interests of Third World *governments* is touched upon in the chapters by Professor Miller and Ralph Pettman. Whatever the politics or psychology of the new agenda, however, it poses some crucial questions. Can economic justice be considered in isolation from a wider conception of justice? If not, as I believe to be the case, what importance should be attached to economic issues? And, more philosophically still, what precisely is it about economic developments that raise doubts about our established notions of justice? In considering such questions what I have to say will, I hope, be relevant to other, more traditional issues of justice in world politics, such as war and intervention.

Justice I take to be a quality of social groups. It refers to the way in which goods — defined in the widest sense to include rights and privileges as well as material possessions — are distributed among members of that group.[1] A concept of justice will normally contain principles about which goods — not necessarily all — are to be distributed and principles about the claims of various classes of people to various kinds of goods. Justice, then, looks at the overall picture so that one can say, given agreement on principles, that a particular society is just or unjust (or somewhere in between). It is clearly important not to assume at the outset that world society, however defined, necessarily constitutes a proper context for justice. As will become apparent, there are arguments for thinking of justice only in the context of the state and arguments about how justice in different kinds of society may or may not correspond.

Justice is, of course, related to the question of right conduct for individuals – 'morality' in perhaps its most usual sense. But there is much room to disagree on how they are related. Many philosophers have noted a general reluctance to accept that a right (moral) action could produce injustice or that a wrong action could promote justice. In such cases an attempt is usually made to depict the 'right' action as not really right in view of all the circumstances – and vice versa.[2] This is a feature of the utilitarian approach to justice. It takes justice – or, more widely, the general good or 'the greatest happiness' – as the standard for judging the rightness of individual conduct. An act is right if it promotes justice, more right than another act if it promotes greater justice.

To put this in the context of world politics, it might be argued that global justice requires – as an absolute minimum – the sparing of as many human lives as possible and that the moral injunction against killing others is (and ought to be) tailored to this end. Now from this conception of justice it may be argued that any involvement in activities which cause death or cause more to die than would otherwise be the case must be accounted immoral; thus support for a business enterprise which pays unduly low wages to its employees in an under-developed country is prohibited to the individual on moral grounds.[3] Global justice and moral behaviour are thus intimately related. Yet this connection is difficult to sustain for two reasons. It is open to the objection that individual acts cannot have any influence on the alleged injustice of business operations or of economic organisation in general. But the more fundamental objection is that such an argument does not correspond with the way people (and many philosophers) normally think about moral rules.

Moral principles are usually identified with individuals. The morality of an act will depend on various factors associated with the actor: his intentions, his reasons for acting, his circumstances, his relationship to the person or persons directly affected. There is a focus on acts such as killing, lying, stealing, which in themselves have little impact beyond those directly involved; their moral or immoral character is such that their ramifications need not be further explored. Norms of conduct, moreover, are frequently regarded as in principle relevant to all men. John Vincent's chapter traces the development of this line of thought in Western philosophy and it is not infrequently found outside Western culture. Moral rules are easily universalised, it would seem, because they deal with the relative simplicities of specific, small-scale events rather than the complexities of social institutions.[4]

These fall rather into the province of justice which looks at the way in which goods ought to be distributed among members of a group. It provides standards by which to judge the competing claims and interests of numerous individuals. The focus is not on motives or immediate circumstances but on the impact of policies, laws, institutions, traditions on a society. In contrast to principles of morality, those of justice take heed of geographical boundaries for they mark off the area in which social interaction occurs. It is precisely because national boundaries appear to some to have been transcended in some areas that the prospect of a wider justice has been raised.

Now a concept of global justice does not seem necessary in order to justify giving aid to the needy and starving. Many individuals feel a moral obligation to give to those less fortunate regardless of national boundaries or political and economic structures. It may well be the case that individuals have a moral duty to assist the needy.[5] As well, some governments are sometimes prompted to give aid by citizens who have a sense of moral duty. Of course, governments may believe that such aid serves their national interest but it would be difficult to prove that this is always the reason for aid or, indeed, that such a reason was necessarily incompatible with genuine humanitarian concern on the part of some decision-makers.[6] The basis of such aid, in short, is morality, not necessarily justice.

But much of the contemporary debate goes beyond this. It is said not to be enough to give even a generous amount of aid, even with the best of intentions. And the reason is not simply the inadequacy of the amount that might be forthcoming. It is rather that the whole economic framework which distributes global resources is unjust. Humanitarianism serves merely as a distraction from this fact and as a palliative which further degrades the dignity of those who receive. What is needed is radical reform of existing institutions, perhaps even their overthrow.[7]

What I have said so far will perhaps have indicated the unwisdom of applying rules of individual conduct (moral principles) to the actions of states, of asking, for example, whether the foreign policy of a particular state is moral in some degree. This may have been appropriate when a nation could be identified with its prince; policies could be examined *in foro conscientiae* and measured against the natural law held to govern all men. But Machiavelli early stressed the special demands of princely office and the prince's need 'not to be good'. The question to be asked of a state's policy is not whether it is moral but whether it is just: how does it affect the distribution of goods among the members of the appropriate society, whether national, international or global?

In domestic policy we are accustomed to judging laws and policies according to principles of justice rather than morality. It is, of course, possible to say that a particular law is immoral (or moral) but this is likely to mean (i) that the law amounts to an immoral act, e.g. provides for capital punishment; or (ii) that the law encourages or discourages individuals in matters of moral behaviour, e.g. laws on prostitution or pornography. It may also be possible to identify certain laws or policies with particular individuals who have taken initiatives or pushed strenuously for change.

In foreign policy, however, these possibilities virtually disappear. Policy and *a fortiori* international law originate rarely from individuals, most commonly from complex and impersonal decision-making organisations or processes. Certain kinds of foreign policy, e.g. war and intervention, do invite moral judgement because they involve individuals in actions, such as killing, against which they are normally enjoined by moral codes. And while it is sometimes possible to identify particular acts of immorality in a war, e.g. those of a Lieutenant Calley, the invitation to moral judgement of a state's policy should in general be declined: firstly, because it blurs the distinction between simple and complex acts and, secondly, because the admission of some acts of foreign policy to the realm of morality is likely to lead to the indiscriminate entry of all.

None of this exempts the individual decision-maker from the demands of his moral conscience. He must attend to these as best he can in the circumstances of his office and he may find that, whatever his decision, he cannot help having dirty hands.[8] What he ought not to do is confuse morality and justice. For this is to deal with groups of people and aggregate interests in the same way as individual and particular interests. An attempt to introduce the latter approach into politics is likely to meet with a flat rejection and a monistic realism. Concern with humanity, with mercy, can be brought into politics only as an integral part of a concept of justice whether within the state or beyond it. Moral vision, in fact, may be necessary to genuine political action.[9]

In politics, then, morality is a second-order concept, subordinate to justice. The question is not, for example, 'Is Chinese foreign policy moral?', but 'What are China's conceptions of justice as evidenced by her policies and objectives?' The concept of 'just war' embodies the correct approach despite its medieval origins: it is concerned not so much with the moral virtue of princes but with the impact of their policies on other princes and peoples. A further example concerns refugees where it is easy enough to see the moral response — and if numbers are small this may be a practical response — but in dealing with larger numbers deeper problems arise. We come up against the interests of groups and their potential impact on other groups, all matters where no simple answers are possible. Similarly, the suggested human right to settle anywhere in the world (or even to emigrate from one's country) asserts a moral principle with total disregard for the rights and interests of groups.

I may be accused at this point, if not earlier, of the sin of states-centrism. But the distinction between the individual and the collectivity — and the principles to govern their behaviour — holds in my view whatever the nature of the groups and whatever the nature of the relations between them. If the world consisted simply of two or more social classes or if there existed dominant and subordinate groups, the dichotomy between the individual and the collectivity would remain. We may wish to develop new concepts of justice to deal with a changed situation but the purpose of introducing moral principles into the debate must be to provide the requisite moral impetus — Weber's 'passion' — not the substance.

The substance of justice must originate with some idea about the nature of those who are the subjects of justice and about the relations between them. In most cases this means beginning with the nature of man. Discovering the true essence of man is, of course, notoriously impossible however essential the search may be. In recent years, moreover, we have come to understand (perhaps to re-learn) that we cannot be certain even about the moment when individuals begin and end their earthly lives.

Now philosophers seek man not only as he is but also as he ought to be, as he once was and as he will be. The first of these approaches identifies a goal or *telos* toward which man ought to move. The second seeks an insight into man's nature by conceiving of an earlier condition, perhaps a state of nature (pleasant or unpleasant), perhaps a time of innocence. The third approach is determinist. It sets out laws of necessity, not principles of moral obligation or eternal justice. Thus Marxism recognises the concept of justice only as the creature of a particular historical epoch; justice is relevant to its own time and cannot be applied to any other epoch. Moreover, since justice is seen by Marx as a formal, juridical and state-bound concept, justice in this sense will have no place in a truly communist society.[10]

There are clearly problems in defining the nature of justice and in identifying the subjects of justice. Of relevance here is the possibility that the subjects of justice may be other than individual human beings. In particular, it can be argued that states — as distinct entities — are capable of creating a special kind of justice amongst themselves, i.e. international justice.[11] A more pessimistic version has it that the intrinsic nature of states leaves no scope for justice at all. The possibility of international justice *per se*, then, arises only with those philosophers who interpret the state not (or not merely) as an institution ordained by God or constructed by men, but as a natural, organic being. The classic statement of the organic view can be found in Aristotle.

For Aristotle the state or *polis* was the supreme institution. It aimed at the supreme good; it was self-sufficient where other associations were not; it was prior to the individual and the household, a whole prior to its parts. As much as man himself, the state was an organism, a creation of nature. Within each community a particular justice could be established based on the precepts of equality and subjection to the law.[12] But Aristotle's conception of justice also transcends the boundaries of the state for it is ultimately founded on reason. Where reason is, so too is justice. Hence in dealing with other states, Aristotle argued, it would be 'completely unreasonable . . . if the work of the statesman were to be reduced to seeing how he could rule others with or without their consent. How could that be regarded as statecraft or lawgiving which is not even lawful in itself?'[13] In practice, of course, as Aristotle well knew, men were not usually inspired by reason, feeling no compunction about dominating other states in a way they would regard as unjust were their own state the victim.

Aristotle's organic view of the state may have created the possibility of a special kind of inter-state justice. But his philosophy stressed rather the role of the state in creating its own justice and where it did go beyond the state it relied on a cosmopolitan conception of men as capable of reason (though some classes of men were, in Aristotle's

view, not capable of reason and therefore fit to be ruled by others).
Other philosophers such as Rousseau and Hegel who have interpreted
the state as in some sense an organic being have stood firm on the
national basis of justice. Rousseau was decidedly pessimistic about
international relations;[14] while Hegel at least saw certain virtues in
conflict between states.[15]

A concept of international justice, it would seem, cannot stand on
its own.[16] It must derive from cosmopolitan ideas or from national
conceptions of justice; and is likely in practice to combine some portion of both. It is true that both sources may undermine international
justice but it is also true that these sources will provide its strength
and resilience. Being derivative does not necessarily mean being weak
and insubstantial. For many purposes international justice can be
thought of as existing in its own right just as international society is
conceived to be a working, if fictional, society. David Hume regarded
justice as an artificial virtue for it is not one of the feelings naturally
found in men.[17] This virtue is acquired readily enough within the state
but in relations between artificial persons justice must be accounted
doubly artificial. The following sections of this chapter will look at the
nature of this artifice within states, among mankind as a whole and
between states.

Traditionally justice has been regarded as a quality of politically
autonomous institutions. Such an organisation holds final authority
over the individuals and lesser groups within it, a sovereignty which is
self-contained and exclusive of the authority of other organisations.
It is in the state that problems of distribution perennially arise. The
social and economic co-operation that facilitates the creation of goods
of all kinds takes place largely within states. In many societies, moreover, the distribution of these goods is something which the central
government can significantly influence. Government, in other words,
offers one means of creating justice at least within its own boundaries.

The business of social co-operation is highly complex, giving rise to
many rights and duties among those participating in the enterprise.
These rights and duties are 'special' in the sense that they are held not
by all individuals but by specific individuals by virtue of the association
or connection between them.[18] Each society, while perhaps accepting
the idea of general rights, will determine for itself what particular rights
and duties (as examples of goods in general) ought to be distributed and
what rules of distribution ought to be adopted. As Hume observed in the

Inquiry Concerning the Principles of Morals, the content of rights and duties varies from society to society and the fact that they exist at all is not a necessary but merely a contingent fact.[19] Only when men come together for some purpose does the possibility of justice arise and then it is limited to that specific group.

It is the stuff of political philosophy to speculate on the nature of political association among men. Explanations are, in the broadest terms, based either on a social contract or on convention. Both approaches seek to account for the fundamental principles which govern a society and must therefore find a place for concepts of justice. This is not the occasion to go over the classical theories, although I shall refer to some of them here and there. I shall instead look at two contributions to the theory of justice — one based on contract, the other on convention — which are of recent date and might be expected to throw some light on the more contemporary issues.

The first work is John Rawls's *A Theory of Justice* which, in the author's words, 'generalizes and carries to a higher level of abstraction' traditional contract theories.[20] For Rawls justice is 'the first virtue of social institutions' (3). It is concerned with 'the way in which the major social institutions distribute fundamental rights and duties and determine the division of advantages from social co-operation' (7). Rawls envisages the basic principles of justice being chosen by free and rational individuals who are willing to co-operate yet concerned for their own interests. In this 'original position' the parties are equal in terms of bargaining power but, most importantly, ignorant of the position which each will occupy in the social structure for which they are drawing up rules. From behind this 'veil of ignorance' two principles are said to emerge. The first states the requirement of equality in apportioning basic rights and duties; the second holds that inequality is justified only if it produces benefits for the whole society, in particular for those least favourably placed. This latter principle Rawls terms the 'difference principle' and adds to it provisions concerning equality of opportunity to enjoy whatever privileges do prove necessary.[21]

Rawls's theory is far richer than this summary might suggest. Two important qualifications which Rawls makes need to be noted here. The first is that justice is not the only prerequisite for a viable society since problems of co-ordination, efficiency and stability must also be solved (6). Secondly, Rawls assumes a society which is more or less self-sufficient (4). It is not altogether clear what Rawls means by this. A community that is self-sufficient both economically and politically certainly fits the description. The whole notion of a contract suggests political autonomy but the consequences of extensive foreign relations and interdependence are not spelled out (though it is only fair to observe that Rawls does not see his theory as complete).

In the tradition of contract theorists Rawls demonstrates the crucial connection between social co-operation and the possibility of justice. Each society requires some notion of justice for without it conflict and coercion will prevail over co-operation. But the creation of justice is necessarily something that sets one group of individuals, the parties to the contract, apart from the rest of humanity. And by uniting with some, as Rousseau has it, we become enemies of mankind.[22] Rawls's theory is also a tribute to the long tradition in Western philosophy which has sustained a vision of the perfectly just society and has thereby provided standards by which to measure existing societies. It is also typical of the Greek inheritance which tends to relegate foreign relations to an afterthought. Rawls's attempt in this direction will be considered in a later section.

The alternative approach to political association relies not on a contract, real or notional, but on the historical fact that groups of human beings have come together for common purposes and have developed through custom and convention principles to govern their relations.[23] This approach bestows the blessing of history rather than of reason on the connection between society and justice. It begins by noting that in no society was there any initial distribution of goods in the sense of a deliberate parcelling out of rights and benefits. Men come together possessed of all kinds of resources and talents, some well endowed, some barely endowed at all. There is no call to justify this state of affairs, however randomly Nature or God might appear to have dealt out the good things of the world. Personal worth or merit has no significance for these initial holdings.

Individuals, furthermore, are free to use or dispose of their resources as they wish: to employ them, for example, to create more resources or to give them away to anyone they choose. The crucial provision governing such changes in holdings is that they do not take place in unfair or immoral ways. As long as this provision is observed, an initial just distribution of goods can only lead to other just distributions, never to an unjust distribution. Those who at any point argue for a redistribution must demonstrate that some goods have been improperly acquired; otherwise they are themselves in a position of infringing moral rules by depriving certain individuals of the freedom to use their resources as they choose. For Nozick, then, a theory of justice has three main components: an account of how goods came to be held in

the first place, rules governing the transfer of holdings, and principles
for rectifying unjust transfers.[24]

The strength of this approach is its rootedness in history rather
than any vision of the future. It may employ various theories to account
for the origin of private property, but stresses the natural liberty of men
to acquire it, use it and transfer it. If men have different talents, abilities ·
and inclinations in these respects, then some will have the means to
secure more benefits than others. To prevent individuals from achieving
this sort of superiority is to interfere with their natural liberty. As with
men, so with states. If individuals can claim exclusive rights to certain
goods, so must a group of individuals be able to enjoy possession of
common goods to the exclusion of other groups.[25] The shift from
individual to group is not automatic but it is reasonable and corresponds
to the practice of groups in their relations with one another. It is,
significantly, a major embarrassment to Marxist theory in that a
communist state in a less than communist world must find itself asserting exclusive property rights over its territory and resources.[26]

A strategic redoubt in the position which sees justice as bound to
the state is the historical function of the state in eliciting effort and
dedication from individuals. In one way or another the state serves to
channel the activities of individuals toward the welfare of the collectivity
— but the national rather than the global community. An important
exponent of such ideas was Friedrich Meinecke, particularly in his work
Cosmopolitanism and the Nation-State.[27] For Meinecke the state was
the ideal form of political organisation for the realisation of human
values; no other community more deserved description as 'man writ
large'.[28] Each nation developed in its own particular circumstances. Not
reason or natural law but geography, family, common fears and so on
determined the nation. And each nation, as an expression of its many
individual members, represented an expression of humanity as a whole.[29]

Cosmopolitan ideas such as natural law halted before this 'abyss of
individuality'.[30] A worldwide community would be both inferior to
national communities and unsatisfactory in itself, and it could in any
case only be achieved by conquest. Hence international relations had to
be seen in national rather than cosmopolitan terms for the latter distracted the statesman and weakened his state. It was not that Meinecke
rejected the ethics of cosmopolitanism; he rejected its apolitical nature
and its tendency to reduce events and issues to absolutes.[31] Cosmopolitanism saw links between men where none were in fact possible
and therefore provided no adequate foundation for justice.

To maintain that justice is essentially national in origin is not necessarily to deny that justice has no place in international relations. One school of thought, epitomised in various ways by Hegel, Machiavelli and Hobbes, does see justice stopping at the water's edge. For them states are morally separate and cannot subordinate themselves to any common principles of justice. Hegel, while recognising universal principles, argued that they could only be made real through the individual state. Similarly, Machiavelli accepted the existence of principles of right and wrong but maintained that they had to be overridden by the demands of the state. Only Hobbes represents a purely positivist view: such moral obligations as exist derive from the command of the sovereign and extend only to the limit of his authority.

But the other school of thought, in which the liberal realist tradition is firmly planted, does see a certain limited scope for justice. States pursue their own interests but, by virtue of a measure of overlapping interests among some or all of their number and of their longstanding interrelationship in a single system, they are able to find room for certain rules of behaviour, including principles of justice, in their relations with one another. What distinguishes the realist from the idealist is simply the extent to which each sees national interests as overlapping. The idealist can discern, actually or potentially, a perfect harmony of interests.

The national approach to justice also finds much support in the practice of states, including many who are vocal in condemning the injustice of contemporary international relations. The principle of sovereign equality has become an axiom, asserting the right of each state to manage its own affairs and hence to create its own principles of justice. Third World states in particular are anxious to confirm their ownership of resources within their national boundaries regardless of their ability or inability to exploit them. Similarly with the world's oceans, states are looking more to expand national control than to an international regime. Demands for justice, it must also be noted, are couched in terms of aid to governments rather than to individuals. For each state wishes to retain control over the manner in which goods are distributed within its boundaries.[32] And while it may be true that this is a demand of governments made for the sectional purposes of a ruling elite, it does not follow that the citizens of such governments would lightly abandon the idea of national autonomy for the sake of an improvement in their food consumption.

Justice, on this view, is founded in the state so that the mere fact of contact between states does not mean that new concepts of justice must replace the old. On the contrary, global economic interdependence has led to a reassertion of the demand for national autonomy. It is leading not to a world society with its own principles of justice but must rather be taken as a warning against the erosion of independence.

It is possible to take issue with the idea of national justice in two ways: by tackling the theories of justice as such or by arguing their applicability to some society other than the state. In recent years the main exponents of this latter line of attack have looked to a broader basis for justice than the state. This will be our focus here, although the tradition of thought that sees salvation in smaller groups is far from extinct.

The arguments against taking the state as the matrix of justice need only be summarised here. They relate, on the one hand, to doubts about the capacity of the state to perform the functions expected of it, e.g. the provision of security against attack and the maintenance of minimum economic standards. Without trying to resolve these issues, it may be noted that they reflect Western anxieties more than global concerns; they are the worries of states which have known security and prosperity but have lost them rather than of states which have never known these blessings. On the other hand, a powerful volley of arguments has been launched by those who stress the changing nature of world economic activity. Modern production, it is claimed, can no longer be walled up within the state; traditional political barriers have been scaled or have been pushed down for the benefit of economic man. Two trends are emphasised: the interdependence of national economies and the dependence of some economies on others.

This is not the place to debate the facts of global economic developments. The conclusions to be deduced from them are another matter. For some the emergence of global economic relations (whether of co-operation or exploitation) necessitates a new basis for principles of justice. No longer can states be regarded as autonomous; they are bound by economic ties and in many cases this means by political ties as well. Others, however, do not reach the same conclusions. Economic interdependence, among states as among men, is seen to breed 'not accommodation and harmony but suspicion and incompatibility'.[33] It is no answer to say that this simply demonstrates the need for a wider conception of justice. The creation of justice, moreover, has typically been possible only when men have submitted themselves to a common political authority. In the absence of world government, global justice appears to be beyond man's grasp.

Nonetheless, speculation about principles of global justice may still be worthwhile. It may offer some vision of the future and also help to explain why the vision is so remote from reality. One such approach to global justice can be developed from Rawls's theory.[34] If we imagine men in the 'original position' who are charged with finding principles of justice to govern the whole of mankind, it is questionable whether they would opt for having states at all. Assumed to be ignorant of their future nationality, they would face an odds-on chance of finding themselves in a country which could barely provide subsistence living.

Surely free and rational individuals would choose a global structure which would ensure a reasonable minimum for all, even if some groups were highly privileged. With this approach to global justice the present momentous accident of birth into one state (and plenty) or into another (and hunger) would be eliminated. Those inequalities that remained would have to be justified on the grounds that they provided the necessary incentives and rewards for those more able to contribute to the general welfare, including that of the least well-off. Inequalities might also serve to improve the efficiency of the system of distribution.[35]

Now one difficulty with this conception of global justice is that it assumes away the importance to men of their sense of nationality. We do not know what sacrifices men would be prepared to make in order to retain the multitude of national groups. An indication may perhaps be found in considering how mankind in the 'original position' would deal with nuclear weapons — on the assumption that they could not be wished away. The problem is to find how such immensely destructive power could be placed in the hands of a group of men without their fellows feeling extreme unease, if not outright fear. A world government could only use nuclear weapons against its own subjects. If placed in the hands of several groups, nuclear weapons would surely promote antagonism between them. In the present international system states always (as far as we know) direct their nuclear weapons against foreign targets. The fact that citizens of some states are nuclear targets of other states serves only to reinforce their sense of nationality.

A second fundamental criticism of this approach to global justice is applicable to many theories of justice. It is not that the principles of justice are unworkable or difficult to uphold but rather that they demand the realisation of a set pattern, a particular distribution of goods. No deviation from the pattern, e.g. equality, can be permitted except as provided for. Nozick contends that such 'patterned' principles of justice focus on criteria for deciding who shall receive goods ('recipient-justice') while ignoring the rights of those from whom goods must be taken. In the standard formula 'to each according to his —

from each according to his —', the first part tends to be carefully spelled out, the latter simply asserted.[36]

Some system, then, would have to be found both for determining who merits assistance and for distributing the world's goods in the right proportions. And, more problematically, some grounds must be found for depriving others of goods which they already have in their possession. The problem of deciding 'why' as well as 'what' and 'how much' is difficult enough in a national society; it promises to be impossible in a world where men have different cultures, religions and outlooks even if they have lost their nationality.

A chief characteristic of this contractual approach to justice is the attempt to nullify inequalities that have arisen through chance or historical fate. The approach to justice based on natural liberty, however, sees no reason to move from the fact of unequal distribution to the norm of equality; redistribution is warranted only in order to rectify the consequences of unjust behaviour in the past. Again, we do not know where men stand on this question: what price are they prepared to pay for natural liberty? If they do prefer natural liberty to a contract providing for equality, it is difficult to deny the right of individuals to form associations for the promotion of their common interests. And we are back to the state as the repository of justice. If the choice is for a contract and equality, we must doubt its credibility in the light of man's longstanding addiction to nationality. Any concept of justice, it would appear, must reckon with the existence of the nation-state.

If principles of international justice are to be found they must recognise the existence of national 'enclaves of justice' which block 'that access to the demands of men and women of all nations which is required for bringing them into a single justice-constituency'.[37] Justice within the state is at once a contribution to global justice and a barrier to it. But international justice cannot ignore the claims of mankind as a whole. For this would be to overlook the strength of cosmopolitan conceptions and to disregard the historical record such as it is. Here I shall look at two contemporary approaches to international justice: one in the tradition of Christian Wolff's *civitas maxima* based on some form of contract between states, the other in the tradition of Vattel emphasising the natural liberty of states.

The chief merit of Rawls's theory of international justice is that it takes the state as the subject of justice. Indeed, Rawls does not even discuss the question of how a community is to be defined for the purposes of his theory of justice.[38] Using the device of a 'veil of ignorance' Rawls would have states confer about the rules to govern their relations without knowing their future identity, whether, for example, there were to be Chad, India or the United States of America. Barry's argument that they would not choose a states system at all loses its force if it is established that states desire to create their own internal principles of justice and are prepared to accept considerable sacrifices to this end. So too does Barry's claim that states meeting in these circumstances would favour strong forms of international organisation possessing a monopoly of weapons of mass-destruction or an effective system of collective security.[39] What states in the 'original position' are likely to agree upon, in Rawls's view, is a series of principles which look remarkably like those which international society has already developed: non-intervention, *pacta sunt servanda*, self-defence and the rules of *jus ad bellum* and *jus in bello*.[40]

One fundamental criticism of this approach is that it does not work in a world of states which are somewhat less than self-sufficient. For interdependence benefits some more than others and, in adding to the world's stock of goods, raises the question of how these goods ought to be distributed. 'In an interdependent world', Beitz argues, 'confining principles of justice to national societies has the effect of taxing poor nations so that others may benefit from living in "just" regimes.'[41] On such a view promoting justice at home takes priority over aid to foreign peoples in need. The benefits which the originally advantaged states have gained from international transfers remain in their hands and there is nothing – save compassion – to oblige them to surrender any part of their possessions.

This is precisely the point which is applauded by those who conceive of state relations in terms of natural liberty. They assert that states, like men, own what they produce or gain through trade. Without security of possession there is no incentive to produce goods, no basis on which to mobilise the citizens of a state; for states, again like men, depend on certain material goods for their survival. In international dealings there are no grounds of justice for wealthy states to accept a lower price for their produce or pay a higher price for others' produce than they need to in the market-place. All are entitled to their holdings, large or small, provided only that they have not been acquired by unfair or immoral means.

An attempt may be made to qualify this line of argument by saying that the better off are obliged to redistribute only that component of their wealth which is due to trade with others, or at least a certain part

of that component. But this is in effect to tax international trade which
will remain worthwhile only so long as some element of profit remains.
It is clear too, that any level of tax would serve to discourage trade so
that both richer and poorer lose the incentive to make exchanges they
would otherwise have made. Moreover, even if the principle of redistri-
buting gains from international transfers were accepted in some measure,
the great difficulty would remain of determining the size of the component to be redistributed. Any figure produced would certainly smack
of guesswork and arbitrary choice.

A further objection to the natural liberty approach is that vast
differences exist and have existed in the natural resources with which
states are endowed. What each has, furthermore, appears morally
arbitrary, reflecting neither moral worth nor desert but the vagaries of
nature. Hence some states happen to be favourably placed to improve
their position in cumulative fashion, while others are unable to make
improvements and simply fall further behind. It was these 'contingencies and biases of historical fate' that Rawls's notion of an international
contract was intended to nullify.[42] Now one response to this objection
is to treat natural resources as comparable to human talents. These also
differ greatly as between individuals and must be recognised as given. It
is absurd to demand that a person justify his possession of great musical
gifts or cricketing ability. So with states it is pointless to require them
to justify their natural endowments.

But then the objection may be pressed further by arguing that
'unlike talents, resources are not naturally attached to persons'.[43]
Whereas no man can be deprived of his talents in the sense that they
can be taken from him and given to another, natural resources can for
the most part be easily transferred once problems of transport and
storage have been solved. Depriving a man of his talents would be a
monstrous act (unless they were talents of evil) for they are intrinsic
to his personality. The same, it is argued, cannot be said of the natural
endowment of the state.

Against this, the libertarians would reiterate the case for a concept
of private property for both the individual and the group and would
emphasise the need to guarantee security of property. A Lockeian
would claim that natural resources require labour in order to make them
useful and that the citizens of a state in applying their labour to such a
purpose create property rights over their product.[44] The life of a
community depends on its possessions, natural and acquired, a significance reflected in the widespread notion of motherland or fatherland.

Moreover, says Locke, 'he who appropriates land to himself by his labour does not lessen but increase the common stock of mankind'.[45] But Locke also assumed that in appropriating what was originally common to all there remained 'enough and as good' for those still unprovided for.[46] This assumption may have been valid for the greater part of human history but recent decades have furnished reasons for doubt in two respects. Here perhaps are arguments which will justify the restriction of natural liberty and necessitate new principles of justice.

First of all, there are some natural resources which are still held in common by the earth's population — notably the resources in and under the oceans. These may be appropriated by states which have the capital and technological capacity in such a way as to fail to leave 'enough and as good' for the rest of mankind. This argument, then, might distinguish between resources which states happen to be sitting on within their national boundaries and resources which do not as yet fall within such boundaries. There are some reasons to quarrel with this distinction since national boundaries have always been subject to determination by agreement (or disagreement) between states; if states can establish boundaries on land, what is to prohibit them from doing so at sea? The distinction looks firmer, however, in the light of a second global problem.

This is the possibility — some would say certainty — that the sum total of the earth's resources will one day be exhausted. Those who exhaust irreplaceable resources today, it is said, are failing to leave enough, even if not as good, for some future generation. And here the advantaged states, the high-consumption societies, appear to be chiefly responsible for bringing closer the point of global scarcity; though it must not be forgotten that the populous states, the less developed of which are striving hard to increase their per capita consumption, must also shoulder some responsibility.

Since these problems are necessarily global, the argument runs, the natural liberty of states must be restrained according to wider principles of justice. Rawls could do this by making states in the 'original position' ignorant of the generation to which they were going to belong or by having representatives from all generations. Rational men would agree on a 'just savings rate' which each generation would maintain for the sake of its successors.[47] Rawls, for some reason not altogether clear, does not follow this approach but requires that a single generation in the 'original position' must care for its successors.[48]

This is in fact the sort of assumption which the libertarian would make: man has a pride in and an incentive to provide for his children and his children's children. A vital aspect of his property rights is the right to transfer or bequeath goods to whomever he chooses. On the basis of what Hume would call a 'natural temper', then, men will provide for their descendants. But the difficulty here is that some in providing for their descendants — whether men for their children or states for the next generation — are likely to do so at the expense of others for whom 'enough, and as good' will not be left. And it remains true that concern for future generations is almost invariably focused on one's own nation. The division of mankind into national groups has until now assisted in the provision for future generations. Whether mankind can continue to provide for its future in this piecemeal fashion has now been brought into question.

While a contractual approach to international justice, particularly one that included some principle of equality, would necessitate major redistribution among states, an approach based on natural liberty does not necessarily produce this conclusion. What is required first is a demonstration that illegitimate transfers have occurred in the past. In the language of the present debate: what was and is exploitation? how can those exploited be paid back? I shall look briefly at some of the problems raised by these questions, although it is my view that ultimately it is more desirable to look forward than to look back.

Exploitation has meaning *either* in the sense of immoral acts committed by individuals against other individuals *or* in the context of agreed principles of justice. In the former case one thinks of enslavement, brutalisation, indiscriminate slaughter and so on, acts of which many early and not so early colonisers were guilty. They may not have thought themselves in the wrong, although it might have occurred to them — as it did to some social critics — that they were acting in ways they would not contemplate in dealing with members of their own nation or race. Such people no doubt lived in societies which generally found such behaviour acceptable, even desirable, and in which it would have taken considerable moral courage to behave otherwise.

Yet even if a verdict of morally guilty is reached it is hard to see what consequences result for the present. The descendants of those who committed such acts cannot be held responsible for deeds they had no part in. The only moral duty they have is that of helping all who have suffered wrongs or who are suffering as a result of past wrongs; and this is an obligation which is shared by all men regardless of what their forebears did. It is on grounds of morality, therefore, not justice, that recompense ought to be made.

The questions raised by earlier injustices perpetrated by states —

more precisely, in the name of states — are yet more difficult. Colonisation is now recognised as an international injustice but it was not so regarded in the past. On the contrary, it was frequently seen as a contribution to the welfare of native populations and as a means of bringing to them the benefits of economic progress. Although some voices were raised against colonialism, they were little heeded until after 1945. Colonialism was outlawed *post hoc*. But the anti-colonialists at first remained forward-looking, seeing independence for non-self-governing territories as their primary goal. And with political autonomy was expected — for some reason — economic independence. It has been the failure to achieve the latter which has given rise to the concepts of neo-colonialism and its cousin structural dependence and which has led to demands for restitution.

The argument is that even if colonialism was not unjust in the past, it is unjust now for states to benefit from the economic transfers that occurred under colonial regimes. And it is a *fortiori* unjust if certain states continue to exploit others, colonies or not. In the case of past exploitation there may be some difficulty in determining who must accept responsibility and who ought to be compensated. The Western colonial powers have generally retained their identity over a period of centuries so that it could be meaningful to talk of the present generation of Britons, for example, benefiting from capital transfers that took place within the Empire. But the same cannot be said of their colonial subjects. Many Third World states are creations of their colonial masters. If their governments have any claim to compensation it is in trust for the various surviving tribes and ethnic groups that experienced colonial rule.

The next problem is to calculate the measure of recompense. Should it be set at the total amount of capital extracted? Or should the net figure be determined by deducting the capital inflow? The latter course would be more in keeping with the idea of compensation. Once figures are calculated, moreover, it will presumably be necessary to convert the sums involved to current prices and there is endless scope for argument as to how this should be done. The final sum reached, however, could well prove quite impractical for one of two reasons: it could turn out to be so great that payment would involve intolerable burdens, or so small that it would not meet the actual needs of the underdeveloped countries.[49] Yet more complex are claims for compensation in respect of spiritual losses. By what criteria could past assaults on human dignity or on traditional ways of life be recompensed?

It will be clear that the concept of compensation does not really address itself to the problems that it is supposed to solve. If economic

advancement is the objective, assistance ought to be calculated in terms
of what is required now rather than what happened in the past. There
will also be states in need of economic aid which have never been
colonies. The argument for compensation, as Stone observes, assumes
a willingness to make major sacrifices on the part of some states and a
great capacity for forgiveness on the part of others; but if these conditions exist the parties concerned could be expected to co-operate
amicably on the basis of existing needs and future objectives.[50] The
idea of compensation is thus not so much a step towards international
justice as a means of focusing attention on global issues.

For the foreseeable future the most effective principles of justice will
be those found within the nation-state. There is no simple way in which
they can be extended to mankind at large. But while national justice
is not a direct contribution to global justice and in fact makes the latter
more difficult to attain, its merits ought not to be overlooked. There is
a common assumption that settling for justice on a national rather than
a global basis is something to be deplored, that it is to settle for second-
best. Yet it does seem that part of man's nature is a sense of belonging
to an exclusive group, a sense which cosmopolitanism seeks to stifle. On
the other hand, the very notion of morality — moral rules which individuals as individuals ought to follow — suggests that man also has a
sense of the universal. It may posit unrealisable goals but it, too, ought
not to be suppressed.

The role of international justice appears to be that of mediating
principles of both national and global justice. To be sure, the former
will predominate, but global justice has not been ignored altogether.
There is some notion of an obligation on the part of states to aid those
individuals who are in the direst circumstances; but states naturally
remain reluctant to accept principles which involve international
redistribution of resources for this would open the door to all manner
of claims against them. This emphasis on retaining autonomy is one that
is shared both by the wealthy states and by those states which at
present condemn the dominance of the rich.

As for economic inequalities in the world, these are indeed enormous. But the market-place perhaps offers more hope of reducing these
differences than any principles of international or global justice. In the
past political power that could be extended overseas gave certain states
the capacity to create and maintain economic advantages for themselves.
If it is the case that power is becoming more dispersed throughout the

globe and more difficult to deploy abroad, then some economic imbalances may be reduced. Again, recent developments have shown that the sources of supply of many raw materials and primary products are widely spread. This will also serve to redress economic inequalities in some degree. And the more interdependent the world economy, the greater the bargaining power of those with goods in short supply.

The most intriguing question of all is how long the total stock of the earth's resources will hold out. If global shortages begin to bite they could lead to a much greater sense of a common predicament for man. Principles of justice to govern the distribution of resources in limited supply might become more appealing. But global shortages could also produce competition between states and present some countries with the opportunity to exploit a monopoly position. If what I have said about the persistence of national outlooks is correct, this more gloomy prospect also looks the more probable.

Notes

1. See W.K. Frankena, 'The Concept of Social Justice', in R.B. Brandt (ed.), *Social Justice* (New Jersey, 1962), pp. 1-3.

2. Ibid., pp. 4-6.

3. For an argument along these lines see Onora Nell, 'Lifeboat Earth', *Philosophy and Public Affairs,* vol. 4, no. 3 (Spring 1975).

4. There are many reasons for treating moral rules as universal and for rejecting relativism. See, for instance, B. Williams, *Morality* (Harmondsworth, 1973), pp. 17-51.

5. P. Singer, 'Famine, Affluence, and Morality', *Philosophy and Public Affairs,* vol. 1, no. 3 (Spring 1972).

6. The issue of humanitarian intervention raises similar problems. For obvious reasons humanitarian aid tends to encounter fewer objections from governments.

7. For a utilitarian, by contrast, the distinction between humanitarian aid and the demands of justice is a second-order one. C.R. Beitz, 'Justice and International Relations', *Philosophy and Public Affairs,* vol. 4, no. 4 (Summer 1975), pp. 360-1.

8. M. Walzer, 'Political Action: The Problem of Dirty Hands', in M. Cohen, T. Nagel, T. Scanlon (eds.), *War and Moral Responsibility* (Princeton, 1974).

9. '. . . the problem is simply how can warm passion and a cool sense of proportion be forged together in one and the same soul? Politics is made with the head, not with other parts of the body or soul. And yet devotion to politics, if it is not to be frivolous intellectual play but rather genuinely human conduct, can be born and nourished from passion alone'; Max Weber, 'Politics as a Vocation', in *From Max Weber,* H.H. Gerth, C. Wright Mills (eds.) (London, 1948), p. 115.

10. On Marx and justice see A.W. Wood, 'The Marxian Critique of Justice', *Philosophy and Public Affairs,* vol. 1, no. 3 (Spring 1972), esp. pp. 257-8, 271.

11. Important here is the idea that only similar entities can be members of the same justice-constituency. Thus men's relations with animals, e.g. hunting or raising for slaughter, are not generally seen as giving rise to questions of justice, although men might be said to have a duty to treat them humanely.

12. '. . . it is preferable that law should rule rather than any single one of the citizens . . . he who asks Law to rule is asking God and Intelligence and no others to rule; while he who asks for the rule of a human being is bringing in a wild beast . . . In law you have the intellect without the passions', *Politics*, Book III, Ch. 16, trans. T.A. Sinclair (Harmondsworth, 1962).

13. Ibid., Book VII, Ch. 2.

14. For an exposition of Rousseau's ideas on international relations, see S. Hoffman, 'Rousseau on War and Peace', in *The State of War* (New York, 1965).

15. S. Avineri, *Hegel's Theory of the Modern State* (Cambridge, 1972), Ch. 10.

16. Julius Stone reaches the same conclusion by a different route, viz. denial of the domestic analogy: 'The aggregate of state entities cannot *as such* constitute a meaningful justice-constituency'. 'Approaches to the Notion of International Justice', in R.A. Falk, C.E. Black (eds.), *The Future of the International Legal Order*, vol. I (Princeton, 1969), p. 435.

17. *A Treatise of Human Nature*, Book III, part ii (London, 1972), pp. 210ff.

18. For the distinction between special rights and general rights see H.L.A. Hart, 'Are There Any Natural Rights?', *Philosophical Review*, vol. 64, no. 2 (April 1955), pp. 183-8. General rights are held by men regardless of any special relationship and are essentially defensive in character, requiring non-interference on the part of others.

19. See W.N. Nelson, 'Special Rights, General Rights, and Social Justice', *Philosophy and Public Affairs*, vol. 3, no. 4 (Summer 1974).

20. (London, 1972), p. 11. Page references in the text are to this work. The main ideas of Rawls's theory are set out on pp. 11-17.

21. For a full statement of these principles and rules of priority see *Theory of Justice*, pp. 302-3.

22. *Discourse on Inequality*, cited in Hoffmann, 'Rousseau on War and Peace', p. 67.

23. The present account follows Robert Nozick, *Anarchy, State, and Utopia* (Oxford, 1974), esp. Ch. 7. A standard exposition can be found in Hume, *Treatise of Human Nature*, Book III, part ii.

24. *Anarchy, State and Utopia*, pp. 150-3.

25. Ibid., p. 178. Nozick does not give any full argument for this shift. This is a potential weakness since the holding of property in common could be said to justify a government with extensive rights over individuals. The whole thrust of Nozick's argument, however, is towards a minimal state.

26. This paradox is pursued in R.N. Berki, 'On Marxian Thought and the Problem of International Relations', *World Politics*, vol. XXIV, no. 1 (October 1971).

27. Trans. R.B. Kimber (Princeton, 1970); the original German edition, *Weltbürgertum und Nationalstaat*, first appeared in 1907.

28. R.W. Sterling, *Ethics in a World of Power: The Political Ideas of Friedrich Meinecke* (Princeton, 1958), pp. 10, 32-3; Meinecke, *Cosmopolitanism*, p. 15.

29. Sterling, *Ethics in a World of Power*, p. 45.

30. Ibid., p. 34.

31. Ibid., pp. 59-60; Meinecke, *Cosmopolitanism*, pp. 20-1.

32. The Chinese concept of aid at grass roots level challenges this view. One may doubt whether governments really welcome this form of aid.

33. Hoffmann deems this 'one of Rousseau's deepest insights, one that shatters a large part of the liberal vision of world affairs'; 'Rousseau on War and Peace', p. 62.

34. Rawls in fact takes a different path, one that leads to *international* justice —see below. The procedure outlined here is proposed by Brian Barry, *The Liberal Theory of Justice* (London, 1973), pp. 129-30.

35. Frankena, 'Concept of Social Justice', p. 16.

36. Ibid., pp. 155-60, 167-73.

37. Stone, 'Approaches . . .', p. 435.

38. Barry, *Liberal Theory of Justice*, p. 128. Rawls's criterion is perhaps implicit in his assumption (admittedly ambiguous) of more or less self-sufficient associations.

39. Ibid., pp. 132-3.

40. Rawls, *Theory of Justice*, p. 378.

41. Ibid., p. 375.

42. Ibid., p. 364

43. Beitz, 'Justice and International Relations', p. 368.

44. 'Whatsoever [man] removes out of the state that nature hath provided and left it in, he hath mixed his labour with, and joined to it something that is his own, and thereby makes it his property . . . it hath by this labour something annexed to it that excludes the common right of other men', John Locke, *The Second Treatise of Government*, J. Gough (ed.) (Oxford, 1956), p. 15 (para 27).

45. Ibid., p. 20 (para 37).

46. Ibid., p. 18 (para 33).

47. Ibid., p. 291.

48. Ibid., p. 292. See the comments in Barry, *Liberal Theory of Justice*, p. 131.

49. It might be pointed out here that the burden of payments could well fall most heavily on the poorest classes in the states concerned.

50. Stone, 'Approaches . . .', p. 442.

6 INJUSTICE AND EVIL IN THE POLITICS OF THE POWERS*

A.L. Burns

In free societies we have some apprehension of injustice in power politics — enough, as Calvin put it, to leave us without excuse — but little apprehension of evil. Ignorance of the evil in ourselves is itself partly evil; but it is also partly innocence, an uncovenanted blessing which obtains just because we are unaware of it.

In the theory and analysis of international relations, including the corpus of international law, the idea of justice and injustice can have factual application, though in no facile way: many annexations, exploitations, the unjust levying of war, and long-term distributions of resources and power which are inequitable and nowadays styled 'structural violence', can sometimes be designated quite objectively as unjust and wrong. After two centuries of the is-ought, the fact-value dichotomy, we can now see it as a philosophers' error of perspective, and recognise that despite it civilised societies since the Middle Ages have increased the discrimination and the range of their judgements of justice and injustice. The societies have not necessarily become more just in themselves; but the codes they subscribe to have progressed in definition and sensitivity.

Thus, a doctoral thesis questioning the justice or otherwise of some internationally significant act[1] would be a possible enterprise. The actuality of evil in power-political and other situations on the other hand, though palpable, is not subject to scholarly demonstration in the same way, except insofar as it has been expressed in specific injustices. Yet profound historical and similar writing can reveal it, as Thucydides' account of demoralisation in Athens does. And of course works of high imagination, such as the great tragedies, paintings and sculpture, are the chief secular teachers of the knowledge of good and evil. But above all that knowledge is made the burden of the Old and New Testaments,

* This chapter is in tribute to Stephen Yarnold, formerly Moderator of the Presbyterian Church of Victoria, and for more than 40 years a powerful and liberating influence, as teacher and pastor, upon his pupils, students and congregations, and many others. He has imparted a sense of history's informing the present moment, and of the depths of the moment. Matt. 16:1-3; Eccl. 11:1.

from Genesis to Revelation. I hope to show how intimately that
scriptural theme is related throughout to the politics of the Powers,
even in apparently so remote an aspect as the forbidding of idolatry
and polytheism.[2]

Evil, then, is a purely subjective or a specially religious concept? So
it was taken, by a leading international scholar whose work is known
worldwide for its shrewdness, lucidity, and sharpness of perception, on
the occasion of this chapter's first presentation. His argument was that
whereas the principles of justice (right and wrong) were rules and
arrangements by which people ordered their relations with each other,
evil and good appertained to the individual's attitude to the devil and
to God (as in Graham Greene's *Brighton Rock*) and so were concepts
not relevant to international relations, nor of much help to non-
believers.

One would indeed expect a sharper sensitivity in these matters from
believers than from non-believers (given always equal experience; for
in our fortunate societies, traditional believers have often been shel-
tered, at least until the present decade). But it is not credible that the
non-believer has no perception of evil in our terrible twentieth century.
Yet the international expert could certainly argue that his analyses need
not refer explicitly to good or evil, much as a psychiatrist might use
precisely the same approach and methods in treating a saintly person
with an intermittent psychosis (a number of saints, we are told, have
suffered episodes of mental illness) and a horrid psychopath. Further,
there is a level of relationship between Powers to which questions about
degrees of evil characterising particular Powers — or for that matter
their several injustices — are not immediately pertinent. The civilian
strategic expert who said

> . . . what king, going to make war against another king, sitteth not
> down first and consulteth whether he be able with ten thousand to
> meet him that cometh with twenty thousand? Or else, while the
> other is yet a great way off, he sendeth an ambassage, and desireth
> conditions of peace[3]

though hardly an amoralist, well understood the relative distinctiveness
of this level of relationship. But analyses that not only begin but also
end at that level, without ever entering the ethical dimensions, are
unrealistic and wrong-headed.

Injustice has its place solely in the dimension of actions and institutions; but evil belongs also to the dimension of disposition, and indeed

has its source there. Two recent reports of evil incidents may bring this out. In one, a crowd chanted, 'Jump, jump, jump!' to a man standing on a high window-ledge. In the other, another crowd shouted, 'Do your own thing!' and 'Right on, sister!' to a girl preparing to slash her wrists. Both crowds were of evil disposition but also did wrong (or injustice in an extended sense); but the element of evil would have been just as great had each member of the crowds *wished* what he did sitting solitary in his room watching television.

From another angle, stark injustice can be done, in a kind of invincible ignorance or error, by pure and even noble characters: there may even be some amongst the murderous Provisional IRA. Tragic paradox, however, is bound to afflict such people, as bitter remorse or as clinical insanity or most often as gradual infection and corruption by self-exculpating anger. Most men and some women, looking within, will be aware of this. It arises from the general disposition to give one's allegiance to some nation, organised movement, state, class, tribe, creed, gang or faction (once, as in the blood-feud, to an extended family) that is or has in it to become a Power, i.e. a group capable of collectively exercising armed force against 'outsiders'.[4] These Powers, into which we have such a tendency to group ourselves, are by their constitution morally ambiguous: the sources of the paradoxical 'well-intentioned' injustices mentioned above, but also now and then of internal justice and freedom; susceptible to overwhelming possession by evil, but also to partial conversion, if not to unqualified goodness, at least to a human decency.

Injustice, even when done in error, is always of course an evil, but evil is not merely injustice only worse: it is not as though the young fiend proceeding to his baccalaureate of wickedness needs only injustice for a pass but must take the course in evil for an honours degree. Reflection will show further aspects of the distinguishable dimensions of the two. As we shall see, for instance, rational progress in the recognition of injustice is possible and has been made. The knowledge of evil comes instead from personal experience. Injustice can sometimes be redressed by action, and free men are under constant obligation to do so. Evil can only be redeemed.

Evidently evil is not an appropriate subject for research. To look for causes of such phenomena as crowds clamouring for suicide, for gladiatorial deaths in the arena, and so on, is beyond the scope of fundamentally historical investigation, such as international politics; for it seems often to arise of its own accord. But there are other and great manifestations of evil for which historically-evolved structures can sometimes be found.

The structures principally considered here are the Powers, which now hold all but universal sway. But from others, whose members each see their particular structure not ambiguous, as in a Power, but instead positively good, great evil may arise, e.g. from churches. One thinks of the Salem witch-hunts, the burning of Servetus in Geneva, the church-encouraged holocausts of witches and heretics, elsewhere and earlier. Precisely because the churchmen more or less responsible for such atrocities usually conceived of a warfare against the forces of darkness (and were not always wholly mistaken as to their victims' intentions: a few of the would-be witches did aspire, like the moor murderers and the Manson family of our day, to wield diabolical powers; some of the heresies were destructive), they could be utterly ruthless in good conscience.

Often, churches could persecute only by compact with the civil Power, so that a structure's giving rise to evil is just another instance of what this chapter chiefly deals with. But more to the point, ecclesiastical sources of evil reveal the importance of fundamental *belief* in its genesis, when some social structure is also present. (To repeat, this is not *necessary* for evil, which often exists willy-nilly.) An example from pagan religion is the belief alleged to have been held by the Aztecs: that the sun would cool and go out if not continually fed with living human hearts torn out of prisoners of war.

Consider that 'belief'. On the one hand, it was not an imaginative figure of speech expressive of some other belief, as in William Blake's

If the sun or moon should doubt,
They'd immediately go out.[5]

Apparently it was literal fact for the people. Yet to us it looks like a blatant rationalisation of the Aztec drive toward conquest and exploitation. We cannot understand how its falsity could remain unrecognised, and suppose the priests must have put it about deliberately as propaganda. But the latter is a naive supposition: the most destructive and lying nonsense in our time has been promulgated by those, e.g. most of the Nazi leaders, who really did believe it themselves.

Not all false beliefs are malignant. From Elizabethan times it was popularly believed that English law made it impossible to tread English soil and remain a slave. The late eighteenth-century lawyers who opposed Grenville Sharp on the slavery issue seem to have been correct at law in denying this popular belief. Thus the Mansfield judgement beneficently validated what may well have been historically false.

Whether our own complex of beliefs are on the whole benign or rather generate evil is a vastly more intractable question. It should be plain from what has gone before that the most careful answers to it cannot be accredited as the products of academic research. Also there are the obvious traps of self-observation; and the ruling beliefs of Western societies form such a complicated structure that one can hardly tell which component is responsible for what. Nevertheless we shall concentrate on one widely-held belief, that the balance of terror guarantees peace at least between the Super-powers and is, because of that, justifiable and necessary. The 'balance of terror' here means the reciprocal deterrence of major and mainly nuclear attack by the known capacity for mass destruction ('counter-resource strikes') in response to the other's most effective 'counter-force strike'. Though actual possession of the weapons that yield this capacity is both necessary and sufficient for ability to deter (no doctrine is really needed beyond a bald description of such weapons and what they can do), each nuclear-weapons Power does spell out its doctrine in its own terms: the US-SU agreement of mid-1972, concluding SALT ONE, generally presupposed the American policy of Mutual Assured Destruction (MAD), though the Soviet Union publicly envisages, in the worst case, all-out war employing all forces, conventional as well as nuclear. The French used to speak of being able to 'tear off a limb' -- an expression which has at least candour to its moral credit. The Chinese and the British doctrines are much less explicit, since their strategic situations involve the capacities of other nuclear-weapon states as well as their own, and are better not spelt out.

The balance of terror and all doctrines expressing it inescapably imply a national will to acquire the nuclear forces that would make the nation able to commit an appalling crime against humanity; yet in some cases (China is a clear one) national leaders may well judge that failing to acquire such forces would be committing just such a crime against their own people.[6] It is as though the sole means available to parents for preventing their children being molested were the ability to torture to death the would-be molester and ten of his nearest relatives. Suppose also that those were the sole methods available to a householder of protecting his liberty, house and property.

That comparison immediately suggests a major countervailing difference: dependence upon the balance of terror is far from direct for the private person whose country is assuredly or possibly under some nuclear umbrella. The doctrine of nuclear deterrence does not so affect his everyday conduct as to reduce him at once to a state of savagery in

the way that re-adoption of the *lex talionis* in the above comparison
would do. All the same, the general assumption of the validity and
application of the balance of terror (i.e. fundamental *belief* in it, and
in the existence of the Powers that operate it) amounts to some acceptance of evil; and anyone who has seen a generation of children grow up
under its shadow will have perceived the rarely expressed but crippling
despair which it creates.

Another effect, combining with that of the televising of the Vietnam
and similar conflicts, has been to promote condonation of, if not positive support for, terroristic ventures. If the president of the United
States can hold scores of millions of foreigners hostage for the prudent
conduct of Moscow and Peking, why should not the PLO or the Red
Army or the Angry Brigade or the IRA make hostage, for their several
objectives, plane-loads of passengers? Though terrorism was by no
means an invention of the 'sixties, what is rather new is the proliferation of these trans-national and ephemeral Powers, ephemeral insofar
as, unlike full-blown territorial Powers, they do not control a producing
economy, or at least not yet. Eire, Israel, Kenya, Algeria and Greek
Cyprus are all now fully territorial Powers (the last not quite so) which
to some extent or another *'grew'* out of the barrels of terrorist guns.
Those of the contemporary organisations, e.g. PLO and IRA, with
connections to particular countries and peoples, may and sometimes do
persist through several generations, turning youthful idealists into brave
and fanatical murderers persuaded that they deserve the status of military combatants. (And why do they not? — Because they are propaga-
ting a national ideal, trying to bring a territorial nation into existence,
and working to redress what they see as historic injustices, not defending family and home. Legal distinctions between combatant and civilian,
and concomitant obligations to prisoners of war, have come to be
recognised in the West because the waging of war came to be seen as at
best a necessary evil for citizens in a polity, whereas when done by
revolutionaries it appears to be a gratuitous act, almost as though it
were a mere crime. I can now see a great deal of sense in that interpretation.) Yet actual evil, in its *extent*, correlates inversely with the
degree of irresponsibility of its perpetrators: criminal gangs can do less
than idealistic terrorists, and they far less than responsible statesmen.

The balance of terror epitomises evil at this time, not by being worse
in itself than anything before — consider the imperialism of the ancient
Assyrians, for instance — but by its worldwide application and its
possible worldwide effects. We have seen that it is also a moral infection
that seems to abet terrorism in lesser forms. Therefore any adult who

lives in a country protected to some extent or other under a 'nuclear umbrella' is despite himself implicated in the evil of the balance of terror. The nature and necessity of this implication takes some understanding. Is one, for instance, similarly implicated in the torture of prisoners of war, should some Australian soldier commit that crime? — No; for it is no part of that nation's defence policy. On the contrary, it is strictly forbidden, and their code of military law has the contrary intent.

Our strategic doctrine and defence policy, on the other hand, predicate a Western nuclear deterrent. We cannot claim, for our conventional military forces, that they depend in no way on the balance of terror. Indeed, the implication of the nuclear umbrella provided by some other Power is morally no different from that of having nuclear weapons of our own. Hence the strong attraction, for Christians and others brought up in a tradition of conscience, of pacifism and withdrawal from an inescapable evil world.

Not only has this way of life been a major influence amongst Eastern Orthodox and Roman Catholics since the third century, when the decline and corruption of Classical civilisation appalled Christian minds who withdrew as anchorites and later as monks and nuns: the earliest biblical stories tell of other, non-celibate, withdrawals such as Abraham's departure from Ur of the Chaldees, and of returns to the nomadic, wilderness existence from time to time in the history of Israel. Under the New Testament dispensation, obedient to the command to render to Caesar what is Caesar's and to God what is God's, there have not been wanting those who, not retreating to the desert, have nevertheless renounced Caesar's protection and defied his power, e.g. the present-day dissident Baptists and Evangelicals in the Soviet Union. Nor have these witnesses all been people who did not really understand the workings of power politics, e.g. not the late Martin Wight, who throughout World War II was a Christian pacifist.[7] As indicated below, evil sometimes so pervades a society or parts of it, e.g. Nazi-occupied Europe, that not only is just treatment unavailable to the individual, but also wholly just action is not open to him as a member of that society. In such cases personal integrity seems to leave no option but withdrawal of social commitment, even though withdrawal may well bring martyrdom.

An argument against withdrawing in order to be in no way responsible for evil which pervades one's country is that one may thereby fail to redress injustices. Suppose you are a citizen of a nuclear-weapon state which has a treaty of military assistance with a smaller non-nuclear state. The latter is attacked without provocation by a more powerful non-

nuclear state. Your government decides to go with conventional forces
to the aid of its ally. But it also deploys, publicly though quietly,
nuclear delivery systems which, though they *could* be used to attack
centres of population, have the obvious purpose of deterring the aggres-
sor from massing either invasion forces or strategic strike forces. The
strong presumption is that these deterrent forces will in any case *not* be
used, because of the powerful inhibition everywhere against being the
first actually to use nuclear weapons since Hiroshima and Nagasaki.
Your nuclear weapon state in fact achieves a satisfactory conventional
victory quite without employment of its nuclear forces; but no one
is prepared to claim that the mere presence of the latter had not affected the outcome. In this instance (contrasting with the actual purpose
of nuclear deployment — to deter *conventional* attack), the terror of
nuclear attack upon mass populations was possible and is of background
moral significance, though admittedly remote.

Even more poignant situations arise when a Power committed to
evil can be effectively resisted only by introduction of some other,
potentially evil, resources. The United Kingdom's (and later, combined
Western allies') project to develop the atomic bomb in order to forestall
Nazi Germany's doing so had its justification in the conscious diabolism
of Hitler's creed and regime, discussed below. (This is not said in miti-
gation of the Allies' mass destruction by conventional weapons, nor does
it apply directly or in the same way to the other issue of the bombing
of Hiroshima and Nagasaki.) Evil sometimes gets built so thoroughly into a society that there may be call to stop it by force. In contrary cases,
e.g. religious persecution as discussed above, there is either magnification
or total misperception of the 'evil' to be overcome, while the injustice,
or indeed the evil, of the means proposed to overcome it is not perceived at all. R.H. Tawney, noble and generous of spirit, once summed
this up, saying that war must be either a crime or a crusade.

If only that were so! Often, undoubtedly, it has been — and much
more often a crime than a crusade. But there have also been other cases,
the English Civil War within England itself providing a clear example,
when each party has had some right on its side and each would have
felt themselves treacherous if they had not resisted. As usual in civil
wars, the one people of England became for the time two Powers, with
a third Power, the Scots, to the north. For armed forces of its day, the
New Model Army campaigned with considerable restraint in England
itself; but in Ireland, where Cromwell and his Roundheads believed they
were combating the Romish Antichrist, the tale was merciless.

Thus even in this exemplary case of the English Civil War as a tragic conflict between causes both of which could lay claim to justice and even to public benefit, the transition to evil and to a kind of lunacy was a short one. And whereas the evil of war with no quarter given has persisted in Ireland to this day (though much moderated now), from the English 'tragic conflict' a development through two and a half centuries of civil liberty, free political institutions, legal justice and, at last, welfare and some small degree of equality can be historically traced. Other societies, in Europe and in the New World, developed similarly, so that from the turn of the century, though interrupted by the terrors of the two world wars and the paradoxical catastrophe — 'poverty in the midst of plenty' — of the Great Depression, an atmosphere of somewhat banal innocence began to prevail in such societies, often contaminated by racial injustice, and always by economic injustice,[8] yet discernible enough.

That atmosphere of innocence had one perilous effect upon those who lived in it: they did not recognise the devil immediately upon meeting him. (There are other, worse effects: one often hears now of many driving past accidents, or stopping only to peer and pry. This used to be rare, with the average person offering help as a matter of course, even at personal inconvenience. I am not thinking of the heroism, sometimes displayed in almost any society, where, say, someone who could have armed himself talks a homicidal maniac who has taken hostages into giving up his weapon instead of picking off the maniac in justifiable self-protection and protection of the hostages. The latter heroism is an instance of the redemptive action.) Specifically, they (or we) did not recognise Hitler.

Melbourne schools in 1939 dealt in one of the history courses with totalitarian ideologies and the contemporary dictators. The textbooks had not been written, so perforce we depended upon original works, including *Mein Kampf*. Its nastiness of tone was at once apparent. We were already informed about Hitler's militarism, employment of crowd hysteria, destruction of liberty and free institutions, use of pan-German nationalism in foreign conquest, and anti-Semitism (though not of the depth and extent of the last), all of which were certainly unjust enough. A very few had learnt of sources of indigenous resistance, e.g. of the Confessing Church and its Barmen Declaration against 'German Christianity', which more than venerated 'the man Adolf Hitler'. But what I for one could not credit were the book's quite explicit indications of his purpose of conquest at least Europe-wide and of establishing a Faustian totalitarian Power based on sheer race. It seemed unbelievable that a society should utterly eliminate the very possibility of public

justice, corrupt children and friends into denouncing parents and
friends, and worship instead blood, soil, and the Führer. We had been
taught that injustices could and should be redressed one by one according to conscience, by what Karl Popper later styled 'piecemeal social
engineering'. The actuality of evil was beyond our experience.

Our failure was a failure of imagination. Yet after the event the
actuality of evil can be conveyed even to the culpably innocent. A
former colleague of Jewish parentage had spent her years from seven
to thirteen (1939-46) in and around Warsaw. Her detailed account of
experiences was instructive, but even more the sense conveyed of the
atmosphere of a society in which public justice was impossible, and
'. . . the blast of the terrible ones . . . like a storm against the wall'.[9]
The evil could be withstood, but at a high cost in risk incurred, and
with little hope. The peril and the fear which battle or a natural disaster
bring, though doubtless as intense, are of a different and less pervasive
order. Borrowing the terminology but not the philosophy of ancient
Gnosticism, Paul sets out that contrast:

> We wrestle not against flesh and blood but against principalities,
> against powers, against the rulers of the darkness of this world,
> against spiritual wickedness in high places.[10]

Those mysterious, supernatural and evil Powers were thought of as
transcending but participating in the earthly 'Powers that be . . .',
which in turn were the scene of a warfare between God who had
ordained them and the Powers of Darkness. When the latter had temporarily prevailed, they were represented in idolatrous form by the
gods of the nations. Hence, from the Mosaic epoch onward, the
prohibition upon idol-making and image-worship, and the Hebrew,
later Iconoclastic and Islamic, recoil from great but idolatrous works
of art as from uncleanness.[11]

By a strange paradox, the allegedly 'subjective' perception of evil is
sometimes stronger and more vivid, and sometimes tells one more about
the state of a society than can the 'objective' analysis of the material
facts. Often, this is because an evil regime destroys the evidence of its
misdeeds, as does the Ministry of Truth in Orwell's *Nineteen Eighty-
Four*; or it fails to produce, and if produced cannot command, the free
enquirers who can assess the evidence from day to day. This partly
explains the widely remarked-on difficulty of evil regimes having no
continuous history, while civilisation and the religious communions
have. (Some secret societies such as the Mafia may be exceptions,

though most of them have not been precisely 'regimes'.) To express
some notions barely half-baked: progress in good, such as the step-by-
step abolition of slavery and serfdom (by which we modern pygmies
have been advanced beyond such giants as Plato and Aristotle) has no
mirror-image in any progress of evil, though an illusion of such 'progress'
may be given by evil's being parasitic upon good. The Assassins of the
ancient Islamic world, and *thuggee* as a worship of Kali in India, could
not 'advance', but at most merely recrudesce, as they and even Nazism
may yet do, even in sterile and artificial forms like the contemporary
recrudescence of witchcraft. But progress in good — say, in civilisation
considered as 'the diminution of the *traces* of original sin' — can never
be guaranteed to be once-for-all: to believe otherwise is to accept the
myth of progress.

That evil can be and is parasitic ephemerally upon good shows up in
the use of the blessings of current psychiatric medicine for purposes of
intellectual and political repression, purportedly done for the benefit
not only of the whole community, but even more of the 'patient' himself. It is at this point that the myth of the Antichrist lends its perspective: upon the occasions of many advances in good, evil men take up as
pseudo-saviours the very advance itself and, worse, persuade otherwise
decent and well-meaning people to accept them as saviours (nevertheless, there is no identifying the historical pseudo-saviour as *the* contemporary Antichrist in the way, for instance, that the antipopes might
once have been identifiable). But in parts of the world, e.g. parts of
Asia, where the Messianic conception is not native, the Antichrist myth
has of course no application. Nevertheless it would be unsurprising if
Eastern traditions with some sense of history should turn out to have
comparable ideas.

Insofar as a society, e.g. a nation-state, continues to afford the
possibility of significant redress of injustice, it remains not wholly
subject to evil: one mark of the nation-state wholly subject to evil is
that it makes impossible the recourse to ordinary, everyday, demon-
strable justice. Redemption in the latter case is worked, if it is worked at
all, by the martyrs and the small martyr-communities, many of whom
will never be known; and no political arrangement can prepare before-
hand to provide and train martyrs. But before a society gets to that
pass, politics and law can do much to set up a structure of freedom and
justice.

Justice and freedom are interrelated, for the essentials of just procedure, logically prior to and more important than apprehension,
charging, adjudicating or sentencing, are the means of publicly establi-

shing the truths of the matter; such means are available only where the truth can be elicited by free enquirers from free witnesses.

The conditions for a society in which there is a good prospect of truth's being thus elicited include a recognisable and accepted body of law, and in particular the principle that no-one can be detained or penalised except according to law. These conditions do not necessarily include electoral or representative democracy in the sense of 'one man, one vote'. The latter, however, is a near-necessity for the further structure that guards against the seizure of power by any single movement, evil or otherwise, by its fragmenting of state power. Though (under the Westminster system, for example) the leader of a governing party has, as prime minister, considerable power, that power is limited in extent by law and by the constitution, and in time by the requirement periodically to face the electors; and *their* power, jointly sovereign, is severally minute. Furthermore, a polity is free and democratic when similar constitutions and systems are accepted, not only at the level of national government, but even, for instance, in private associations and clubs. All the citizens of such a polity could, admittedly, succumb to evil at the same time, in which case the free and democratic polity would soon be overthrown; but that is much less likely than in a concerted and corporate society.[12]

Along with the rather uninteresting innocence and ignorance of evil referred to at the beginning of this chapter, we labour under an unawareness of our freedom: for us it is, and it should be, taken as much for granted as the air. Yet though it is not perhaps directly detectable, its absence is. If you cannot leave the society, that nation-state is not free. The greatest political difference in the world is between those Powers that maintain their frontiers only to keep outsiders out, and those which also and even more maintain them to keep insiders in.

Notes

1. E.g., the UN Congo forces' closure of airports and the radio station in Léopoldville on 5 September 1961, following the former Prime Minister Lumumba's attempted deposition of Kasavubu, the Head of State. In that instance the rights and wrongs of the action, by no means immediately clear, could be disentangled, with care: see A.L. Burns and Nina Heathcote, *Peace-Keeping by U.N. Forces: from Suez to the Congo* (Praeger, New York, 1963).

2. No derogation is suggested of the scriptures of other religions, such as Islam, Zoroastrianism or Buddhism, with which we are much less familiar.

3. Luke 14:31-2.

4. This idea is pursued further in A.L. Burns, *Of Powers and their Politics* (Prentice-Hall, Englewood Cliffs, 1968), especially pp. 85-90 and 267-80.

5. William Blake, *Songs of Innocence and Experience*. The belief Blake refers to is that 'the just shall live by his faith', faith being thought of by him as creative energy, which resembled the physical energy that radiates light from and to natural objects.

6. This dilemma is considered at length in A.L. Burns, *Ethics and Deterrence: a nuclear balance without hostage cities?*, Adelphi Paper No. 69, International Institute for Strategic Studies (London, 1970).

7. Hedley Bull, 'Martin Wight and the theory of international relations', *British Journal of International Studies* (1976) vol. 2, p. 103.

8. Economic injustice, and the nihilistic power-hungry evil which often arises from it, are not dealt with in this essay, principally because it is a distinct theme and, even more, because I have no substantial knowledge of it. But it does seem that one can distinguish two phases of exploitative evil — the first, in which labour is exploited, without a qualm about injustice, by virtue of the scarcity of the necessities of life (a situation currently perpetuated in totalitarian regimes by the causing of 'artificial' scarcity of these necessities); and the second, the notorious consumerism, in which new demands are elicited for novel goods by methods amongst which advertising is only one, and the workers who produce such goods are also given a vested interest in the sustaining of demand for them. The two phases of course often co-exist, as in the major capitalist economies nowadays. When, in the first phase, some compunction about wage injustice is shown, and when, in the second phase, exploiters hold back to some extent from eliciting demand for destructive or debilitating 'goods', a hope can be entertained for reform. But when in either phase the exploitation is sheerly nihilistic, then it often combines with the evil of unbridled power-politics to cause, say, the Opium Wars.

9. Isaiah 25:4.

10. Ephesians 6:12. It is odd that this dark saying, when received as a depiction of the history of the last 60 years, seems merely matter-of-fact.

11. See further G.B. Caird, *Principalities and Powers* (Oxford, 1956), and the present author in *Of Powers and their Politics*, pp. 77-85. The foregoing paragraphs do not invoke Scriptural authority on behalf of a particular interpretation of international politics; they assert a mainly biblical origin for the concept of 'the Power' as an international actor; and they attempt to show how the historical international order appears from a biblically-formed perspective. Concepts like 'the Powers' and 'the Antichrist' are not abstract ones under which to find specific historical instances, as Aristotle found many such instances under his abstract concept of *'the constitution* of a city-state': to attempt to find instances leads straight to the literalist millenarianism which seeks the identity of the current Antichrist or the Book of Daniel's Fifth Monarchy. These biblical concept-images are generative ideas that set and (I believe) widen and deepen a perspective upon history and upon today's world, and that stimulate one's analyses.

12. The fragmentation of power is not the same as (the illusion of) pluralism. Free democracy comprises a strong, strict and rather narrow set of values, but in matters indifferent its principle is to remain indifferent. Matters indifferent are the illusory realm of pluralism.

PART TWO: PRAXIS

7 RACE, CONFLICT AND LIBERATION IN AFRICA

Jan Pettman

In the late 1950s and early 1960s colonialism and racism appeared on
the retreat before the triumphant demands of African nationalism. The
retreat was halted at the Zambesi, leaving white Southern Africa in a
strong defensive stance against the black north. Confrontation included
liberation wars within the white preserve. In 1974, the *coup* in Portugal
found Africa's oldest imperial power acknowledging the right of its
colonies to independence. With the frontiers of white power contrac-
ting, South Africa joined forces with Western governments to legitimise
a moderate form of majority rule in Rhodesia and the 'independence'
of Namibia, and began to seek acceptance within the continent as an
African state.

In the years that separate the two stages of African decolonisation,
the political, economic and ideological forces in Africa have changed
profoundly, and with them the bases for moral claims[1] made on behalf
of African peoples. There is some continuity in the assertion of African
identity, since shared colonial experiences and being judged by others as
'Africans' led to feelings of common victimisation,[2] but in the mid
seventies the issues have become decisively more complex. Previously,
African leaders claimed rights on behalf of their fellows against their
colonial masters, and demanded control of their own destinies. These
demands were articulated in terms of race, colour and access to wealth
and power, and were summed up in slogans of anti-colonialism, anti-
racism and rights of national self determination. Africans did not seek
to establish rights of a new kind or on a different philosophical base
from those already accepted within the Western tradition, but required
of Europeans that they extend these rights to Africans, and so close the
gap between the liberal rhetoric and the colonial reality. Africans
asserted the universal applicability of these rights, and denied the
legitimacy of alien rule, and of a privileged caste system based on race.
They thus claimed the right to rebel, to resort to violence in the face of
their continued exclusion from the political processes of their country.

In this way, African leaders not only pursued claims on behalf of
their fellows, but saw themselves as a moral force, 'teaching' the
decadent, inconsistent European powers to live by their own moral
principles. This dimension, an added self-righteousness, stemmed from

the African self-image as being the most victimised of peoples.[3] A sense of injury, and of innocence as victim compared with the guilt of the aggressors, helped fuel the struggle against colonialism.

By the mid seventies, however, the debate had become much more complicated and critical. The key issue is no longer the challenge to formal colonial rule, but rather the very nature of the post-colonial state in Africa, and of its relations with the wider, Western-dominated, economic, political and cultural system. The lines of conflict are no longer simply black against white but reflect deep divisions within the black ranks. Many African leaders, both of independent governments and of aspiring political movements in Southern Africa, continue to couch their claims in terms of majority rule and political independence. They are countered by others who speak of liberation and social revolution, of armed struggle and the need to create alternative structures within the state, to create new relationships capable of sustaining and defending the rights of Africans against those who continue to deny them. These rights are no longer claimed for Africans *per se*, or for those within a certain territory, but for those who are in an exploited, subordinate position. The claims are made as much against the African elite as against outsiders. The issue has become 'who speaks for whom?', with competing spokesmen representing different kinds of interests and competing notions of the good society, with its consequent rights and duties.

There remains a considerable moral element, no longer seeking morally correct behaviour from the colonial powers, but rather recognising the psychologically crippling and morally compromising effects of colonialism on the colonised.[4] In this sense, liberation becomes a search for African moral regeneration, the rediscovery of integrity through assuming responsibility for self, and establishing African autonomy.

The overwhelming facts of 'independent' Africa's existence are its extreme weakness, and subsequent vulnerability, and its profound dependence on external forces. All the black African states are poor,[5] insecure, dependent on their military forces for internal use, and lacking the instruments or basis for economic development or effective political control. State borders do not on the whole coincide with ethnic, racial or cultural frontiers, but are the creation of colonial regimes whose legitimacy has now been denied. At independence, all the units of the polity – the government, the state and the nation – were underdeveloped and, in the last case, almost non-existent. In this situation 'it is not the country that is in danger of attack or conquest, but the government that is in danger of overthrow or collapse. Insecurity is thus endemic, inherent, and political, rather than specific, external and military'.[6] Anti-national threats are often internal, sub-national ones — from tribal, ethnic or regional groups, or stemming simply from alternative elites like the military. Government rests on so slender a base that little power is necessary to topple it.[7]

This weakness has crucial implications for the external relations of African states. A dissatisfied group within the country may, through external support, provide itself with the means to overthrow the government. This support may take the form of a covert guarantee from the ex-colonial or dominant external power that it will not intervene against the *coup*-makers. But the government is vulnerable to other kinds of intervention or outside influence — to the threatened withdrawal of a desperately-needed loan, or insistence on changes in domestic policy as a precondition for the loan; to a fall in prices for the principal export crop, since the export-dominated, externally-orientated economy of most African countries is mono-cultural; or to the advice and aid of 'experts' whose guidance may be sought voluntarily by governments appalled at the gap between policy formulations and the instruments which are available for government action.

At independence, then, African leaders found themselves charged with responsibility for pursuit of the 'national interest'. Because the government was obliged to create the nation, as much as assert its independence, national security was often defined in terms of the survival of the government. Defence of both the state and its government led, therefore, to attempts to argue and implement the rights of state sovereignty and continental hegemony, to protect the country against intervention by either African neighbours or extra-continental powers.

Independent Africa's search for its own ground-rules, for consensus on the rights and duties of African states, thus reflects African vulnerability and fear of intervention. The Organisation of African States, an all-inclusive grouping established in 1963, has attempted to regularise intra-African relations, based on such norms as non-interference in the domestic affairs of others, and the peaceful settlement of disputes.[8] The functioning of these rules depends upon coexistence and compromise, on values of good neighbourliness and mutual forbearance, thus guaranteeing the status quo. Hence only four African states recognised Biafra's right to secede, despite its claim to national self determination, a moral claim viewed as universally valid in the colonial context.[9] So the anti-colonial movements, on becoming successor governments, assert the legitimacy of colonially-drawn boundaries, and accept the Western international law bases of state sovereignty and non-interference.[10] Such a mutually agreed-upon stand-off thereby allows governments to turn their attention, and their minimal resources, to the more urgent threats to their security, that is, internal opposition, and extra-continental penetration and manipulation.[11]

Calls for African unity do reflect the emotional identification which comes from shared colonial experience and racial humiliation. They also reflect awareness that the 'Balkanisation' of Africa, now divided into over 50 countries, invites further external intervention.[12] However, lack of ideological consensus, lack of clearly-demonstrated short-run economic advantages, and the unwillingness of any existing leaders to surrender what power they do have, makes the commitment to unity little more than rhetorical. No leader, except possibly Nkrumah, seriously considered jeopardising his state's sovereign rights in an all-African supra-national government. What African unity does assert, however, is Africa's claim to continental jurisdiction — that Africa has the right to solve its own problems, without external intervention.[13] Thus African unity represents not an attempt to challenge state sovereignty, but to bolster state sovereignty by mutual collaboration to insulate the continent from those external forces which would exploit Africa's vulnerability for their own ends.

Such a defence, through alliances and organisations and the assertion of on-going rights of self-determination, is a desperate attempt to manipulate symbols and so convince others to forgo their comparative power advantage.[14] The moral rights of the poor and downtrodden must be legitimised and recognised for the poor lack the resources to defend themselves against the strong. Such pleadings are unlikely to succeed, both because Africans have no sanctions to enforce their claims, and because Africa is already so deeply enmeshed in the global capitalist system that intervention is everywhere an on-going, structural and total reality. Every 'independent' African state is profoundly shaped by external forces, tightly linked into relations of dependence, and thoroughly penetrated by patterns of unequal economic interchange.[15] The non-autonomous nature of African states results from their role as periphery, integrated into and shaped by wider systems of trade, investment and direction. Thus Zambia, one of the 'richest' and comparatively strongest African states, depends on copper for 96 per cent of its export income, and 64 per cent of its government revenue.[16]

Lacking administrative, technical or financial resources to do more than paper-nationalise the main assets of the country and to demand a slightly larger share for its elite, the government is itself a peripheral mechanism, a transmission belt through which the wider economic and more potent political directives may sometimes flow. To this extent, not only the state's independence but the government itself as little more than a fiction, and the right of national self-determination is removed from the realm of reasonable political possibility. So weak is the government, and so dependent itself on external support and finance, that the cry of non-intervention is either a convenient disguise, or a plea against hostile anti-government intervention, or, at best, the desperate claims made on behalf of an exploited people, in no position to assert their rights or interests against foreign interests.

In the two decades since the first advances of African nationalism, the realities of the wider international system and the distortion of African forms through integration into that system have acted to deny the very rights which African leaders thought they had won. The earlier claims for national self-determination, against alien rule and racial injustice, were gradually replaced by attacks on neo-colonialism.[17] For most African leaders this simply meant that political independence was not enough, and did not, in fact, exist if every important aspect of the economy remained in foreign hands, or was shaped by external forces far more powerful than the new African governments. Africa's right to control its own destiny then became more an issue of economics, no longer couched in Lockean terms of moral rights to individual freedom, or dignity, or humanity, but in terms of material claims, rights to the control of national resources for the national good, and the rights of Africans to a more equal share in the wealth of the world. Development replaced freedom, and the vocabulary and terminology shifted subtly from that drawing on the rhetoric of the former colonial masters, rhetoric in the liberal-democratic tradition, to that loosely selected and adapted from another alien source, Marxism.[18] Exploitation became the greatest evil, although exactly how to define the corresponding right, and how to base and justify it, was less certain. Thus a changed political situation fostered an evolving ideology which incorporated alternative definitions of rights, and different assessments of those against whom these rights were claimed. Morality became a function of ideological purity, and of recognition of the conflicting sectional and class interests of various groups.

Here, the confused nature of contemporary African political claims became evident, for while many African leaders used Marxist terms, they did not accept the logical implications of their rhetoric, nor the assumptions which they appeared to articulate. The most common response was to blame the international capitalist system for Africa's exploitation, but few (except, perhaps, Tanzania)[19] seriously tried to insulate themselves from this system. More often, they attempted to improve their position, within the rules of the system's game, seeking an economic development based on diversity of exports and import substitution which might make the state, or at least its elite, marginally more wealthy. At the same time, African Socialism was redefined, moving from its earlier version — asserting the value of African traditional communalism as an indigenous and valid form of political and economic organisation — to a policy of selective nationalisation and elaborate state planning through parastatal and government bodies (usually staffed and directed by expatriates, often the former owners or administrators, now richly compensated and bearing management contracts).[20]

Franz Fanon predicted, at the beginning of African independence, that African rights and freedoms would not be guaranteed by formal political statehood. He foresaw the subversion of African rights through the nature of African leadership, the succession governments — the intermediary elite.[21] This elite was racially representative of its people, perhaps, but was the creation of the colonial system — of its values, its education system, and its allocation of administrative and other occupational roles. The elite was not only created by the alien 'other', but remained dependent upon it for its continued existence. Lacking its own independent power base, as well as its own, or national, values or goals, it did not act to transform the polity or economy, but acted as the agent for outsiders, who continued to monopolise effective power and decision-making. Such a group might resent its inferior status, or wish for a larger share in the national wealth, but it lacked the popular base, the authentic nature, the national or ideological integrity, to pursue claims on behalf of indigenous interests and so challenge the deeprooted colonial structures. Thus independence localised the political system — and, less so, the economic management — but it did not alter either the domestic power realities or the imperial connection.

'The problem of the nature of the state created after "independence" is perhaps the secret of the failure of African independence.'[22] Nowhere in the first round of African independence did governments oversee a structural revolution of the sort necessary to create national forms able to establish and defend national independence, or even define its objectives in terms that represented a substantial break with the colonial past and neo-colonial present. Growing awareness of this fact has coincided with and reinforced another, the radicalisation of some segments of the liberation movements in Southern Africa, and the shift of claims from majority rule to liberation, from political independence to social revolution.

The liberation movements began, as did most African nationalist movements, as mass parties committed to non-violent protest and constitutional demands for political rights. In the early sixties, Southern African parties found the road to peaceful change closed, their leadership decimated, their followers harassed, their demands denied all political or moral legitimacy. They became, by default, parties of revolution. They claimed the right to rebel, labelled their own violence 'defensive' and justified because they were given no choice but surrender or revolt.[23] So they became clandestine, seeking the external support, internal strategies and ideological justification for armed struggle. Some movements, especially the MPLA in Angola, Frelimo in Mozambique, and ZANU in Zimbabwe, developed an elaborate definition of African realities which was far more radical than any represented by independent African governments. The role of ideology was stressed, not only as an essential component in raising peoples' consciousness, as part of the mass mobilisation necessary for successful guerrilla warfare, but also to guard the movements against the pitfalls of moderate African politics — to clarify priorities and to identify the enemy more rigorously.[24]

Not all liberation movements have a commitment to thoroughgoing social revolution. The ambiguities of their origins are aggravated by continuing ideological, as well as political and personal, divisions.[25] However, the issues are no longer framed in terms of black and white, but also, and except in South Africa itself, mainly, as a conflict between competing African views of the good future society, and differing definitions of social, as well as racial, justice.

The radicalisation of some segments of African politics led to the cry for liberation, for the total destruction of the structures of dependence and exploitation, which have proved so strong. But liberation still appears remote. When Frelimo's leader Samora Machel became President of Mozambique, he said: 'the State is always an organized form through which a class takes power in order to fulfil its interests'. He went on: 'We are aware that the apparatus we are now inheriting is, in its nature, composition and methods, a profoundly retrograde and reactionary structure which has to be completely revolutionized in order to put it at the service of the masses'.[26] The process of radicalisation has led, then, to the articulation of new moral claims, and the identification of far more thoroughgoing obstacles to these claims than Africa's early independence leaders ever suspected. But still the priorities stemming from this alternative view of Africa's lack of freedom must be reconciled, in government, with Africa's lack of power and dependent status. Thus Frelimo, while at war, cried: 'Smash Caborra Basa', and condemned any connection at all with South Africa. After independence the Frelimo government allows Portugal to manage Caborra Basa, and pays for the hydroelectric scheme by selling electricity to South Africa, and announces that it will still send workers to South Africa. Such phased disengagement sounds little different from statements by the Zambian government in earlier independence. Even the more morally rigorous and radical leaders, then, have been forced to compromise in the face of the objective realities of African weakness and dependence. Yet the rhetoric, the perception of the issues at stake, has changed.

The key issue is: who rules? and for whom? For whom are rights claimed, and against whom? The history of African independence, thus far, is dominated by claims advanced by Westernised, city-based leaders who claimed representativeness on the basis of shared race and their shared exclusion from full humanity and responsibility. With few or marginal exceptions, they then exploited their formal political rule for their own, or their sectional group's profit or security. Power did not pass to the people, but to selected elites. The question in the mid-seventies is whether decolonisation in central-southern Africa will merely repeat this process.

In September 1976 Rhodesia's Ian Smith capitulated, and accepted the principle of majority rule and the right of Africans to at least a share in political power.[27] Here again, the non-authentic nature of African politics emerges. The negotiations toward majority rule in Zimbabwe have depended from the outset on external intervention. The relative strength or role of any particular African leader lies, not on his following within the country, so much as in the support and recognition he receives from outside. South Africa's Prime Minister Vorster and American Secretary of State Kissinger brought Smith to the conference table, but the five front-line Presidents (of Zambia, Tanzania, Botswana, Angola and Mozambique) dictated terms to the Zimbabwe nationalists. The crucial significance of sponsors, and of host countries' facilities, offered to or withheld from national liberation movements or leaders, have constantly distorted internal power relations and decisions. Such manipulations from outside make nonsense of the claim of national self-determination, in the name of which much of the intervention is made.

The explicit attempt, by South Africa and the Western Powers, to foreshorten the armed struggle, to halt the process of radicalisation within the liberation movements, and to install a moderate black government in Zimbabwe,[28] brings us back to the crux of the problem: 'What is basically at issue is not the *whether* or *when* of majority rule, but *what kind* of independent state is to emerge. In particular, is there any prospect for a form of national liberation which provides a democratic alternative to the neo-colonial state?'[29] It has yet to be demonstrated that Africa's options include the possibility of the creation of political and economic structures sufficiently autonomous to justify the description 'national independence'.[30]

The problem of competing moral claims in Africa is brought into sharpest relief in South Africa's struggle to assert its right to exist — even, indeed, to hegemony — in Southern Africa. Here, the issue is not colonialism, with its extracontinental dimension, but racism. The dominant white minority is a settler minority, a group which has staked its existence, as well as its claim to exclusive privilege, within the domestic context of an African country. Like other states in Africa, South Africa relies heavily on external finance, arms, assistance and sponsorship. But South Africa is unique in that it is the only state in Africa with real power, with a developed infrastructure, with organisational and comparative military and economic strength. South Africa produces 22 per cent of the entire African Gross Domestic Product, and 40 per cent of its industrial output, as well as possessing its strongest military forces.

The place of South Africa in Africa is one of the crucial issues facing the continent.[31] The question would remain, although in changed form, even if the white government fell. However, the likelihood of internal revolution is extremely remote,[32] and the chances of external intervention in support of revolution are likewise minimal. The South African government was increasingly isolated in Africa, and the world, after 1960.[33] Then, in the late 1960s, its capacity to survive and the failure of significant intervention against it, led to the new outward-looking foreign policy, seeking dialogue with black African states, and trade and investment through a proposed common market for Southern Africa. Dialogue faltered as the liberation wars of Angola, Mozambique and Zimbabwe accelerated in the early 1970s, and reached crisis point in Angola in 1975. The racial and ideological war, long predicted by Kenneth Kaunda and many others, appeared a belated reality. Angola became 'independent' in the midst of a war whose ramifications included Great Power confrontation on a scale not witnessed in Africa since the Congo.[34] The radical Marxist MPLA was backed by Soviet and Cuban advisers, in opposition to Unita, which had South African

military support, and the FNLA, which was partly financed and armed
by the United States. Henry Kissinger considered Angola the post-
Vietnam testing ground for American will and power, and declared that
'the United States will not accept Soviet intervention in other parts of
the world',[35] especially where it had 'no historical interests' (conveniently overlooking the fact of continued Soviet arms and support to
the MPLA over a period of 15 years, a period during which America
had chosen, first, to support the Portuguese colonial regime which
MPLA had opposed, and then to endorse the anti-Soviet, non-radical,
forces against MPLA).

Angola was indeed a testing-point for South Africa and the West.
Kissinger argued to continue support for the anti-MPLA parties. But the
American Senate, seeing Angola as remote and unimportant to
America's security and national interest, passed an amendment to the
Defence Appropriation Bill in December 1975, and forbade the Ford
administration to grant further aid. South African leaders then faced
the choice to intervene, without massive Western aid, against the forces
of African liberation, or to accept African rule along its borders and
seek a new relationship with independent Africa. They decided that
they could not fight for the West alone,[36] withdrew their military
forces from Angola, pursued partial co-operation with the Mozambique
government, declared themselves in favour of majority rule in Zimbabwe
and of independence in Namibia. Working closely with Zambia's
President Kaunda, Vorster sought to establish a statesman's role,
accommodating even radical governments, and cosmetic changes were
made in apartheid as evidence of South Africa's goodwill and desire for
peaceful change. A number of moderate black leaders responded by
differentiating it from the colonial problem in Zimbabwe and Namibia,
and South Africa was granted status as a fellow African state.[37] Such
recognition is exactly what South Africa currently seeks, reducing the
possibility of hostile intervention against it, depriving its own African
nationalists of nearby bases and support, and securing an external
market that allows it to escape the need to restructure its own domestic economy. The alternative — the stimulation of a local black demand
sufficient to support its expanding industrial output[38] — is politically
inadmissible.

South Africa represents an extreme case of white privilege and white
power, a regularised and tightly structured system of domination.
Domestic African nationalism has reflected the evolution of the movements further north — first claiming rights on the basis of grievance
and deprivation, then asserting claims to self-determination and, after

Sharpeville, claiming the right to rebel.[39] Then began the painful transformation from mass political parties to 'illegal' liberation movements, committed, at least in theory, to armed struggle and social
revolution.

The doctrine of apartheid excludes the possibility of power-sharing
or the granting of formal political rights to the majority of South
Africa's population. In the past, South Africa has justified apartheid
on grounds of white superiority and civilisation, technical competence,
and the concept of guardianship of those racially, or at least culturally,
more backward. This defence was linked with the more general notion
of Western, Christian society, in a battle against Communism and
chaos. South Africa also attempted to insulate itself from outside
pressure or criticism by declaring its racial policies to be matters of
domestic concern, protected by state sovereignty, and the right of the
state against external interference. Lately, however, the position has
changed. The South African government has pursued the logic of
apartheid by deliberately internationalising the issue, and so readjusting
the basis on which apartheid is justified by its proponents.

Apartheid has long been defended in terms of the separate identities
of the peoples involved. Rejecting the pluralist model of different but
basically compatible cultures or interests, or the alternative assimilation-
ist model, South Africa opts for a conflict model, where only strict
separation will both preserve the differences, and ensure that the
different peoples do not destroy each other. These groups of 'peoples'
are defined as separate nations. Thus apartheid's 'basic premise today
is not one of race or colour relations, but one of national relations'.[40]
Black South Africans are denied citizenship or land rights within the
dominant society, but are granted the right of 'national' self-determination and management of their own affairs in their own homelands. The
first homeland to achieve formal independence, the Transkei, did so in
October 1976. What began as a system of internal colonisation, and
became a convenient mechanism of control over a cheap labour pool,
has led to a process of legitimising and institutionalising a lack of black
rights within the Republic, on the grounds that Africans can enjoy these
rights within their own national territories.

These territories are even more fragmented, penetrated, vulnerable
and dependent than are the pseudo-independent states further north.
Many black Africans will continue to live outside them, in white areas.
There may be partial accommodation of any aspiring black elite within
domestic politics which will allow for some movement towards a class
system, but this should coincide on the whole with traditional racial

stratification.[41] Any changes that do occur will be aimed at strengthening white domination, so that the realities of power will change little by granting 'independence' to the homelands, or by granting Africans the right to buy houses in Soweto. However, South Africa points to the homelands as evidence of its contribution to African nationalism, to national self-determination and political independence, and so justifies its domestic and foreign policies in rhetoric not unlike that of the African nationalists of the 1950s and 1960s.

Most African governments, as presently constituted, claim rights against other states in terms of a perception of international relations which is basically statist and conservative, despite the ritualistic rhetoric of liberation against illegitimate, non-African regimes. The vocabulary, the claims themselves, the very choice of the questions asked, are, on the whole, alien. The education system which granted Africa's leaders positions in administration and government was a Western one.[42] The price of success within that system was approximation to the Western ideal, and through the school Africans exchanged the village and the land for the city and the office. The personal rewards have been enormous in terms of wealth, power and status, and the cost has often been cultural alienation, or cultural schizophrenia.

Ali Mazrui suggests that the most profound impact of colonialism is cultural.[43] Dependency lies, not only in political and economic structures, but also in the minds of men. Colonialism represented ideological aggression, for it established a system of domination and subordination in which the subordinate became passive, fundamentally compromised by their own failure to overthrow it. The psychological effects of implicit collaboration in a system which devalued the majority — the arbitrary distinctions and the denials of human equality and full responsibility — cannot be underestimated.[44] It is more than symbolic that Africans have used the language of the oppressor to make their claims against that oppressor, and even, often, to communicate with one another. For the choice has been that of acquiescence in exclusion, or attempting to overcome exclusion by accepting the framework of domination, and seeking access to its rewards through assimilation.

The process of acculturation of Africa's ruling elite, together with the long colonial heritage of dependence, of powerlessness, is little altered by formal political independence. Despite some hostility to Western groupings and values,[45] Africa continues dependent on Western forms, its governments define development as closer approximation to Western designs, and seek acceptance into, or better terms within, the dominant system, rather than the assertion of African rights or roles outside that system.

There is, for example, within the 'Dar' school in Tanzania,[46] and within MPLA and Frelimo, an alternative world-view, asking different questions and making moral claims of a different kind. This view, too, draws on a radical critique which did not originate in Africa, and is based on a reaction to an analysis of the wider international system in which Africa finds itself enmeshed. It is, however, substantially different from the more conventional 'imitate-integrate' response of most of the older-established African governments. For it advances the possibility of an alternative set of relations, of the destruction — or at least reduction — of those bonds of dependence and exploitation which currently paralyse Africa. In economic terms, it seeks a development model on an inward-looking, self-directing and self-generating base; in political terms, it seeks the creation of structures of participation and control which would destroy foreign-sustained intermediary elites.

How authentically African this response is, or whether, given the global power structure, there is any room for Africanicity in any but the most marginal way, is as yet undetermined. But many of those urging a radical alternative look to the achievement of a moral, as well as a functional, autonomy, which would re-establish African initiative, giving Africans the right to create and not simply emulate,[47] to determine their own priorities, and to decide for themselves whether or not the progressive-popular state can preserve indigenous values. Such urgings attempt to give meaning to the claims of national — or racial — self-determination; to demand independence in forms which challenge the on-going system of domination which has kept African states as the weak and manipulated products of forces beyond their shores.

Notes

1. Moral claims are determined by the political interests and ideological perspectives of the claimants, whose moral arguments and principles both reflect their notions of what is justified and good, and also represent an effort to improve their own material, political or psychological position *vis-à-vis* others.

2. A.A. Mazrui, *The Anglo-African Commonwealth* (Pergamon, 1967), p. 81.

3. Ibid., pp. 82-7.

4. See e.g. G. Balandier, *The Sociology of Black Africa* (London, 1970); F. Fanon, *The Wretched of the Earth* (Penguin, 1967), and *Black Skin, White Masks* (Penguin, 1967); A. Memmi, *The Coloniser and the Colonised* (Boston, 1965).

5. W. Zartman, *International Relations in the New Africa* (Prentice Hall, New Jersey, 1966), p. 145; R.O. Matthews, 'Interstate Conflict in Africa: a Review',

International Organization (Spring 1970), p. 360. Shaw points to the growing stratification, the inequality within Africa itself, as middle powers capable of acting as regional centres establish a complex hierarchy in intra-African relations. However, these middle powers remain dependent on external forces and collaborate closely with the great Powers. In global terms, these are weak and ineffective actors. T.M. Shaw, 'Discontinuities and inequalities in African International Politics', *International Journal* (Summer 1975), p. 386.

6. Zartman, *International Relations,* p. 49.

7. 'Arrest the person of the President, and you arrest the state', R. First, *The Barrel of a Gun* (Penguin, 1970), p. 4.

8. See e.g. F.C. Okoye, *International Law and the new African States* (Sweet and Maxwell, London, 1972), pp. 124-73.

9. Tanzania, Zambia, Ivory Coast and Gabon.

10. For a detailed examination of African governments' overall acceptance of international law see Okoye, *International Law,* especially pp. 179-82. Those aspects of international law which African governments have challenged are those most affecting state sovereignty, e.g. a state's rights to control its own natural resources, and questions of foreign investment and 'appropriate' compensation for nationalisation. See also the wider 'Third World' attempts to rework the international economic system, especially in areas of trade and investment. B. Gasovic and J.G. Ruggie, 'On the creation of a new international economic order', *International Organization* (Spring 1976), pp. 309-46.

11. In some circumstances, 'Africanity' becomes a principle overriding state sovereignty -- thus the independent African states refused to recognise the white governments of Angola, Mozambique and Rhodesia, and intervention against these becomes a higher African duty in defence of the rightful claimants, the African people. Some African leaders, e.g. Julius Nyerere of Tanzania, extend this principle to South Africa too, while others, e.g. Kenneth Kaunda of Zambia, have always stressed South Africa's 'different' status, as a legitimate sovereign state. See Julius Nyerere, 'Why We Must Fight in Southern Africa', *Objective: Justice* (United Nations Publication, March 1971); Kenneth Kaunda, *Canberra Times,* 21 September 1976; D.C. Anglin, 'Zambia and Southern African "detente" ', *International Journal* (Summer 1975), pp. 497-8.

12. Kwame Nkrumah, *Africa Must Unite* (Heinemann, London, 1964), p. 172; A.A. Mazrui, *Towards a Pax Africana* (Weidenfeld and Nicolson, London, 1967), pp. 74-96.

13. Nkrumah, *Africa Must Unite,* pp. 109-28; A.A. Mazrui, *Violence and Thought* (Longmans, London, 1969), p. 240.

14. Zartman, *International Relations,* p. 145.

15. Arghiri Emmanuel, *Unequal Exchange: A Study in the Imperialism of World Trade* (Monthly Review Press, New York, 1972); Samir Amin, *Neo Colonialism in West Africa* (Penguin, 1973); W. Rodney, *How Europe Under-developed Africa* (Bogle L'Ouverture, London, 1972); Colin Leys, *Underdevelopment in Kenya: The Political Economy of Neo Colonialism* (Heinemann, London, 1975).

16. J. Pettman, *Zambia, Security and Conflict* (Friedmann, London, 1974).

17. Kwame Nkrumah, *Neocolonialism: the last stage of Imperialism* (London, Nelson, 1965).

18. For analyses of some sources of African rhetoric see A.A. Mazrui, *Anglo-African Commonwealth,* pp. 11-23; Introduction and K. Grundy, 'The Political Theory of Kwame Nkrumah' in W.A.E. Skurnik (ed.), *African Political Thought* (University of Colorado, Denver, 1967), pp. 67-91; and R. Gibson, *African Liberation Movements* (OUP, London, 1972), p. 10.

19. Tanzania -- a partial and contradictory exception. J.S. Saul, 'African

Socialism in One Country', in G. Arrighi and J.S. Saul, *Essays on the Political Economy of Africa* (Monthly Review Press, New York, 1973); J.S. Saul, 'The State in Post-Colonial Societies: Tanzania', *Socialist Register* (London, 1974), pp. 349-73; Tanzanian Studies no. 2, *The Silent Class Struggle* (Tanzanian Publishing House, Dar es Salaam, 1974).

20. Gibson, *African Liberation Movements,* p. 11; Tanzanian Studies no. 1, *Towards Socialist Planning* (Tanzanian Publishing House, 1974).

21. F. Fanon, *The Wretched of the Earth* (MacGibbon and Kee, London, 1965), pp. 305-21; Saul, *Socialist Register* 1974, pp. 349-72; I.G. Shivji, 'The Silent Class Struggle', in Tanzanian Studies no. 2, pp. 1-60.

22. Amilcar Cabral, quoted in *Review of African Political Economy,* 5 (1976), p. 1.

23. Mazrui, *Anglo-African Commonwealth,* p. 21; R. Blackey, 'Theories of Revolution: Fanon and Cabral', *Journal of Modern African Studies,* 12 (1974), p. 205.

24. Ideology 'created the conditions for transforming the armed struggle into a people's war, for going over from a liberation struggle to the higher phase of a people's democratic revolution', Samora Michal, 'The Struggle Continues', *Review of African Political Economy,* 4 (1975), p. 18. See also Kwame Nkrumah, *Handbook of Revolutionary Warfare* (Paraf, London, 1968); Grundy in Skurnik, *African Political Thought,* p. 91; Amilcar Cabral, *Revolution in Guinea* (Stage I, London, 1973), pp. 73-90; Henri Oren, 'The Ideological Work of African Liberation Movements', *African Communist,* no. 56 (1974), pp. 82-90.

25. Competing ideological, ethnic and regional groupings aggravate personality differences, and all are compounded by the 'frustrations of exile'. Propaganda activities and lobbying for outside support and finance become crucial in a situation where there is no means of mobilising or assessing popular support or political effectiveness.

26. Machel, 'Struggle Continues', p. 19. See also J. Saul, 'Free Mozambique', *Monthly Review* (1975), p. 13.

27. Nathan Shamuyarira, *Crisis in Rhodesia* (Transatlantic Arts, New York, 1966); Ben Mtshali, *Rhodesia: Background to Conflict* (Hawthorn, New York, 1967); J. Nkomo and J. Nyere, *Rhodesia: the case for majority rule.*

28. For issues of intervention and Zimbabwe see *Review of African Political Economy,* 5 (1976), Editorial and Briefings. Henry Kissinger told a press conference on his return from central and southern Africa on 13 May 1976, 'The radical elements were gaining the upper hand. The Soviet Union was appearing from the outside as a champion. The moderate regions were coming under increasing pressure, and therefore all the moderate Governments in Africa were in danger and all the Western interests in jeopardy. I think with this trip the [American] Administration started a process which can lead to negotiation of the so-called arms struggle in Southern Africa and permit Black and White populations there to work out a way to live together . . . I think it protected the Western interests in a moderate, constructive evolution of African Affairs.'

29. Editorial, *Review of African Political Economy,* 5 (1976), p. 4. See also J.S. Saul's question 'smash the post colonial state, or use it?' *Socialist Register,* 1974.

30. Some African states have achieved a measure of 'autonomy' or at least a lack of efficient external direction, by virtue of their very weakness. Thus Saul describes Amin's Uganda as 'unhinged', an unsteady state which is 'too weak and too internally compromised to stabilise society and economy and thereby effectively guarantee the on-going generation of surplus and accumulation of capital'. 'The Unsteady State', *Review of African Political Economy,* 5 (1976), p. 12.

31. Mazrui, in F.S. Arkhurst (ed.) *Africa in the Seventies and Eighties* (Praeger, New York, 1970), pp. 60-61.

32. Armed struggle in South Africa 'falls little short of suicide', H. Adam, 'Conquest and Conflict in Southern Africa', *Journal of Modern African Studies,* 13 (1975), pp. 627-8. See also Sheridan Johns, 'Obstacles to Guerrilla Warfare – a South African Case Study', *Journal of Modern African Studies*, 11 (1973), pp. 267-304. The consequences of the Soweto riots, leaving 176 Africans dead in June 1976, have yet to be assessed.

33. J.E. Spence, 'South Africa's "new look" Foreign Policy', *World Today,* (April 1968), pp. 137-45; Sam Nolutshungu, *South Africa in Africa: a study in ideology and foreign policy* (Manchester University Press, 1975); Anglin, 'Zambia . . .', pp. 471-503. ·

34. John Marcum, 'Lessons of Angola', *Foreign Affairs,* vol. 54, 1976, pp. 407-22; A. Gupta, 'Collapse of the Portuguese Empire and the Dialectics of Liberation in Southern Africa', *International Studies,* 14 (1975), pp. 1-20; Azinna Nwafor, 'The Liberation of Angola', *Monthly Review,* 27, 9 (1976), pp. 1-12.

35. *New York Times,* 24 December 1975.

36. *The Star* (Johannesburg), 21, 23 December 1975.

37. At the Ninth Extraordinary Meeting of the OAU Council of Ministers in April 1976, Tanzania, Zambia and Mozambique urged separation of the colonial problems of Zimbabwe and Namibia from South Africa's situation, and defended dialogue with South Africa. Opposition to this distinction, and a demand that all African governments shun South Africa's diplomatic 'offensive', was led by Kenya and Nigeria, two 'middle powers' who see their influence threatened by South Africa's increasing role in black Africa.

38. Saul, *Socialist Register,* p. 147.

39. N. Mandela, *No Easy Walk to Freedom* (Heinemann, London, 1965); A. Luthuli, *Let My People Go* (Collins, London, 1966); T. Karis and G. Carter, *From Protest to Challenge: a documentary history of African politics in South Africa 1882-1964* (Hoover, Stanford, 1972); *Sechaba* (African National Congress Newspaper, London).

40. D.P. de Villiers, *The Case for South Africa* (Stacey, London, 1970) p. 45 see also Eric H. Louw, *The Case for South Africa,* ed. by H.H.H. Biermans (MacFadden, New York, 1963).

41. Adam, 'Conquest and Conflict', p. 639.

42. For an analysis of the functions of Western education as role-allocator and social mobility agent, see e.g. P. Foster, *Education and Social Change in Ghana* (London, 1969). But see Mazrui's assessment of Uganda's President Amin, and other East African military men, whose parochial, rural background and minimal acculturation sets them apart from civilian politicians and from West Africa's military elite, and may signal a 'selective retraditionalization' in certain African states. 'Soldiers as Traditionalizers', *World Politics* XXVIII (1976), p. 269.

43. Ibid., p. 267; G. Groks, 'Difficulties of Cultural Emancipation in Africa', *Journal of Modern African Studies* 14 (1976), p. 66.

44. A. Moumouni, *Education in Africa* (Deutsch, London, 1968); A. Memmi, *The Coloniser and the Colonised;* G. Balandier, *The Sociology of Black Africa;* F. Fanon, *The Wretched of the Earth.*

45. Mazrui, 'Racial Self-Reliance and Cultural Dependency: Nyerere and Nkomo', *Journal of International Affairs,* 27 (1973), pp. 105-7.

46. D. Deroon and A. Kuper, 'The "New Historiography" in Dar es Salaam', *African Affairs,* 69 (1970), pp. 329-49; *Tanzanian Studies* papers (Tanzanian Publishing House, Dar es Salaam).

47. Mazrui, 'From Social Darwinism to Current Theories of Modernization', *World Politics* XXI (1968), p. 76.

8 MORAL PRECEPTS IN CHINESE FOREIGN POLICY: THE CONCEPT OF INDEPENDENCE

Michael B. Yahuda

Most students of Chinese affairs who admire and appreciate China's achievements in socialist construction are conscious of the moral qualities of the ideological and indeed practical frameworks which guide decision-making at all levels in Chinese society. All students of contemporary China are highly conscious of the collectivist ideals and the collective morality which pervade Chinese society. Few can be unaware of the moral dimensions of the debates as to how best to narrow urban and rural differences and as to how to reduce the gaps between the elites and the masses, mental and manual labour, etc.

There are very few, however, who are prepared to discern such moral concerns in the conduct of China's foreign policy. Indeed, many of those who most admire China's domestic achievements deliberately eschew careful analysis of Chinese conduct of foreign affairs. Foreign affairs, after all, in China as elsewhere, belongs to the domain of elite politicians. Moreover, it is the arena of contingency accommodations where, to quote Chou En-lai:

> The necessary compromises between revolutionary countries and imperialism must be distinguished from collusion and compromise between Soviet divisionism and US imperialism. Lenin put it well: 'there are compromises and compromises. One must be able to analyse the situation and the concrete conditions of each compromise, or of each variety of compromise. One must learn to distinguish between the man who gave the bandits money and firearms in order to lessen the damage they can do and facilitate their capture and execution, and a man who gives bandits money and firearms in order to share in the loot'.[1]

It is not the intention here to seek to examine such compromises, nor is it the intention to examine the general principles underlying China's foreign policy. Here one should note that the Chinese argue that their principles are constant, but it is their tactics that are flexible and that if there are changes in their foreign policy this has to do with changes in the external environment.

Nevertheless even within the framework of Chinese terms of reference it can be questioned as to whether all their declared principles are
wholly compatible with each other. For example, there is the problem
of promoting revolution abroad while simultaneously defending China
as a socialist country. Put in another way, it is a problem of co-ordina-
ting Party to Party relations, involving revolutionary minded Marxist-
Leninist organisations committed to armed struggle, with state to state
relations with the country in which these operate. Already a public
incident has occurred over Peking's moral support for the Communist
Party of Malaya which was regarded officially by the Malaysian Government as interference in Malaysia's internal affairs.[2] Non-interference in
the affairs of another country is one of the cardinal constituents of the
Five Principles of Peaceful Coexistence — regarded by the Chinese as
the best framework for the conduct of international relations and as
such it features in the Joint Communiqué establishing diplomatic relations between China and Malaysia in 1974. The Chinese explained that
Party to Party relations were conducted on totally different levels from
those of the state to state variety so that the Malaysian protests were
misplaced. Intellectually and organisationally the Chinese may distinguish between the practice of revolution and the diplomacy of inter-
state relations, but the relevant state which is receiving both dimensions of these policies does not. Moreover, there are grounds for
believing that the dimension of China's state interests and orientations
decisively affects the extent of support given to revolutions in other
countries.[3]

Another kind of conflict can be seen in the contrast between the
pursuit of revolution at home and the conduct of foreign policy on the
basis of compromise and contingency accommodation abroad. For
example, this has been graphically illustrated by the pictures showing
Chairman Mao happily receiving President Nixon in early 1972 and
then the former President four years later in 1976. Although the
receptions for Nixon can be defended on the grounds of Maoist
principles by reference to the exploitation of contradictions indicated
in the earlier quotation from Chou En-lai, these receptions nevertheless
contrast sharply with the fierce struggles on revolutionary purity
carried on at home.

In this essay, however, we are mainly concerned with general questions of morality, or what have been called in this volume 'moral
claims'. Clearly this is not just a question of consistency. It is rather a
question of asking whether or not foreign policy statements and actions
are based on something larger than the instrumental concerns of

security and utilitarian self interests. For example, are they based more on general principles deducible or defendable in Marxist-Leninist terms? We must examine the question as to whether or not there are certain kinds of moral values genuinely preferred and promoted which underlie much of China's attitude and conduct in world affairs. In classical Western philosophical terms we are concerned here with the question of whether foreign policy in China is dominated in the final analysis by a view of the good life in societal terms, and as to how this good life may be achieved.

One of the most dominating moral concepts in China's foreign policy since 1949 is the concept of independence. As advanced by the Chinese this is a complex concept imbued with considerable moral force and passion. The concept may be said to have dominated Chinese thinking about foreign affairs both in terms of the role of the Chinese state in the world arena and in terms of the basis on which a new and more moral world order can be built. The concept, which in Chinese usage also means self-renewal based on genuine popular support, is one which arises deep from within China's historical experience over the last 150 years. The careful development and application of the concept of independence may be seen as one of the main reasons for the success of the Chinese Revolution under the leadership of the Communist Party headed by Chairman Mao. It is this concept, too, which sharply demarcates the different approaches of the Soviet Union and the People's Republic of China to questions of imperialism, proletarian internationalism, national liberation, and so on, as well as their different approaches to Third World issues and their attempts to establish a new world economic order.

The Maoist concept of independence is one which goes well beyond legalistic notions of the trappings of statehood with its formal freedom from overt external subordination. For Mao in particular, but also for the Communist Party of China as a whole, the creation of a new China was always more dependent upon the mobilisation, regeneration and indeed revolutionisation of the Chinese people themselves than upon the simple exclusion of imperialist influences from China. Indeed a comparison between Mao Tse-tung's main writings in the 1930s and 1940s and those of Chiang Kai-shek, as expressed for instance in his book *China's Destiny*, shows that the latter put far greater emphasis on the imperialism factor as the primary source of China's ills than did Mao. In Mao's slogan of the time imperialism was but one of 'the three mountains' that was addressing the Chinese people. (The other two were feudalism and bureaucrat-capitalism.)

It is not the intention here to review Mao's strategy in the Chinese revolution. Nevertheless a few points are worth mentioning from our perspective so as to underscore the main aspects of the Maoist and (as they have now become) the Chinese concepts of independence. Much of this may be familiar ground, but the concern here is to show that it is a dominant element in Chinese thinking about international affairs and it is necessary to review certain aspects of China's foreign relations.

Clearly for Mao, the socialist period of the present was one dominated by struggle -- one might almost say dominated by a passionate, moral drama between the two roads of socialism on the one side and the bourgeois road on the other, or public versus self.[4] For his socialism was not, and the move towards communism was not, just a question of abundance. His criticisms of Khrushchev's 'goulash communism' are particularly pertinent here.[5]

Having identified the meaning of communism, the Chinese found Khrushchev's approach wanting in all respects. The comment on raising public consciousness is especially relevant:

> Going forward to communism means moving towards enhancing the communist consciousness of the masses. A communist society with bourgeois ideas running rampant is inconceivable. Yet Khrushchev is zealously reviewing bourgeois technology in the Soviet Union and serving as a missionary for the decadent American culture. By propagating material incentive, he is turning all human relations into money relations and encouraging individualism and selfishness. Because of him, manual labour is again considered sordid and love of pleasure at the expense of other people's labour is again considered honourable. Certainly, the social ethics and atmosphere promoted by Khruschev are far removed from communism, as far as can be.[6]

The clearest disdain for Khrushchev's approach is apparent in the following passage:

> Khrushchev's 'communism' is in essence a variant of bourgeois socialism. He does not regard communism as completely abolishing classes and class differences but describes it as 'a bowl accessible to all and brimming with the product of physical and mental labour'. He does not regard the struggle of the working class for communism as a struggle for the thorough emancipation of all mankind as well as itself but describes it as a struggle for a 'good dish of goulash'. There is not an iota of scientific communism in his head but only

the image of a society of bourgeois philistines.[7]

At the same time, there are very practical instrumental aspects to the Chinese criticisms and the advocation of alternatives. Thus later in the same commentary the Chinese spelt out a programmatic view of the future including a commitment to thoroughgoing modernisation. Nevertheless the moral tone of the objections to Soviet practices are evident. There is also a passionate yearning for tapping the creativity and initiative of the Chinese people.

This in some ways goes back to what has sometimes been called the 'Yenan syndrome'. By this is meant the way in which under conditions of scarcity and isolation the Chinese communists were able to create a new revolutionary society. Here one should note the reports of many foreign journalists and indeed the representatives of the American government who visited Yenan at the time and contrasted the whole demeanour of the people there with that of those they found in the Kuomintang areas.[8] One of the major reasons for the Chinese communists' ultimate success can be seen firstly in their ability to translate the demands of the Chinese Nationalist movement for social revolution into practical concerns. This is something in which the Kuomintang failed utterly after 1927, even though land reform measures were passed by legislatures in Nanking. Because the Kuomintang's power was based ultimately upon landlords, these excellent programmes on paper were not in fact carried out and practised. Chinese communists by contrast were able to create even in their revolutionary bases tremendous social changes along these lines. A second aspect linked to this has been the way in which the Chinese communists, particularly under Mao, were able to provide a new moral framework within which the Chinese people were able to link their own local needs and aspirations to larger universal principles. Fundamental was the complete independence within which the Chinese communists operated.

The nationalist strain had always been a deep one in Mao's thinking. It antedates his embrace of Marxism-Leninism and it stayed with him throughout his life. Indeed the most complete text available of an extensive essay by Mao written in the period between 1917-23 (that is *The Great Union of the Popular Masses* written in 1919), carries the following vivid passage:

Our Chinese people possess great inherent capacities! The more profound the oppression, the greater its resistance: that which has accumulated for a long time will surely burst forth quickly. I venture to make a singular assertion. One day, the reform of the Chinese people will be more profound than that of any other people, the society of the Chinese people will be more radiant than that of any other people. A Great Union of the Chinese people will be achieved earlier than that of any other place or people. Gentlemen! Gentlemen! Our golden age, our age of glory and splendour, lies before us![9]

Against the objection that this was written nearly 60 years ago and that it belongs to a phase of Mao's life long since past, consider this quotation from a piece published at the beginning of the Great Leap Forward in 1958:

Apart from their other characteristics, China's 600 million people have two remarkable peculiarities; they are first of all poor, and secondly, blank. That may seem like a bad thing, but it is really a good thing. Poor people want change, want to do things, want revolution. A clear sheet of paper has no blotches, and so the newest and most beautiful words can be written on it, the newest and most beautiful pictures can be painted on it.[10]

Four months before this was published Mao was telling the other Chinese leaders in confidence:

Whenever we talk about it we say that our country has such an enormous population, it is such a vast territory, abundant resources, so many people, 4,000 years of history and culture . . . we have bragged so much about this, yet we cannot compare with a country like Belgium . . . now our enthusiasm has been aroused. Ours is an ardent nation, now swept by a burning tide. There is a good metaphor for this: our nation is like an atom . . . when this atom's nucleus is smashed the thermal energy released will have tremendous power. We shall be able to do things which we could not do before.[11]

These kinds of considerations are predicated on the fact that such a movement must be independent. Without that there is little that can be achieved. In this sense Mao always linked the necessity of independence with the successful conduct of revolution. In 1936 he told Edgar Snow that the Chinese revolutionaries were not fighting for the emancipation of China in order to turn the country over to Moscow. More than 20 years later Mao recalled Stalin's opposition to the Communists' armed struggle with the Kuomintang after World War II:

The Chinese Revolution won victory by acting contrary to Stalin's will. The fake foreigner (in Lu Hsun's *True Story of Ah Q*) did not allow people to make revolution. But our Seventh Congress advocated going all out to mobilize the masses and to build up all available revolutionary forces in order to establish a new China.[12]

Internationally the Chinese experience has been very different from that of the Soviet Union. Whereas the early Bolshevik leaders began their revolution on the assumption that it could only survive if it sparked off revolutions in the more advanced industrialised countries, a moving away later from the notion of internationalism towards the concept of socialism in one country was in a sense a fall from grace. One only has to note the big debates that preceded the Brest-Litovsk agreement to see how deep this went. The majority of the Bolsheviks at the time argued that as internationalists it was their duty not to sue for peace with the advancing German armies. Rather they should allow the German armies to continue their penetration in the conviction that this would enable the Bolsheviks to instigate a class conflict between the German officers and men which would lead to revolution in Germany. Starting in a minority position, Lenin maintained that the actual hard war revolutionary achievements in Russia should not be lightly given up for the unrealistic hopes of subverting the German armies. Lenin's arguments finally won the day.[13] But it can be argued that it was a costly victory. The passionate internationalism of the Bolsheviks was seen to be at loggerheads with the needs of socialism in Russia and, what is more, it was the interests of the latter which assumed priority. Yet the Bolsheviks had begun their revolution on the basis that if it were to be contained within an isolated backward Russia socialism would hardly survive, let alone develop and prosper.

For China, on the other hand, there has never been any question but that the Chinese people will be able to pursue socialism within the boundaries of the Chinese state. It is well known that their embrace of Marxism-Leninism was in many respect a product of radical nationalist considerations rather than some kind of internationalism. The Chinese insistence that revolution cannot be exported is something that arises fully out of their own experiences. There is no Chinese equivalent to Lenin's march on Poland. Indeed, one may go further and argue that the Chinese concept of proletarian internationalism has always been in many fundamental respects different from that of the Soviet Union. China has had no experience of running the Comintern. On the contrary, the Chinese experience of the Comintern is one in which the Comintern meddled in Chinese affairs. Indeed in 1948 one Chinese leader, in a famous piece, argued that in order to be an internationalist one has to be a nationalist first, and that there was a direct correlation between the two. China's message to other revolutionaries and to other countries has always been that it is the internal factors which are primary and the external ones which are secondary. It is not too farfetched to state that this has dominated China's approach to foreign relations in so far as the revolutionary factor is concerned. There is no example of a revolution in another country to which one can point as having been promoted and conducted by the Chinese. Since 1949 they have always seen it as their internationalist duty to help what they regard as genuine movements of national liberation and genuine Marxist-Leninist organisations. But never to the point whereby the Chinese, as it were, take over the conduct of such movements; never to the point at which the Chinese dictate to the movement concerned what it should do and what it should not do at any key point in time. To be sure, the Chinese have tended at various times to argue that there are general principles which others should follow, but here the Chinese approach seems to be much more that of a didactic teacher than that of an actual behind-the-stage general conducting a vast array of forces.

Interestingly, the one area in foreign relations where Mao is known to have acknowledged a serious error on his part concerns the question of judging in the late 1940s and early 1950s the quality of the independence which several Third World countries had gained from their colonial masters:

> In the initial period after the founding of our state, some people, including myself as well as Comrade XX, took the view that the parties and trade unions of Asia and the parties of Africa might suffer serious damage. It was later proved that this point of view was incorrect: it did not turn out as we expected. Since the Second World War, thriving national liberation struggles have developed in Asia, Africa and Latin America year by year.[14]

This error arose at the time from the conviction that not having arisen out of the revolutionary armed struggles for genuine independence like that of China the independence of a country like India could only be a sham. The Indian government could not but be a puppet of imperialism. Thus on 19 November 1949 Mao wrote to the Secretary General of the Indian Communist Party:

I firmly believe that India, relying on the brave Communist Party of India and the unity and struggle of all Indian patriots, will certainly not remain long under the yoke of imperialism and its collaborators. Like free China, a free India will one day emerge in the socialist and peoples' democratic family . . .[15]

By 1953-4 the mood had changed to the extent that Chou En-lai emphasised the commonalty between China and the newly independent countries of Asia and Africa in his Bandung diplomacy of 1955.[16] As John Gittings has pointed out, Mao began to differentiate between national independence and national liberation. The former could be won from a colonial power whether the movement had been led by the proletariat or the national bourgeoisie. Whereas the latter suggested a more thoroughgoing revolutionary process. Thus while India had gained its independence China had undergone a process of liberation.[17]

In fact the Chinese continued to have doubts about the fundamental readiness of national bourgeois governments to stand up to imperialist pressures in the interests of independence. It was not until 1968 and the fundamental realignment of world politics as seen by the Chinese leaders that they began to feel confident that the general trends of world affairs meant that Third World countries would have to stress the policies of independence in preference to dependency relationships with centres of imperialism or neo-colonialism. Thus in October 1959 *Red Flag,* the Chinese theoretical journal of the Party's Central Committee, carried an article by a Deputy Foreign Minister which argued that because of the basic bourgeois character of the national bourgeoisie 'even the national independence they have won is by no means secure'. By pursuing a capitalist road 'in the final analysis, they can never escape from the control and bondage of imperialism'.

In the early 1960s, following the break with the Soviet Union, the Chinese found a further reason to distinguish between the independent Afro-Asian states. This centred on the issue of genuine opposition to the United States. Those who were genuinely opposed to US imperialism, in the Chinese view, necessarily had to exclude the Soviet Union too from any putative international united front. It was not until the 1970s that China's confidence in the genuineness of the independence of the Third World countries has been continually affirmed without question. Nevertheless some issues concerning the point still remain unsettled and we shall return to them at a later stage.

Regarding the question of imperialism, the Chinese, or rather Mao, had developed an approach which from the beginning was different

from that of the Soviets.[18] It was in 1946 that Mao painted a scenario
in which he argued that the danger from the United States arose less
from its preparedness to strike out at the Soviet Union than from its
desire to gain control in the first instance of the vast zone between the
Soviet Union and the United States. Only when such areas had come
under US control would the Soviet Union come under direct military
threat. This contrasted very sharply with the view of the struggle
between the two camps as outlined for example by Zhdanov in 1947.
In the Soviet view at that time the main danger was that the United
States might seek to attack the Soviet Union itself. Therefore revolutionaries throughout the world had, in the Soviet view, to avoid
taking unnecessary risks which would provoke the United States into
making such an attack. It was primarily because of considerations such
as these that Stalin, for example, advised the Chinese communists
during their civil war not to engage in armed struggle, but to bury their
weapons and seek to reach an accommodation with Chiang Kai-shek.
Mao. by contrast, argued that since the Americans were in the first
instance trying to build up their strength and gain control of the vast
zone between Russia and the United States, it was resistance in those
countries which could best stop the United States. It was most important that the Chinese revolutionaries carry on the civil war because in
that way they would deny China to the United States and in that sense
they would help to postpone a new world war for a long time. Indeed,
the logic of the position was that by building bases in many foreign
countries the United States, in the Chinese view, was attacking in the
first instance the people of those countries. Therefore if the peoples of
those countries rose in armed resistance against the United States, this
would help the Soviet Union and China and that would also help the
development of revolutionary forces throughout the world. During
the period of the Sino-Soviet alliance this view of the world and the
nature of imperialism was rather superseded by Soviet concepts. In
1958, however, the concept of the intermediate zones lying between
the two camps surfaced once again in Chinese thinking, and it came even
more to the fore once the break with the Soviet Union had become
complete. This is indeed the view that the Chinese advance today in a
more sophisticated form on the basis of the division of the world into
three parts or Three Worlds: The First World consists of the two superpowers; the Third World is made up of those countries with an historical
experience of imperialist exploitation and a current situation of being
less developed economically; and the Second World consists of the
small and medium capitalist countries lying in between these two. In

the Chinese view there is a danger of a new world war arising out of the struggle between the two superpowers, but one of the most effective ways of preventing this is for the countries of the Third World in particular, but those of the Second World too, to resist being dominated economically and otherwise by the two superpowers. Regarding Third World countries the Chinese have gone further. They have identified them as the revolutionary motive force in world history at the present stage.

Since 1968 the Chinese have held that the Soviet Union has become a 'socialist imperialist' country. That is a country which flaunts the banner of socialism while in reality behaving as an imperialist power. Because of this development the Chinese claimed that the socialist camp had ceased to exist.[19] The Chinese nevertheless believe that the general global trends are positive but highly complex. Since the Chinese argue that the principal contradiction in the world today is between imperialism and social-imperialism on the one side and the people of the world on the other, it follows that the main focal point of resistance to the spread of superpower influence and dominance should be regarded as a revolutionary motive force for change. This is reinforced by the fact that many of the governments in the Third World not only resist superpower claims, but they also advance alternative visions of world order and offer practical proposals for changing the present distribution of power and wealth in international society.

The Chinese message to the Third World is quite simply to stress the importance of independence. In the Chinese view if Third World countries struggle for this they will become less and less dependent on exploitative economic relationships and economic dependencies, particularly with the superpowers, and secondly they will begin to become much more self-reliant. In the Chinese view there seems to be a link between pursuing independence of this kind and the growth of more revolutionary developments in the long run. This is expressed in their slogan 'Countries want independence, nations want liberation, and people want revolution'. In fact Chinese commentaries regard this as an objective analysis of the main trend in world affairs.

The Chinese, having identified their country as a socialist member of the Third World, have assumed a rather didactic role with regard to other Third World countries. They do not seek to lead the Third World as a bloc among blocs in world affairs; rather they seek to offer example and instruction. The message is very simply to maintain independence, aim for self reliance and support each other. Consider, for example, the following extract from the speech by the Chinese Minister of Foreign

Trade to the UN General Assembly special session to discuss reform of
the international economic system:

> To be independent and self-reliant, the developing countries must
> first of all smash the heavy fetters imposed on them and free
> themselves from imperialist and particularly superpower exploita-
> tion and control while at the same time eliminating the imperialist,
> colonialist and neo-colonialist forces at home so as to create the
> necessary conditions for the development of national economy.
>
> By self-reliance, we mean that a country should mainly rely on the
> strength and wisdom of its own people, control its economic life-
> lines, make full use of its own resources, work hard, increase produc-
> tion, practise economy and develop its national economy step by step
> and in a planned way. Each country should make a distinction be-
> tween different circumstances and determine its own way of practi-
> sing self-reliance in the light of its specific conditions. Many deve-
> loping countries have followed the road of self-reliance in con-
> formity with their own characteristics and conditions and, after
> making sustained efforts and overcoming all sorts of difficulties, they
> have achieved gratifying successes in developing their national industry
> and agriculture, striving for self-sufficiency in foodgrain, developing
> communications and transport and training their own scientific, tech-
> nical and managerial personnel. Facts show that it is entirely feasible
> for the developing countries to develop their national economy inde-
> pendently and self-reliantly.
>
> We have learnt from our own experience that in the course of
> developing the national economy independently and self-reliantly
> it is essential to correctly handle the relationship between agricul-
> ture, light industry and heavy industry. In the light of her own
> conditions, China has formulated a general policy of taking agri-
> culture as the foundation and industry as the leading factor in deve-
> loping the national economy and made her national economic plans
> according to this order of priorities: agriculture, light industry and
> heavy industry. Priority is given to the development of agriculture
> to solve the people's food problem, supply industry with raw
> materials and a market and accumulate funds for it. *It must be
> stressed that if a country is not basically sufficient in foodgrain but
> has to rely on imports, it may be taken by the neck at any time
> and find itself in a very passive and dangerous position.* In developing
> industry, we have adopted the policy of putting emphasis on small
> enterprises while combining small, medium and big enterprises, and

based ourselves on domestic needs and capabilities, relied on our own resources, built up our industries from scratch and expanded them step by step.

Self-reliance in no way implies 'self-seclusion' or rejection of external assistance, but means relying mainly on our own efforts while making external assistance subsidiary. Experience has shown that in the development of the national economy it is both beneficial and necessary for countries to carry on economic and technical exchanges on the principles of mutual respect for state sovereignty, equality and mutual benefit and the exchange of needed goods, thus making up for each other's deficiencies and learning from each other.

Mutual assistance and economic co-operation among developing countries are especially important. We are all developing countries, and we understand best each other's difficulties and needs, so we should support and help each other. Such co-operation is based on genuine equality and has broad prospects. (Emphasis added)[20]

The dominant theme is one of independence. A country which is not independent in its economic affairs cannot expect to be so in political terms either. A country which depends on imported foodgrains, as the underlined passage puts it very graphically, 'may be taken by the neck at any time'. The message which the Chinese continually hammer home is that sovereignty and independence extends beyond the trappings of international law. For these to have meaning and substance the people of a country through their leaders must be able to determine their own objectives free of external dependencies. Ultimately this means, to quote Li again, that 'a country should mainly rely on the strength and wisdom of its own people'. It is therefore a moral message and not an instrumental one that the Chinese are passing on. Li is at pains to point out in the extract quoted above that he is not calling for self-sufficiency or autarkic self-seclusion, but rather he is asking fellow Third World countries to rely 'mainly on our own efforts while making external assistance subsidiary'. He then went on to outline how foreign trade and aid could be carried out in such a way as to support and enhance independence. Indeed in a latter part of his speech, Li Chiang went on to assert that the developed countries had a role to play too: 'The developing countries demand that the developed countries should make and honour explicit commitments in such matters as international trade, finance and currency, shipping, the transfer of technology and aid. These demands are entirely justifiable'.

It may be questioned, however, whether most Third World countries are either willing or able to carry out such a programme. Many of them are led by elites who in Chinese parlance would be called 'comprador bourgeoisie' — i.e. the class in developing countries which acts basically as agents for foreign companies and which actively supports dependency economic relationships. Others are led by a variety of strata and class groupings none of whom would find it in their interests to carry out a Chinese type programme.

A further problem concerns the sheer capacity of most of the Third World countries to follow the Chinese programme even if the will were not lacking. Few countries are as richly endowed with natural resources as China. Still fewer have undergone the enormous revolutionary transformations that have characterised China's modern historical experience. It is this experience which enabled the Chinese people to 'stand up' and move forward. China's socialist programmes of self-reliance may be said to be the product of the energising national self regeneration of the people's revolution. It may be doubted whether a people which has not been energised and mobilised in this way can in fact follow the Chinese way. It is certainly highly questionable whether leaders thrown up by a non-revolutionary process and not committed to revolution (like Chinese leaders) would be prepared to embark on the Chinese road of self-reliance. Really to follow that road would be to make fundamental changes in the fabric of the social and political processes which brought most of these leaders to power.

Even though most Third World countries may not be able to implement the full programme as outlined in Li Chiang's speech, it is nevertheless true that China's general message has been highly influential throughout the Third World. This is partly because of the international impact of China's domestic achievements in pursuit of self-reliance, combining both emphasis on production with continued revolution. But it is also partly because of China's international role as a fellow member of the Third World which points out a genuinely independent path of development. That role is sustained also through extensive aid programmes which have long been regarded as unique and as models to be emulated by others.

Despite being a relatively underdeveloped economy China has spent several thousand million dollars on aid to the Third World since the late 1950s. The bulk of this aid was spent in the 1970s.[21] The figures are all the more remarkable if it is considered that most of China's aid consists of low capital cost projects emphasising intensive labour and intermediate technology. Since 1964 no interest charges have been applied to loans. No dependency relationships are established. At the earliest possible opportunity the projects concerned become entirely self managed and operated locally. Arrangements are made so that even spare parts can be manufactured locally and where possible local materials only are employed. Chinese workers and technicians on aid projects invariably work at the local rates of remuneration.[22] There is no evidence to suggest that the Chinese use their aid to exercise political leverage. To be sure countries which have special links with China, such as Tanzania or Albania, are especially favoured. Likewise countries which embark on policies particularly liked by China, such as Egypt's severing Russian ties, are frequently offered more extensive aid by the Chinese. The aid is linked to China's foreign policy preferences. But there is no evidence that the Chinese have sought to use their aid as a means of pressurising governments to act in ways they would not do otherwise.

There can be no question but that China's whole approach on these issues arises out of the moral perspectives within which her leaders have operated. Just as the Chinese have been anxious to avoid following a foreign trade pattern which leads to dependency relationships on other countries, so China's pattern of aid distribution is designed to encourage economic independence in others. China does not seek to lead a bloc of Third World countries tied to and dependent upon her. On the contrary, the preferred pattern of development in the Third World as seen from Peking is one in which Third World countries progressively assert their economic independence and establish supportive links with each other. Much as the Chinese support regional associates in the Third World they have taken care not to join such associations themselves. Nor have they suggested that such countries either individually or collectively link themselves to China in a bid to establish alternative economic relations to those which they have with capitalist countries.

This contrasts sharply with the approach advanced by Soviet spokesmen. They still view the world in basically bi-polar terms. Despite the emphasis on détente and on the relaxation of international tensions, the Soviet leadership still maintains that there is a capitalist or imperialist camp headed by the United States which is in conflict with the socialist camp headed by the Soviet Union. To be sure the Soviet view of the capitalist world is much more complex than that of Stalin's day and Soviet foreign policy is tactically much more flexible. Nevertheless at the most fundamental level the Soviet view is still a bi-focal one. The two camps still exist and the socialist one headed by the Soviet Union is still seen as representing the forces of the future. It is still seen as the repository of genuine proletarian virtue. In so far as the Soviet leaders detect positive developments in world affairs these are ascribed to the beneficial consequences of the growing influence and might of the socialist camp headed by themselves. It is this allied to the internal problems and contradictions in the capitalist camp which, in the Soviet view, augurs well for continued détente and for eliciting gradual incremental changes in that camp towards a more socialist future. Those who support or are instrumental in helping such a development, by encouraging closer links with the Soviet Union and its institutions, are regarded as more or less progressive, while those who oppose this are condemned as reactionaries.

With regard to the Third World, variants of this approach are followed. Soviet leaders tend to call upon Third World countries to try to link themselves much more with the socialist bloc. Indeed at times they have identified certain kinds of countries in the Third World as being 'socialist-orientated' countries. Soviet spokesmen have pointed to what they call the road of non-capitalist development, by which they mean state-led industrialisation linked with exclusive trade aid relations with socialist bloc countries. The Soviet leaders see no special virtue in independence *per se* unless this involves an anti-Western posture and a leaning to the Soviet side. Indeed they see positive virtues in newly independent countries establishing dependency economic links with socialist bloc countries. Far from conceiving the Third World as a unified whole, Soviet spokesmen tend to divide the countries concerned (or rather their leaders) into those who are more or less progressive and those who are more or less reactionary. Therefore the Soviet Union has far less compunction than China in actively intervening in the domestic politics of other states. At the same time in the Soviet Union there is profound irritation and anger with the Chinese approach. Consider, for example, the following criticism by the theoretical journal of the Central Committee by the Communist Party of the Soviet Union:

The Chinese leaders discredit the idea of a socialist orientation and the non-capitalist road of development for the developing countries. Maoist propaganda hushes up the fact that progressive social changes can be effected only in the countries which have embarked upon non-capitalist development, and this road is not only the sole alternative to neo-colonialist subordination but it also ensures radical social transformation. The evolution of the developing countries towards scientific socialism and towards closer co-operation with the socialist community would have been much faster but for Peking's disorientating activities.

The same piece goes on later to decry the 'imposing of the Maoist schemes of economic development upon the Third World' and the discrediting of the policy of developing heavy industry.[23]

To a certain extent it may be argued that both the Soviet Union and China are seeking to transform the Third World after their own image. The Soviets stress heavy industry, the Chinese agriculture. The Soviets emphasise the importance of the industrialised European socialist bloc headed by themselves as the central gravitational point for the future progressive development of the Third World. The Chinese, however, stress the importance of the Third World of which they are a key member, as the current revolutionary motive force propelling world history forward. From a Soviet perspective there are indeed moral claims to their position, yet they clearly run counter to those of the Chinese.

The Chinese passion for independence, as we have seen, arises deep from within their historical experience in general and the revolutionary experience in particular. It was one of the main causes of the Sino-Soviet split and it has dominated China's international outlook since. Firstly, there was the emphasis in 1963-4 and 1965 on the revised concept of the intermediate zones and on the revolutionary content in them. In this phase the Chinese looked for signs of independence and genuine resistance to imperialism amongst Third World countries and also in countries such as France.[24] Secondly, the Cultural Revolution itself may be seen in terms of one notion of Chinese independence, namely that of total isolation. Viewing China as the 'bastion of socialism' China's leaders sought to pursue 'socialism in one country' by insulating that socialism from all external influences. The revolutionary people of China stood alone in their purity with the revolutionary people of the world defying all other states and the two superpowers in particular. Thirdly, in the period since the Cultural Revolution the Chinese have opened much more to the world but on a basis of emphasising state sovereignty and independence above all. The operational framework of analysis was built around Maoist concepts of contradictions. That is of using the contradictions between the two great imperialist powers, the USA and the USSR, on the one hand, and also using the contradictions between them and the rest of the world on the other. The units of analysis were and continue to be states and nations rather than classes. Likewise in the attempt to set up a broad international united front against the two superpowers the units to which the Chinese appeal are independent sovereign states. No other country in the world today stresses the importance of the concepts of sovereignty and sovereign equality of states more than China.

Yet China is still committed to revolution. Proletarian internationalism figures prominently in both the Party and the State constitutions.
China's new leader, Hua Kuo-feng, has gone out of his way to emphasise
the importance of the commitment to revolution and proletarian internationalism. How can this be accommodated with the principled
commitment to the independence and sovereignty of states? The
Chinese Communist Party maintains links with over 70 organisations it
regards as genuinely Marxist-Leninist. By and large these have tiny
memberships and are without influence in the states in which they
operate. They basically take their cue from Chinese publications on
general ideological issues. There is no evidence that the Chinese impose
their views on them or that the Chinese seek to have just one such
organisation as representative of a single country. Thus some West
European countries have several independent organisations recognised
by the Chinese as genuinely Marxist-Leninist.[25] Chinese recognition
gives these organisations a kind of ideological legitimacy, but clearly
the Chinese do not follow here the Leninist practice established in the
Third International of 1919 of recognising only one Communist Party
as the representative of the working class of that country. The orthodox
Leninist view was that the working class can only have one core political
party. Moreover, that party had to be closely linked with and super-
vised by the Communist International. There is no evidence that the
Chinese seek to direct the domestic political activities of such organisations. At another level the Chinese have encountered problems in South
East Asia in particular in seeking to maintain revolutionary party to
party links while also maintaining separate but good state to state relations at the same time. Thus as we have already seen Malaysia formally
protested to the Chinese government regarding the moral support given
by Chinese leaders (wearing their Party hat) in formally congratulating
the Communist Party of Malaya on its 45th Anniversary.[26]

A separate but related problem concerns China's relations with those
countries still considered by China to be socialist. According to Marx's
and particularly Lenin's concepts of proletarian internationalism, fellow
genuine Communists were bound by definition to have a common view
of the principal characteristics of the current world situation. Yet China
has not sought the acceptance of her own views as to the nature of the
balance of world forces at the present time. Fundamental to China's
new international position is the view that the Soviet Union has restored
capitalism at home, and indeed has gone far toward establishing a monopoly capitalist system which is even worse than that of the United

States. It is this which in the Chinese view makes the Soviet Union a more dangerous and expansionist power than the United States. It would have been natural for a leadership so keen to establish its Leninist orthodoxy to have tried to pressurise other socialist countries into accepting its fundamental line. Nevertheless the Chinese have not done so. To take but one example, there is a great contrast between the views of the Vietnamese and their Chinese comrades on this. The Vietnamese still see the Soviet Union as socialist and they argue that the socialist camp continues to exist. China's entire foreign policy is predicated on entirely the opposite view. The Chinese, however, have not demanded that the Vietnamese change their line.

In the Chinese practice of proletarian internationalism it is the principle of respect for the independence of others which predominates. The Chinese leaders must surely consider that their analysis of the Soviet Union and the analysis of the main forces at work in the world today belong to the level of general principles rather than tactics. Their tolerance of the deviance of fellow Marxist-Leninists, therefore, can only be justified in theoretical terms by arguing that the Chinese position is absolutely correct and that it is based on objective facts so that in time the others will *independently* come to recognise its validity too.

It has been argued in this essay that the moral claims of the Chinese leadership regarding international affairs centre on the principle of independence. It permeates their view regarding the relationship between pursuing socialism domestically and conducting foreign affairs with an external world largely made up of non-socialist states. The development of socialism within China may be seen as a variant of socialism in one country. There is quite a conscious refusal to have any kind of dependence on outside forces. Even the case of possible reparations from Japan arising from the 1931-45 conflicts was refused.[27] However much as the Chinese may support the claims of developing countries in their demand for a new international economic order and for the transfer of technology, the moral basis for it does not rest on the argument that the industrialised world profited initially from exploitation and that it must now give back what it has taken. The moral basis for the Chinese support is that the current international economic system is an exploitative one and it is for that reason it must be changed.

The way to change the exploitative international economic system is by stressing sovereign independence and self reliance. For the Chinese, however, that is not simply an instrumental device useful for tactical purposes, but, at a deeper level, it is also a moral and revolutionary principle. For a state to be genuinely independent and for it really to pursue a policy of self-reliance it must, in the Chinese view, 'rely on the strength and wisdom of its own people'. The Chinese adage that the weak can defeat the strong and the small can defeat the big is predicated upon the assumption that the movements or countries concerned must be genuinely independent and therefore able to tap the creative forces and impulses of the people. In the long term, the Chinese argue, such movements or countries will prove indestructible. The moral qualities of the argument here are unmistakable.

The Chinese also maintain at a simple moral level that where there is opposition there will be found also resistance to that oppression. It is this conviction which makes the Chinese leaders believe that the Third World will play the positive role which they assign to it. Explaining this to the United Nations Sixth Special Session on 12 April 1974 Teng Hsiao-ping, representing the view of his government, put it as follows:

> The numerous developing countries have long suffered from colonialist and imperialist oppression and exploitation. They have won political independence, yet all of them still face the historic task of clearing out the remnant forces of colonialism, developing the national economy and consolidating national independence. These countries cover vast territories, encompass a large population and abound in natural resources. Having suffered the heaviest oppression, they have the strongest desire to oppose oppression and seek liberation and development. In the struggle for national liberation and independence, they have demonstrated immense power and continually won splendid victories. They constitute a revolutionary motive force propelling the wheel of history and are the main forces combating colonialism, imperialism and particularly the superpowers.[28]

There is still the problem, however, that while China may be able to follow the policies of independence and self-reliance this may not be possible for most Third World countries. As we have seen China is in a very special position in having undergone probably the greatest revolution of the modern era. That position is based on a long history of a proud people largely independent of the outside world. Other countries lack a similar tradition, nor have they experienced a revolution of such dimensions. Furthermore, China is abundant in resources and is one of the world's great powers. While China may be able to insulate her economy from the vagaries of the international economic system this is not necessarily possible for most Third World countries. Even if the Third World countries have been the most oppressed and the most exploited and even if some of them have been 'awakened' in the Chinese sense of the word, it is still true that many of them are led by comprador elites whose very existence is dependent upon the maintenance of special kinds of relations with stronger external forces.

Thus the Chinese stand on independence ultimately has significant and deep revolutionary qualities. It calls for reliance by the leaders upon the people. The term 'people' for Mao always had revolutionary connotations. As he put it on innumerable occasions 'reactionaries are excluded from the ranks of the people'. The Chinese have maintained for several years that the slogan 'countries want independence, nations want liberation and people want revolution' is descriptive of an objective fact describing the general long-term trend in world affairs.

There can be no question, however, that revolution had a higher claim in Mao Tse-tung's thinking than independence. As a characteristic quote from Mao puts it:

> I stand for the theory of permanent revolution. Do not mistake this for Trotsky's theory of permanent revolution. In making revolution one must strike while the iron is hot — one revolution must follow another. Revolution must continually advance. The Hunanese often say, 'straw sandals have no pattern — they shape themselves in the making'. Trotsky believes that the Socialist revolution should be launched even before the democratic revolution is complete. We are not like that.[29]

The democratic revolution is by no means complete in most of the countries of the Third World. Since in the Chinese view socialist revolutions are a long way ahead, to be measured in terms of centuries perhaps, it follows that for the present it is the concept of independence which is the more dominant in shaping Chinese approaches and attitudes towards international affairs. It is certainly the concept which would be the more useful in resisting the encroachment of the Soviet Union. As we have seen, however, in Chinese usage the term independence is imbued with moral qualities and values which at times exceed established Leninist norms.

Notes

1. Chou En-lai, 'Political Report to the Tenth Congress of the Communist Party of China', *Peking Review,* Joint No. 35 and 36, 7 September 1973.

2. A congratulatory message by the Central Committee of the Communist Party of China signed by Mao and Chou En-lai to the Communist Party of Malaya on its 45th anniversary was printed prominently in the *People's Daily* of 29 April 1975. The text is in *Peking Review,* No. 18, 2 May 1975. The Malaysian government then lodged an official protest with the Chinese government as this was regarded as interference in Malaysia's internal affairs. See *The Annual Register of World Events in 1975* (Longman 1976), p. 268.

3. See Peter Van Ness, *Revolution and Chinese Foreign Policy* (University of California Press, 1970), for a careful analysis which leads to the proposition (p. 190) that 'whether a foreign non Communist Country was seen to be "peace loving" or ruled by "reactionaries", or whether a Communist Party state was viewed in Peking as "socialist" or denounced as "revisionist" largely depended on the extent to which that country's foreign policy coincided with China's own.'

4. This view was first outlined publicly in a systematic way by Mao Tse-tung in 1957. See 'On the Correct Handling of Contradictions Among the People', in *Selected Readings From the Works of Mao Tse-tung* (Foreign Language Press 1967), pp. 350-87.

5. 'Scientific Communism has a precise and definite meaning. According to Marxism-Leninism, Communist society is a society in which classes and class differences are completely eliminated, the entire people have a high level of Communist consciousness and morality as well as boundless enthusiasm for and initiative in labour, there is a great abundance of social products and the principle of "from each according to his ability, to each according to his needs" is applied, and in which the state has withered away'. From 'On Khrushchev's Phoney Communism and Its Historical Lessons for the World — Ninth Comment on the Open Letter of the Central Committee of the CPSU' (14 July 1964). In *The Polemic and the General Issue of the International Communist Movement.* (FLP, Peking 1965), p. 459.

6. Ibid., pp. 461-2.

7. Ibid., p. 464.

8. See, for example, the accounts quoted in Kenneth T. Shewmaker, *Americans and Chinese Communists, 1927-1945* (Cornell University Press, 1971).

9. Translated by Stuart R. Schram in *China Quarterly,* No. 49 (January/March 1972), pp. 76-87.

10. Translated by S.R. Schram, *The Political Thought of Mao Tse-tung* (Penguin, 1969), p. 352.

11. 'Speech at the Supreme State Conference', 28 January 1958. Translated in Stuart Schram (ed.), *Mao Tse-tung Unrehearsed* (Penguin, 1974), p. 92.

12. Ibid., p. 102.

13. For a brief summary of the debate and for references to the Russian sources see M. Fainsod, *How Russia is Ruled,* (OUP, 1963), p. 90 and 141-2.

14. 'Speech at the Tenth Plenum', 24 September 1962. In Schram, *Mao Tse-tung Unrehearsed,* pp. 191-2.

15. Cited in Schram, *Political Thought,* p. 379.

16. See the study of the Bandung Conference and the reproduction of its main documents in George McT. Kahin. *The Asian-African Conference* (Cornell University Press, 1956).

17. John Gittings, *The World and China 1922-72* (Eyre Methuen, 1974), p. 211.

18. For a clear analysis of this see Gittings, *World and China,* particularly pp. 35-115, for the period up to the end of World War II.

19. See in particular Chou En-lai's speech of 2 September 1968, at the National Day Reception given by the Vietnamese Ambassador in Peking, for the claim that the Soviet Union 'had long since completely destroyed the socialist camp which once existed'. *Peking Review,* No. 36 (6 September 1968), pp. 6-7.

20. Speech by Chairman of the Chinese Delegation, Li Chiang, to the Seventh Special Sesssion of the United Nations in *Peking Review,* No. 37 (12 September 1975).

21. For the figures on the extent of China's aid see Carol H. Fogarty, 'China's Economic Relations with the Third World' in *China: A Reassessment of the Economy,* A Compendium of Papers Presented to the Joint Economic Committee, Congress of the United States of America (July 1975), p. 730.

22. For a Chinese account see *People's Daily,* 22 September 1974, 'Mutual Support and Sincere Cooperation', also available in *China Quarterly,* No. 60 (December 1974), Quarterly Chronicle and Documentation, pp. 836-8.

23. A lengthy editorial entitled 'The Maoist Regime at a New Stage' in *Kommunist,* the theoretical organ of the Central Committee of the CPSU. Translated in two parts in the publication of the Soviet Embassy in London, *Soviet News,* 9 and 16 September 1975. In particular see 16 September, p. 321.

24. It should be noted that as late as 11 May 1964 Mao Tse-tung still had grave misgivings about De Gaulle. A inner Party speech rejected the Soviet Union as a 'dictatorship of the bourgeoisie, a dictatorship of the big bourgeoisie, a dictatorship like German fascism, a Hitler type of dictatorship, they are a pack of ruffians, *even worse than De Gaulle*' (emphasis added). Quoted in Gittings, *World and China,* p. 256. Yet three months earlier in February of that same year Mao contrasted the French favourably with the Russians as still having 'some notion of business ethics'.

25. See, for example, *Peking Review,* No. 3 (16 January 1976), which published condolence messages on the death of Chou En-lai *inter alia* from three separate such organisations in Germany, two in France and two in Japan.

26. See note 2.

27. For an account of the Chinese refusal of Japanese offers to pay reparations for war damage see *China Quarterly,* No. 52 (October-December 1972), Chronicle and Documentation, section on Japan.

28. *Peking Review,* Special Supplement to No. 15 (12 April 1974).

29. 'Speech at the Supreme State Conference', 28 January 1958, translated in Schram, *Mao Tse-tung Unrehearsed,* p. 94.

9 MORAL PRECEPTS OF CONTEMPORARY SOVIET POLITICS[1]

Vendulka Kubálková

The Soviet and East European conception of morality is at the same time related to and distinct from its Western counterparts: related in so far as it has evolved from the same intellectual tradition, distinct because it has gradually developed several characteristics which could seem to separate it from Western conceptions by an increasingly potent intellectual barrier. Thus, to contrast Soviet and Western moral precepts, I would suggest describing the former as an *explicitly ideological-militant paradigm* and I shall try to substantiate in this chapter why I think it merits the introduction of a category of its own.

Moral precepts are central to Marxism-Leninism. The Soviet and East European systems derive their very legitimacy from the moral creed inherited from Marx; in fact the whole of Marxist-Leninist ideology is erected on a set of beliefs and values derived from Marxist classics and interpreted by Party leaders and Party ideologues. Philosophy, including moral philosophy, is sharply distinguished from ideology in the non-Soviet world. In the Marxist-Leninist terms of reference it is closely related to the point of merger, in the sense that philosophy is subordinated to ideology. The task of the Soviet philosophers (if they want to remain in business) is not to strive to understand the totality of social reality on the basis of human experience and reason in a critical and ostensibly value free manner (as their Western counterparts attempt to do), but to make their ideology more intellectually viable, acceptable, believable, consistent, coherent and teachable. Although philosophy in the Soviet and East European societies displays a certain degree of independence, one should bear in mind this close link. The other side of this coin of subservience to ideology is, of course, that the works of the approved philosophers are much better known than those of philosophers in the West, with an audience ready made by decree and waiting. Thus they exercise a considerably greater degree of influence on public affairs than Western philosophers whose views, frustratingly, often do not reach beyond a small academic circle.

In tying moral conceptions to ideology one also pre-empts their fate, given, that is, the esteem in which Western international relations theorists seem to hold 'ideology'. The highly contentious issue of the merits of ideologies in general, and of their place in the understanding of world politics in particular, is obviously beyond the scope and intention of this chapter. Let me, however, by way of introduction draw attention to some rather randomly selected aspects of what is still a minority counter-argument — that the study of ideologies from the point of view of world politics is a worthwhile enterprise, particularly those aspects with a direct bearing on the question of the relevance of studying moral conceptions.

First of all it is probably correct to say that there is nothing in Soviet and East European international behaviour that could not be understood in practical terms and along power political lines. There is no need whatsoever for recourse to Marxist theories, and this applies to moral conceptions in particular. In fact, the argument might run, Marxist ideology is something one can well do without in the theory of world politics. And this is probably correct for any individual international event taken in isolation: one can say that Marxism-Leninism does not prescribe any particular course of action and indeed in any particular instance an indefinite number of actions could be compatible with Soviet ideology. But this would be the case with any other system of beliefs and values, not only the Soviet one. It can be argued, however, that the conduct of international affairs over a period of time can be understood correctly only by keeping ideological motivations in mind: the theory that supplies the *end* to which all communist actions are explicitly directed.

Secondly, as Brzezinski for one has pointed out,[2] dismissing ideologies seems to postulate that Soviet leaders have greater effective (if not supernatural) powers than those they certainly seem to possess. Though they set in motion the machinery for political socialisation (and the existence of this process is not being questioned) in the attempt to inculcate the official ideology, and morality in particular, into people's minds, they themselves are miraculously exempt from the same socialisation process. They themselves, in other words, follow in their decision-making different values from those that they try to inculcate.

Such an argument, and this leads us to point three, postulates the universal validity of a set of moral precepts (obviously Western ones) common to all humankind; Soviet precepts are seen as some devilish aberration, or at least as something completely spurious and alien to human nature, bound to degenerate and 'return back' sooner or later to these universal values. Given this attitude there is very little one can say about the moral virtues of the Soviet political system and of Soviet behaviour, let alone the way the system tries to explain and justify its own rule: in relation to Western values Soviet ones often appear to be their actual negation, and everything to do with that system may be branded as amoral because of its oppressive attitude to the individual and individual values. In the history of human thought such an approach, referred to sometimes as 'external analysis', has frequently been used to reject another philosophical system rather than mount a rebuttal of it: each system as a rule carries its own definitions of truth and criteria of evidence to be used, and 'external analysis', from the standpoint of 'other truth' and evidence, can only lead to conflict and deadlock. In order to be able to refute effectively a system of thought one should therefore use the method of 'internal analysis' or 'imminent critique'[3] which does not *a priori* reject any part of that system. One seeks instead for logical inconsistencies, rather than those that appear in contrast to one's own set of axiomatic postulates.

Fourthly, the dismissal of Soviet ideology might still have been justifiable in the time of Stalin perhaps, but dismissal would be totally out of date now: it would overlook important intellectual developments in the Soviet and East European situation. The practical requirements and the real disappointments associated with a body of Marxist teaching, grown gradually stale in its dogmatic version, have succeeded where the armies of Western critics and revisionists have totally failed.[4] Marxist ideology and its moral component is increasingly perceived as a social instrument for achieving certain internal and external ends, more reliable and less painful than the Stalinist methods of open terror and brutality. To achieve this a perpetual updating and revision of the ideology and its credibility is required, which does not necessarily indicate ideological erosion; perhaps the very opposite. As a side effect of this process, one should add, there is an emerging group of philosophers, in most cases wholly educated in the Marxist-Leninist *Weltanschauung*, who are no longer satisfied with a non-critical apologists role. They are sometimes referred to as 'New Marxists'[5] (in distinction from Western 'Neomarxists'). These 'New Marxists' are not simply Marxologues. They would identify themselves with most of Marx's heritage and, unlike most of the Neomarxists, would still be committed to the construction of communist society and the fundamentals of dialectical and historical materialism, but they represent a new breed of Marxism which is certainly not to be overlooked, particularly from the point of view of its influence on the development of Soviet ideology in the future. From their writings as well as from the writings of dissidents one could reconstruct several moral countercodes, but to discuss them as well will not be possible within the scope of this chapter, where attention will be paid strictly to the official orthodox ideological version of morality.

Fifthly, one of the arguments of the New Marxists against the rejection of Marxism is that, because there is no way to deduce a political system and political action from Marxist thinking, *ergo* Marxism cannot be blamed for the emergence of any particular sort of system and behaviour.[6] Thus, for instance, Stalinism and everything negative that it represents does not follow from Marxism. Marxism is still seen as the most valid methodological approach. If anything the moral crisis that Marx observed in the capitalist system still exists, and what is more has extended to the planet as a whole, with initially intrasocietal inequities now spread on a global scale. Marxism is perceived by New Marxists (and in this respect they and the Western Neomarxists would agree) as still best equipped for this analysis.

Sixthly, there is the well-known argument based on the perceived heuristic sterility of all theories that are likely to come from the Soviet section of the world. Even if it is true to say that there is not yet a Soviet ethics, or if there is, it is either too eclectic[7] or 'pedestrian'[8] to have much to say to Western moral philosophers about the problems of their subject, one should not mix ethics and actual morality. Even if the Soviet and East European regimes totally fail in their attempts to reform their societies through the inculcation of specific values (which they openly declare as their task) these values in one form or another will still be held by a large proportion of the population of a perpetually shrinking world, and they should at least be noted as one of the symptoms of the diseased condition of the world today.

Last, but not least, I believe that, as Richard T. de George has aptly put it, 'to try to understand either Soviet society or Soviet politics without a knowledge of the foundations of Soviet thought is in many respects like trying to understand the Middle Ages without a knowledge of Christianity'.[9] To put it even more bluntly a simile with opera is offered. The refusal to study Soviet ideology could be likened to the refusal of an audience to read a libretto and its claim that the same degree of appreciation and understanding of the plot can be reached on the basis of the music alone. This is partly true – the orchestration and harmony and the acting on the stage are 'universal' and enable one to *follow* and guess the plot, particularly with an occasional word here and there that sounds familiar (detente, peace, freedom, etc.). Needless to say, however, misunderstandings and illusions about the plot could easily arise.

Let us first of all take a brief look at the essential characteristics of Soviet moral conceptions and proceed to a similarly brief outline of how these moral conceptions fit in with Soviet international relations theory.

There is quite a range of definitions of morality[10] to be found in the perpetually growing bulk of Soviet literature on the subject,[11] from a 'functional' definition (as a 'social institution for regulating man's behaviour'[12]) to wider descriptive ones such as 'the totality of principles or norms of men's conduct which regulate their relations to one another, to society, to a certain class, to the state, country, and so on, supported by personal conviction, tradition, education, the force of public opinion of a whole society or of a certain class'.[13] The philosophical theory dealing with morality is referred to as the 'science of morals',[14] in contrast to bourgeois ethics which cannot by definition ever become scientific.[15]

The Marxist pedigree of the 'science of morals' is slightly precarious to say the least. Marxologues still argue whether Marx had a clearly discernible ethical position, explicit or only implicit, and if so where precisely he stood.[16] Thus as in many other cases the view of a Marxologue would not help one very far in understanding Soviet ethics. The Soviet ethical position is in fact more Leninist, or rather Stalinist, than it is Marxist, and from Marx it got a somewhat shaky start. There is a broad moral framework deducible from Marx's whole work, i.e. the moral message of indignation which his works *in toto* convey (although Marx did not devote himself to a separate study of morality), and there is the commitment to the moral goal of communism argued out on the basis of a collectivist understanding of man. The Soviet ethical position, however, did inherit from Marx one serious error. This error consisted in the assumption that morality more or less automatically followed as a part of the social consciousness of the development of social existence (also called social being). The pairs 'social existence/social consciousness' and 'base/superstructure', although they are at the very heart of Soviet thinking, leave a great deal to be desired from the point of view of conceptual clarity and meaning. In the discussion about them their content and relationship has not yet been concluded.[17] Social existence, in standard Marxist understanding, is defined as 'the material life of society, the production of material goods and those relations (in a class society these are class relations) into which men enter in the process of production'. Social consciousness then consists of 'views, notions, ideas, political, legal, aesthetic, ethical and other theories, philosophy, morality, religion, and other forms of consciousness'.[18] Not only have these terms been the subject of controversy amongst Marxists since Marx[19] (because of the conveniently vague and obscure character of

Marx's original formulations), but together with the changing emphasis on objective and subjective factors and their importance in human history (i.e. the varying degrees of perceived determinism or voluntarism), the mutual relationships of social consciousness and social existence and base and superstructure have undergone frequent reinterpretations from one Marxist school to another. In the original determinist interpretation which one can derive from Engels and less directly from Marx,[20] it would seem to follow that there is no need to have a theory about morality: when economic conditions change, the social reflection of it as a part of both superstructure and social consciousness will follow suit, to the eventual disappearance of morality together with such other institutions as state and law in communist society.

Soviet society has painfully discovered, however, that this is not the case. Morality has not begun to change as dramatically as its ideological forebears had supposed, and certainly not in the first three decades of the existence of the Soviet Union. Thus it was Stalin who, paradoxically, became the founding father of Soviet ethics as an independent theory. Continuing in Leninist footsteps in so far as the subjectivist emphasis is concerned, he coined the concept of 'relative independence of certain parts of the superstructure' causing 'lag of superstructure behind social existence'. Particularly after Stalin's 1950 discourse on linguistics a considerable amount of chaos was introduced into the twin notions of base and superstructure and social existence and consciousness. Some social phenomena (e.g. language) were actually declared as not belonging to either base or superstructure.[21] This was, in a way, the only way of 'rectifying' Marxism and explaining why morality did not undergo the changes that classical Marxism had anticipated. At the same time it opened new fields for theoretical activity that might be reconciled with the classical legacy. Short of this 'error' the classics did not leave any recipe for their ideological descendants, and one can thus (although there are other reasons) explain the body of theoretical writing on the subject[22] that shares with the classical Marxist nonformulated ethics only its broad framework, and the conception of man from which moral goals are derived.

Let us attempt to characterise, within Western terms of reference, the official Soviet conception of morality in so far as one can generalise about it from the voluminous Soviet literature. There is a strong similarity to pragmatism, utilitarianism, ethical relativism, Darwinian evolutionism, natural law ethics and Christian ethics,[23] although Soviet ethics is an admixture of elements of all these and is not reducible to any one of them in particular. Soviet ethics is also not without precedent in its self-assuredness, self-containment[24] and highly intolerant attitude to other moral conceptions: it regards itself as not only superior to all 'bourgeois' ethics but also exclusively capable of providing 'true answers'. It thus rejects all other moral conceptions,[25] and refuses to make a distinction between normative and critical ethics (or metaethics) on the basis that the two merge to such a degree that they cannot be meaningfully separated.[26]

In its approach to morality Soviet ethics is historical:[27] morality appears at that moment in history when a split occurs between individual and social interests.[28] Moral diversity is attributable to differing physical and economic conditions. Morality as a part of social consciousness [29] appears and develops with the social consciousness.[30] Thus the existence of morality is bound up with the existence of society and in this respect the Soviet position approaches that of some ethical relativists, with the modification that the morality of any particular society is never relative but always objectively given and necessary for a particular stage of the development of society. In a class society, it would follow, there is always dual if not multiple morality. 'People have always been and will continue to be silly victims of deception and self-deception in politics, as long as they will not learn to search in any moral, religious, political, social phrases, declarations, promises, the interests of one class or another'.[31] Together with Nietzsche the Marxists would postulate that what is good for one is by definition bad for the other. But unlike Nietzsche the Marxists see an end to this highly undesirable state of affairs, since in communist society there will be no classes and the interests of all members of society will coincide. Every morality in history is assumed to have always contained elements of what Marxist-Leninists describe as 'all-human morality',[32] or 'common moments of morality of different human collectivities and classes'[33] representing the 'minimal conditions of moral life'[34] which are negative (do not kill, do not steal, do not fornicate, etc.) and positive (work, respect old people, be brave, etc.).[35] However, the full development of this all-human universally valid morality is to be expected only in communist society. Correcting Marx, the contemporary Marxist-Leninists believe that morality will not 'wither away' with the state but will in fact flourish and replace law (which will 'wither away') and with which morality is seen to be increasingly enmeshed.[36] Thus in communist society there will be for the first time only one morality, the universal one, which will express the interests and feelings of all humankind or most of it. In fact Soviet morality, 'the noblest and most just morality' [37] is already represented as a harbinger of communist morality, and coincides with the morality of all working mankind. It will we are told, 'express the interests and ideals of the whole of working mankind' and will encompass 'the fundamental norms of human morality which the masses evolved in the course of milleniums as they fought against vice and social oppression . . .'[38] The Soviet position is thus basically objectivist: moral norms for each society are the objective norms necessary for its development. Separate moralities are assessed on the basis of their proximity to a moral ideal which is absolute but of a non extra-terrestrial or extrahuman source.

For such an approach it becomes obvious that the *moral ideal* assumes paramount importance. Let us look at the Soviet definitions of their moral ideal. We discover that their position is basically teleological, resembling utilitarian and self-realisation theories. At the root of the Soviet understanding of 'moral' and 'good' (used interchangeably) are still Lenin's formulations, dating from 1920 and 1922.[39] Whatever promotes the revolution is good and moral, and after the successful revolution, it is obviously whatever serves the achievement of communism that serves as a moral criterion. One should not allow oneself to be misled by some roundabout Soviet formulations that say that 'good' is what promotes the interests of society, and that is the construction of communism.[40] The ultimate moral ideal, the absolute moment in the relativity of moral judgements and the criterion by which all actions should be judged, is the ideal of communism.

Apart from setting out unequivocally their main moral criterion, the Soviet treatment of good and moral leaves much to be desired. This applies to the notions of 'right', 'duty', 'happiness', 'justice', etc., too, in so far as they all are derived from the concept of good. Generally speaking, 'good' in non-Soviet formulations is assumed by Soviet writers to be a relative concept, and one that has 'kept changing historically from one epoch to another'.[41] Thus they would not agree with G.E. Moore that good cannot be defined,[42] nor with Mill and Bentham that it is equivalent to pleasure. By defining moral and good the way they do, i.e. as serving the advancement of the construction of communism, they sanctify whatever means that are necessary to that end. All means as long as they lead to this goal are *ipso facto* moral. Thus anything can be justified in the name of necessity, and the meanings of what is 'necessary' and 'expedient' merge. That the means used to achieve the desired end can negate it as a moral ideal becomes obvious; this way of defining 'good' leaves a blank space which can be filled with any action whatsoever.

If the ultimate moral criterion is communism then obviously its precise meaning assumes a crucial importance for the whole of the Soviet conception of morality. This is, however, another stumbling block. The notion of communism is important for every Marxist-Leninist theory, and yet it is not quite clear what precisely it is supposed to mean.

Marx himself defined communism in a very sketchy way[43] and rather negatively, i.e. in terms of what will not exist, rather than what will, and all subsequent definitions have been plagued by a similar problem. Soviet Marxist-Leninists became aware of the need for a less ambiguous formulation of the actual goal of their society, and the most complete outline comes from the 1961 Programme of the CPSU adopted at the 22nd CPSU Congress.[44] This Programme, third in the history of the Soviet Communist Party, was actually designed for the period of the immediate eve of communist society, and outlines the route that is to be taken to ensure the successful entrée of that society into the communist stage of development. According to this Programme

Communism is a classless social system with one form of public ownership of the means of production and full social equality of all members of society; under it, the all-round development of people will be accompanied by the growth of the productive forces through continuous progress in science and technology; all the springs of co-operative wealth will flow more abundantly, and the great principle 'From each according to his ability, to each according to his needs' will be implemented. Communism is a highly organised society of free, socially conscious working people in which public self-government will be established, a society in which labour for the good of society will become the prime vital requirement of everyone, a necessity recognised by one and all, and the ability of each person will be employed to the greatest benefit of the people.[45]

Again, it would be beyond the scope of this chapter to analyse such a definition; however, the crucial fallacy of Soviet ethics is derived from this definition. Regardless of any attempt to clarify the situation elsewhere in the Programme, it would seem that 'communism' remains extremely loosely defined. Despite its vagueness, the notion of communism is not only given great importance but it is seen to perform a multiple role: on the one hand it is a moral goal as well as a moral criterion, and on the other it is also a political system. What would happen to moral ideals when communism as a political system gets established is not quite clear. Furthermore, by mixing the usage of the term communism, without distinguishing clearly in what sense it is to be used, one creates considerable confusion. The vagueness of the definition, the fact that to a great extent it is still a negative one while it leaves room for positive elements to be added as they evolve, makes for arbitrary usage in practice. Furthermore it is not at all clear who is to decide that the society is a communist one. Perhaps, as in Stalin's time, it will like socialism simply be declared. And on what authority will the communist party, in whose hands the promulgation of communism obviously rests, come to know that it actually is communism? The mixing together of the functions of communism, establishing its content being left to the party, is presented as an advantage however. This is epitomised in the Stalinist notion, reiterated *ad nauseam*, of the 'moral-political unity of the society', and expresses the merger of political aims with moral goals. While striving, at least nominally, toward this still distant political end (although the Programme declares that communism in the USSR should be achieved 'in the main' in the 1980s),[46] whatever the party decides to do automatically becomes by definition 'moral' and 'good'. One should add, however, that at critical junctures like the denunciation of Stalin after the 20th CPSU Congress in 1956, this looseness has posed a serious problem for Marxism-Leninism. Stalin's amoralities (in a Marxist-Leninist sense) still wait for a scholarly explanation.

Many Western critics tend to accuse Soviet moral philosophy of being no more than a secular religion: the facts merge with values (something which Marxism-Leninism presents as a positive achievement). It is argued that such statements as 'communism is the goal of all mankind', or many other frequently repeated slogans, cannot be empirically tested, therefore they are merely values, spuriously presented by the Soviets as fact. However, as we have said at the outset, the Marxist-Leninist system of thought carries its own definitions of truth. When accused of presenting the goal of communism as a fact rather than value, the Soviet answer would be twofold.

Because dialectical and historical materialism assume that society operates according to discoverable laws, the fact that these laws can be identified, leading historically from one type of society to another, prompts them to believe that the coming of communism can, by the same token, be 'scientifically' predicted. In other words they do not seem to distinguish, like some Western theorists do, the elements of explanation and prediction.[47] The occurrence of certain developments in the past, and the existence of 'objectively' existing laws that derive from them, allows Soviet theorists to predict 'scientifically' the occurrence of certain events in the future. Obviously Marxist-Leninists, in contrast to most Western theorists, answer the question about the possibility of prediction in social theory in the affirmative, adding as a scientific test the capacity of social theory to control future events. Thus since Marx, one of the characteristics of Marxism (in the Leninist-Stalinist and contemporary Soviet line of thought) is the belief in the factual *inevitability* of the advent of communist society. It is a future for the whole of mankind. A belief in the knowledge of the objective laws that lead to communism, however, is only the first part of the answer to *why* the notion of communism plays such an important role in the whole system of Soviet thought. The second part of the Soviet defence would be based on an analysis of the human being who, they believe, can come to fulfilment only in a communist society. Thus the justification of communism is made in terms of man, the 'most valuable entity in the world'.[48]

Starting with Marx's sixth thesis on Feuerbach and quotes from the *Economic and Philosophical Manuscripts of 1844*,[49] we find that Soviet theorists understand human nature as a collectivist entity: '. . . the human essence is no abstraction inherent to each single individual. In its reality it is the ensemble of the social relations'.[50] In contrast with most ethical positions in the West (although not all) a man is seen as a collective being — fully externalised, i.e. with no values of his own except those which derive from his place in a certain collective. This is another paradoxical part of the Marxian heritage: it seems beyond any doubt that the ultimate goal of Marx's theory was to liberate man, and yet his liberation can only be achieved within and through the collective. Only in a fully fledged communist society can man be free to develop all of his inherent human characteristics and achieve universal happiness; only in communist society can there be freedom of expression for everybody, universal justice and material plenty. Only within or *despite* the collectivity will his interests and those of everybody else for the first time fully coincide. Until then, however, and in order that this may be achieved, they have to be tailored to do so. Thus from Marx onwards Marxism has contained a paradoxical, one may say, 'schizophrenic', value system; for the ultimate achievement of the desired end, the same values that one strives for and advocates can be negated. Means are justified by their ends; in Lenin's simile, the chips fly when the forest is cut down; or in English, the eggs must be broken for an omelette to be made. Thus Soviet morality is somehow prepared to prescribe great personal sacrifices in the name of the distant future of man. This 'postponement' of moral gratification is not without precedent in Western ethical systems either, though Marxism-Leninism, in contrast to Christianity for instance, brings gratification forward and does not leave it to another world of existence beyond *this* one. The recipients will be different, however, from those preparing the way *now* for their future happiness.

Thus one may characterise the bulk of Soviet ethics, particularly in the case of the theory of international relations, as an attempt to devise a system of levers to synchronise conflicting interests and to transmit them to communist society where all interests will not only be compatible but will coincide. The ubiquitous dialectic is invaluable of course in explaining how the incompatible is made compatible, although as has been frequently pointed out since Stalin's version to say that something is 'dialectically related' is not an explanation, rather it restates the problem tautologically.

To restate the point: after the Soviet revolution, which was designed it was believed according to Marx's recipe, the predictions of the classics went badly awry and did not occur; new social relations did not develop with the new economic relations, and if in Stalin's time a doctrinal proviso had not been devised it would have been very difficult to avoid rejecting historical materialism *in toto*. The *deus ex machina* was once again located in the notion of the relative independence of certain parts of the superstructure and their active functioning with respect to the base, i.e. economic conditions.[51] The debate thus started is still far from concluded and parts of it implicate the very essence of historical materialism, that is to say the distinction between social existence and social consciousness. If some parts of the social consciousness, morality in particular, are allowed to play a role as important as parts of social existence, the very distinction between the two seems to be pointless.

From the notion of the relative independence of the superstructure (i.e. its lagging behind or 'running ahead of' the substructure), which was consistent with the subjectivist emphasis introduced by Lenin generally and caricatured in the extreme by Stalin, there followed *inter alia* a very important conclusion which is central to this chapter: communism is historically inevitable *but* – it will not happen of itself, its inevitability has to be assisted, communism has to be built. After the disappointing experience of a Soviet society which 'refused' to behave according to classical expectations, the whole attitude to Marxist determinism had to be modified. A need was recognised for 'laws of the development of communism' — economic, psychological, sociological — which was an admission by Soviet society that the classical Marxist recipe no longer held, since it had not anticipated a fraction of Soviet social reality and practice.

What is the practical implication of this relatively new emphasis on the active part of the subjective element, almost overwhelming the role of objective economic factors? If a new man is not formed by virtue of a change in economic conditions, then there is obviously a need to form him artificially, to mould him and his ideas and his values; his mind itself must be reached and changed directly by some other means. Thus morality clearly assumes a functional role, reinforcing law and the state. Morality becomes 'one of the basic types of social regulation'.[52] What is required by Soviet law is *ipso facto* required by Soviet morality. In a recent formulation all of this boils down to the perceived need to transform the *ideological into the psychological,*[53] that is to say, 'the knowledge of the moral principles of socialism has to become not only a matter of deep-rooted conviction but one of habit'.[54] But can a functional use of morality not be dismissed as strictly amoral, if not immoral? The Soviet response is, no. In their definitions of morality[55] they openly say that morality is a social institution for regulating human conduct, and this functional role is openly admitted. Soviet writers would argue that bourgeois morality does this just as strongly as the socialist one because, like socialist morality, bourgeois morality is passed from generation to generation, is designed to perpetuate and reinforce the capitalist system, and that its values and beliefs are inculcated just as much as in Soviet society. Morality is always a means, never an end in itself, and its function of strengthening the system is repeated *ad nauseam.*[56]

Awareness of the need to inculcate and educate in order that communism would not be missed by default has led to an unprecedented ideological campaign,[57] particularly after the promulgation of the Soviet *moral code* (!) as part of the 1961 CPSU Programme. The rules enumerated in this code are to be assimilated by every Soviet citizen as a *conditio sine qua non* for the achievement of communist society. The code, we are informed, is supposed not to be an artificial construct but a 'voice of the future'. With such a promulgation the question arises, of course, of the merits of its promulgator — the party, and the paternalistic position which it usurps in Soviet society. The party places itself in the position of moral mentor, which in itself can be described as an amoral act.[58] The party — whose patterns of recruitment and self-perpetuation are more than doubtful — does not provide a guarantee that it consists of the 'most advanced members of the society' who may assume the right to correct every other member of that society, who by definition are never 'mature', possess no independent moral conscience of their own, and remain subject to lifelong supervision and education. With this said we may now be witnessing one gigantic social experiment to prove in practice that, first of all, there is one universal morality which is neither born with man nor received from some external divine agency but is historically evolving, and in this respect objectively given for every stage of societal development, and that secondly, the last stage, before the achievement of universal morality, has to be strongly 'assisted' by social agencies to help human beings to get rid of the 'muck of ages' (to paraphrase Marx) — the surviving remnants, that is, of previous moral conceptions because — last but not least — social consciousness in itself is prone to exhibit considerable staying power and considerable delay in adjusting itself to changing economic conditions.

Let us take a brief look at the moral code,[59] particularly those points of it that are directly relevant to Soviet thinking on international relations. We should emphasise that all that has been said above about moral ideals is explicitly valid for the world as a whole. Advancing the achievement of communism all over the planet serves also as the criterion of morality in international relations. Thus, it would follow that Soviet foreign policy, being a means to this end, is presented to the population as moral by definition and meriting moral support. Perhaps that is why Stalin, despite his supposedly total removal from Soviet history books, seems to have received at least silent approbation for his international successes: it was after all under his command that (via the doctrine of socialism in one country) the Soviet state survived, 'capitalist encirclement' was broken, and the first paragon of communism maintained on the map.

First of all we should once again repeat that the Soviet morality is a collectivist one: thus it seems to be by definition better tailored to collectivities, states, etc., than to individuals. This is the opposite situation to that arising in the West, where individualistic moralities, when stretched to the level of states, seem to crack at the seams and tensions and incompatibilities arise.[60] In Marxist ethics it would seem to be rather the other way around. Soviet morality (although in the name of Man) is obviously designed for groups, classes, states, socio-economic systems, and other such collectivities. Secondly, it is important to bear in mind the closely argued and interconnected nature of the Marxist

Weltanschauung as a whole: thus, for example, its theory of international relations is bound to be closely consistent with its moral
conceptions, at least in formal terms. In fact one cannot begin to understand the Soviet theory of international relations without an understanding of Soviet moral conceptions: it would not make any sense if
taken separately. The Soviet moral code is, one could argue, a 'moral
code of international relations'. Moral conceptions lie at the root of the
main characteristic of Soviet international relations theory, i.e. the
strict differentiation of types of international relations, not according
to their content, but according to the participant in a particular relation.
This is so because in ethical terms Marxism does not distinguish
between the good and a gooddoer and a wrong and a wrongdoer, but
only between gooddoer and wrongdoer. Whatever the former does is
by definition good, whatever the latter does is bad and amoral. In other
words the same action is never judged by the same moral yardstick but
in terms of *who*, i.e. what class, state or socio-economic bloc, under-
takes it. It is an extension and a making absolute of Marx's distinction
of 'just' and 'unjust' in his reference to wars.

A first glance at the moral code reveals, beyond any doubt, that the
world is divided into Greeks and Romans, or in New Testament terms,
into capitalist 'goats' and socialist 'sheep'.[61] Soviet understanding of the
world coincides with this scheme. The world is divided into two main
socio-economic systems (capitalist and socialist), which have been
created as a spillover of the basic two antagonistic classes. The addition
of the 'Third World' makes a triangular model which, however, is still
fully consistent with a basic 'dialectical' dichotomisation because the
'Third World' apex of the triangle is in a state of flux. The triangularity
is obviously regarded as a transitory stage before bipolarity is achieved
(when the tug-of-war of the two main systems over the 'Third World' is
concluded obviously in favour of the Soviet one). This will be in its
turn a transitory stage on the way to achieving a monolithic communist
world.

Identifying sheep and goats does not completely coincide with the
triangular Soviet organisation of the world either, or its present stage
(and indeed class) structure. The 'sheep' are obviously the three groups
of 'progressive forces' which create 'a militant alliance of the main
revolutionary forces of our day'.[62] They are located in the capitalist
world (the international working class plus other progressive anticapita-
list forces), in the Third World (the anti-colonial national liberation
movements), and (as the third progressive force) the totality of the
world socialist system. For the sheep thus defined the moral code

provides a newly found streak of humanism, but because it is exclusive to this group, it is a very limited humanism. Within these 'revolutionary forces' norms not so very different from the biblical Ten Commandments apply, with the possible modification that work — regarded by some ethical systems as a necessary if not degrading evil — is 'promoted' to a moral duty. (This is obviously because of the perceived need to 'build' communism.) Toward the capitalist goat (i.e. the capitalist world *minus* the proletariat and other anti-imperialist progressive forces, and plus some 'Third World' pro-capitalist regimes) the moral code proclaims 'an uncompromising attitude'.[63] This amounts to a declaration of open hatred toward a considerable part of the world, which seems a sad state of affairs in the second half of the twentieth century. An 'uncompromising attitude', in the self-conscious symbolic jargon of communism, would sanctify whatever means the progressive forces' might choose to harm the 'goats'. Wars of national liberation movements are once again described as 'just' wars; similarly 'just' would be the encouragement of any subversive action, industrial or otherwise, that undermines the capitalist system, the 'goodness' and 'morality' of such actions being once again assessed in terms of the advancement of the worldwide communist cause (as perceived by the SU).

In comparison with Marx's time the institution of the state, from the point of view of its moral content, has undergone considerable change. Whilst morally negative in classical Marxism, since by definition it was an oppressive instrument of one class against all other classes, it has since Stalin become a good and worthy institution.[64] In the absence of antagonistic classes the state in fact allegedly assumes a highly positive and laudable role; it becomes a surrogate for the traditionally postulated dynamic provided by the antagonistic relationship between the two main classes. Now that the relations of classes are of a 'nonantagonistic' nature the state may set in motion a revolution 'from above' and perform highly desirable societal functions. In addition to this 'internal' function the state performs an important 'external' role (i.e. the 'sheep' state in the socialist and 'Third World') — it acts as a protective bulwark against capitalist influence, and Soviet law goes into great detail as to the respect with which socialist and Third World states should be treated by capitalist countries. Thus, and this would no doubt cause some surprise to Marx and Engels, the moral code actually makes the love of one's country (i.e. state) into a moral obligation.[65] The 'class approach to international relations'[66] results in a concept of state of various content; likewise sovereignty, and the concept of nation. Patriotism, we are told, has an economic (social ownership of the means of production and a socialist system of management), political (the Soviet state system, Soviet democracy) and ideological-theoretical (the teaching of Marxism-Leninism) basis.[67] Thus 'patriotism is totally different from bourgeois cosmopolitanism, which always expresses the interests and the spirit of the ruling classes, and disguises the necessity of class conflict'.[68] In contrast to bourgeois cosmopolitanism, proletarian internationalism is 'that moral quality which expresses itself in the attempts to harmonize national and all-human interests, to consider all nations'.[69] With a class understanding of patriotism and proletarian internationalism it is, of course, possible to conclude that proletarian internationalism 'does not hinder national sovereignty',[70] a sovereignty which is similarly defined in class terms.

Notions such as state, sovereignty, nation and internationalism are treated variously according to whom they are attributed. International relations is also divided into neatly delimited groups according to the same criterion. The inter-state relations amongst countries within the socialist system go under the composite label of 'socialist internationalism' and are presented as the 'prototype of international relations, which will fully and individually prevail in the world when the revolutionary transition from capitalism to socialism is completed on a world scale'.[71] The 'passport' into the 'socialist world' is in sharing the same economic foundation and the corresponding political and legal superstructure, and the same moral-political common goal is a commitment to the construction of communism. Thus the socialist state is endowed with *communal morality*. It is assumed that the 'harmonic connection between international and national interests' is achieved not only because once in the socialist system the national interests of all states begin to coincide, but because individual states can flourish only within the bloc. The occasional contradictions are of a 'nonantagonistic nature',[72] or in a less Stalinist way, they are referred to as merely 'partial conflicts' and are easily resolvable. Thus the meaning of socialist internationalism as a kind of international relations is an addition to the standard list of minimal requirements for international relations (respect for sovereignty, independence, the national interests of states, full equality, and non-interference in internal affairs.)[73] The socialist states owe each other 'fraternal and mutual aid'.[74] This 'fraternal mutual aid' not only changes the meaning of the other requirements of international relations but adds a moral (and also legal) right, and duty, for these states to 'protect their unity and mutually assist one another in the struggle against capitalism', as well as to 'co-operate and mutually to assist one another in building socialism and communism in a com-

radely manner'.[75] This merger of the moral and the political is
expressed in the merger of the moral and the legal; the documents and
declarations of communist parties [*sic*] and governments constitute
international agreements *sui generis* and in fact are considered as a
source of international law valid amongst the socialist states.[76] Thus
socialist internationalism places a moral duty upon all socialist states
for the joint protection of socialist achievements.[77] In other words the
'Brezhnev doctrine' is not only not denied by Soviet ideology, but is
morally sanctified by it. In so far as it can be argued that socialist internationalism is arrived at by an extension of the old classical principle of
proletarian internationalism[78] the 'Brezhnev doctrine' is not so much
Brezhnev's as Lenin's and Stalin's, its essence deeply embedded in
Soviet Marxist-Leninist thought.

But obviously the moral goal of communism should not be a privilege open only to socialist states and those countries of the Third World
taking the 'non-capitalist path' of development. Soviet Marxism-Leninism still argues that all humankind 'inevitably' heads in that direction,
well aware of the classical postulate, defeated by Soviet experience in
this century, that communism cannot be achieved in a smaller geographical area than that of the world as a whole, and all at once. Thus
one could argue that if this is the case 'peaceful coexistence' (as applied
to capitalist countries, capitalist oriented Third World countries, and of
late also to China — hence applied to the 'antagonistic enemy') seems
to be by definition immoral, if not an overt *contradito ex adjecto* within Marxist terms of reference. Particularly since, as we have seen, the
emphasis has been placed on the need to *build* communism (domestically) rather than wait for it. The idea of peaceful coexistence at best
would seem to indicate a passive attitude. Would not the idea of peaceful coexistence and détente, therefore, run counter to the moral duty
the socialist states perceive that they possess?

Western audiences are still unaware of what exactly the Soviet leaders mean by peaceful coexistence. As Brzezinski has pointed out some
of the blame for this must be laid on Kissinger's doorstep when he
advised Nixon on his first trip to the USSR to include the phrase
'peaceful coexistence' in the American-Soviet statement as the founda-
tion-stone of the East-West relationship — and this has been the case
ever since. Thus the Russians can dictate the semantic framework of
the relationship in an 'age of instant and universal communications,
[when] words are politics'.[79] But what do the Soviet leaders mean?
It is beyond the scope of this chapter to describe the changing theoretical reasoning behind the idea of peaceful coexistence since Lenin's

times; let us only briefly note that it does not contradict the ultimate
goal of communism as much as one would think at first sight. First of
all it is not a class principle; it applies exclusively to inter-state relations.[80] And it does not in the slightest hamper the ideological and class
conflict, which in fact we are told is to intensify in the period of
détente. Intensified ideological hostility does not, however, have to
stand in the way of economic co-operation. In fact, as Marshal Shulman
has argued, between socialist countries and capitalist ones economic
co-operation is a substitute for costly Soviet internal reforms.[81] Thus
the tension, often unnoticed in the West, that arises from Soviet statements that they want to co-operate with the West, at the same time
informing us that they want to destroy the West.[82] Peaceful coexistence,
which in this last form emerged at the time of Khrushchev's 'discovery'
that the 'atomic bomb does not observe the class principle' and would
destroy more sheep than goats (because in absolute terms there are
more of them) has added to the Marxist-Leninist moral treasury chest a
value of peace. But peace with a very important qualification — *world
peace.* Soviet morality therefore does not reject all wars, but only those
which cannot be kept to local size. Thus the notion of peaceful coexistence by no means ends the battle between the 'two camps' and does
not make the battlefield into a playground. Peaceful coexistence remains
as a long-term strategic-tactical shield under the shelter of which the
'sheep' of this world can in fact better proceed in their respective corners
to assist 'historical inevitability'. Thus peaceful coexistence did not pre-
clude 'fraternal and mutual aid' to Vietnam, or the Middle East. Indeed,
this type of assistance is still regarded as a moral duty.[83] Peaceful coexistence is declared to be an objective necessity in this epoch and for
various reasons as extremely advantageous to the communist cause: the
general peaceful climate creates more favourable opportunities for the
struggle of the working class in capitalist countries, and facilitates the
struggle of the peoples of the developing countries for their liberation.
The economic co-operation of the socialist and capitalist countries
greatly assists the internal 'building of communism' in socialist countries, whilst at the same time capitalism, because of the increasingly
sharp conflict between the more and more socialised forces of production and the still private relations of production, has 'no future'.[84] Thus
it is naive to expect that détente will mean the relaxation of the ideological grip within the socialist countries or that it will mean the abandonment of the current Soviet ideological campaign, or the avoidance of
war. 'War can and must be banned as a means of resolving international
disputes. But we must not "ban" civil or national liberation wars. We

must not "ban" uprisings, and we by no means "ban" revolutionary mass movements aimed at changing the political and social status quo.'[85] The November 1975 issue of *Communist of the Armed Forces* once again reaffirmed, in fact, Moscow's acceptance of the permissibility of nuclear war, endorsing yet again 'the premise of Marxism-Leninism on war as a continuation of policy by military means'. 'The description of the correlation between war and policy is fully valid for the use of weapons of mass destruction' which makes the value of world peace less than absolute and shows how much some Western writers misunderstand the USSR when they claim that this Clausewitz, Marxist-adopted dictum was abandoned long ago in the SU because of nuclear arms.[86]

There is an end to where the study of a system of thought can take us. Many Sovietologists would hasten to add that Soviet theory and practice are far removed from each other; for instance, that 'neither force, nor tolerance nor synthetic "authority" can put the communist Humpty-Dumpty together again'[87] – if it ever held together – and that the Soviet Union long ago abandoned the revolutionary content of its ambitions, and does not in fact wish a change in the status quo at all. Its moral conceptions, however, remain Manicheanly militant. Therefore their intellectual and heuristic adequacy or inadequacy (some features of which I have tried to demonstrate in this essay) is to a great extent beside the point. Indicating the intellectual blunders of their doctrine will not stop many Soviet citizens from believing that 'happy generations of one communist world will live according to the principles of our [i.e. Soviet] more developed and accomplished communist morality'.[88] Only the next generations will be able to tell. In the meantime one should, at least for their sake, try to follow how the Soviet Union proposes to go about realising its moral goals, not only in practice but also in theory.

Notes

1. I would like to acknowledge the linguistic assistance given to me by Dr Ralph Pettman in connection with the preparation of this chapter.

2. Z. Brzezinski, *Soviet Bloc: Unity and Conflict* (Harvard University Press, 1967), pp. 388ff.

3. See H. Marcuse, *Soviet Marxism: A Critical Analysis* (Penguin, 1971), p. 16.

4. G. Fischer (ed.), *Science and Ideology in Soviet Society* (Atherton Press, New York, 1967), p. 78.

5. See e.g. Richard T. de George, *New Marxism: Soviet and East European Marxism since 1956* (Pegasus, New York, 1968).

6. Ibid., p. 140.

7. E. Kamenka, *Marxism and Ethics* (Macmillan, St Martins Press, 1969), pp. 1-2, 64.

8. E. Kamenka, *The Ethical Foundations of Marxism* (Routledge and Kegan Paul, London, 1972), p. 186.

9. R.T. de George, *Patterns of Soviet Thought: the Origins and Developments of Dialectical and Historical Materialism* (Ann Arbor, The University of Michigan Press, 1970), p. 2.

10. Cf. Soviet selection of definitions in *Moral'i eticheskaia teoria* (Morality and Ethical theory) (Moscow, 'Nauka', 1974), pp. 9ff.

11. Richard T. de George in his *Soviet Ethics and Morality* (Ann Arbor, University of Michigan Press, 1969), p. 177, which is without a doubt the best study in the English language, says that a complete bibliography of Soviet writings on ethics and morality from 1924 to 1968 would include 600 items, and of the 338 Soviet authors on the subject, only 14 have written more than three items. Thus in surveying the field it is difficult to establish the importance of individual writers or make generalisations about the subject.

12. *Kratkii slovar po etike* (Short dictionary of ethics) (Moskva, 1965), p. 226.

13. *Filozofskaia enciklopedia* (Philosophical encyclopedia) (Moskva, 1964), vol. 3., p. 499.

14. A.F. Shishkin: *Osnovy marksistskoi etiki* (Essentials of Marxist Ethics) (Moskva, Izdatel'stvo IMO, 1961), p. 14.

15. A.A. Guseinov, *Social'naia priroda nravstvennosti* (Social nature of morality) (Izdatel.stvo Moskovskogo Universiteta, 1974), pp. 14ff.

16. See for instance Svetozar Stojanović, 'Marx's Theory of Ethics', in N. Lobkowitz (ed.) *Marx and the Western World* (University of Notre Dame Press, Notre Dame, London, 1967), pp. 161-72.

17. For the debate about these categories see e.g. A.E. Furman, 'O predmete istoricheskogo materializma' (About the subject-matter of historical materialism), *Filozofskie nauki* (1965/6), pp. 85-90; M.S. Dzhunusov, 'O vsaimosviazi osnovykh poniatii istroricheskogo materializma' (About the relationship of basic notions of historical materialism), *Voprosy filozofii* (1965/7), pp. 144-6; M. Kammari, 'Nekotorye voprosy teoria bazisa i nadstroiki' (Some questions of theory of basis and superstructure (1956) 10, pp. 42-58; V.P. Tugarinov, 'O kategoriakh' obshchestevennoe bytie 'i' obshchestvennoe soznanie' (About the categories 'social existence' and 'social consciousness'), *Voprosy filozofii* (1958), 1, pp. 15ff.

18. *Filozofskii slovar* (Philosophical dictionary) (Moskva, 1965), p. 318.

19. G. Fischer (ed.), *Science and Ideology*, pp. 61-2.

20. F. Engels, *Anti-Dühring: Herr Eugen Dühring's Revolution in Science* (Lawrence and Wishart, London 1969), Chs. IX, X, XI.

21. J.V. Stalin, *Marxism and Linguistics*, in *The Essential Stalin: Major Theoretical Writings, 1905-1952*, Bruce Franklin (ed.) (Anchor Books, Doubleday & Company Inc., Garden City, N Y , 1972).

22. The Soviet authors themselves acknowledge the differences amongst their views resulting from the 'relative youth of their discipline', cf. Bandzeladze G, *Etika: opit izlozhenia systemy marksistskoi etiki* (Ethics: an attempt to systematise Marxist ethics), 2nd ed., Izdatelstvo, 'Sabchota Sakartvelo' (Tbilisi, 1970), p. 4.

23. Cf. de George, *Soviet Ethics and Morality*, pp. 13 and 27.

24. Bandzeladze, *Etika*, p. 17.

25. Guseinov, *Social'naia*, p. 19; also *Moral'i eticheskaia teoria: nekotorye aktual'nye problemy* (Morality and the ethical theory: some topical problems) (Moskva, 'Nauka', 1974), p. 47.

26. Despite the fact that recently the expression 'metaetika' has been increasingly frequently used, in the sense suggested by a Polish author M. Fritzhand in *Glowne zagadnienia i kierunki metaetyki* (Warsaw, 1970), p. 29, as the 'epistemology and methodology of normative ethics, or more broadly speaking, ethical

discourse', it is obvious that its meaning is confined to the 'methodology of Marxist ethics' with no sharp distinction along Western lines. For the debate on the subject see P.B. Petropavlovskii, 'Metodologicheskie problemy etiki' (Methodological problems of ethics), in Guseinov, *Moral' i eticheskaia teoria*, pp. 228ff.

27. Bandzeladze, *Etika*, pp. 55, 78.
28. Guseinov, *Social'naia*, p. 27.
29. Ibid., p. 19; *Moral' i eticheskaia teoria*, p. 47.
30. Bandzeladze, *Etika*, p. 66.
31. Lenin quoted in Guseinov, *Social'naia*, p. 5; see also ibid, pp. 19ff.
32. Guseinov, *Social'naia*, pp. 133 and 190, *Moral' i eticheskaia teoria*, p. 41.
33. B.C. Shtein, 'Problema prostykh norm nravstvennosti i spravedlivosti v marksistsko-leninskoi etike' (Problems of simple norms of morality and justice in Marxist-Leninist ethics), in *Aktual'nye problemy marksistsko-leninskoi etiki* (Topical problems of Marxist-Leninist ethics) (Tbilisi, 1967), p. 168.
34. Ibid., p. 164.
35. Guseinov, *Social'naia*, p. 133.
36. N.A. Trofimov, 'O perspektivakh razvitia morali i prava v ikh vzaimnom otnoshenii' (On prospects of the development of Morality and Law in their mutual relations), *Voprosy filozofii* (1962) 5, pp. 24-6.
37. *The Road to Communism: Documents of the 22nd Congress of the CPSU*, Moscow, 1961, p. 566.
38. Ibid., p. 566.
39. From 'The Tasks of the Youth Leagues', speech at the 3rd All-Russian Congress of the Russian Communist League (2 October 1920); and 'On the significance of Militant Materialism', a letter written to the periodical *Pod znamenem marksizma* (Under the Banner of Marxism) in 1922.
40. Bandzeladze, *Etika*, p. 5.
41. *Moral' i eticheskaia teoria*, p. 46.
42. G.E. Moore, *Principia Ethica* (Cambridge University Press, 1971), pp. 9ff.
43. K. Marx, *Economic and Philosophical Manuscripts, 1844, London* (Lawrence and Wishart, 1959), p. 103; K. Marx, *Critique of the Gotha Programme* in K. Marx, F.Engels, *Selected Works in One Volume* (Lawrence and Wishart, London, 1970), pp. 327-8, 320.
44. *Programme of the CPSU* (Foreign Languages Publishing House, Moscow, 1961).
45. Ibid., p. 59.
46. Ibid., p. 62.
47. Carl J. Hempel and Paul Oppenheim, 'Pattern of Scientific Explanation', in Herbert Feigl, May Brodbeck, *Reading in the Philosophy of Science* (New York, Appleton-Century, Crofts Inc., 1953), pp. 322ff.
48. A.F. Shishkin, 'Chelovek kak vysshaia tsennost' (Man as the highest value), *Voprosy filozofii* (1965) 1, pp. 3ff.
49. Guseinov, *Social'naia*, p. 10.
50. *Selected Works in One Volume*, p. 29.
51. The functional dependence of social existence and social consciousness is expressed in the philosophy of Marxism in the shape of a *law of reverse influence of social consciousness on social existence*, complemented by the *law of the increasingly active part of consciousness* (italics added), A.S. Molchanova, 'O social'no-reguliatornoi funkcii soznania' (On the social-regulatory function of consciousness), *Problemy social'nykh issledovanii* (Problems of social research) (Tomsk, 1972), p. 34.
52. Guseinov, *Social'naia*, p. 20; see also M.G. Zhuravkov, *Socializm i moral': nekotorye cherty i osobennosti formirovania morali sovetskogo obshchestva*

(Izdatel'stvo 'Nauka', Moskva, 1974), pp. 145ff.

53. Krapivensky, *The Revolution and its Moral Mission* (Novosti Press Agency Publishing House, Moscow, n.d.), p. 85.

54. Ibid., p. 88.

55. See above p.177.

56. M.A. Zhuravkov, 'XII S'ezd KPSS i nekotorye voprosy etiki' (XIInd Congress of the CPSU and some problems of ethics), *Voprosy filozofii* (1962), pp. 3ff. L.F. Il'ichev, 'Current Trends in the Party's Ideological Work', *Pravda*, (19 June 1963), in *Current Digest of the Soviet Press* (3 July 1963), pp. 5-11.

57. *Filozofskie nauki* (1966) 6, p. 123. *Voprosy filozofii* (1966) 9, p. 129.

58. P. Ehlen, *Die philosophische Ethik in der Sovjetunion* (München und Salzburg, 1972), p. 113.

59. The Party holds that the moral code of the builder of communism should comprise the following principles: devotion to the communist cause; love of the Socialist motherland and of the other socialist countries; conscientious labour for the good of society — he who does not work, neither shall he eat; concern on the part of everyone for the preservation and growth of public wealth; a high sense of public duty; intolerance of actions harmful to the public interest; collectivism and comradely mutual assistance: one for all and all for one; humane relations and mutual respect between individuals — man is to man a friend, comrade and brother; honesty and truthfulness, moral purity, modesty, and unpretentiousness in social and private life; mutual respect in the family, and concern for the up-bringing of children; an uncompromising attitude to injustice, parasitism, dishonesty, careerism and money-grubbing; friendship and brotherhood among all peoples of the USSR; intolerance of national and racial hatred; an uncompromising attitude to the enemies of communism, peace and the freedom of nations; fraternal solidarity with the working people of all countries, and with all peoples. *The Road to Communism*, pp. 566-7.

60. I refer here to John Vincent's chapter.

61. Most students of Soviet morality point out this striking similarity. See e.g. de George, *Soviet Ethics and Morality*, p. 103.

62. Brezhnev's speech at the 25th CPSU Congress, *Pravda* (25 February 1976), p. 2.

63. See note 59 above.

64. Stalin, *Report to the Eighteenth CPSU (Bolshevik) on the Work of the Central Committee* (10 March 1939), in *The Essential Stalin*, p. 384.

65. See note 59 above.

66. F.V. Konstantinov (ed.), *Sociologicheski problemy mezhdunarodnykh otnoshenii* (Sociological problems of international relations), (Moskva, 'Nauka', 1970), pp. 5ff.

67. Bandzeladze, *Etika*, p. 358.

68. Ibid., p. 366.

69. Ibid., p. 367.

70. Ibid., p. 368.

71. V. Granov, O. Nakropin 'Socialist Foreign Policy: Its Class Nature and Humanism', *International Affairs* (1965) 11, p. 11.

72. Josef Mrázek, 'A Code of Socialist international Law', *Nová Mysl*, No. 2 (February 1976), translated in RAD Background Report/63 (15 March 1976), p. 9.

73. This is, incidentally, the content of the inter-state relations between socialist and capitalist countries, i.e. 'peaceful coexistence' to which 'mutually advantageous economic, trade, scientific, technological and cultural ties' are sometimes added: e.g. *International Affairs* (1969) 10, p. 45.

74. Quoted from R.H. McNeal (ed.), *International Relations amongst*

Communists (Prentice-Hall, 1967), pp. 99-100.

75. Mrázek, 'A Code . . .' p. 7.

76. Ibid.

77. See also *Documents Adopted by the International Conference of Communist and Workers' Parties* (Moscow, Novosti, 1969).

78. F. Konstantinov, 'Internationalism and the World Socialist System', *International Affairs* (1968) 11, p. 3.

79. Z. Brzezinski, 'From Cold War to cold peace', G.R. Urban (ed.) in *Détente* (Temple Smith, London, 1976), p. 266.

80. Brezhnev's speech (see note 62). p. 4.

81. Brzezinski, 'From Cold War'.

82. Ibid.

83. Brezhnev's speech (see note 62), p. 4.

84. Ibid.

85. *Soviet World Outlook,* vol. 1, no. 2 (12 February 1976), p. 7.

86. W. Zimmermann, 'International Relations in the Soviet Union: the Emergence of a Discipline', *The Journal of Politics*, vol. 31 (1969), no. 1, p. 64.

87. Alexander Dallin, 'The USSR and World Communism', in J.W. Strong (ed.), *The Soviet Union under Brezhnev and Kosygin* (Van Nostrand Reinhold, New York, 1971), p. 223.

88. Bandzeladze, *Etika,* p. 453.

10 CONCLUSION

A little book like this one cannot pretend to have covered the water-front. Though the topic does occur in a number of the chapters the treatment of distributive economic justice in world society, for example, remains too brief. There is nothing said on the concepts of 'just war' and of 'private international violence', and American foreign policy, which post-Vietnam and with President Carter's human rights initiatives became highly conscious of moral issues, is not discussed. This said, however, the study does draw attention to a very important and a relatively neglected subject area as well as introducing the key dilemmas in the field as these appear to political practitioners and to academic analysts alike. There are limits on how many practical questions can be considered in a work of this length, and the choice of essays on China and the Soviet Union was quite deliberate since considerably less is known in the West of the moral dynamics that underpin the foreign policies of these two great powers. What American and European statesmen appear to believe or would have us believe is more readily available to the interested reader, and the fundamental terms of the debates they conduct are more familiar as well.

The racial conflict in Southern Africa is placed in the wider context of claims made by contemporary black African leaders in their pre-colonial and post-colonial predicaments. The issue is a topical one, but it also demonstrates clearly a more general phenomenon — the way morality is contingent upon politics, how claims for 'right' or 'just' consideration depend upon the possession and exercise of socio-economic power; and how possession of such power enables one to co-opt cultural perspectives and define for others what is the 'right', the 'good' and the 'true'.

In many ways, this is the heart of the matter, and it is a perennial problem that readily bears periodic restatement. Professor Miller argues that it is the lesson of experience alone that group or national moral claims are stronger than those based on humankind as a whole. One could extend this case further and argue, as Reinhold Niebuhr has done, that moral conduct is an effective option only for the individual:

> Individual men may be moral in the sense that they are able to con-
> sider interests other than their own in determining problems of

conduct; and are capable, on occasion, of preferring the advantages of others to their own. They are endowed by nature with a measure of sympathy and consideration for their kind, the breadth of which may be extended by an astute social pedagogy. Their rational faculty prompts them to a sense of justice which educational discipline may refine and purge of egoistic elements until they are able to view a social situation, in which their own interests are involved, with a fair measure of objectivity. But all these achievements are more difficult, if not impossible, for human societies and social groups. In every human group there is less reason to guide and to check impulse, less capacity for self-transcendence, less ability to comprehend the needs of others and therefore more unrestrained egoism than the individuals, who compose the group, reveal in their personal relationships.

This phenomenon Niebuhr attributes to 'collective egoism', and to the 'difficulty of establishing a rational social force which is powerful enough to cope with the natural impulses by which society achieves its cohesion'.[1]

While the utopian may be 'naive', this 'realist' position, as has been argued many times, is a distinctly 'unreal' one. The fact remains that there *are* moral judgements that transcend the national community. We may all too readily overstate their appeal, and realists argue that any universalist ethic will remain a minority point of view of limited political efficacy. Here, as E.H. Carr has pointed out, is the 'fundamental dilemma of international morality. On the one hand, we find the almost universal recognition of an international morality involving a sense of obligation to an international community or to humanity as a whole. On the other hand, we find an almost equally universal reluctance to admit that, in this international community, the good of the part (i.e. our own country) can be less important than the good of the whole'.[2] He concludes himself, however, and it is a good statement of the position, that:

Just as within the state every government, though it needs power as a basis of its authority, also needs the moral basis of the consent of the governed, so an international order cannot be based on power alone, for the simple reason that mankind will in the long run always revolt against naked power. Any international order presupposes a substantial measure of general consent. We shall, indeed, condemn ourselves to disappointment if we exaggerate the role which morality is likely to play. The fatal dualism of politics will always keep consideration of morality entangled with consideration of power. We shall never arrive at a political order in which the grievances of the weak and the few receive the same prompt attention as the grievances of the strong and the many. Power goes far to create the morality convenient to itself, and coercion is a fruitful source of consent. But when all these reservations have been made, it remains true that a new international order and a new international harmony can be built up only on the basis of an ascendancy which is generally accepted as tolerant and unoppressive or, at any rate, as preferable to any practicable alternative.[3]

This last argument becomes even more significant in the light of 'dependency' theory and a world view that complements the fact of nation-states with a consideration of global classes. If we adopt, as neo-Marxists and neo-Leninists urge us to, a picture of humankind in terms of its unequal capacities to produce, distribute and exchange goods and services, a pattern emerges of class inequalities between states and within them and a world heavily loaded in favour of the overdeveloped industrialised sectors of the globe against the rest, that goes far to explain the macro-phenomenon of exploitation. Such a picture is used to endorse claims for radical modifications to the existing world order; for a less oppressive socio-economic regime.

Doomed, as John Herz would argue,[4] to the final frustration of their idealist resolve, those who feel that the present structure of world affairs is hardly the most rational dispensation under which we might labour urge its revision. Hypocrisy, mixed motives and opportunism abound. Any success would be ambiguous at best, probably marginal, and could be brought about only at considerable cost. The feeling is a fact of world affairs, however, and from it flows the desire for change. And so it goes; our competing ideas about what is, and our diverse predilections, where we dare admit them, for what should be. We stand ever, and it is an effective symbol of our enduring plight, with water in the left hand and fire in the right.

Notes

1. Reinhold Niebuhr, *Moral Man and Immoral Society: a study in ethics and politics* (Charles Scribners' Sons, New York, 1934), pp. xi-xii.

2. E.H. Carr, *The Twenty Years' Crisis* (Macmillan, London, 1958), pp. 166-76.

3. Ibid., pp. 236-7.

4. J. Herz, *Political Realism and Political Idealism* (University of Chicago Press, Chicago, 1956), pp. 39-42.

CONTRIBUTORS

H. Bull	Balliol College, Oxford University
A.L. Burns	The Australian National University
V. Kubálková	University of Queensland
J.D.B. Miller	The Australian National University
J. Pettman	The Canberra College of Advanced Education
R. Pettman	The Australian National University
W.H. Smith	The Royal Military College, Duntroon
R.J. Vincent	The University of Keele
M. Yahuda	The London School of Economics and Political Science

INDEX

apartheid, *see* racism

balance of terror 119, 120

capitalism 26, 60, 135, 173, 185, 186, 188; bureaucratic 149
class 26
class war 28
colonialism 26, 73, 87, 110, 131, 132, 134, 139, 141, 142, 166, 194; decolonisation 138
communism 176-82, 186, 187, 188; Chinese 150; Khrushchev 150; morality, view of 53; scientific 150
cosmopolitanism 90, 98, 101, 105, 111; bourgeois 186; partisan 10

dependency 28, 61, 103, 106, 134, 142, 162, 196
determinism 175; Marxist 181, 182
development: global 24
distributive economic justice, *see* justice-distributive
duty 42, 79, 177; Machiavelli 42

elites 11
equality 10, 66, 67, 74, 97, 99, 109; racial 11, 87
ethics: Christian 23, 175; Machiavellian 23, 95; Marxist 183; personal 22; political 22; presumptive 30; Soviet 174, 175, 176, 178, 181; universalist 195
exploitation 11, 28, 135, 165

fact/value dichotomy 17, 18, 115
feudalism 149

globalisation 26

human rights 10, 17, 25, 63, 68, 69, 72, 74, 79, 80, 81, 82, 84, 85, 88, 90, 96, 194
humanism 185
humanitarianism 94

idealism 10, 62, 65, 73, 74, 102
imperialism 26, 60, 147, 149, 154, 155, 163, 166; in Africa 131; social 157

independence: Chinese concept of 11, 149, 150, 157, 159, 163, 165, 167; economic 161
individualism 81
injustice 11, 115, 116, 117; economic 123; racial 123, 135
internationalism 153, 154; proletarian 149, 153, 164, 165, 186, 187; socialist 186, 187
intervention 71, 83; non-intervention 70

justice 11, 17, 39, 48, 49, 52, 53, 60, 63, 70, 92, 95, 97, 99, 108, 115, 125, 177; as compensation 109, 110, 111; as fairness 54; corrective 54, 68; distributive 10, 54, 68, 92, 94, 98, 100, 105, 106, 194; economic 28, 87, 92; global 93, 94, 103, 104, 111; international 97, 98, 105, 109, 111; Marxian concept of 97; national 98, 102, 111; Nozick's theory of 100, 104; Rawls's theory of 29, 61, 99, 100, 104, 105, 106, 107, 108; social 30, 40; universal 180

liberation movements: in Africa 136, 137, 139

materialism: dialectical 179; historical 179, 181
Marxism 135, 173, 180; Marxism-Leninism 170
morality: as science 174; bourgeois 182; Christian 55, 56, 115, 126; Greek concept of 18, 54; group 36; Marxist 172, 174; socialist 182; Soviet 183, 188; universal 36, 47, 48, 50, 52, 53, 65, 74, 176, 183

nation: state 11
national independence 139, 143, 155, 166
national interest 37, 133
national liberation 149, 154, 155, 166; wars of 185, 188
nationalism: African 131, 135, 142; Chinese 151
natural law 23, 24, 25, 39, 41, 46, 53,

THE MYTH MAKERS

THE
MYTH MAKERS

Literary Essays

V.S. Pritchett

Random House
New York

Library of Congress Cataloging in Publication Data
Pritchett, Victor Sawdon, Sir, 1900—
The mythmakers.
Bibliography: p.
1. Literature, Modern—19th century—History and criticism—Addresses,
essays, lectures. 2. Literature, Modern—20th century—History and
criticism—Addresses, essays, lectures.   I.   Title.
PN761.P7   1979   809   78-21801
ISBN 0-394-50472-0

The essays in this volume are revised versions of work originally published
in *The New Statesman, The New York Review of Books* and *The New Yorker.*
Acknowledgments are made by the author to the editors of these periodicals.

Manufactured in the United States of America

2 4 6 8 9 7 5 3

FOR MY WIFE

Contents

PASTERNAK

Unsafe Conduct

THE SUPPRESSION OF *Dr Zhivago* in 1957 exposed the obsequious proceedings of the Union of Soviet Writers to international ridicule and contempt. We know now that after publishing a portion of autobiography, *Safe Conduct*, in 1931, Pasternak had published no original work under the Stalinist repression between 1932 and 1943 and that he was silenced by the absurd gauleiter Zhdanov from 1946 to 1954. Cautiously Pasternak planned a collection of poems to introduce an *Essay in Autobiography*, his natural mode, which would have prepared the way for a fuller understanding of the novelist's idiosyncrasy and imagination, and the changes they passed through since *Safe Conduct* was written.

The *Essay* was translated by Manya Harari in 1959. It is short enough to give some idea, Pasternak says, 'of how in my individual case, life became converted into art and art was born of life and experience'. It is a reminiscence touched upon tactfully and confined within the narrator's intimate circle. To take the story further and describe a 'world, unique and not to be compared with any other', a writer would have to write 'in such a way as to make the hair rise and the heart falter'. So the book is a reticent sketch, but does draw at least an outline. As Edward Crankshaw says in his warm introduction, Pasternak's battle has been with himself. Is there any other battle for an artist? His achievement is to have upheld the fact of the artist's conscience in a time when committees, programme makers, administrators and so on, thought literature had obligations to *them*! 'I dislike my style before 1940,' Pasternak says, 'just as I quarrel with half

9

of Mayakovsky's writing and some of Yesenin's. I dislike the disintegrating forms, the impoverished thought and the littered, uneven language of those days. It is more important in life to lose than to acquire. Unless the seed dies it bears no fruit.' *Safe Conduct*—the earlier autobiography—dies: *Dr Zhivago* is born. *Safe Conduct* is a congested poetic embryo.

Part of Pasternak's tenacity comes from his upbringing and an inherited, strong yet evasive gaiety of spirit. The *Essay* sketches a family and circle of like-minded friends dedicated to the arts. The father, a painter, was a friend of Tolstoy; the mother, a distinguished pianist. Scriabin came to the house and the young Pasternak decided to become a composer and pianist. The portraits are less reminiscent than active, for Pasternak's prose, even in translation, has the present clarity of notes struck on the keys of a piano. The preoccupation with the ideas of resurrection and rebirth must have, I think, a link with the re-creating effect of music which never embalms a past. Scriabin and the elder Pasternak went for walks:

> Scriabin liked to take a run and then go on skipping along the road like a stone skimming the water, as if at any moment, he might leave the ground and glide on air. In general, he had trained himself in various kinds of sublime lightness and un-burdened movement verging on flight.

He defended Nietzsche, and we find in Pasternak's comment the traditional Russian feeling for the limitless. It was also Dostoevsky's:

> Scriabin's defence of the superman was an expression of his native Russian craving for the superlative. Indeed, it is not only true that music needs to be more than itself if it is to mean anything, but that everything in the world must surpass itself in order to be itself. There must be something limitless in a human being and in his activity for either to have definition and character.

The elder Pasternak had to make a drawing of Tolstoy on his deathbed at the station of Astapovo; the son went with him. In the corner of the room lay

> a wrinkled old man, one of the dozens of old men invented by Tolstoy and scattered through his books. The place bristled with fir saplings which stood round the bed, their outlines sharpened by the setting sun. Four slanting sheaves of light reached across the room and threw over the corner where the body lay the sign of the big shadow of the crosspiece of the window and the small childish crosses of the shadows of the firs.

Outside the World Press 'brayed' and waiters at the station restaurant were galloping about with plates of 'underdone beef steaks. Beer flowed like a river'. The word 'underdone' evokes the whole of journalism in one of its raw and macabre news-gathering fiestas.

Pasternak gave up music because he found he lacked perfect pitch. He was sent to Germany for his education, travelled to Venice. He was the equipped intellectual. He felt the excitement of that iconoclasm which was to provoke the last glories of art in Europe. The poets Mayakovsky, Yesenin, Marina Tsvetayeva and Paolo Yashili come in. There is excitement and argument and then the aftermath; the tragic list of suicides—Mayakovsky killing himself (out of pride); Yesenin (without thinking it out) carelessly; Marina Tsvetayeva because she could not put her work between herself and the reality of daily life any longer; Yashili bewitched by the purges. There is compassion for the wretched Fadaev, the novelist who sold out:

> And it seems to me that Fadaev, still with the apologetic smile which had somehow stayed with him through all the crafty ins and outs of politics, told himself just before he pulled the trigger: 'Well, now it's all over. Good-bye, Sasha'.

Fadaev once told me that the decline in the drawing of grotesque characters in the Soviet novel was due to the fact that, under Communism, people were better integrated!

To go back 28 years to *Safe Conduct* is to meet the affected Pasternak. His self-criticism is just. Edited by Stefan Schimanski, it was first published abroad in 1945 and has been reissued with an introduction by J. M. Cohen. The translation is by Beatrice Scott. Robert Payne has done the stories, which include *Aerial Ways* and *The Childhood of Luvers*. Mr Cohen translates the poems. Another version of *Safe Conduct*, the stories and poems, comes from Alec Brown and Lydia Pasternak-Slater. I prefer the Beatrice Scott translation: Mr Alec Brown is heroically literal when dealing with the images, but he is conventional and commonplace in the straightforward writing. It is not surprising that translators differ and that they should drop sentences in the dazzle they have to face. Here are two versions of the firework scene in Venice. From Beatrice Scott:

> Under the open sky the faces of the audience glowed with a clarity which is characteristic of the baths, as in a covered wonderfully illuminated hall. Suddenly from the ceiling of this imaginary ballroom fell a slight shower. But hardly had it begun when the rain ceased. The reflection of the illuminations simmered above the square in a coloured dimness. The bell tower of St Mark's cut like a red marble rocket into the rose mist in wreaths halfway up to its summit. A little farther off dark-olive steams circled, and as in a fairy tale the five-headed shell of the Cathedral hid within them.

Mr Alec Brown's version is rhetorical. It begins:

> The outdoor audience was drenched in a bathhouse froth of brilliance, as if in a magnificently illuminated ballroom. All at once a fictitious ceiling began gently sprinkling it as if the assembled audience were a seminal square of the far north. Scarcely had a shower of another sort begun than it suddenly ceased.

In what way can a square be seminal? Mr Brown has 'whorls of dark purple vapour' for Miss Scott's 'dark olive steams'. Miss Scott's renderings of Pasternak's reflections on the fertilizing conflicts in European culture are far clearer than Mr Brown's and the two translators have a serious difference of meaning in the passage on the roles of the genius, iconoclast and rebel. In Pasternak, the stress on tradition is strong; without it, he says, the rebellious are 'empty-handed'.

Safe Conduct is a longer, richer, denser autobiographical work than the *Essay* is. It contains a throbbing account of the poet's relationship with Mayakovsky and of the wild scene of grief at his death. Simplicity and the sense of the limitless favour the Russians in the expression of extreme emotions. The Western reader toils to impose order as he reads. One sees this again in the story of Pasternak's short love duel with his pretty cousin in Marburg in his student days. Each moment of this experience— and of all others—is so sensuously active that we have the characteristic Pasternak vision of chaotic sense impressions, all spring and the effervescence of the blood, yet enclosed as by a serene medallion. The affectations of style and the teasing out of the thought have their difficulty, which is a torture for translators who cannot catch the tone of a poet whose mind has been formed by music and, to some extent, by painting. One has one's doubts, in prose at any rate, about the value of putting one art to the service of another. In the story *Childhood of Luvers*, the beauty of the tale and the deep perception into a girl's life take time to emerge from the orchestration.

Pasternak never looks from society to the individual. Society is some formless thing, a general fate or flux of circumstance which, in his lifetime, has been riven by events that are like inexplicable storms and lightning—a symphony of which he does not know the score, but he does know that it cannot exist without him. Only, much later on, in the far future, will it be possible to understand what happened and what the symphony was.

There, once more, is the traditional Russian nostalgia for the future. It is a faith in distance. Pasternak is not a closed and accomplished egoist. His feeling for the autobiographical comes from a capacity for living and re-living and putting passion into it. His continual reflections on memory are those of one who thinks of memory not as a fixed picture, but as a force in motion, perhaps like a storm that has passed, but is still banked up and reverberating. The present has its *élan* because it is always on the edge of the unknown and one misunderstands the past unless one remembers that this unknown was once part of its nature. For this reason Pasternak is able to raid the past and carry off people and places from it with the gleam of their own passion and bewilderment still on them. Such a view of life is poetic in the absolute sense. It is as hostile to the academic attitude to literature—Pushkin's feelings for his wife are more important than Pushkinism—as it is to the -isms of religion, politics, history and economics. It is the role of the poet to look at what is happening in the world and to know that quite other things are happening.

Those who expect some kind of counter-revolutionary or anti-Soviet journalism from *Dr Zhivago* will be disappointed. It is not, in that sense, a political novel at all, although it is entirely about the effects of the revolution of 1905, the first world war, the 1917 revolution and the last war, upon a group of families of the upper-class intelligentsia and others. Pasternak is a-political. His temper is Christian; Marxism is dismissed scornfully as half-baked folly and pomposity. The ground is cleared for an account of what really happens to people in catastrophe and the human, moral and spiritual loss. Pasternak has written a confession of anguish. We see it largely in the experiences of Dr Zhivago, a young doctor and poet who is neither for nor against the regime, but who suffers and endures. The son of an alcoholic, wild millionaire whose suicide is unforgettably described in the opening chapter, Zhivago is a man

torn in half by events. He survives for a long time partly because
he is a doctor. He sympathises with the revolutionary desire for
social justice but many of his friends are on the White rather
than the Red side. His chief idea is to save his wife and family
and to get away from Moscow to some peaceful spot. He gets
them, after an appalling journey, to Siberia. He is separated
from them when he is taken prisoner by Partisans who need a
doctor, although he frankly tells them he is not of their party.
When he escapes he finds his wife has got away to Paris. He is
starving and pursued but—cool, indecisive, numbed in heart by
suffering—he makes no attempt to join her; neither, at the end
of his long and moving love-affair with a woman called Lara—
whom we have met earlier as a seduced schoolgirl—does he
stick to her and save himself. Wrecked in health and demoral-
ized, he goes to pieces in Moscow, marries a peasant girl, deserts
her and dies, eventually, of a heart attack while trying to open
the window of a Moscow tram. He is the complete Soviet non-
hero; yet at his death, his poems and diaries are treasured by the
young generation. They recognize the integrity of the irre-
claimable citizen who has only a grudging respect for the Soviet
system.

As a novelist's just interpretation of the rights and wrongs of
history and revolution, *Dr Zhivago* is useless. A political critic
would say that it wilfully left out half the drama and argument.
Pasternak would agree. He would add that people who are
living history cannot know what history really is. Dr Zhivago
himself is a passive and truthful character—a man out of E. M.
Forster—and he survives, as long as he does, by submission to
fate. This is a strength because he is inflexible in the sense
of vocation. He reminds one of Chekhov.

The temper of Zhivago's mind can be judged best in a few
passages. Back from the Front in the first world war and seeing
the revolution, he finds his upper-class friends colourless:

The fooling, the right of idleness enjoyed by the few while the majority suffered, could itself create an illusion of genuine character and originality.

But how quickly, once the lower classes and the rich had lost their privileges, how these people faded! How effortlessly they had given up the habit of independent thought—which at this rate could never in fact have been genuinely theirs!

On the leap from peace to 'mass insanity and to the savagery of daily, hourly, legalized, rewarded slaughter', Zhivago says:

> It was then that falsehood came to our Russian land. The great misfortune, the root of all the evil to come, was the loss of faith in the value of personal opinions. People imagined that it was out of date to follow their moral sense, that they must all sing in chorus, and live by other people's notions, the notions that were being crammed down everybody's throat. And there arose the power of the glittering phrase, first tsarist and then revolutionary. . . . Instead of being natural and spontaneous as we had always been we began to be idiotically pompous with each other.

He is sick of 'claptrap in praise of the revolution and the regime'. He can't accept that 'they' are all radiant heroes and he 'a mean little fellow'. A brilliant diagnostician, he is interested in mimesis in organisms. He gives a lecture, and there is a party outcry against his 'idealism, mysticism, neo-Schellingism'. The vulgarity of it disgusts him. Antipov—the husband of Lara, Zhivago's mistress—is a commissar whose star is beginning to fade. He is infected by obsessive self-criticism and the desire to confess:

> It was the disease, the revolutionary madness of the age; that in his heart everyone was utterly different from his words and the outward appearance he assumed. No-one had a clear conscience. Everyone had some reason to feel that he was guilty of everything, that he was an impostor, an undetected criminal. The

slightest pretext was enough to launch an orgy of self-torture. People slandered and accused themselves, not only out of terror but of their own will, from a morbidly destructive impulse, in a state of metaphysical trance, carried away by that passion for self-condemnation, which cannot be checked once it has been given free rein.

Zhivago's perennial longing is to get away from the emptiness and dullness of human verbosity and to take refuge in nature, in sleep, in grinding labour or understanding 'rendered speechless by emotion'.

But Zhivago's musings are a small part of a book which has countless precise pictures of revolutionary happenings, as they appeared to the private eye of the characters. Some, like the young Zhivago, the young Lara, the young Pasha, the young Tonya, have grown up in quiet intellectual circles; but there are the railway workers, the peasants, individuals taken out of the Russian mass and soon to be scattered, martyrized or transformed. In twenty-odd years they became unrecognizable to one another. The shy Pasha will become the truculent commissar; Lara, the sensual, tormented girl who was seduced while still at school, will become the austere hospital nurse, the difficult wife and—after her sufferings—the tragic mistress. Fatal separations come sooner or later to all and destroy the heart.

From the point of realism, Pasternak's use of far-fetched coincidence to bring about meetings with his characters is absurd; but this book is really a romance in which the novelist is seeking the lineament or texture of a fate, not the detail of adventure or a construct of event and character. He jumps, without explanation, to new places and situations. How does Zhivago escape arrest after his unpopular lecture? How does he get to his hiding place in the forest? How did he intrigue? What happens to Lara when she is torn from Zhivago and goes off to degradation in China? These things are left out or are slurred over. The very slurring adds to our sense of the immeasurable quality of the general disaster. He conveys that cataclysms observably remove *meaning* from people's lives without leaving them futile.

Several large episodes stand out in the book, especially the long, quiet and unforgettable account of the Zhivago family's journey of escape by cattle-truck to Siberia. It takes them into the heart of the civil war, and yet (by a freak of war) into a village which is little touched by it and still living the old life. There are small episodes like the grotesque death of the revolutionary soldier Gintz who slips into a water-butt when he is making a speech. Simply because this happens suddenly and he looks so silly, a Cossack shoots him. Pasternak has an eye for the gratuitous actions of life; it deceives both in its fears and assurances. When the street fighting breaks out in Moscow, the Zhivago family is far more preoccupied with a fanatical attempt to make their stove work. Their child gets a sore throat and temperature and the guests they are sheltering bore them with ceaseless chatter. That is how revolution comes. Everywhere people are carrying their core of private life about with them. There is no cliché of invention in Pasternak; there is no eccentricity either. He has the eye of nature. Another refreshing quality is the freedom from the Anglo–American obsession with sex. In love, he is concerned with the heart. It is hard to imagine an English, French or American novel on Pasternak's subject, that would not be an orgy of rape or creeping sexuality.

Dr Zhivago is a great mound of minutely observed particulars and this particularity is, of course, expressive of his central attitude—his stand for private life and integrity. Even the look of the newspaper in which Zhivago reads the first news of the revolution is described. He stands reading, overwhelmed, in the snow which 'covered the pages with a grey, rustling, snowy gruel'. There is a similar instantaneous detail in the lovely observations of nature. The snow melts, the forest comes to life in the smoking and steaming months of the thaw.

Ancient pine trees, perched on dizzy heights, drank moisture almost from the clouds and it foamed and dried a rusty white at their roots like beer-foam on a moustache. The very sky, drunk with spring and giddy with its fumes, thickened with clouds. Low clouds, drooping at the edges like felt, sailed over the woods, and rain leapt from them, warm, smelling of soil and sweat, and washing the last of the armour-plating of ice from the earth.

Yury woke up, stretched, raised himself on one elbow and looked and listened.

At another point, in a vermin-infested house, he writes of the rats, flopping down and squealing in their 'disgusting, pitiful, contralto voices'.

Dr Zhivago might be called an autobiography which breaks the rules and turns novel, reckless of form and restrictions of point of view. Pasternak never resists any hour of life that can be crystallized and fixed for ever, even if it is a digression. But we can guess, from Dr Zhivago's notes and especially from one which defends the 'seemingly incongruous jumble of things and ideas in the work of the Symbolists against the charge of stylistic fancy', that Pasternak's writing lives in the instant. The chief characters appear and then dive out of sight into time. Moving, urgent, vivid, they are suddenly swept away into nothingness. Zhivago's mistress vanishes into the street, was probably arrested (he says) and died in some labour camp 'as so many people did in those days'.

This does not make them seem futile. Zhivago's demoralization has the effect of giving edge to his moral criticism. He is scornful when two of his friends, who are jailed and 're-educated', boast of their reformation: Dudorov taking the textbook orthodoxy of his sentiments as a sign of humanity. 'Men who are not free, he thought, idealize their bondage,' says Zhivago.

Health is ruined by the systemic duplicity forced on people if you say the opposite of what you feel, if you grovel before what you dislike and rejoice at what brings you nothing but misfortune. Your nervous system isn't a fiction, it's a fact of your physical body and your soul exists in space and is inside you like the teeth in your head. You can't keep isolating it with impunity. I found it painful to listen to you, Nicky, when you told how you were re-educated and grew up in jail. It was like listening to a circus horse describing how it broke itself in.

The doctor is the self-perfecting man and saint who goes downhill as a citizen. He refuses to be neutered by mediocre optimism. His story marks the return to the compassion of the great Russian tradition and repudiates the long, long reign of highly-coloured journalism and neo-Victorianism in Soviet writing.

SOLZHENITSYN

The Gulag Circle

As a novelist Solzhenitsyn is very much in the powerful tradition of the nineteenth-century Russian novel as it appears in the prophet-preacher writings of Tolstoy and Dostoevsky, now one, now the other; as a polemical writer, in the tradition of Belinsky and Herzen. If history has altered his ground, another difference seems to me important. As far as one can judge he is far removed from the influences Western genius had upon his predecessors—for example, Shakespeare, Cervantes, Sterne, Dickens—his indoctrination as a young Komsomol was political and scientific. It is true that he was a poet, had read the poets of the revolutionary period and intended to be a novelist, but the tendencies of his youth drew him to the documentary and his unrest to a documentary which defied the Stalinist political monopoly of this mainly 'useful' form of writing. Since he is a passionate man, equipped with searing powers of irony, he was certain to find that man does not live by the record alone, but by the myths he creates, myths which contain his private thoughts and that sense of being 'elsewhere' when dogma becomes despotic. From Tolstoy and Dostoevsky, and as a man of imagination, he learned to hate contemporary materialism. There is a passage in the last of the Gulag volumes which makes the point:

> We don't mind having a fellow countryman called Lev Tolstoy. It's a good trade-mark. (Even makes a good postage stamp.) Foreigners can be taken on trips to Yasnaya Polyana. . . . But my dear countryman, if someone takes Tolstoy seriously, if a real-life Tolstoyan springs up among us—hey, look out there! Mind you don't fall under our caterpillar tracks.

Not exactly the *style* of Tolstoy; it is closer to the crowd style of Dostoevsky.

Solzhenitsyn's reputation was made by the simple stark reporting of the horror and degradation of the labour camps, in *One Day in the Life of Ivan Denisovich*. The title phrase 'one day' is not only a clue to its immediacy, but far more to the tradition that the Russian novelists do not move by plot-time—which is an artifice—but by the felt hours of the day that run into each other. In its simplicity this 'story' is still the finest and most apprehensible thing he has written, for the prophet-preacher does not obtrude upon the simple character whose humble tale is told. He became a novelist in *Cancer Ward* and *First Circle*. Here documentary and the novel merge. The autobiographical element is strong but the symbols grow larger than the personal report of the author's own story. *Cancer Ward* is close to his own history. A twenty-six-year-old Captain of Artillery in East Prussia, with a university degree in mathematics and physics, he was sentenced to eight years of forced labour, for making derogatory remarks about Stalin. He was not freed until 1956. In exile in Kazakhstan where, in his time, Dostoevsky had also been sent—Solzhenitsyn was treated for a tumour and recovered. In this picaresque novel—the sick are the picaros of contemporary life—we get a day-by-day account of the life of an overcrowded cancer hospital, an exhaustive analysis of how cancer distorts the life stories of the patients and the doctors, and this is a way of describing what Russian life is really like outside. Hospital is like prison; it isolates. Every man and woman has his tale on his tongue; having cancer is a way of life. The people are all far from home, owing to the war or exile, and one sees the part played by distance, anarchy, and chance. The hospital is really an obscene Collective. Illness and overwork pretty well destroy private relationships; the irony is that the unanswerable punishments of Nature free one from the malice of the Secret Police and one has a brief liberty before one dies. The comedy is black: a philologist, for example, gets cancer of the larynx! No more languages for him. If you are a Party man, like the careerist Rusanov, you are astonished that your power has gone. His bed lies between the beds of two men condemned to exile:

> If Pavel Nikolayevich were the same man he had been before he entered hospital, he would have gone and raised the question as a matter of principle—how could they put executive officials among dubious, socially harmful elements? But in the five weeks that the tumour had pulled him about as if he were a fish on a hook, Pavel Nikolayevich had either mellowed or become a simpler man.

Rusanov is quietly drawn as a Iudushka or hypocrite—see Shchedrin's classic portrait of the Russian Judas in *The Golovlyov Family*—a tedious, self-complacent, and exacting bureaucrat: he thinks he has the right to be the first to read the Party newspaper when it is brought to the ward; he is a glutton for all the boring articles about economics and politics. At first illness terrifies him, but as he recovers, his arrogance returns. Still, he has been a little mellowed until a new fear arises from the news that a new Presidium has been elected and that an investigation of the delinquencies of Stalinism will take place. He is calmed by his awful go-getting daughter who has written a few poems and has just intrigued her way into the Union of Soviet Writers. She tells her father that he need not worry; its only a question of knowing the ropes and she has learned the tricks. He need not worry too much about that shameful intrigue by which he arranged to have someone sent to a labour camp in order to get the man's apartment.

The cancer ward is, of course, a symbol of Russia under Stalinism. The patients talk of their lives and their beliefs, and above all of the conflict between those who believe in power and those who rebelliously think of private happiness. Most accept the Communist society; it is daily life. But the experience of one or two has shown them what has been lost: the moral ideal of socialism. (The loss is like the loss of the American dream.) The ward is a sort of confessional. So far the limits of the novel are familiar; but halfway through there is a scene which shows Solzhenitsyn breaking new ground. He gives us that portrait of a happy family, the simple, ingenuous Kadims who, expecting nothing from the life of harsh exile, had found an absurd happiness with their dogs and cats: it recalls the idyllic pages of *Oblomov*. Solzhenitsyn is opening a window on a subject that has so far been obsessive and claustrophobic. In *First Circle*, he is quietly in command of powers that were scattered and now, like the great novelists, can control an orchestrated theme. The idea is taken from Dante. The first circle of Hell in Dante is the fate of the pre-Christian philosophers who are doomed to live there for eternity, and it is represented by the Mavrino Institute for scientific research on the outskirts of Moscow. The year is 1949, Stalin is ageing and becoming more ruthless. The Institute is staffed by scientists, engineers and academicians who have been taken out of the labour camps to do technical work under conditions only slightly less awful than the brutal conditions of the camps, for though they eat better, they are still cut off almost completely from their families. Most have been prisoners for ten years; at the end of it, their terms will probably be extended to twenty-five. They know they are there for eternity. With them, under the efficient police system, work a number of free workers from outside who go home at night and who act, together with some of the prisoners themselves, as informers. Eternal damnation could not be more certain. If their particular usefulness comes to an end, the prisoners will be returned to the savage camps and die at last in the prison hospital. It is exactly like the system applied to foreign workers by the Nazis during the war: feed them little, exhaust their muscles and brains, and let them die.

But eternal damnation is a kind of freedom, just as having cancer is. The prisoners of Mavrino have adapted themselves to their fate. Among them is the brilliantly drawn Rubin, a Jew and Party member, a philologist who was an organizer of sabotage in Germany during the war: then there are Nerzhin, a mathematician who has been a soldier; Pryanchikov, an engineer; Spiridon, a peasant and glass blower who has been taken on by mistake: Doronin, a young double agent: Sologdin, a designer, a recalcitrant in for a twenty-five year stretch. Their task is sinister: to design an apparatus for codifying speech patterns and tracing telephone calls—a machine that Stalin has specially asked for. It will lead to a huge increase in arrests and the novel indeed opens with a scene in which Innokenty Volodin, a diplomat, foolishly uses the telephone to warn a friend not to give a certain medicine to a foreign professor. By the end of the novel the completed apparatus traps him. It is typical of Solzhenitsyn that women play only a small part in the book. They are lost, touching, lonely figures and in only two or three chapters do they have any part. Incidentally, one characteristically Victorian aspect of the book is its scant interest in the perverting of sexual life in prison. Love is sorrow and sex is 'outside' and regarded as rather disgraceful. The idea owes something to Russian puritanism.

Within Solzhenitsyn's scheme, we see the curious nervous eagerness of life in prison, listen to the life stories, watch the effect of prison on character—on the guards and officials in charge. The prisoners are known as *zeks*:

. . . One of those age old prison arguments was in progress. When is it best to be imprisoned? The way the question was put presupposed that no one was ever destined to avoid prison. Prisoners were inclined to exaggerate the number of other prisoners. When, in fact, there were only 12 to 15 million human beings in captivity, the zeks believed there were 20 or even 30 million. They believed that hardly any males were still free. 'When is it best to be imprisoned?' simply meant was it better in one's youth or in one's declining years. Some zeks, usually the young ones, cheerfully insisted that it was better to be imprisoned in one's youth. Then one had a chance to learn what it meant to live, what really mattered and what was crap; then at the age of 35, having knocked off a ten year term, a man could build his life on intelligent foundations. A man who'd been imprisoned in old age could only suffer because he hadn't 'lived right', because his life had been a chain of mistakes, and because those mistakes could no longer be corrected. Others—usually these older men—would maintain no less optimistically that being imprisoned in old age is, on the contrary, like going on a modest pension into a monastery; one had already drawn everything from life in one's best years. (In a prisoner's vocabulary 'Everything' narrowed down to the possession of a female body, good clothes, good food and alcohol.) They went on to prove that in camp you couldn't take much hide off an old man, whereas you could wear down and cripple a young man, so that afterwards he 'wouldn't even want to get a woman'.

Rubin, the logical Jewish Communist, accepts prison, because 'the ways of Socialist truth are sometimes tortuous'. He has a violent row with Sologdin, the unrepentant designer, that goes to the heart of the novel. The row is about ends and means. An excellent distinction is made: Rubin's situation 'seemed to him tragic in the Aristotelian sense'. He had been

dealt a blow by the hands of those he loved the most (the Party). He had been imprisoned by unfeeling bureaucrats because he loved the common cause to an improper degree. As a result of that tragic contradiction, in order to defend his dignity and that of his comrades, Rubin found himself compelled to stand up daily against the prison officers and guards whose actions, according to his view of the world, were determined by a totally true, correct and progressive law.

The other zeks are against him and persecute him. The quarrels are wrecking the health of this clever, emotional man. Sologdin is his worst persecutor.

> Sologdin knew very well that Rubin was not an informer and would never be one. But at the moment the temptation was great to lump him with the security officers. . . .

Sologdin says:

> 'Since all of us have been imprisoned justly and you're the only exception, that means our jailers are in the right. Every year you write a petition asking for a pardon . . .'
> 'You lie! Not asking for a pardon, but for a review of my case.'
> 'What's the difference?'
> 'A very big difference indeed.'

As a Party member, though in disgrace, Rubin makes his Jesuitical point.

'They turn you down and you keep on begging,' Sologdin reports. And, Sologdin says, *he* would never demean himself, by begging. (And in fact, he doesn't: Sologdin is a student of human weakness. He shrewdly waits till he has a brilliant idea about the encoding device and boldly plays one prison official off against another in a feat of blackmail which is the only thing officials are frightened of.)

And now we see Solzhenitsyn's mastery as a novelist: he is able to see the consoling contradictions of human nature and how they fertilize character. Rubin is not only the subtle and passionate Jewish Marxist and 'sea-lawyer': he is also the born Jewish comedian: he entertains the prisoners with a farcical historical parody of their own trials, filled with faked evidence from poetry, prison slang and innuendoes. And there is even more to this richly sympathetic man. His successes make him miserable and he becomes the practical Jewish mystic who is working on a plan for ritualizing Communist life by introducing Civic Temples!

The density of Solzhenitsyn's texture owes everything to the ingenious interlocking of incidents that are really short stories. This is the form in which he excels. His philosophical and political debates are always in this lively and purposive story form. He never fails to move forward. And the stories build up the central idea. The later tendentious Tolstoy is an obvious influence, more marked than Dostoevsky's in *The House of the Dead*. Our eye is on the most tragic character: Nerzhin, and his concern with what a man must do with his life. It is through his sorrow that we see that, bad as the lot of the prisoners is, the lot of their wives whom they can scarcely ever see or write to is a worse imprisonment in the open. They dare not easily admit that their husbands are political prisoners, for they will be shunned. Guilt by association is like plague: one is unclean. Nerzhin is a genuine stoic—in contrast to the endangered diplomat Volodin who is a genuine epicurean. Both men know they are doomed. In his early days as a Communist Nerzhin had noticed that educated or 'liberal' prisoners always let him down in a crisis; he turned idealistically to 'the People' in the labour camps and found they were worse.

> It turned out that the People had no homespun superiority. . . . They were no more firm of spirit as they faced the stone walls of a ten-year term. They were no more far-sighted than he during the difficult moments of transport and body searches. They were blinder and more trusting about informers. They were more prone to believe the crude deception of the bosses. . . .

With great tact Nerzhin nevertheless cultivates the peasant Spiridon who feels tragically the separation from his family, because in the family he saw the only meaning to life. He can never argue or think much but hits the nail on the head, peasant-fashion, with a proverb. His eventual reply to the question 'How can anyone on earth really tell who is right and who is wrong? Who can be sure?' is devastating:

The wolfhound is right and the cannibal is wrong.

(Solzhenitsyn has read Hemingway and this scene reminds one of the only good thing in *For Whom the Bell Tolls*—the long talk with the Spanish peasant at the bridge in the Guadarrama.) Spiridon's view of life (Nerzhin sees) has an important and rare characteristic: it is his own. Nerzhin reflects:

> What was lacking in most of them (the People) was that personal *point of view* which becomes more precious than life itself.
>
> There was only one thing left for Nerzhin to do—to be himself ... the People is not everyone who speaks our language, nor yet the elect marked by the fiery stamp of genius. Not by birth, not by the work of one's hands, not by the wings of education, is one elected into the people.
>
> But by one's inner self.
>
> Everyone forgets his inner self year after year. One must try to temper, to cut, to polish one's soul so as to become *a human being.*
>
> And thereby become a tiny particle of one's people.

Nerzhin's integrity detaches him from the others; on matters of regulation and principle he risks everything with the officials and guards and insists on straight or cold ironic confrontations. They fear his powers of irony. Naturally—and he knows it—he will be sent back to the labour camp. He has understood the awful words 'For ever' as few of the others have; the words mean 'You have exhausted your power to hurt me'.

A passionate and agonized book like Dostoevsky's *The House of the Dead* owes much to the Romantic belief in the supreme value of suffering which is often said to be fundamental among Slavs. Prison has the monastic lure. Many of Solzhenitsyn's characters are haunted by this acceptance, but there is nothing mystical or romantic in him. He is quite clear that the Mavrino is not the Chateau d'If or Gorky's Siberia, that something has gone morally wrong and that courage in a changed attitude to the self is the important thing. He is, as I have said, more Tolstoyan than Dostoevskian.

The novel is not a sprawling, flat panorama, in spite of its range of scenes inside and outside prison. It has a serene command of space and time. It has architectural unity, and once the uneasy opening chapters are over, it is unshakeable. This beginning does contain, in my opinion, one weakness: the novelist has, with a daring which I find merely journalistic, introduced a live portrait of the ageing Stalin alone in his rooms. I simply do not believe the following words:

> But reviewing in his mind the not-so-complex history of the world, Stalin knew that with time people would forgive everything bad, even forget it, even remember it as something good. Entire peoples were like Lady Anne, the widow in Shakespeare's *Richard III*. Their wrath was short-lived, their will not steadfast, their memory weak—they would always be glad to surrender themselves to the victor.

A word about Solzhenitsyn's style: in these novels it is close to the vernacular and spiced with slang and proverbs and in two respects resembles the plain style of Swift: it sways between savage, educated irony and the speech of the people. Solzhenitsyn delights in exposing official prose and its deceits. There are two passages in *First Circle* which comment on the 'popular' or 'newspaper' style used by the poets when they addressed 'the People'.

> Mayakovsky, for instance, considered it an honour to use a newspaper clipping as an epigraph for a poem. In other words he considered it an honour not to rise above the newspapers. But then why have literature at all?

For a good reason

a great writer—forgive me, perhaps I shouldn't say this, I'll lower my voice—a great writer is so to speak a second government, that's why no regime anywhere has ever loved its great writers only its minor ones.

Whether Solzhenitsyn still intends to complete the historical trilogy he began in *August 1914* and continued in the fragment *Lenin in Zurich* is not clear. The influence of the Tolstoy of *War and Peace* is explicit. The subject of *August 1914* is the invasion of East Prussia and the military disaster of Tannenberg and that is the perfect Tolstoyan subject. It contains all the ironies: a General Staff corrupted by court favouritism and more concerned with seniority than battle; a muddled and ill-prepared campaign; yet a defeat which nevertheless did draw off so many German troops from the West that it enabled the French to save Paris at the Marne. There were two rival and out-of-date plans of campaign; drive into East Prussia with overwhelming manpower, cut off the East Prussian salient at the shoulder and encircle it: or force the way through to Berlin. If we check Solzhenitsyn's account with what the military historians have said, we find he is completely accurate. The actions of General Samsonov, the commander of the second Russian army that was destroyed, are set out correctly; the fact that the sad general was the victim of rival generals and criminally ill-equipped and cut off from information, is set out in the history books, down to such details as the lack of wire for his field telephones and the neglect of signal codes, so that he had to send out all messages *en clair*.

The other figures in the High Command—Danilov, the master strategist, the Grand Duke Nicolas, Zhilinsky who cheated, the obsequious Yanushekevich who buried his incompetence in paper work—are drawn to the life and, at the end of the book, there is a searching account of their behaviour at the conference table when the white-washing of their responsibilities is completed. Solzhenitsyn has examined all the records. But until I read all this elsewhere I was often lost in his account of the confusion of the campaign: the great Tolstoy was a master of confusion in the field. He made the disposition of forces clear: one follows him easily without a map. To follow Solzhenitsyn without a map is very difficult. Still, in Vorotyntsev, the staff officer and fictional character who carries the moral burden of the narrative, we have the well-drawn portrait of both a feeling man and an intelligent professional soldier who can not only guide his remnant out of the mess, but who can guide us too.

Solzhenitsyn has Tolstoy's eye for the meaninglessness and the futilities of war—the town captured and then evacuated for no reason that is clear to the army; the loss of contact; the mystery of one's situation; the contradiction of orders; the jealousies of the officers; the baffled faces of the fatalistic troops; and when there is a question of action any given incident is vividly done and without journalistic rhetoric. One is struck, when Solzhenitsyn singles out an officer or a common soldier, by the fact that it is their particular type of mind that is thoroughly presented to us: they are thinking animals rather than the frightened, mad, simple, hysterical or violent men who appear in nearly all post-Tolstoyan books on war and in which war is turned into orgy. In the narrative the horror tends to be generalized, but here we notice an odd innovation. It seems that Solzhenitsyn either intended two kinds of war narrative, one to be read and the other to be filmed; or that a film director has inserted intervals of script-writing in which the physical horrors of war are set up for the exploiting cameraman. This insertion of film frankly destroys the illusion and if it is a new literary device it is a disaster and strikes one as cynical.

There are two exceptionally fine moments in the narrative. We have seen General Samsonov in all his moods but when the debâcle comes, he splits: half of him thinks he has an army still, the other wanders about with an innocent, mad smile on his face, raising his cap politely to his soldiers who themselves don't know whether they are soldiers any more. This and other passages are as good as anything in Vigny's *Servitude et grandeur militaires.* The other is a long episode describing the escape of Vorotyntsev and his remnant, through the forests and through the encircling German advance. They will succeed. We know from history what their lives are likely to become and by this hindsight it would have been easy for the author to show them with bitter irony as the marionettes of fate, but Solzhenitsyn rejects that; rather he speaks for them as the novelist should, feeling with the ignorance of each one in his different way and himself moving with their changes of feeling. This sensibility to change in the mind and heart is important to the book's intention, which is to show both the innocence and the ignorance of these men's involvement as they advance into their own and their country's future. He is clearly working up to a humane, sceptical exploratory conception of Russian history that will grow more and more at variance with official conclusions.

The war therefore is folly; when the son of one of the advanced families joins up patriotically he is regarded by his young friends as a traitor to an enlightened education. They are not part of the rootless intelligentsia; they are sincere, without being seriously deluded in their desire to get closer to the people. They, too, can't know their future and Solzhenitsyn has presented their innocence with the slow-moving care that he is to show in portraying the soldiers. One's picture of Russians of this kind in this period has been so stereotyped by Gorki and the melodramatic denigration of Marxists that one is astonished by the absence of the usual teeth-grinding doctrinal hatred and by the evidence of a free witness. Underlying the book is the criticism of the dogma that history can be rationally known or governed. History, says a teasing old professor to one of the ingenuous young students in the story, grows like a living tree.

Lenin in Zurich consists of a number of chapters which Solzhenitsyn cut out of *August 1914* because they ran too far ahead of the time scale of the huge historical chronicle he had in mind. These chapters have a natural intensity and unity, and something of the scenario for a film. We are plunged suddenly into Lenin's mind without preparation, as he stands with his wife and mother-in-law on an Austrian station platform staring at the engine of the train—frightening image of impersonal power— which will soon carry them to Cracow. The 1914 war has taken the logician by surprise. So deep in the tactics and mechanics of conspiracy is he that he simply has not expected the onset of a stupendous act of history and is utterly unprepared for its accidental element. Once more—as in 1905—the conspirator finds real life has outpaced the tactician. When the train gets to Cracow his situation has again changed; he will have to make for neutral Switzerland. But at Cracow, where the first Polish wounded are arriving and the crowds of women are weeping over the stretchers, he has already been revived by an exultation that will keep him going:

> Piss-poor, slobbering pseudo-socialists with the petit-bourgeois worm in them would try to capture the masses by jabbering away 'for peace'. They must be hit first and fast. Which of them has the vision to see and the strength of mind to embrace the great decision ahead: not to try and stop the war, but to step it up? To transfer it—*to your own country.*
> 'Peace' is a slogan for fatheads and traitors! What is the point of a hollow peace that nobody needs, unless you can convert it immediately into *civil war with no quarter given*?

In the next three years Solzhenitsyn puts us inside Lenin's mind, crushes us against it, entangles us with it, takes us down into the pit of his rancours, the frustrations and the hatred that sustain him, as he keeps the political machine in his mind oiled and free of rust, while he is forced to live in limbo.

The thing was to be immediate on shifting ground. The war was a gift in itself to revolutionaries, but now—where would the revolution start? Russia was inaccessible. The one idea the war made plausible was the idea of permanent revolution, i.e. permanent civil war. Why could it not begin in neutral Switzerland? The idea came to nothing: the 'swinish' Swiss socialists were pusillanimous. They were in love with 100 years of petit-bourgeois neutrality; and were more interested—how could you believe it!—in defending their country? This failure made him furious with himself; why hadn't he seen that Stockholm was the place to set the world revolution going? In the end, the Germans were plotting to use him against the Tsarists and he had the humiliation of hearing from others not condemned to inactivity (writing pamphlets in the Zurich library), and—in 1917—he was once more taken by surprise and did not for a long time believe that the Revolution had begun in Russia.

Of course, this is a gross simplification of Solzhenitsyn's chronicle. *That* depends on his plausible if hostile estimate of Lenin's introspections, as they torment his mind and become minutely argued decisions. Solzhenitsyn says that the dialogue in the book is documented and close to the dreary language of the dialectic in which Lenin and his conspirators habitually chatted. One can be sure of that, and it is a relief to come upon two scenes in which Lenin is brought to life by rogues, the fantastic Parvus, the millionaire conspirator and the brilliantly cynical Radek. This journalist is at his merriest when it comes to writing articles or letters of eager duplicity. The sight of shamelessness so happy and inspired is almost cheering. As for the fat Parvus who has made millions in Turkey and delights in getting funds for revolutionaries out of capitalist financiers—he is a sort of stage magician. He knows money is power and simply loves playing with it in order to buy women, chateaux and, in a most disinterested way, leaders. Thus he has been invaluable to the conspirators. The Red millionaire had no faith, we are told, in

the Bolsheviks' organizing ability. He attacked Lenin's concessions to the peasants. He ended by building himself an opulent
house on the island of Schwanenberger in Germany and lived
there to enjoy his orgies for the rest of his life.

CHEKHOV

A Doctor

THE MARK OF genius is an incessant activity of mind. Genius is a spiritual greed. By the time of his death from tuberculosis when he was in his early forties, Chekhov had spent whatever breath he had, in every minute, not only in the writing of his hundreds of stories, his plays and his research on the convict island of Sakhalin—where he even took a census—but in exhausting work as a doctor, a founder of clinics and hospitals, schools and libraries, as the practical manager for many years of a small estate, as an indefatigable traveller in Russia, Europe and Asia.

From the age of nineteen he supported his family—a bankrupt despotic shop-keeping father, his fretful mother, a string of bickering relatives and hangers-on—mainly by his writing, under knockabout domestic conditions which were farcically at variance with what a serious artist is supposed to need. He appointed himself—even at nineteen—head of this tribe, who were 'depressed by the abnormality of living together' and who were people (he wrote in one of his letters) 'pasted together artificially'. They were touchy, lazy, talkative, noisy, pretentious and incurably hard up. Simply to listen to the noise they made drove him to despair and made him dizzy. To his brother he wrote—I quote from David Magarshack's *Anton Chekhov: A Life*:

> You know that I have a whole multitude of grown-up people living under the same roof with me. Because of some inexplicable set of circumstances we don't find it possible to separate: mother; sister; Michael who won't leave till he has finished his

37

university course; Nicholas who is doing nothing and who has been jilted by his lady love and is always drunk and walking about in rags; auntie and Alexey who live with us rent free; Ivan who spends all his time here from three in the afternoon till late at night . . . and father. All of them extremely nice and cheerful people but vain and full of themselves, always talking, stamping their feet, and with never a penny in their pocket.

(He could lose his temper too.) They hung on to the precocious son and brother like leeches—and by mixing his pride with his comic sense, he hectored and coughed them into order. Although he was broad and strong as a young man, he was soon in bad health; he is the classic case of the doctor and consumptive who refuses to admit his case and neglects it.

On top of all this, Chekhov found time to write over 4,000 vivid letters, many of them merry, many of great literary importance, to critics, editors, novelists, friends and to women who were in love with him and whom he was evading. The notion of the melancholy, passive, defeated Chekhov vanishes when one considers these letters alone, and especially when one meets the candour, spontaneity, the humour sharp as horseradish and the intimacy of his correspondence. The man is alive to the tips of his fingernails and has the knack all good letter writers have of springing in person before the reader's eyes. In letters a writer projects a large number of impromptu disguises, and, since he was often secretive in a self-preserving way, we do not get the whole of Chekhov—whatever that was—but we always see him in the hour he is living through.

A few of Chekhov's letters were published soon after his death. They were followed by a six-volume edition edited by his sister who adored him though she did make decorous cuts. There followed some of his letters to his wife, the actress Olga Knipper whom he married in the last years of his life. In 1948–1951 an official Soviet collection appeared and was revised and expanded in 1963–1964 to the number of 4,200 items. From this edition Avrahm Yarmolinsky has extracted some 500 of the 'most telling'—helped by the excellent translator Babette Deutsch. In another edition Michael Henry Heim and Simon Karlinsky have selected 185. Heim is the translator and Karlinsky gives a thorough critical commentary.

The editors of the two new volumes speak gratefully of the work of the Soviet scholars but cannot conceal their amusement or irritation with the well-known vagaries of Soviet censorship. The Russians have long been prudish about sex and the bodily functions, and in these matters Chekhov was often outspoken and sportive: after Pushkin (Simon Karlinsky points out), Russia became genteel as did the West, but the censorship in the Soviet Union has, uniquely, held on to nineteenth-century prudery. In a passage like:

> There is no outdoor privy here. You have to answer the call in nature's very presence, in ravines and under bushes. My entire backside is covered with mosquito bites,

the word 'backside' has been deleted.

In matters of ideology, Chekhov's admiration of certain things in the West to the detriment of Russian efforts has been cut—yet not always in every edition. But here, when one considers how subversive Chekhov's ideas on artistic and personal freedom are, and how generally opposed to the tenets of official doctrine in the Soviet Union, the tolerance of the editors surprises. They pay their tribute to Caesar by cutting out what Chekhov said about the superiority of European actors to Russian actors, and other matters that offend Russian chauvinism, but the rest suffers little. The American editors have not found it difficult to put back much of what may have been tampered with.

The two selections of the letters now offered overlap, particularly in the important ones. Both volumes are well annotated. After a short and pleasant introduction the Yarmolinsky edition leaves Chekhov to speak for himself. There are more of his letters to his wife, Olga Knipper, than in the Heim and Karlinsky edition: they bring out more variously the harassed passion of the one powerful—and belated—love of Chekhov's life; and the letters written during the Sakhalin journey convince one of the revival of Chekhov's vigour. Both editors dismiss the notion that the journey to Sakhalin was undertaken because of a love affair with Lydia Avilov: they agree with Ernest Simmons that the lady imagined the affair when she wrote her book. (Chekhov would be the last man wholly to gratify the lady or indeed our curiosity on the point.)

The smaller Heim and Karlinsky selection is critical and informative and is framed in a general thesis. They group the letters in periods, each section preceded by an account of Chekhov's growth as a writer from phase to phase, so that the background is set out in some detail. This is invaluable. They are particularly concerned with his hostility to the long socio-political tradition of Russian criticism and the misapprehension this has caused. Where Yarmolinsky calls Chekhov 'the incomparable witness', they go deeper into the nature of his witness. They show that the precocious success of Chekhov at the age of twenty-eight annoyed the intelligentsia because he was held to be a man 'without principles'—which infuriated him: his belief in the freedom of the artist was a principle. They also show why, in the later years of fame, his opponents adroitly denigrated him by defining him as the moody, twilit poet of futility and despair. They were too partisan to see his truthfulness and grace.

Since then many Soviet critics have seen him as an incipient revolutionary and have even distorted his language to demonstrate this. Through either blindness or disingenuousness, they mistake the nature of the one or two apparently directly political stories—*The Anonymous Man* or *The Bride* for example—which are not dogmatic assertions. In a well-known letter Chekhov said that it was not the artist's business to solve questions, but to pose them correctly. Marxists do not allow the posing of the question: they state the answer first and then create the question. Chekhov wrote when he was twenty-eight:

> I am neither liberal nor conservative, nor monk, nor indifferentist. I would like to be a free artist and nothing else and I regret God has not given me the strength to be one . . . Pharisaism, dull-wittedness, and tyranny reign not only in merchants' houses and police stations. . . . I see them in science and literature among the younger generation. I look upon tags and labels as prejudices. My holy of holies is the human body, health, intelligence, talent, inspiration, and the most absolute freedom imaginable, freedom from violence and lies, no matter what form the latter two take.

Or in a letter to Pleshcheyev about *The Name-Day Story*:

> It's not conservatism I'm balancing with liberalism—they are not at the heart of the matter as far as I am concerned—it's the lies of my heroes with their truths. . . . You told me once my stories lack an element of protest and that they have neither sympathies or antipathies. But doesn't the story protest against lying from a start to finish? Isn't that ideology?

And in defence of *Mire*:

> A writer is a man bound by contract to his duty and his conscience.

These replies are a defence against the accusations of the orthodox radicals who accused Chekhov of selling himself to the reactionary millionaire Suvorin and his paper. He was at once critical of Suvorin and his grateful friend.

Here we come to the continuous argument of the Heim and Karlinsky book: Chekhov was a subversive writer in the Russia of the Eighties and Nineties. He was exceptional in not belonging to the gentry class: he was one of the few writers—Leskov was another—whose elders had come from below. Although he was opposed to Tsarism, his opposition had not been formed by the radical tradition of the literary intelligentsia, that is to say the tradition which, starting with the great Belinsky, demanded a didactic social content in literature and which was continued by Chernyshevsky, Pisarev and Dobrolyubov. (Lenin admired the last of these for turning a discussion into a 'battle cry, into a call for activism and revolutionary struggle'.) Chekhov believed that the radical utilitarians (with the exception of Belinsky) neither liked nor understood literature, and he was 'as subversive of the sociological presuppositions of a Russian Populist such as Mikhailovsky as of the Christian mysticism of Lev Shestov'. He was accordingly attacked for 'lack of social relevance', Karlinsky says, and the letters confirm him, that

> . . . politically the most subversive aspect of Chekhov's thinking is his systematic demonstration of the illusory nature of all labels, categories and divisions of human beings into social groups and social classes, which are the starting point of all political theories of his time and ours.

The explanation is that Chekhov's intellect had been formed by the medical and biological sciences: his well-known practical work in hospitals, in building of schools, in the new local councils and in the clinics in the fight against cholera, brought him a great deal closer to the people and gave him a deeper knowledge of them than most writers of the time had. This has been awkward for some Soviet critics. In *The House with the Mezzanine*, the girl Lida (one of them complains) is doing exactly what Chekhov was doing in real life: dedicated social work. Yet Chekhov exposes her as an authoritarian and political fanatic who brutally wrecks her idle sister's life and he makes the reader admire the sweeter, weaker girl. In life Chekhov would no doubt have admired Lida's work. But, as Karlinsky says, he sees that Lida is a fanatic who will not tolerate opposition and indeed wishes to dominate the family. She will use any means to break those who oppose her beliefs. The story is not an attack on social concern but on the inhumanity and tendency of a particular humanitarian.

Chekhov's independent response to the pressure of the orthodox left-wing establishment is that of the working doctor: he is modestly self-accusing. He is bothered by abstract programmes and speculations. He wishes he were a 'great writer'. The best writers, he says,

> . . . are realistic and describe life as it is, but because each line is saturated with the consciousness of its goal, you feel life as it should be in addition to life as it is, and you are captivated by it. But what about us? We describe life as it is and stop dead right there. We wouldn't lift a hoof if you hit us with a whip . . . there is an emptiness in our souls. We have no politics, we don't believe in revolution. . . . No one who wants nothing, hopes for nothing, can be an artist.

That Chekhov was influenced for a time by Tolstoy's teachings —especially by the idea of non-resistance to evil—is true: but he soon returned to his own nature. As an artist he exposed himself. His purpose as a man was practical and he admired the intelligentsia when they went out to the villages and fought the cholera epidemic. One has the impression that the power to believe—in the doctrinal sense—was destroyed in his childhood by the violence and tyranny of his father: 'What aristocratic writers take from nature gratis, the less privileged pay for with their youth'—though they have had the triumph of their liberation. Unprotected by radical doctrine, Chekhov nevertheless exposed himself as an artist to the full misery of Russian poverty in such stories as *The Ravine* or *The Peasants* which may have been prompted by his reading of Zola. (He read widely in European literature.)

The Peasants is less a story than a collection of incidents that convey what poverty is like, in the sense that it is a sub-culture of its own. Everything depends on the choice of the right detail and showing it as an aspect of living. A broken Moscow waiter decides to move back with his parents and children to the home where he was brought up in the country. His childhood memories have deceived him. How to describe the crucial shock of arrival? Chekhov describes him looking into a filthy hut, not a house, but a shed half-filled with a dirty stove, covered with soot and flies on which a ragged girl is sitting. The parents are out in the fields and the child says nothing:

> A white cat rubbed itself against the fire irons on the floor. Sasha [the waiter's child] beckoned to it.
> 'Puss, puss. Come here pussy.'
> 'She can't hear,' said the little girl. 'Deaf.'
> 'Why?'
> 'Someone hit her.'

By a single line we are prepared for squalor, rancour, drunken fighting, the rabid greed of poverty, the blaspheming grandmother, the loose-living daughter who comes home stripped of her clothes. A neighbouring hut catches fire and no one knows how to put it out; the tax collector comes for arrears and takes the samovars from every hut. He is an obsessive collector of samovars and lines them up in his own place. One young girl can read and, in a conceited way, breaks into Gospel reading. Yet there is nothing Zola-like in Chekhov's descriptions of the vile: they are not rhetorically vile. The waiter dies and his wife and her child leave to beg on the road. The wife thinks:

> Yes, they were frightful people to live with. Still, they were men and women, they suffered and wept like men and women,

and there was nothing in their lives for which an excuse could not be found. . . . She now felt sick with pity for all these people and kept turning back to look at the huts.

What is striking about *The Peasants* is that Chekhov was able to catch every small drama in the lives of the community he describes in thirty pages.

One suspects that Chekhov's worry about 'purpose' had a good deal to do with his inability to write a long novel; he complained that he could not sustain a philosophic plan. The truth is that he lacked the novelist's vegetative temperament; he was avid for new beginnings and new 'good-byes'. His one serious attempt to write a long novel—it was scrapped after two or three years—collapsed from what he called 'fatigue' and because of the 'unreasoned' overcrowding of events, places, people, motives.

> Oh if you knew what a wonderful subject for a novel sits in my noodle. What wonderful women, what weddings, what funerals! If I had money I would make off to the Crimea, seat myself under a cypress and complete a novel in two months. . . . However, I am lying; if I had money in hand I would live it up.

Even in writing his stories he complained that he was a man of splendid beginnings who went flat from exhaustion in the middle and did not know how to go on. This self-criticism is of course absurd when one considers his very long stories *Ward 6*, *The Duel*, *Lady With a Dog* or *In the Ravine* in which he is certainly as great an artist as Tolstoy. Karlinsky quotes the hero of *Dr Zhivago*:

> Of things Russian, I love now most of all the childlike quality of Pushkin and Chekhov, their shy lack of concern over such momentous matters as the ultimate fate of mankind and their own salvation. They understand all that very well, but they

were far too modest and considered such things above their rank and position.

The letters indeed show that Chekhov did 'understand all that'. He attacked Suvorin, his friend and editor, on two crucial occasions: for the anti-Semitic articles Suvorin published at the time of the Dreyfus affair and the trial of Zola, and for Suvorin's attitude to the student riots of 1899:

> No one can pass judgment in print on the disturbances when all mention of the facts is prohibited. The state forbade you to write, it forbids the truth to be told, that is arbitrary rule. . . . Right and justice are the same for the state as for any juridical person. If the state wrongly alienates a piece of my land I can bring an action against it and the court will re-establish my right to that land. Shouldn't the same rules apply when the state beats me with a riding crop?

About anti-Semitism at the time of Dreyfus:

> Little by little a messy kettle of fish began stewing, it was fueled by anti-Semitism, a fuel that reeks of the slaughterhouse. When something is wrong we seek the cause from without and before long we find it: it was the French who messed things up, it was the Yids, it was Wilhelm. . . . Capitalism, the bogeyman, the Masons, the syndicate and the Jesuits are all phantoms, but how they ease our anxieties. . . .

Even if Dreyfus were guilty,

> Zola is right, because the writer's job is not to accuse or perse-cute but to stand up even for the guilty once they have been condemned and are undergoing punishment. 'What about politics and the interests of the state?' people may ask. But major artists and writers should engage in politics only enough to protect themselves from politics.

As Karlinsky says, Chekhov's greatness does not lie in what he said about the culture of the time, indeed he often contradicts himself. It lies in his invention of 'dazzling literary forms' and particularly in finding a way of seizing the dramatic value in our very inability or unwillingness to communicate fully with each other. Rather pretentiously Karlinsky elaborates this as 'the semantic tragedy', and 'the changes in the texture of time's fabric which cause every attained goal to be different from what it was at the planning stage and which make a teleological approach to any undertaking or any personal relationship an absurdity'. What Chekhov saw in our failure to communicate was something positive and precious: the private silence in which we live, and which enables us to endure our own solitude. We live, as his characters do, beyond any tale we happen to enact. So, in the saddest as in the most sardonic of Chekhov's tales, we are conscious of the simple persistence of a person's power to live out his life; in this there is nothing futile. What one is most aware of is the glint of courage.

The letters do not say much about the making of this fabric. The most we learn is that his head was packed with people, that his early trash, as he rightly called it, was written by a very bright reporter and for money. Chekhov began by laughing at his stories. In 1883, in his 'trash' phase, he told his elder brother how to write a short story:

1) The shorter the better.
2) A bit of ideology and being up to date is most *à propos*.
3) Caricature is fine, but ignorance of court and service ranks and of the seasons is strictly prohibited.

In 1886, when the serious Chekhov first appeared, the instructions were drastic and in fact describe almost any good story he ever wrote:

1) Absence of lengthy verbiage of political-social-economic nature.

2) total objectivity.
3) truthful descriptions of persons and objects.
4) extreme brevity.
5) audacity and originality: avoid the stereotype.
6) compassion.

He hated publicity and the pushing of his career. He was a self-perfecter and resented that he had to make money. He was an enormously responsible man who liked to pass as a reckless fellow. He was very susceptible to women and, indeed, said wine and women always set his imagination going. He wrote with more sympathy and understanding of women and was more their liberator than any other Russian writer except Turgenev. His many love stories are really woman stories in which the women are presented whole. If his own love affairs were generally short, his affection for the women concerned was lasting. Love did not turn into hatred. He was by nature too restless, too hard-working to be either a resounding romantic amorist or a compulsive seducer. He would marry, he often said, if he could be sure that the lady and he could arrange to live apart. Such love letters as survive are a mixture of fantasy, playfulness and farcical insults—'There is a great crocodile ensconced within you, Lika'—and are really letters of friendship, in which his determination on his own independence is frank but unwounding.

One understands his curious, defensive insistence that the 'sad' plays are not only comedies but in fact farces. He is asserting that life is a fish that cannot be netted by mood or doctrine, but continually glides away between sun and shadow. And this feeling, his letters show, is at the bottom of the value he put on his freedom. Gorki reports that Chekhov did not like conversations about 'the deep questions with which our dear Russians assiduously comfort themselves'. And he certainly did not like the 'Chekhovians':

Once a plump, healthy, handsome well-dressed lady came to him and began to speak à la Chekhov. 'Life is so boring, Anton Pavlovitch. Everything is so grey: the people, the sea, even the flowers seem to be grey. . . . And I have no desires . . . my soul is in pain . . . it is like a disease.'

'It is a disease,' said Anton Pavlovitch with conviction. 'In Latin it is called *morbus fraudulentus*.'

Like a great many, perhaps all Russian writers of the nineteenth century, Chekhov caught people at the point of idleness and inertia in their undramatic moment when time is seen passing through them and the inner life exposes itself unguardedly in speech. He caught people in their solitude.

The comedy of Chekhov lies in the collisions of these solitudes. That is why, despite Stanislavsky and the Moscow Arts Theatre, Chekhov insisted that his plays were not dramas, not tragedies, but comedies and even farces. The tragedy, if there was one, lay in the very fact of farce: and the farce existed because it displayed people speaking innocently out of their own natures; the gigantic Pichchik believes he is descended from Caligula's horse; he calls out, astonished at himself, in the middle of a dance that he has had two strokes; he cries like a baby when he says goodbye to his friends. He is acting out his inner life. It is at once farcical and sad that a man has an inner life.

We shall misunderstand Chekhov if we do not grant him this starting point. Again and again his impulsive letters help to bring this out.

TOLSTOY

The Despot

THE LIFE OF Tolstoy is a novel that might have been written
by Aksakov in its beginning, by Gogol in the middle and by
Dostoevsky in the years following the conversion. He was not
so much a man as a collection of double-men, each driven by
enormous energy and, instinctively, to extremes. A difficulty
for the biographer is that while we grin at the sardonic comedy
of Tolstoy's contradictions and are stunned by his blind egotism, we are also likely to be infected by his exaltation: how is
this exclamatory life to be brought to earth and to be distributed into its hours and days? And besides this there is the
crucial Russian difficulty which the Russian novel revels in and
which mystifies ourselves: there seems to be no such person as a
Russian alone. Each one appears in a crowd of relations and
friends, an extravagantly miscellaneous and declaiming tribal
court. At Yasnaya Polyana the house was like an inn or cara-
vanserai. There is the question of avoiding Tolstoy as a case or a
collection of arguments. And the final affront to biography is
the fact that Tolstoy exhaustively presented his life nakedly in
his works.

One's first impression of Henri Troyat's remarkable Life is
that we have read all this before and again and again, either in
the novels or the family's inveterate diaries. So we have, but
never with M. Troyat's management of all the intimacies in the
wide range of Tolstoy's life. He was a man always physically on
the move, even if it was only from room to room; even if it
was simply gymnastic exercise, riding, hunting at Yasnaya
Polyana. He is in Petersburg or Moscow, in the Caucasus, in

Georgia, in Germany, England, France and Italy; and when he moves, his eyes are ceaselessly watching, his impulses are instantly acted on. His military career, his wild life, are packed with action and mind-searching. In sheer animality he outpaces everyone; in spirit and contradictions too. The amount of energetic complexity he could put into the normal search for a girl to marry, outdoes anything that the most affectable sentimental novelist could conceive. Marriage, when it did come, was abnormal in its very domesticity. M. Troyat writes:

> Sonya was not sharing the destiny of one man but of ten or twenty, all sworn enemies of each other; aristocrat jealous of his prerogatives and people's friend in peasant garb; ardent Slavophil and Westernising pacifist; denouncer of private property and lord aggrandising his domains; hunter and protector of animals; hearty trencherman and vegetarian; peasant-style Orthodox believer and enraged demolisher of the church; artist and contemptuous scorner of art; sensualist and ascetic . . .

M. Troyat has managed to make this live with the glitter of the days on it. His book is a triumph of saturation. He has wisely absorbed many of Tolstoy's small descriptions of scene and incident and many of his phrases into the text. So when Tolstoy rushes off to one of his outrageous bullyings of his aunts in Moscow, we are at once back in a drawing room scene in *Resurrection*; and one can see M. Troyat going adroitly to the novels for exact moments of the life. He has learned the master's use of casual detail. He has learned his sense of mood and also of 'shading' the characters. He does not lose an instance of the ironic and even the ridiculous in Tolstoy's behaviour, but—and this is of the utmost importance—he keeps in mind the tortured necessity of Tolstoy's pursuit of suffering, and his knowledge of his situation. The conscience of the prophet often performs farcical moral antics, but fundamentally its compulsions are tragic. One can be angered by Tolstoy's hypocrisies, but also know that they agonized Tolstoy himself.

A test for the biographer is the exposition of Tolstoy's great quarrels. They are so absurdly jealous that the temptation must be to leave them in their absurdity. M. Troyat does better than this. The row with Turgenev, the breach and the reconciliation years later when Turgenev had become a garrulous old man, has never been so well-placed and made to live, as in this book. The comedy of the reconciliation brings laughter and tears to the eyes. There Tolstoy sits at the family table making enormous Christian efforts to repress his undying jealousy of the elegant and clever man who enraptures the family. Tolstoy grunts while Turgenev shows the girls how one dances the Can Can in Paris. It is a farce that contains the sadness of the parting of irreconcilables; even more than that, for Turgenev is a dying man and does not fear death. He is interested in his disease and is sure that death is the end of all. The still vigorous Tolstoy is terrified of death; his flesh demands immortality. The search for God, was really a return to childhood, an attempt at rejuvenation, but in Turgenev, Tolstoy was faced by a man who lived by an opposite principle. At thirty-five Turgenev had hit upon the infuriating device of attaining serenity by declaring his life was over, and then living on as a scandal until his sixties. One is present at a country house scene in a heart-rending play by Chekhov, where the elders are tortured and the young people laugh.

The story of Tolstoy's marriage is one of the most painful stories in the world; it is made excruciating by the insane diary-keeping of the parties. They exchanged hatreds, crossed them out, added more; from the very beginning the habit of confession was disastrous and brutal. Like the Lawrences and the Carlyles, the Tolstoys were the professionals of marriage; they knew they were not in it for their good or happiness, that the relationship was an appointed ordeal, an obsession undertaken by dedicated heavyweights. Now one, now the other, is in the ascendant. There is almost only one genial moment, one in which the Countess conquered with a disarming shrewdness that put her husband at a loss. It occurs when the compromise about the copyrights is reached. The Countess decides she will publish her share of his works herself and consults Dostoevsky's widow, who has been very business-like in a similar undertaking. The two ladies meet enjoyably and profitably; the Countess is soon making a lot of money, she is happy—to Tolstoy's annoyance. The art he had denounced was, as if by a trick, avenging itself on his conscience. He was made to look foolish and hypocritical. And yet, after all, they were short of money and his wife had proved she was right.

If there had been no struggle for power between the couple— and on both sides the feeling for power was violent—if there had been no struggle between the woman who put her children and property first and the man who put his visions before either; if there had been no jealousy or cruelty, there was enough in the sexual abnormality of both parties to wreck their happiness. Even though mere happiness was their interest for only a short period of their lives. She hated sexual intercourse and was consoled by the thought that by yielding to his 'maulings', she gained power; and he, whose notions of sexual love approached those of primitive rape, hated the act he could not resist. His sexuality tortured him. He hated any woman after he had slept with her. Conscious of being short and ugly, he was appalled that women were magnetized by him. Into this question—so alluring to psychologists—M. Troyat does not go very far; he simply puts down what is known and, of course, a great deal is known. It is an advantage, and in conformity with his method, that M. Troyat has not gone on the usual psychological search. He would far sooner follow Tolstoy in his daily life, tortured by lust or remorse, than dig into the unconscious. The fact is that Tolstoy seems to have known something nearer to love in his devotion to his aunts and to one or two elusive and distinguished older women.

About the Works M. Troyat has many interesting things to say. Because he was many men Tolstoy was able to get into the skins of many men, and the Countess understood that he was most fulfilled and made whole by the diversion of his protean energies into imaginative writing. On that she is unassailable; even his messianic passion produced religious fables of great purity and beauty; and in *Resurrection*, the recognition of the moral integrity of the prostitute is a triumph of Tolstoy's psychological perspicuity in a novel that does not promise it. Tolstoy's fear of death had a superb imaginative expression in *The Death of Ivan Ilich*—but, it is to be noted, this was not written in one of the passionate phases of his life, but in a period of coldness that was almost cynical. M. Troyat has a sentence which describes Tolstoy's love of quarrelling and his promise to reform, but only for the pleasure of going back on his promise, a sort of moral slyness, which contains a comment on his nature as an artist:

> Impenitent old Narcissus, eternally preoccupied with himself, he blew on his image in the water, for the sheer pleasure of seeing it come back when the ripples died away.

It is at the rippling stage, when he has dissolved himself, that he is an artist. And, of course, very conscious of what he is doing. He is watchful as an animal that sees every surface movement, he builds his people from innumerable small details of things seen. A misplaced button may tell all. He 'shades'—that is to say, he builds out of contradictory things: a cold dry character will be shown in a state of surprising emotion partly because this is true to nature, but also because that gives him an extra dimension that will surprise the reader. Tolstoy rewrites a scene again and again in order that the reader shall not know in the course of a conversation whose side he is on. He makes a great point of impartiality. Although *Anna Karenina* strikes the reader as a novel with a clear idea, set out in orderly manner and of miraculous transparency, the fact is that Tolstoy did not know what he was going to do when he started, and many times, in altered versions, changed the characters and the plot. He groped very much as Dostoevsky did, though not in a fog of suggestion, but rather among an immense collection of facts. The Countess and her daughters had to copy out many versions and the printers found on his pages a mass of re-writing which even Balzac cannot have equalled. One can see—and this is true of many artists—that the trivial idea from real life takes its final form only as the subject is finally assimilated to the self or experience of the author. He is edging towards a vicarious self-analysis.

It is fitting that this Life should have been done in Tolstoyan fashion with constant attention to the vivid and betraying surface. Not a single incident among the thousands of incidents fails in this respect. Yet the whole is not novelized. There is no imagined dialogue: it finds its place out of the immense documentation. The commentary is ironical, but a just sense of the passions involved is there: perhaps M. Troyat leans more to the side of the Countess but she is drawn as a woman, not as a cause, and we see her change, just as we see Tolstoy as an incalculable man. The complexity of the long final quarrel and the flight is made clear, and the narrative, at this dreadful point, is without hysteria. One can't forget such things as the old man sitting on a tree stump in the wood, secretly altering his will; or the Countess rushing out half-naked to pretend to drown herself in the pond. Then comes that awful train journey in the Third Class: the dim, inadequate figure of the worshipping doctor who went with Tolstoy; the whispers of the passengers who knew they had the great man with them; the bizarre scene at the station when the Press arrived and were not allowed to take pictures of the station because it was illegal to photograph railway stations: the face of the demented Countess at the window as she looks at her dying husband to whom she is not allowed to speak—the whole scene is like the death of a modern Lear. As Isaiah Berlin wrote in *The Hedgehog and the Fox*, Tolstoy

died in agony, oppressed by the burden of his intellectual infallibility and his sense of perpetual moral error: the greatest of those who can neither reconcile, nor leave unreconciled, the conflict of what there is with what there ought to be.

GONCHAROV

The Dream of a Censor

ON THE FACE of it, it is extraordinary that one of the great comic novels of the Russian nineteenth century should have come from the hand of the most pedestrian, industrious and conservative of state officials, Ivan Goncharov, a man outwardly devoid of fantasy and lacking inventive powers. From what leak in a mind so small and sealed did the unconscious drip out and produce the character of Oblomov, the sainted figure of nonproductive sloth and inertia; one of those creatures who become larger and larger as we read?

The simple view—still held by some Soviet critics and encouraged by remarks of Goncharov himself—is that *Oblomov* was a solemn exposure of the laziness and ineffectiveness of the landowning class; but as it grew in the slow process of the writing (which took between ten and thirteen years) the novel became far more than that. Several contemporary critics have even suggested a prophetic kinship with Beckett and have noted the protest against the work ethic that has created a sense of emptiness and boredom in the modern world. Everyone exclaims at the influence of *Don Quixote*, to which Russian novelists so often responded; but, thinking of Goncharov's case, one could say that it is just as extraordinary that the Cervantes of the neat *Exemplary Novels* should also have burst the formal bonds of his period. All one can say is that literature has a double source: one in life, the other in literature itself, and if one is going in for the influence game, Goncharov's admiration for *Tristram Shandy*—the corresponding English comedy of domestic lethargy—may have helped to awaken his dilatory and very literary mind. From Sterne he learned to follow a half-forgotten tune in his head.

The interest of a new study of Goncharov by Milton Ehre lies in his close knowledge of Russian critical writing and his observation of the detail of Goncharov's impulses and methods as a novelist. *Oblomov* appears to be a work of objective realism as minute in this respect as a Flemish picture done from the outside, yet in fact it comes from the inner secret anxiety of an organized, even carefully dulled temperament. This anxiety arises from a haunting nostalgia for what has been lost, an edginess suggesting fear of a hidden 'abyss' that lies close to one who, torn between the ideal and the practical, has opted for the respectable golden mean.

There is, at times, an air of fret in Oblomov's nature that makes him seem on the brink of madness from which surrender to his sloth, perhaps, saved him. This madness came out in the form of paranoia in Goncharov himself toward the end of his life when he accused Turgenev and even Flaubert of stealing his ideas. Goncharov was State Censor and, maybe, the man who had such political power over the works of his contemporaries had been quietly boiling with the jealousies of the unconscious and the temptations of a right-thinking profession which hates the imagination. Censors go mad, just as prison governors come to feel, as prisoners do, that the only righteous people are those inside. The curious fact is that the unconscious of Goncharov, a lifelong bachelor, pushed him in old age into a fate like Oblomov's: will-less, drowsy, isolated, petulant, fond of food, he surrendered himself to the care of his manservant's widow, whom he called his 'nursemaid' and 'little mother', and he left his fortune to her and her children, whom he had virtually adopted.

Before making his closely analysed study of Goncharov the artist who wrote only three novels in his life, Professor Ehre points to the important wounds and compensations in the personal story. It is a little like Gogol's, if it is less harrowing. It has some not dissimilar seeds of instability, and since Goncharov's writing was very autobiographical—and in this sense unimaginative—the real life is important. He came from a well-off family of the merchant class—and was the child of the second marriage of an elderly man and a girl of nineteen. The father died when the boy was seven, and a rich relation of the land-owning class, an educated man of the world, took charge of the family. This Tregubov is one of the sources of the character of Oblomov. The boy had thus two fathers: the real one, a religious fanatic, dedicated to ritual and Byzantine formalism, and a melancholic; the other, an aristocrat, an intellectual, a humanist, a disciple of Voltaire and the Enlightenment, full of charm and totally indifferent, in the manner of the Russian landowners, to the practical demands of running his large estate at Simbirsk, a region often ridiculed for its sleepy and comic provinciality.

The place was an Oblomovka in itself and is precisely evoked in Oblomov's famous dream: one of the almost beautiful fantasies in Russian literature. As so often happens in countries where the males are denied a ruling political role, the women become the power figures: Goncharov adored his mother who was, however, one of those strict and practical Varvara Petrovnas who rule the Russian novel. She saw severely to his education, got him to Moscow University, and fitted him to become the efficient civil servant he eventually became. He was nevertheless uneasy in aristocratic company—rather jealous too—and among talented contemporaries like Belinsky, Herzen and Turgenev he was obliged to be only a spare-time writer. The truth is that his upbringing and temperament were as much to blame as his feeling of social inferiority for the neurotic indecisiveness which plagued and protracted his attempts to write. Indecisiveness also ensured that his one known love affair—the model for Oblomov's love of Olga—should fizzle out. There is a failure to adapt romantic idealism to natural feeling and action, to give up the pleasures of talk for the risk of the deed; the personality is split and, in the end, the deep boredom or ennui so familiar in Russian literature of the time becomes a sort of governing secret society in his nature.

Such maladies can be an enormous advantage to the man who can goad himself into the writing of a masterpiece. Cold, cold, cold, Chekhov complained of Goncharov; but knowing he had talent, susceptible if not inventive, turning self-mockery into play, frightened of the possibility of losing his talent, Goncharov dragged on year after year, forcing *Oblomov* to become a work of art. It is typical of the paralysing indecisiveness of his nature that he was working on another long novel, *The Precipice*, at about the same time and that while *Oblomov* was a study of stagnation almost without direct narrative and plot, *The Precipice* was sternly political and acted out with crude bad temper in dramatic episodes. This book was a failure.

But it would be wrong, as Professor Ehre shows, to think of Goncharov groping or blundering in his methods. The most revealing chapters of Ehre's study are those that follow in detail Goncharov's clear understanding of what he was doing, and the principles he stuck to and the value he put upon the need to allow memory and the unconscious to ripen and form his work. He knew he was a conservative artist, that a form in which life stood still was indispensable; that he was dealing in types which would cease to be types and become symbols, that the more realistic his scenes were the more subjective must be the moving force.

In the chapter on the novelist's aesthetic views, Ehre quotes two passages from Goncharov's letters that show he had an exact notion of what he was doing and that Oblomov is not an oddity blown up to sprawling proportions:

[The writer] should write not from the event but from its

reflection in his creative imagination, that is, he should create a verisimilitude which would justify the event in his artistic composition. Reality is of little concern for him.

Art represents nature as a refracted image. Reality was too 'varied' and 'original' to be taken as a whole. He said much the same thing in a letter to Dostoevsky. If the Western calendared attitude to plot and precise action escaped him, he had on his side the Russian sense of the hours of the day running through his scenes and people like a stream or continuous present.

Since I do not know Russian I cannot comment on Goncharov's style and its rhythms, though I do see that plain or average styles such as his have to be consciously achieved. Writers who have no style are as obtuse as people who have no manners, either good or bad. Since Oblomov, like all extreme or outsize characters, is on the point of being mythical, I can, with some resistance, almost accept Ehre's references to Freud in his comments on Goncharov's relationship with his mother as suggesting the sun, warmth, a refuge from the Petersburg winters; and I can also see that if one looks back on childhood as an Arcadia one will have to recognize that one of the attractions of childhood is that it is lived under a system of magical rules whose chief use is that they give shelter to the imagination.

But we do not enact myths only in our lives. It is just as satisfying when thinking of Goncharov's difficulties in love to attribute these to the influences of Romanticism, in which it was natural even in split personalities both to idealise and fear 'ladies' as distinct from 'women'. Goncharov solved his difficulty by the ironic mockery of his feelings, i.e., by playing the game of being a man of the world. Oblomov, after all, is reluctant, not sexless but sly. In his early comedy of manners, *A Common Story*, Goncharov was content with the ironic reversals of idealism in love and to show, with some relish, the price of worldliness: the young hero becomes as cynical as his uncle—a Tregubov figure—and the uncle attempts disastrously to recover the follies of his youth and heart. But in *Oblomov*, the novelist broke out of this neat formula, with the result that the critics have been divided by the account of Oblomov's love of Olga and her marriage to Stolz; and Ehre is very suggestive.

At first reading Stolz is a virtuous stick and Olga is not much better; at later readings, Olga strikes one as being a remarkable portrait of an unformed sentimental girl acquiring the will of a real woman, and one can take the whole episode as a very penetrating study of the deceits of Romanticism in its watery mid-century form. When Oblomov falls into the arms of his servant and has children by her, Stolz feels the sluggard is lost and has taken the plunge into the 'abyss'. He has, so to say, gone native and Stolz breaks with him; but Olga begins to see him as one who, resisting the modern world's worship of will and activity, has preserved the quality called 'heart'. Perhaps Oblomov is self-indulgent; but Stolz remains stolid, and one understands, in theory, Olga's unrest in her sensible marriage to a responsible man.

If we accept this, it remains true that the Olga–Stolz episodes are unsatisfactory, but for another reason: one of style. How important that tune in the head is! The moment we get away from Oblomov himself the narrative becomes flat and toneless: as Ehre says, it becomes dry, argued, and conceptualized. One can even suspect here he had stolen from Turgenev a theme that was beyond his own sensibility.

Goncharov's unconscious had no living or literal material to offer when marriage or romantic love were the subjects. In his next novel, *The Precipice*, all the petulance and jealousy came out in the ageing Censor. He could not use the tongue of the younger generation. His particular genius lay in the prolonged and loving farming of his only aristocratic estate: his private evil.

DOSTOEVSKY

The Early Dostoevsky

WHEN DOSTOEVSKY WAS a cadet in the Academy of Engineers—the story runs—he designed a nearly perfect fortress, but forgot the windows and doors. A guide to the novels: the reader is dropped into the novelist's claustrophobia, and it must be said that the enormous amount of Dostoevsky criticism since 1880 makes the walls thicker. The task of tunnelling one's way out of his labyrinth is exhausting, and there is disappointment (if there is also relief) in discovering that the great artist was often, like Balzac and Dickens, also a journalist who skids into a phantasmagoria of 'the topical and *au courant*'.

This is a phrase of the Czech critic Václav Černý: all the critics have their phrases. We are helped for a moment and then we are forced to discard: the *âme slave* was the first to go; it was followed by Dostoevsky as 'the key' to the Russian character; we hesitate over the surely conventional theory of Dostoevsky as the product of medieval Russia in collision with capitalism. Too many 'ideas' occur to us. The root of the trouble is that the artist, the man in the act of writing, is lost—he was before anything else an improvising artist. As Mikhail Bakhtin put it in his well-known and difficult book, *Problems of Dostoevsky's Poetics*, which first appeared in Russian in 1929 and was expanded in 1963,

> The subject is not a *single* author-artist, but a whole series of philosophical statements made by *several* author-thinkers— Raskolnikov, Myshkin, Stavrogin, Ivan Karamazov, the Grand Inquisitor and others. . . . The critics indulge in polemics with

63

the heroes; they become their pupils, and they seek to develop their views into a completed system.

Such criticism is concerned with ideology alone and not with the evolving storyteller, at home in the slipshod but struggling against it, and autobiographical to the point of apotheosis.

For the biographer who sticks for the moment to the early pre-Siberian Dostoevsky, as Joseph Frank does in *The Seeds of Revolt*, the ground is clearer. (There are three volumes still to come.) The great novels are not yet here to obscure the man whom Siberia enlarged and transformed. We are able to see the young man painfully growing. The story has gradually become well known, but it still contains its mysteries and Mr Frank's very long book can be called a work of detection and collation at its scrupulous best. Every detail is considered; evidence is weighed and fortunately the author has a pleasant and lucid style, unleadened by the fashionable vice of fact-fetishism. He brings a clearer focus and perspective to things that have been often crudely dramatized, especially in Dostoevsky's childhood and youth, and we have a more balanced and subtler account of this period than we generally get.

There is no prophetic assumption, for example, that Dostoevsky's father was a rough, miserly, flogging, lecherous brute like the older Karamazov. The home itself could not be the source of Dostoevsky's knowledge of abandoned or lethargic poverty. Childhood was happy, if youth was not. The anxious father was ambitious, energetic, strict, but thought constantly of his children's piety, education, and future; the mother was deeply loving. The boy had his father's energy and determination and dash. Where was the flaw that made both father and son unstable, jealous, envious and instantly suspicious? When one looks at Dr Dostoevsky's past one sees how powerfully he was influenced by the dream of rank and advancement; even his narrow religion was the dreaming sort of dissident Puritanism which urges the family up the social ladder. This was very much a nineteenth-century dream. The worm in the heart of Dr Dostoevsky's success in achieving rank in the lowest grade of the Russian nobility was the knowledge that he had been merely admitted to the new service 'aristocracy' invented by Peter the Great and could never become part of the traditional gentry, in fact or in his attitudes.

The crowded Dostoevskys lived very much to themselves. They dwelled in the legend—perhaps it was a fact—that their forebears in the sixteenth century belonged to the old Lithuanian gentry class. Their history has a suggestive religious aspect. The ancient Dostoevskys were scattered and divided in nationality and creed.

The Orthodox Dostoevskys, falling on hard times, sank into the lowly class of the non-monastic clergy. Dostoevsky's paternal great-grandfather was a Uniat archpriest in the Ukrainian town of Bratslava; his grandfather was a priest of the same persuasion; and this is where his father was born. The Uniat denomination was a compromise worked out by the Jesuits as a means of proselytizing among the predominantly Orthodox peasantry of the region: Uniats continued to celebrate the Orthodox rites, but accepted the supreme authority of the Pope. Dostoevsky's horrified fascination with the Jesuits, whom he believed capable of any villainy to win power over men's souls, may perhaps first have been stimulated by some remark about the creed of his forebears.

The debate about reason and faith would have had an ancient edge and force to it if it ever occurred in the doctor's small apartment in his hospital. The Dostoevskys differed from the real gentry in a more important respect. The real gentry had become merely lax in religion and tended to be sceptical Voltaireans. Aristocrats like Tolstoy and Turgenev had had no religious education. But for Dostoevsky:

The very first impressions that awakened the consciousness of the child were those embodying the Christian faith. . . . Dostoevsky was to say that the problem of the existence of God had tormented him all his life . . . it was always emotionally impossible for him ever to accept a world which had no relation to a God of any kind. . . .

If aristocrats like Turgenev's mother flogged their sons, the domineering doctor never once struck his children. Whether he flogged his serfs when his new status allowed him to own land and he bought a poor estate in the country is not really known; but he sent his elder sons to a private school in order to shelter them from brutality: until then he had been their strict schoolmaster. He saw they were taught Latin and the indispensable French well.

Yet if the childhood was happy, it lay under a lid: the strain of the father's anxiety for rank and success became hysterical after his wife's death. He had awakened a deep love of literature in his children, yet, still pursuing conventional status, sent Feodor to the Academy of Engineers against the boy's will. The Academy was a great drain on his pocket and the father was so beside himself that he had a stroke when Feodor failed to be promoted in his first year. Feodor became extravagant and wanted, in his turn, to cut a 'noble' figure, and we get the first signs of duplicity and guilt in the sanctimonious begging letters to the father.

At this point Mr Frank deals with Sigmund Freud's famous essay on the Oedipal nature of Dostoevsky's conflict with his father. Freud believed Feodor had become parricidal and, in fantasy, homosexual; and that his epilepsy now occurred as a discharge of the guilt he felt when his father, now deep in drink, was murdered by his serfs. (Dostoevsky's silence on this subject is extraordinary, and indeed the murder did not, in any case, become known until long after his death. It had, for respectability's sake, been hushed up.) Freud's case was easily demolished by E. H. Carr in his *Life* published in 1931. Mr Frank agrees with Carr and believes that Dostoevsky's disease did not appear until just before his imprisonment in Siberia or just after. If he was mentally ill in adolescence this is likely to have been so because, like his father, he had little control of his nerves and his temper.

In the ambivalence of Dostoevsky's relations with the father he resembled, and in his fluctuations between resentment and filial piety, Dostoevsky had his first glimpse of the psychological paradox. He came to seek 'self-transcendence, a sacrifice of the ego', and, says Mr Frank, 'whether one calls such a sacrifice moral masochism, like Freud, or more traditionally, moral self-conquest', is a matter of terms.

We move on to the early struggles of the writer and a far closer view of the literary scene than the foreign reader is usually given in other Lives. Russian culture in the 1830s was moving from German Romanticism and Idealism towards French Realism or Naturalism. The influence of George Sand, Balzac and Victor Hugo on young Dostoevsky was enormous (he translated *Eugénie Grandet*) and in Russian literature so were the influences of Pushkin and Gogol. We move on to the conflict with Belinsky who had praised *Poor Folk* and to the interminable debates on socialism with or without free will and Christian faith that lead us eventually to the Petrashevsky conspiracy, the climax of the trial at which Dostoevsky declared, 'Socialism is a science in ferment, a chaos, alchemy rather than chemistry, astrology rather than astronomy.' Mr Frank goes on to quote from the *Memoirs* of Alexander Milyukov, who suggests that there was a small Populist wing in the Petrashevsky group and that this is where Dostoevsky may possibly be placed.

The account of the Petrashevsky meeting is given at length, and if Mr Frank is not vivid—others *have* been—his account is gripping as a piece of detection among ideas. For 'What are your convictions? What are your ideas?' set the note of discussion in the many 'circles'—satirized at the time by Turgenev—that were characteristic of a society where there was no freedom of the press. Dostoevsky wandered in and out of these discussions, occasionally bursting out with emotional attacks on the tsarist bureaucracy, but in the main he simply floated giddily among the Radical speakers. Only one political question preoccupied him passionately: the emancipation of the serfs. The tsar himself was hesitating in the matter.

There was a change in Dostoevsky when the extraordinary, dramatic figure of Speshnev appeared among the drab and circuitous intellectuals. A few years earlier in his life Dostoevsky had been bowled over by the perfect aristocrat: Turgenev ('I love him'). Speshnev, too, was an aristocrat; wealthy, cultivated, travelled, cold and strong. His melancholy feminine appearance fascinated (Semenov remarked that 'he could well have served as a model for the Saviour'). He was to become the model for Stavrogin in *The Devils*.

There is the report of Dostoevsky's doctor, who found the novelist irritable, touchy, ready to quarrel over trifles and complaining of giddiness. There was nothing organically wrong, the doctor said, and the trouble would pass. 'No, it will not,' Dostoevsky said, 'and it will torture me for a long time. I've taken money from Speshnev'—500 rubles in fact—'and now I am *with him* and *his*. I'll never be able to pay back such a sum, and he wouldn't take the money back; that's the kind of man he is. Now I have a Mephistopheles of my own.'

Speshnev was a sinister example of 'the double' who brings about catastrophe. The money, of course, was meaningless to Dostoevsky, the perpetual borrower, living the hard life of an unsuccessful writer; it was the will of Speshnev that was irresistible. It drew him towards what he abhorred—some form of revolutionary activity. What appalled him, Mr Frank argues, was that he had, in his unstable way, lost his moral freedom. Later in life he told his second wife that but for the *providential* accident of his arrest he would have gone mad! The strange thing is that living for contradictory extremes, Dostoevsky was one of those neurotics who recover their health and even their serenity when disaster at last occurs.

Mr Frank's first volume stops with the arrest and trial. The last hundred pages deal with the novels and stories Dostoevsky had written up to this point. If we except *The Double* and *White Nights*, these belong to the Dostoevsky few people read, for although there are flashes of talent, they are derivative of Gogol, Hoffmann, Sand, clumsy in construction, garrulous and tedious. Mr Frank is conscientious in his hunt for signs of a developing moral insight, but I am afraid his exhaustive summaries of the stories and the examinations of the characters do not make the tedious less so. In one Hoffmannesque tale of incest and demonic possession, *The Landlady*, one does see (as Frank says) a new theme emerging: the crushing of the personality under traditional Russian despotism and, in the portrait of Katerina, there is his first study of masochism. (Katerina says, 'My shame and disgrace are dear to me . . . it is dear to my greedy heart to remember my sorrow as though it were joy and happiness: that is my grief, that there is no strength in it and no anger for my wrongs.')

When one tackles these stories, one has to admit there is a certain mastery and even a tenderness in evoking masochistic sensuality. But one also sees how this derives from literature. He had not read the Gothic novels in vain; he was a great borrower and already an expert in pastiche and parody. *Netotchka Nezvanova* is Russified George Sand and is for me, though not for Mr Frank, unreadable. It has the turgid air of obsessive conspiracy which certainly became a characteristic element of Dostoevsky's genius, but here the artist is cramming too much in. The one thing I miss in Mr Frank's reading is a real response to Dostoevsky's comic irony, although he does praise the brilliant hack's pastiches of the bedroom farces of Paul de Kock.

Dostoevsky was surely, from the beginning, a master of dialogue and situation, and one of the great comic wits. His morbid insight into psychological contradiction, his habit of seeing the conflict of inner and outer life, not only as a quest but an imbroglio, are constantly attended by the sardonic spirit when he reached the height of his powers. And it is in this, rather than in his religious or moral utterances, whether they are subtle or overweening, that one feels the iron quality of forgiveness which elsewhere is sentimental.

'Without art,' Dostoevsky once wrote, 'man might find his life on earth unlivable.' And, one must add, he might find the novelists and, above all, a certain kind of academic critic, hard labour. In Mikhail Bakhtin's *Problems of Dostoevsky's Poetics* the originality of this great Soviet scholar's work is obscured by a structuralist prose so opaque that one has to translate to oneself as one struggles on. An inventor of awful words in Russian— 'characteriology' for example—he has been a great trouble to his apologetic translators. But Bakhtin does understand that Dostoevsky is creating his own means as an artist. For him Dostoevsky is the inventor of a new genre, the polyphonic novel. His characters are not the author's voiceless slaves but rather 'free people who are capable of standing *beside* their creator, or disagreeing with him, and even of rebelling against him'. There is a plurality of voices inner and outer, and they retain 'their unmergedness'.

He goes on:

> Therefore the hero's word is here by no means limited to its usual functions of characterization and plot development. . . . The hero's consciousness is given as a separate, a *foreign* consciousness. . . .

The traditional European novel is 'monological', a thing of the past, and if Dostoevsky's novels seem a chaos compared, say, with *Madame Bovary*, so much the worse for the tradition. Man is not an object but another subject. As for Dostoevsky's ideas, they are

> artistic images of ideas: they become indissolubly combined with the images of people (Sonya, Myshkin, Zosima); they are freed from their monological isolation and finalization, becoming completely dialogized and enter into the great dialogue of the novel on completely equal terms with other idea-images (the ideas of Raskolnikov, Ivan Karamazov and others). . . .

Dostoevsky's principle as a novelist is simultaneity. There is no doubt that Bakhtin exactly describes the originality of Dostoevsky; one has indeed the impression of being among people whose inner lives are dangling at the ends of their tongues. The lasting defect is that so much self-dramatization drives one into the ground. Not all tongues are equal. Polyphony suffers from the excess of voices. Only in *The Brothers Karamazov*, where the effect is of theatre, has Dostoevsky really brought them to order. Where Bakhtin becomes most stimulating is in his remarks on Dostoevsky's shameless indulgence in literary genre: the detective novel, the story of adventure, parody, pastiche, boulevard farce, grotesque and melodrama. Dostoevsky has prolonged periods of seeing life as an enormous scandal or as a revival of the ancient folk traditions of Carnival in which the types are contemporary and not mythical.

At this point Bakhtin takes a long, effusive, learned flight into the history of the scandalous Carnival tradition and is immensely suggestive. It is delightful to see a scholar going too far. I am surprised to read that these scenes in which—to use Bakhtin's metaphor—the drawing room becomes a public square, are thought by many critics to be artistically unjustified. Surely, no longer? They are at the height of his comic achievement. This kind of scene is organic, nothing invented in it (as Bakhtin says), though when he says such scenes really go back to the 'underworld naturalism' of the menippea of Petronius and Apuleius, I enjoy the scholarly trapeze act but I don't believe a word of it.

On the whole, European criticism of Dostoevsky has not paid much attention to him as a novelist at work; it has concentrated on his ideas. This is natural: the hunger for apocalypse has recurred, reviving, exhausting itself and reviving again, in every decade of this century as the human situation gets worse. One can see why Dostoevsky, the prophet and 'gambler who doesn't dare not to believe' is still the master; he moves forward with us as the sense of our own danger changes. We reject, as people fifty years ago did not, his preaching of the Russian Christ which so blandly overflowed into military chauvinism, for the notion of the man-God was Victorian and Dostoevsky's irrationalism offered us something unpleasantly close to the herd-God of fascism. But we were left with his insights into Russian history. When the West recovered from the catastrophe that he had accurately prophesied, there was still the great psychologist of the 'mystery of man'. And when that required counter-checking, we now find in him the authority on such strange elements in the Russian character as the communal personality and the morbid habit of confession. If anyone took up alienation as a profession it was he.

Yet we would not be reading him at all if he had not wrenched his great and his minor novels out of the chaos and contradictions of his own mind by a strictly artistic process. He was a novelist first and last. His very characters are storytellers. It is the novelist who contains the prophet, the sensationalist, the rather smug hair-raising journalist and the often disingenuous mystic. To an exalted and agonized lady who thought he, above all, surely must know the synthesis that would heal the dualism tormenting her, he replied cheerfully that dualism has its delights as well, and that, for his part, he was lucky: he could always turn to writing. A wise remark, but one does have the impression that the gambler who played for the highest spiritual stakes had an unfair resource when he had lost all his money.

One turns therefore to a Russian critic for a sharper, native view of these matters. Professor Mochulsky died in Paris in 1948 and his admired book on Dostoevsky appeared in Paris the year before. A professor at Odessa and the Sorbonne, Mochulsky experienced a religious conversion and became a disciple of Berdyayev. For the reader who expects a new approach to Dostoevsky, this is ominous news. We have already had so much about Dostoevsky's spiritual struggles. Ernest J. Simmons, E. H. Carr and others had already used most of the immensely important notebooks, letters and journals which were available, and have made economical and skilful use of them; they caught also some of Dostoevsky's irony. And although Mochulsky does, in minute detail, shows us the novelist struggling to arrive at his 'idea', changing and re-changing his plots and his characters until the idea becomes plausible life, we are far more aware, in the end, of the message than we are of the novel. It is no news that Dostoevsky's novels are dramas of conscience and belief; but they are great novels because he is able to translate this into specific acts and scenes of believing, and because he creates imbroglios of extraordinary physical vividness. He is a sculptor of molten figures.

Of course, it is important to see how the famous conflicts arose (the love-hate in the conflict with Belinsky, the utilitarians and the humanists; with the landowner tradition and the effect of being forced into the company of criminals) and he forged the contradictions of belief and nature into people; but there is far too much synopsis in Mochulsky's book, and far too little exposition of Dostoevsky's power of theatrical scene, of his gift of hallucination, his narrative whose strongest effects somehow arise from their disorder; and there is not enough about his humour and comedy. A hurried but classically constructed novel like *The Eternal Husband* might be a conscious parody of the great tragedies; but it points to the barbed, sardonic laughter which makes his pages of exaltation, or tortured doubt and terror, finally human. The recurrence of the great scandal scenes—on which Mr Ronald Hingley was very good in *The Undiscovered Dostoevsky*—and indeed the fact that nearly all Dostoevsky's characters are seen in a scandalous light for his own purposes and even by compulsion, are matters which a less religious critic would have attended to. And there are questions like Dostoevsky's ability to put a whole houseful, a whole set of people, an officeful, on the page instantly. This is his *biographical* gift. Life stories of endless complexity hang shamelessly out of the mouths of his characters, like dogs' tongues, as they run by; the awful gregariousness of his people appears simultaneously with the claustrophobia and the manias of their solitude. Dostoevsky contrives always to select so that he is able to show everything happening at once, without freezing into dead statement, and without thereby exhausting his subjects at the outset. Dostoevsky's sense of time is a sense of bursting, continuous instants. A whole life, past and present, breaks open this minute and will go on bursting in every minute that follows.

Some of these things *are* implicit in Mochulsky's analyses of the books and he is properly aware that since Dostoevsky is a confessional writer, the links with his own dramatic life are important. He was experienced in finding enemies to whom he could glue himself, upon whom he could fawn, and with whom he could fight. Like the saints, he knew how to hit below the belt. Mochulsky knows that the novelist is theatrical—one can often grasp Dostoevsky far more easily on the stage than in the novels—that he is poetic, that his struggle to find a form for his work was part of the spiritual struggle; that he is, as he said, an expressive rather than a descriptive artist—one of the reasons for his attraction today. Mochulsky is good about his literariness, about Dostoevsky's growth out of literary forbears like

Gogol, Hoffman, Balzac, Hugo; the importance of Shakespeare, Cervantes and of Dickens. He was much swayed by foreign writers. He welcomed confusion. One sees him switching from an intended novel called *The Drunks* to *Crime and Punishment*, stopping to write *The Gambler* in a month and then putting *The Drunks* into *Crime and Punishment*. Raskolnikov was at first to be another Rastignac. The novel was to be a first person confession; this was abandoned for an outside narrator. Initially in *Crime and Punishment* the idea was to be that crime leads to moral rebirth and redemption. Suddenly Rastignac is replaced by Napoleon and we have Dostoevsky's involvement with the 'strong' character and the questions of pride, power and living beyond good and evil. At the end of the novel he looked for a compromise that would reconcile his conflicting ideas about Raskolnikov's fate:

> The 'vision of Christ' and his heroism at the fire had to be discarded; Svidrigailov and not Raskolnikov fell heir to the solution of suicide. An exterior dénouement still remained; his giving himself up to the authorities, the trial, his deportation to the penal colony; but this did not suffice for an interior spiritual development. Raskolnikov did not repent and did not 'rise' again to a new life. There is only a promise of his resurrection in the concluding words of the epilogue . . . 'the miracle-working force of life will sustain him' . . . The murderer has not yet been saved, but he can be saved if he will completely give himself up to a spontaneous, irrational love of life.

The changes in the conception of the character of Prince Myshkin are even more extraordinary. At first he is quite the opposite of the final character: he is to be a power figure, a spiritual brother of Raskolnikov. (Dostoevsky swings giddily from one extreme to the other.) Myshkin is to be an epileptic. Then he is to be like Iago—another instance of a bookish choice —cold, envious, vindictive; after a glance at Turgenev, the enemy, he becomes 'a superfluous man', an idle power. Then he turns into a Stavrogin, a character whom we see trying to be born in other novels. After that he is the opposite, the 'holy fool'. Dostoevsky is really looking for the most dangerous solution. He finds it in 'a beautiful individual'—Christ, Don Quixote, Valjean—even Pickwick is considered. The idea was never certain for him until the fourth part of the novel and he was harassed by the feeling that the Prince ought to be, like Don Quixote, a comic character.

And, in fact, it is as a comic character that he almost succeeds. Dostoevsky's nearest approach to Quixote (though a more mundane one and untroubled by selflessness and the imagination; he is simply bullied and is an old liberal with out of date ideas) is the figure of Stepan Trofimovitch Verhovensky in *The Devils*. He is a reminder that there are periods of untheatrical tolerance and ripeness in Dostoevsky. There was a good deal of the sinful humanist left in the mystic; a good deal of slyness, of never quite letting the right hand know what the left was doing. It is here that prophet and novelist come together.

Mochulsky is clear that Dostoevsky is without landscape, is uninterested in nature, ignorant of peasant life—which makes nonsense of his mystical exaltation of the Russian people. Much to the taste of the Symbolists and some contemporary critics is the suggestion that he was seeking to enact basic human myths: 'the enchanted bride', 'the revolt against Mother Earth', 'the stranger'. He certainly portrayed the Man-God and the Covetous Knight. I find Mochulsky most informative about Dostoevsky's style: it is a talking style in which his own voice and the voices of all his characters are heard creating themselves, as if all were narrators without knowing it.

Founding Father

IT IS SAID that among foreigners only the Baltic Germans can see Pushkin's genius as a lyrical poet at once. The rest of us who have no Russian and read his poetry in English or French translation echo the remark made by Flaubert to Turgenev—'Il est plat, votre poète'; it expresses our polite embarrassment before a mystery. To the dramatic poet-novelist in *Eugene Onegin*, to the prose tales and above all to his marvellous letters, we do respond. In the last we hear the natural voice of the man that goes leaping along beside the cooler voice of the conscious artist and we at once see why the Russians think him the greatest of their letter writers. He is there before us: 'In casual letters of confession/One thing inspired his breath, his heart/And self-oblivion, was his art!/How soft his glance, or at discretion/How bold or bashful there, and here/How brilliant with his instant tear'. We learn to 'mourn for Russia's gloomy savour, Land where I learned to love and weep'. We see the courtier trapped by the Court; we see the rake who wears his nails long and who looks like a monkey, the aristocrat of two aristocracies: the Court and Art; the patriot who, like the Spanish Cid, is struggling with a false king. Pushkin had the art of appearing suddenly dishevelled or elegant, out of the very hour he was living. He is as concise as impulse itself. He is as clear as ice, as blinding as snow.

It is true that a lot of Pushkin's letters are mystifying—who are all these people? What is it all about? By now biographers have picked out the important ones, but it is still startling in the three volume edition translated into English by an American scholar, J. Thomas Shaw, to find how all still have their instant upon them and bring out Pushkin's voice. It is a good idea to have a life of Pushkin handy when reading them; but Professor Shaw's exhaustive notes pin down a long list of minor writers, actresses, mistresses, social figures and officials, and point the detail of adventures, projects and scandals. A half-elegant, half-barbarous scene is there if one can piece the fragments together; and when this is too much for us, Pushkin is there from youth to just before his death, never failing in accent or gesture. His mood, because it is so changeable, switching at every sentence, may seem careless at first. Looked at more closely almost all the letters are as certainly works of art as the letters of Byron are.

Pushkin has the appetite for life and, more important from a letter-writer's point of view, a genius for playing with it, for changing his tone, for leaving some things sardonically unsaid and others spoken bluntly. He is entranced by his laughing mastery of all kinds of style from the drily formal, the eloquent, the witty to the hotly argued and tenderly felt. He enjoyed rewriting. He was a keen tester of phrase. Each sentence rings like a true coin. For the moment he is all ours and we, on hearing him, are all his.

Here he is held up in quarantine because of the cholera and distracted because of the family quarrels concerning his marriage:

All you say about society is just: all the more just are my fears that aunts and grandmothers and little sisters may start turning my young wife's head with folderol. She loves me, but look, Aleko Pletnov, how *the free moon goes its way*. Baratynsky says that only a fool is happy when he is a fiancé, but a thinking person is disturbed and agitated about the future. Up to now it has been I . . . but now it will be we. A joke! This is the reason I have been trying to hurry my mother-in-law along; but she, like a peasant woman of whom only the hair is long, did not under-

stand me and was fussing around about a dowry; to hell with
it! Now do you understand me? You do? Well, thank God!
... I should like to send you my sermon for the local peasants
on the cholera; you would die laughing, but you do not
deserve this gift.

Pushkin is not one who, self-entranced, takes one under-
ground into the labyrinth of introspection. He takes it for
granted that he is known and that we know what it is to be a
man. He is modest. He is expressive but neither tortuous nor
exhibitionist. His stress is not on the egotist's 'I' because he is
multifarious. He writes rather as the messenger or familiar of a
human being called Pushkin who, though perpetually in some
sort of scandal or trouble, is like a swimmer who knows how to
survive in a storm of his own making and who will make no
fuss if he sinks. The appetite for life is not simply a matter of
extroversion; it is inseparable from the appetite for putting it
into words. Yet he does not live in words alone. Once every
three days he is in love with a new woman; he is quarrelling
with the censorship, travelling on awful roads, drinking, gamb-
ling, listening to his old nurse, eagerly describing his poems,
amusing himself in villages, flung into bouts of inspiration,
driven forward by whim, never frosted with doubt and never
green with guilt or remorse. These, he says, he never felt. He
looks like a monkey and is as lithe and restless; and he has a
touch of dangerousness too. He insists that he is an aristocrat.
But he insists, too, that he writes to make money, for that frees
one from the servilities of patronage.

Pushkin's biographers have all pointed to the powerful self-
control he must have had and the letters show that he has
reserves; but one thinks of him not so much as a man wrestling
with his passions or in conflict with himself, but one who is in
command of his experience. He is inhabited by a genius that
guarantees his integrity; but his is not a mad genius: it is sane,
orderly, generous, serene in feeling. It is impossible to imagine

ourselves trusting the judgment or good sense of a Dostoevsky
or a Tolstoy. Egotism distorts them. Pushkin one entirely trusts.
He is so open. His follies expose the corruption of the society he
lived in, rather than falsity in himself. Pushkin lived very much
like other men of his class, very much in the world. The early
letters are those of a brilliant, dissipated character living the
loose life society willingly allowed to the young and well born.

> Everything is going as before; the champagne, thank God, is
> lasting—the actresses likewise—the former gets drunk up and
> the latter get f . . . Amen. Amen.

To women 'who have too much sense to be prudes', he writes
with flattery and innuendo:

> I shall imitate a monkey, I shall slander, and I shall draw for
> you Mme de . . . in the 36 poses of Aretino.

(Professor Shaw, who belongs to the exhaustive tradition of
American editing, does not forbear from telling us that
Aretino's erotic work has 38.) To Mme Kern, one of his
mistresses who wants to leave her husband, Pushkin writes

> My God, I'm not going to preach morals. But yet respect is due
> to a husband, else nobody would want to be one. Do not
> oppress the vocation too much, it is necessary in the world.

There is a more dangerous female who was to be with Pushkin
all his life:

> Give my greetings to the censorship, my ancient girl. I do not
> understand what in my elegiac fragments could have troubled
> her chastity . . . One may and must deceive the old woman for
> she is very stupid.

In obtaining the right to be censored only by the Tsar, who

used the pretext of saving Pushkin from himself, the poet saw
he was caught in a cruel comedy that was to be played out
coldly to the end of his life.

> They deprive me of the right to complain (not in poetry but in
> prose, a devil of a difference) and then they forbid me to be
> enraged . . . The right to complain exists in the nature of things.

At thirty young men of Pushkin's class were expected to
marry and settle down. Obedient to convention Pushkin settled
down. The rake turned with sudden tenderness to the 'necessary vocation' of being a husband and enjoyed the novel pleasures of family anxiety. He was captivated. But he was caught
between a rancorous mother-in-law, a cunning Tsar and a
coquettish wife. His marriage which mellowed him also destroyed him. That was tragic and yet, of course, both as a man
and an artist, Pushkin got what was vivid and valuable in his
life and work from venturing; not from change itself, but from
the capacity to make it. His vitality jumps out in every sentence.
For one who scattered his life in storms and comedies, he is
astonishing for a fundamental seriousness. And what he read!
Byron, Shakespeare, Corneille, Goethe, Scott and Voltaire, of
course. Racine to quarrel with and Mme de Staël to defend. He
hated German metaphysics. But he knew enough about Addi-
son and Steele and the system of patronage in English literature.
He could recall lines from the low characters of Fielding. He
treats literature as a form of action.

Even when he picks an obscure friend's poem to pieces, he
enhances as he criticizes. His literary letters are entirely mixed
in with the life of the moment:

> The next day I ran across Nikolay Raevsky in a bookshop.
> 'Sacré chien,' he said to me with tenderness, 'pourquoi n'êtes-vous
> pas venu me voir?' 'Animal,' I answered him with feeling,
> 'qu'avez-vous fait de mon manuscript petit-Russien?' After this we

set off together as if nothing had happened, with him holding me by the collar in plain sight of everybody, to keep me from jumping out of the calash.

This is from one of his letters to his wife, a touching correspondence beginning in awestruck devotion, going on to the tender, the possessive and playful and ending in the painful attempts to allay his dismay at her sexual coldness and her jealousy. It is a comedy in the French fashion, with a cold undertone and a dire end.

On one question that was to become crucial to later generations, the split between Westerners and Slavophils, he has a letter of great importance. The letter is a criticism of Chaadaev's famous pamphlet which argued that, having fallen into the hands of Greek orthodoxy, Russia had had no real history, culture or tradition. Chaadaev was arrested and declared mad. Pushkin wrote to him, before this official persecution occurred, agreeing with Chaadaev's attack on Russian social life, but rejecting the religious argument:

> We have taken the gospels and traditions from the Greeks, but not the spirit of puerility and controversy. The customs of Byzantium were never those of Kiev.

This is the characteristic view of the man of the world: the Russian clergy are backward because they wear beards and are not in good society; then patriotism is stirred:

> What? Are the awakening of Russia, the development of its power, its march towards unity (Russian unity of course), the two Ivans, the drama that began at Uglich and concluded at the Ipatiev Monastery—is all this to be not history, but a pallid and half-forgotten dream? . . . Do you believe that (the future historian) will place us outside Europe?

Pushkin was deep in European literature. He was avid for the remodelling of literary forms; in a *Selection* of his literary letters, another editor, Tatiana Wolff, says:

> When Pushkin wrote of his calling as a poet he did not write of afflatus: on the contrary he always wrote of himself as a crafts-man. The Muse was his gossip and his mistress with whom he did not have to be on the best behaviour—powdered and in pumps. The letters came in spate, full of comments on the books he had read, requests for more books, praise, blame, vituperation, enthusiasm. He questioned, argued and swore . . . There was a note of increasing urgency in Pushkin's determination to replace the influence French literature had on Russian with that of German and English.

His letters are always dashing in their candour:

> I sing as a baker bakes, as a tailor sews, as Kozlov writes, as a doctor kills—for money, for money, for money—such I am in my naked cynicism.

When we turn to Pushkin's prose tales, the common opinion is that he writes in frozen, formal, well-corseted style that seals the subjects from the outside air. In a very fine study, *Pushkin: A Comparative Commentary*, Mr John Bayley disposes of this view, gracefully and with learning. Pushkin was indeed so deep in English and French eighteenth-century writing that it is per-haps natural to see that classical style as having been transposed without change when, in fact, he was a pillager of styles. He was, as Mr Bayley says, fascinated by the way in which modern literature had imposed its stereotypes on the men and women of the period, a process particularly marked in Russia where the upper class tended to identify itself with a current European model. 'It made a contrast, sometimes a grotesque one with the solid ramifications of Russian life.' Pushkin is less a giant than Proteus, as Shakespeare was, presenting new forms with the laughing boldness of a Renaissance figure. Form is of the greatest importance and it is on this subject, particularly—to my taste—in his discussion of *Eugene Onegin* and the prose tales, that Mr Bayley is most penetrating. For there is a paradox here: the strictly formal artist is one who brings to Russian writing the sensation we have that the doors and windows of the closed house are open and that more than one person lives there to tell its tale. The watching writer can make no rigid claims because he himself is watched by other selves within himself or, maybe, only by the sky:

> *Eugene Onegin* and *The Bronze Horseman* . . . have a formal perfection and inevitability, combined in being provisional and open-ended, a paradox that has a parallel in the structure of the greatest Russian novels.

The carefully insured impersonality or evasiveness of the writing is warm: there is none of Flaubert's chill.

On the surface *The Queen of Spades* or *The Stationmaster* are no more than skilful anecdotes in an antique setting—which was one reason for Mérimée's regard for them. They emerge from 'old papers', hearsay or after-dinner talk, in the conventional manner, and a tale like *The Stationmaster* looks at first sight like a simple reversal of the Prodigal Son story, as it might be retold by Maupassant. On a second reading one sees that this is not so. At the end we do not give a shrewd grin at the expense of the poor stationmaster's mistaken belief that his daughter's 'fall' will be a moral disaster, when it has turned out to be a most respectable success. Indeed, the success is not the sort of paradox enjoyed by a man of the world, but is humanly moving. We see a life unexpectedly surviving the clever or stupid misunderstanding of experience, and compassion cuts the claws of irony. In the last lines of the flat ending, life, doubting life, assimilates not only father and daughter, but the narrator himself. The 'closed' end is really open. The same may be said of the far richer *Queen of Spades*, where the terse picture of a society and an obsession with meaningless luck can be read on several levels and where the curious Russian gift of exact portraiture-by-accident or devastating miniature puts an indelible glitter on the people. The story melts into the interests of other lives.

Pushkin was a constant literary collector, but he changed what he collected. He is an example of the writer who shocks old subjects into life by a gay and intelligent search for new means. It is interesting that the incident in *The Captain's Daughter* where the girl goes on a journey to the Empress to plead for the life of her betrothed was taken from the *Heart of Midlothian*, yet with what new dramatic ease or innocence of eye! The economy and the impudent bravura of these tales are shapely, but the sense of the open, passing hour is always there and it will pervade all the great Russian novels that follow.

The longest and most illuminating essay in Mr Bayley's commentary on Pushkin is the one on *Eugene Onegin*. To English ears the manner and the voice are Byron's and in the opening book Pushkin seems to be explicit. The young dandy is a fop, spending three hours before the looking glass, a pedant of fashion:

> Porcelain and bronzes on the table.
> With amber pipes from Tsaregrad;
> Such crystalled scents as best are able
> to drive the swooning senses mad,
> with combs, and steel utensils serving
> as files, and scissors straight and curving,
> brushes on thirty different scales;
> brushes for teeth, brushes for nails.

The loot of Paris and London. Then the sudden twist of irreverent comment

> Rousseau (forgive a short distraction)
> could not conceive how solemn Grimm
> dared clean his nails in front of *him*,

the brilliant crackpot: this reaction
shows freedom's advocate, that strong
champion of rights, as in the wrong.

He's off to Talon's, to hear the corks go flying up, as he sits
before his bloody beef, his truffles

and pâté, Strasbourg's deathless glory,
sits with Limburg, vivacious cheese
and *ananas*, the gold of trees.

He'll shout at the ballet, alarm the ballrooms. Don Juan is on
the prowl. Soon he will be Childe Harold, 'glum, unpleasant,
caught by the British *spleen* and the Russian *chondria*'. Who is
he? Is he Pushkin himself, or is he being Byron out of sheer
vivacity?

I regularly take much pleasure
in showing how to tell apart
myself and Eugene, lest a reader
of mocking turn, or else a breeder
of calculated slander should
spying my features, as he could,
put back the libel on the table
that, like proud Byron, I can draw
self-portraits only—furthermore
the charge that poets are unable
to sing of others must imply
the poet's only theme is 'I'.

This is Mr Bayley's moment. The autobiographical surgery of
Constant's *Adolphe* is in the poem; but Pushkin is deep in
Clarissa, in Fielding, Scott and above all in *Tristram Shandy*: he
is parodying the novel of sentiment. For Mr Bayley this poetic
novel is far more closely related to *Tristram Shandy* in form than
to *Don Juan*. As in *Dead Souls*, *Don Juan*, *Finnegans Wake* or *The
Waves*—Mr Bayley says—

The impression is one of constant and brilliant improvisation, problems and contingencies recurring in endless permutations . . . under the guise of a dazzling helplessness. . . . The author escapes at every moment into the new pattern of the structure that he is creating.

The poem is, so to say, one of the earliest anti-novels, and it is achieved by conscious art. Mr Bayley's great attraction is that he shows the pleasure of the poet at work and brings him closer to us by his asides. Pushkin shares with Joyce and Sterne

an easy relationship with poetic facility and cliché. What Wordsworth and the romantic poets forget in their stricture on the poetic diction of their predecessors, was that the best poets who used it never took it very seriously, just as a great rhetorician does not take the rhetoric he makes use of very seriously.

The clichés of Pushkin are 'aware of their own obviousness and emphasize it with gusto'. Another good comment, which takes one back to the 'openness' conveyed in this stylized work, is that *Eugene Onegin* is not depressing—certainly not in the manner of the nineteenth-century realists. The daily life of Russia in Petersburg and the country sparkle; and if ennui follows the frustration of love, recollection has its tenderness; there is a kindness in the acceptance of experience.

The very incomprehension of one character by another, the abyss of distance between them, is as much an earnest of possible happiness as of deprivation. When Tatyana says 'yet happiness was so possible, so near . . .' her words have something more than the pathos of illusion . . . The perspective of 'life's humble journey' opens out from every point in *Eugene Onegin* where artifice, irony and the patterning of the novel of sentiment are most dazzling and triumphantly in control.

Possibly the changes of mind Pushkin went through during the years of writing the poem were a help. More important are the nonchalant changes of point of view in the narration. The elusive narrator-within-a-narrator gives the poem that circular, round-and-round view which was to become common in the Russian novel, so that the personages are at once 'we' and 'I'. The sentiments, the passions, are a dream; we are mocked but without ill-will. We dream, we wake up. Time passes through us as we pass from youth to age. We are defined and re-defined as the days melt and remake us.

STRINDBERG

A Bolting Horse

AN INTELLIGENT EDITION of Strindberg's anti-feminist stories, *Getting Married*, has been done by Mary Sandbach. The commentary is detailed and valuable to those of us who have seen many of Strindberg's plays but who do not know him thoroughly as a prose writer and know even less about the tensions in Swedish life in the last half of the nineteenth century.

Among the Ancient Mariners who arrive to stop guests from getting into the wedding feasts of the European middle classes in that period, Strindberg has the most frenzied and unrelenting grip. The calms that lie between the bouts of paranoia are themselves dangerous. We can easily 'place' the sexual guilt in, say, *The Kreutzer Sonata*, for Tolstoy has immensely wider interests. But except, apparently, in his historical novels (which few people outside Sweden have read), Strindberg's personal obsession rarely ceases. He is the perpetual autobiographer who has at least three albatrosses—his three wives—hanging from his neck, and it is not long before he is telling us that the birds shot *him*. One of the surprising consolations of his life was that he liked going out into the country for a day's shooting, and it is a striking aspect of his lifelong paranoia in human relationships that he loved what he killed.

Strindberg's strange upbringing as the unwanted son of a successful businessman and a domestic servant, and as the victim of a stepmother; his poverty as a student; his quarrel with the Anabaptists and Pietists of a respectable society, who had him prosecuted for blasphemy because they hadn't the courage to bring him to court for his public campaign for sexual freedom;

his flight from literature into experiments with sulphur that drifted into a half-insane obsession with something like alchemy; above all, his instability as a husband or lover—all these torments kept him at white heat. What astonishes is the lasting fertility—in his work—of these ingeniously exploited obsessions. I can think of no other writer with the possible exception of D. H. Lawrence who retold himself in so many impassioned ways.

One thought one had seen his case analysed and dramatized for good in *The Father*—where he is the sea captain, in fact the Ancient Mariner in person, who was driven mad by the cunning calculations of a respectable bourgeois wife—or in *Miss Julie*. Yet, in 1903, much later, the whole personal story is retold as a legend, folk tale or saga for children, in the droll story called 'Jubal the Selfless'. This tale appears to be serene, but its playfulness and resignation are deceptive. The title itself is misleading. Jubal's selflessness is not that of the saints. It is the selflessness of an opera singer who, in old age, realizes that his ego or will has been systematically destroyed by a conspiracy between his father, his mother, and his wife (an actress who uses him in order to supersede him in his career). When he looks into his mirror—this is typical of Strindberg's brilliant theatrical imagination—he sees he is a body without a face. It is only when he finds his lost mother and puts his head in her lap that he recovers his ego—and, needless to say, dies!

The fable is a characteristic experiment with Strindberg's own history and it contains a truth about him as an artist and a person: the history and character are *disponible*. He is a model for the early nineteenth-century concept of Genius: the genius is free and without character but compelled to seek martyrdom. This is a matter for Strindberg's biographers. The work is far more important. Reading any story, particularly in the first section of *Getting Married*, one sees the link between the short story writer and the dramatist. He is a master in the use of overstatement; and one knows at once he is attacking a sententious and cliché-ridden society by the abrupt use of the offhand, natural voice:

> They had been married for ten years. Happily? As happily as circumstances allowed.

or:

> The couple met at dinner and at night, and it was a true marriage, a union of souls, and of two bodies into the bargain, but this they never mentioned, of course.

A young wife is fretting because she is not pregnant. The husband

> . . . had a confidential talk with his wife, and she went to see a doctor. Bang! Six weeks later the trick worked.

The word 'Bang'—used by many translators—seems to come, with a grin, from Strindberg the sportsman but it also shows his sense of theatre. A singer begins to get fat and to lose her audience—this is from 'The Tobacco Shed':

> She really began to get somewhat corpulent. She began so slowly and cautiously that she did not notice it herself until it was too late. Bang! You go downhill fast, and this descent took on a dizzying speed . . . the more she starved the fatter she got.
> 'It wasn't fat,' said the prompter. 'It was conceit.'

This devilish, grinning abruptness gives his stories a swinging elation. In play writing and story, the cutting from outside to inside the people has to be drastic and fast. There is no doubt of Strindberg's enormous talent; so that, in these stories, when he moves from one marriage to the next, one finds that as a realist with a message Strindberg is at ease in his mixture of the pugnacious, the pitying and the revealing.

Mary Sandbach says that Strindberg's misogyny has been overstressed; that he is as much concerned with the false values of a powerful upper merchant class which produces the unbending man and the cunning, idle female. His attack on 'Amazonian' women who wish to have careers or non-domestic interests is rooted in deep private jealousy of them—as in his first marriage—but he is talking of women who are 'idle' only because they have a huge supply of working-class girls as servants.

The message in the first series of the stories is that men *and* women must be liberated. In the second series, the excellent little scenes of life in town and country, the delight in the sea journeys and outings which bring out his high quality as an imaginative writer give way to arid, harsher analysis and polemic. But in the first part of one tale, 'The Payment', one gets that compelling and shrewd power of social analysis which D. H. Lawrence was to take further. The story is a full statement of Strindberg's case: the stifling of the sexual instincts leads women to use sex as a weapon, so that the men become the slaves while the women grasp occupational power outside the home. It must be read in the context of nineteenth-century life, but it approaches the Lawrence of 'St Mawr'.

Helène, the young woman in the story, is the daughter of a general. In her home she sees the exaggerated artifices of respect paid to women and grows up to regard all males as inferiors.

> When she rode she was always accompanied by a groom. When it pleased her to stop to admire the view, he stopped too. He was like her shadow. She had no idea what he looked like, or whether he was young or old. If anyone had asked his sex she would not have been able to answer, for it never occurred to her that a shadow could have any sex.

One day she is out riding in the country alone—she in fact hates nature; it makes her 'feel small'—and when she gets off

her mare the animal bolts off to mate with a stallion before her
eyes. She is shocked and disgusted. In the next phase she takes to
the out-of-date library in her father's house and becomes in-
fatuated with Mme de Staël's *Corinne*, and this leads her

> . . . to live in an aristocratic dream world in which souls live
> without bodies. . . . This brain-fever, which is called roman-
> ticism, is the gospel of the rich.

After the horse-riding episode, the analysis of the mind of a
frigid, proud and ambitious girl as it grows degenerates into an
essay, but it is nevertheless very thorough and alive. As Mary
Sandbach says, 'For Payment' comes so close to the portrait of
Hedda Gabler that many critics thought Ibsen must have read
it. In the end Helène marries in order to trade on her scholarly
husband's political reputation and get herself into public life:
she is a recognizable high-bourgeois female type.

I think Mary Sandbach is right in disagreeing with those
critics who say it is incredible that Helène's husband should
submit to her rule even though, sexually, she has swindled him.
This would be exactly in Strindberg's own character but—
more important—there have been many observable and well-
known instances of this armed frigidity since his day. Strindberg, the impossible, sincerely loved the recalcitrant woman,
even if he reserved the right to take it out on her and then, with
chronic masochism and double-mindedness, to crawl back for
forgiveness. Strindberg's story fails not because it is false—
emancipated groups, classes or individuals are often likely to be
tyrannical and reactionary when they get power, as every revolution has shown—but simply because in the later part of this
story the artist has been swallowed up by the crude polemical
journalist. He has turned from life to the case book. Trust the
tale, not the case history.

The original artist in Strindberg survives in his imaginative
autobiographies, in the powerful and superbly objective and

moving account of his breakdown in *Inferno*; in certain plays, and in the best of these stories. In many of these, a curious festive junketing, a love of good food and drink, a feeling for the small joys of Swedish life, and the spirit of northern carnival, break through. In 'Needs Must', the story of a bachelor schoolmaster who runs into a midsummer outing in the country and is eventually converted to a marriage which is very happy—'no part of this story', says Strindberg drily—Strindberg suddenly flings himself into the jollities of the trippers. The schoolmaster listens to the accordion and 'it was as if his soul were seated in a swing that had been set in motion by his eyes and ears'. It is a story that contains one of his happiest 'Bangs':

> Then they began to play Forfeits, and they redeemed all their forfeits with kisses, real kisses bang on the mouth, so that he could hear the smack of them. And when the jolly bookkeeper had to 'stand in the well' and was made to kiss the big oak tree, he did so with comical lunacy, putting his arm round the thick trunk and patting it as one does a girl when no one is looking, that they all laughed uncontrollably, for they all knew what you do, though no one would have wanted to be caught doing it.

If there is elation in the black Strindberg it springs like music out of his sunny spells. One is always compelled by something vibrant and vital in him. He is a bolting horse whatever direction he takes; and, as Mary Sandbach says, he brought new life to Swedish prose by his natural voice and his lively images. He was, as some have said, a cantankerous Pietist or Anabaptist turned inside out. His lasting contribution was his liberation of the language. The reader feels zest of that at once.

KAFKA

Estranged

AT THE BEGINNING of his Investigations of a Dog', Kafka wrote—in Willa and Edwin Muir's translation—

> When I think back and recall the time when I was still a member of the canine community, sharing in all its preoccupations, a dog among dogs, I find on closer examination that from the very beginning I sensed some discrepancy, some little maladjustment, causing a slight feeling of discomfort which not even the most decorous public functions could eliminate; more, that sometimes, no, not sometimes, but very often, the mere look of some fellow dog of my own circle that I was fond of, the mere look of him, as if I had just caught it for the first time, would fill me with helpless embarrassment and fear, even with despair.

The flat bureaucratic style strikes one as being a mask: Kafka notoriously did not know where he belonged. He was a Jew not quite in the Christian world; as a non-practising Jew—at the beginning anyway—he was not quite at home among Jews. The German critic Günther Anders, from whom I take these remarks, goes on:

> As a German-speaking Czech, [Kafka is] not quite among the Czechs; as a German-speaking Jew not quite among the Bohemian Germans. As a Bohemian he does not quite belong to Austria. As an official of a workers' insurance company, not quite to the middle class. Yet as the son of a middle-class family not quite to the working class.

In his family he wrote that he is 'more estranged than a stranger' and at the office he is alien because he is a writer. In love he is in conflict with literature. Because he was an extreme case which was exacerbated by fatally bad health, Kafka was able to enlarge, as by a microscope, the sense of exile which becomes visible as a characteristic of our experience in this century, its first martyr to 'alienation', which has become something of a cult.

When we turn from his books to his letters we have a series of self-portraits desperate and courageous, always eager and warm in feeling; the self is lit by fantasy and, of course, by drollery. His candour is of the kind that flies alongside him in the air. He was a marvellous letter writer. For these reasons alone the present translation of the *Briefe* first published in 1958 and collected by his great friend Max Brod is worth having. Richard and Clara Winston, the American translators, tell us that it is based on that volume and it is not clear to me whether 'based' means the whole or a selection from that volume—I fancy, the whole. (Other parts of Kafka's large correspondence have been translated, notably the important *Letters to Felice* by James Stern and Elisabeth Duckworth in 1973.) The present volume does contain now the full text of his long letter explaining his break with Julie Wohryzek to her sister, and the whole of the long letter to his parents a few days before he died in 1924 at the age of forty-one. There are also a few letters (of slight interest) to Martin Buber.

We hear the authentic Kafka when he is writing in a girl's album that words cannot carry memories because they are 'clumsy mountaineers and clumsy miners'; or to a fellow student when he is nineteen:

> When we talk together, the words are hard; we tread over them as if they were rough pavement. The most delicate things acquire awkward feet. . . . When we come to things that are not exactly cobblestones or the *Kunstwart* [a cultural magazine, of Nietzschean tendency, edited by a nephew of Richard Wagner:

another kind of paving], we suddenly see that we are in mas-
querade, acting with angular gestures (especially me, I admit),
and then we suddenly become sad and bored. . . . You see,
we're afraid of each other, or I am.

Later on, letters are comparable to 'mere splashings of the
waves on different shores: the waves do not reach one'. In 1916,
quick to admit that his stories are painful, he adds proudly that
he wants to be 'truly a man of his time'. In 1922 when his many
illnesses have united to become the fatal tuberculosis of the
larynx, he writes to Robert Klopstock, the young medical
student who was often with him in his last years, that he wants
no indissoluble bonds, beyond the tacit, with men or women:

> Is there anything so strange about this anxiety? A Jew, and a
> German besides, and sick besides, and in difficult personal cir-
> cumstances besides—those are the chemical forces with which I
> propose to straightaway transmute gold into gravel or your
> letter into mine, and while doing so remain in the right.

That may sound bitter, but he is really thinking about his role
as a writer of fables who reverses the classic manner of fable in
order to be truly that man of his time. Again:

> The writer . . . is a scapegoat of mankind. He makes it possible
> for men to enjoy sin without guilt, almost without guilt.

He sways between assertion and qualification, between reaching
out to the gold of friendship and retiring into defensive strategies. They are necessary, especially in his relations with women,
in order to pursue literature and nothing else. Such manoeuvres
have a sick man's pedantry, but in fact the self-irony, the kindness, the nimbleness, the fantasy, mask the pain. When it is certain
that he is terribly ill he begs that this shall be kept from his
parents and adds that his

earthly possessions have been on the one hand increased by the addition of tuberculosis, on the other hand somewhat diminished.

He imagines a battle of words going on between brain and lungs; talks of clinging to the disease like a child to the pleats of his mother's skirts. During a longish period at the house of his beloved sister Ottla at the village of Zürau he is plagued by country noises. A girl plays the piano across the street, children scream, men chop down trees, next comes the scream of the circular saw, then the loading of logs onto an ox wagon, the noise of the oxen, the shunting of the trains going away. A tinsmith starts hammering. Noise, he says, is the scaffolding within which he works; perhaps in the end, he says, noise is a fascinating narcotic. And then the house is alive with mice and the long half-farcical, half-obsessional drama continues for many letters. The creatures race round the room—he has the fancy that he can frighten them off by making his eyes glow like a cat's. He gets a cat in, the cat shits in his slippers; when the cat quietens the mice he still sits up half the night 'to take over a portion of the cat's assignment'.

Certainly this fear, like an insect phobia, is connected with the unexpected, uninvited, inescapable, more or less silent, persistent, secret aim of these creatures, with the sense that they have riddled the surrounding walls through and through with their tunnels and are lurking within, that the night is theirs. . . . Their smallness, especially, adds another dimension to the fear they inspire.

We see by his speculations about a Mouse Sanatorium that he is on the edge of one of his breakdowns and that soon he will once more find himself in hospital.

In love, Kafka sought perfection, knowing that it was an impossibility; knowing also the ideal served as a defence as

ingenious as an insurance company's refusal to admit a claim.
The most honest statement of this defence is in the long letter
to Julie's sister, a confessional document of pitiless and subtle
self-searching and, as always, frankly expressing his guilt—
elsewhere he said that guilt so easily turned to nostalgia. The
sincerity, and above all the sensibility to friendship, in letters to
women, give them a spontaneous grace. The self he is preserving
is in no way hard but clearly expatiated. Yet it glows under the
friendship he receives and also offers.

As a sick man he is, one might say, negotiating a life which he
knows is diminishing. He has the patient's ironical interest in
the clinical state of his condition; and when he says, for
example, that there is something fundamentally childlike in the
Czechs of Prague, he describes a trait many foreigners have
noted in the most tormented of all European cities, and a quality
he shares. There is something of Italo Svevo, who was also
partly Jewish, in his exploration of his condition: illness is a kind
of second self that has cleverly moved in on him.

There is scarcely anything about the 1914–1918 war—illness
secluded Kafka—although he does have a few incidental lines
about the shortage of food and, afterward, some anxious joking
about German inflation, especially in Berlin. He is even detached about anti-Semitism: this is interesting because it shows
how active anti-Semitism was in the early Twenties in Germany; he makes a distinction between the Eastern European
and the Western European Jews: the former were beginning to
go to Palestine, to which he too was emotionally drawn and
from which he withdrew: a spectator.

Kafka's most revealing things come most naturally in the
letters to Max Brod, who is the strong, ever active, positive,
generous and successful writer. Kafka reads Brod's latest works
as they come out, comments on them with enthusiastic interest,
and also takes over Brod's marital troubles in the manner of a
brother exhaustive in advice. There is a letter to Brod in 1923,

written from Berlin-Steglitz, which shows the continuous circ-
ling of Kafka's self-awareness:

> It is true that I do not write to you, but not because I
> have anything to conceal (except to the extent that conceal-
> ment has been my life's vocation), nor because I would not
> long for an intimate hour with you, the kind of hour we
> have not had, it sometimes seems to me, since we were
> together at the north Italian lakes. (There is a certain point in
> my saying this, because at the time we had truly innocent inno-
> cence—perhaps that's not worth regretting—and the evil
> powers, whether on good or bad assignments, were only lightly
> fingering the entrances through which they were going to pene-
> trate some day, an event to which they were already looking
> forward with unbearable rejoicing.) So if I do not write, that is
> due chiefly to 'strategic' reasons such as have become dominant
> for me in recent years. I do not trust words and letters, my
> words and letters; I want to share my heart with people but not
> with phantoms that play with the words and read the letters
> with slavering tongue. Especially I do not trust letters, and it is
> a strange belief that all one has to do is seal the envelope in
> order to have the letter reach the addressee safely. In this respect,
> by the way, the censorship of mail during the war years, years
> of particular boldness and ironic frankness on the part of the
> phantoms, has proved instructive.
>
> I forgot to add to my remark above: It sometimes seems to
> me that the nature of art in general, the existence of art, is ex-
> plicable solely in terms of such 'strategic considerations', of
> making possible the exchange of truthful words from person to
> person.

Letters like this take one straight across the bridge from
Kafka's private life into *The Castle* and *The Trial*, both of course
unfinished and published after his death. There was a great deal
of Swift (whom he read attentively) in Kafka's 'mad' imagination, above all in his habit of seeing people and sensations
exactly, microscopically, as objects. He was much taken by

Swift's inflexible remarks on marriage and the bringing up of children. The letters to women have even something of Swift's advisory playfulness, and are all gentle to a degree one would have thought unlikely in a man so self-enclosed, alone, and perhaps even proud, with some delicacy of manner, of being incurable.

A Modern Nihilist

IN THE MOST literal sense of the phrase, Genet is a writer who has the courage of his convictions. Out of the lives of criminals, and following a tradition in French literature, he has built an erotic mystique, even a kind of metaphysic. Just as Zola was romantically stimulated by the idea of heredity as a fate, and by sex as a mindless habit of brutal instinct, so Genet is moved by an aspiration to the state of Absolute Evil. One thinks of him as a Vidocq without the gaiety, slipperiness and hypocrisy—a Vidocq who has read Dostoevsky; the autodidact of the jails.

Absolute Evil implies the existence of Absolute Good at the opposite extreme; but there is no sign of that in his writing. Absolute Evil is not the kingdom of hell. The inhabitants of hell are ourselves, i.e., those who pay our painful, embarrassing, humanistic dues to society and who are compromised by our intellectually dubious commital to virtue, which can be defined by the perpetual smear-word of French polemic: the bourgeois. (Bourgeois equals humanist.) This word has long been anathema in France where categories are part of the ruling notion of '*logique*'. The word cannot be readily matched in England or America, and simply has associations of the grotesque in Germany. Although 'bourgeois' has a definite place in Marxist hagiography, it is hard to appoint a certain place for it in our empiricism. Some believe that its emotional force in France comes from the violent overthrow of the Commune in 1871. Possibly the self-love, the trim, pedantic obduracy of the French middle class, owes a great deal to its roots in the satisfactions of a successful peasantry. (They got what they wanted after the Revolution and, frugally, what they have they hold.)

Again, there seems to be a Manichaean overtone in discussions about the class: the conflict is between the children of light and the children of darkness. In Genet's novels, his criminals, traitors, male prostitutes, pimps, collaborators and Nazis are known by adjectives that convey light and brightness. Those of us who close his works in anger and disgust at his sacrilege live in the outer darkness of right thinking. Hell is not an extreme; it is in the middle.

Absolutists put their money on Being rather than Action: they are after our souls. If Genet can be said to have mystical claims they are in his interest in the 'dark night' of the soul; but the soul, in Christian thought, emerges from its 'dark night'— see the lives of the saints. Genet's murderers and cheats do not emerge. They live out of drama impenetrable to others. For Genet's experiences as a thief, a reformatory boy and burglar, and one who has seen murder (but is not a murderer) have taught him—because he is a gifted man, a sort of poet and rhetorician—that criminals are a stupid, dingy lot of short-sighted morons. Their 'dark night' is really a grey night. Having opted out of society, and narrowed by their monotonous hatreds, they find their momentarily experienced liberty is a wilderness: they long for punishment in the extremely complacent society of prison in which they spend most of their lives if they survive the treacheries of their friends. (Anyone who has had a passing acquaintance with the convicted knows that many consider the wicked are outside of jail.) Genet draws portraits brilliantly in detail with all the passion and *parti pris* of prison society: he admires what can be called the *virtu* of the profession like an aesthete. A good burglar may be self-condemned, but he has pride in his superstitions, his techniques and rituals. Reform is a loss of skill. To be incurable is both a fate and a vanity. He is unknown to loyalty, mercy, pity or charity (i.e., *bonté*).

How does it come about that Genet, a writer so committed to his theme, is able to be without illusions about the criminal? A Sade sees himself as a revolutionary energy; a Dostoevsky, who can so thoroughly abandon himself, for a time, in the idea of 'beyond good and evil,' sees Christ and Salvation. Genet sees nothing. He is a total nihilist, angered by *ennui*. In a really admirable exposition, Richard N. Coe describes him as a lucid schizophrenic and makes a very convincing (and anti-Sartre case) for Genet as one living between those disparate poles that at a touch create the electric spark of poetry. Philip Thody, in a cooler but equally searching work—written, I think, in 1968—contains a little more biographical material, and suggests, if I read him aright, that Genet was a 'made' criminal and not a born one, relying on Genet's words that he became a thief because he was called a thief. It was the result of shock. And that he was able to 'cure' himself by a truly astonishing discovery of language; he entered not a moral world, but a world of words and images.

It is certainly true that his prose is very fine, and that his virtuosity as a writer is enormous: he proceeds from criminal ritual to the literary, without losing his innate interest in violence. He has a marked humour. The paradox and the ambiguity that floor the critic who tries to formulate Genet's thought are the sparks flying off from the brutal hammer-on-anvil of experience. He was born existential. His work is autobiographical but more forcefully so for anticipating the masks, the disguises, the involvement of the reader, assumed by later writers of the *nouveau roman*.

An important feature, also, is Genet's preoccupation with Things. Things exist, have a magnetism, and are as inciting as persons: the majority of his characters are homosexual, but it is the holster, the belt, the jackboot, the badge, the uniform of the male lover that allure: the picturesque argot of buggery, its un-ecstatic clinical detail, are themselves like objects in a 'black' museum at police headquarters. It is true there is a passing sexual tenderness and naïvety. Particularly in a book like *Funeral Rites*—which critics think to be a falling off and which shows an ambiguous and provocative attraction to Nazism—one seems to be in a collector's gallery. In defence of this book it must be said we have forgotten the seamy side of the Libera-tion in Paris.

The poetry of Genet's novels is fragmentary. This has a special force, because of the abrupt and necessarily fragmentary nature of the criminal's life: he never sees beyond his nose as he heads toward punishment or his own death. Genet's virtuosity lies in his management of rapid discursiveness and sudden clinch-ing scenes, in the skill in moving back and forward in time, and in the convincing though arbitrary way in which the author takes himself with a sort of effrontery from the outside to the inside of character. The defects are sudden descents into banal reflection and in over-all pretentiousness. We are not all that far from the idealization of the criminal. There is a theatrical suggestion—especially in the German references, the hatred of France, and so on—of 'the twilight of the Gods'.

And it is both the originality and the tedium of the writer that his impulse is one of personal revenge. (There are scarcely any women in Genet's novels and although this is due to his homosexuality, which is passive and feminine, it has an obvious root in his rage at being abandoned by his mother, who was a prostitute.) The hymn of hate springs from sterility, though it is relieved by a savage humour and by one or two remarkable big scenes. The locale is always deeply there: I think of the eerie seduction in the Tiergarten, or the horror of the hot stink of shooting, fear and rape in the long rooftop scene in the Paris street-fighting.

Genet is the natural production of an age of violence, a natural cult-figure for those who feel guilty because they have escaped martyrdom. He offers everything to the voyeur in ourselves. Sartre tried to push him into politics but except in his play *The Blacks* that has not borne results. I find the interest in the orgies of disgust in the novels, and the attempt to shock us by half-arguing for Hitler and the Nazis, monotonous as scandals. One gets in the novels something of the self-caressing dreariness and pettiness that date, I suppose, from a much better writer like Restif de la Bretonne. The lack of charity is an appalling defect and one rebels against the claustrophobia. His characteristic material is seen to my mind to far better effect in the theatre, simply because the theatre is drastic and has design. The scene in *Funeral Rites* where the drunken Nazi shoots at his Other Self in the mirror is pure theatre.

Genet's rather portentous conceit of the Self, the mirror Self and the Double, works well in the theatre and draws out his extraordinary technical skill. It emphasizes the dream or nightmare frame in which his violence is set and which establishes him as an artist as well as a pornographer. *The Maids* is as good as anything in Strindberg's theatre.

Without the aid of commentators like Thody and of Coe I do not get far with the novels. Coe warns us not to stop at the fact that Genet's novels interpret criminal psychology; he tells us to see the symbolism. This puzzles me. Genet's paradoxes and contradictions seem to be native to the poet of violence and not to a thinker. It is a good argument that Genet is a taboo breaker rather than a law-breaker.

What I got from *Funeral Rites*, after its view of the hoodlum temperament and passive homosexuality, was his capacity to evoke a really frightening sadness, the *tristesse* of the incurable. It is a novel about hatred and sex, lived by people grieving in a void or limbo. The void is all the worse for being small, a place —if that is the word—where people exist only as bodies with sexual or bullet holes in them. Coe thinks that there are signs of something more than a factitious virility in Genet's later work. It would be striking to see Genet achieving the masculine instinct for responsibility and a sense of proportion, but perhaps this would silence him as a writer. Inside his great vanity, a serious artist is clearly at grips with his conflicts.

ZOLA

Zola's Life

ZOLA STANDS IN his time, the latter half of the French nineteenth century, when the energies of industrialism and social
change throbbed, a time above all of awakened appetites for
power. Zola, as we see him from the outside, is Appette in
person, a continuous consumer. Like some powerful locomotive, he eats up facts and lives as if they were so much coal,
choking us with enormous clouds of smoke which were both
dream and nightmare. This was what his public, on which he
kept a close eye, looked for. Their lives were drab. They were
looking for dramas of escape, the satisfactions of desires which
had been repressed by the work ethic and, being the children of
'Get Rich' Guizot and his educational reforms, they were new
to literacy and a little leisure. The scientific pretensions of Zola's
Naturalism, his social concern and his half-poetic violence and
melodrama, were exactly their meat.

Professor Hemmings's *Life* is the first biography in English
for twenty-five years. He has collated the new material now
available to scholars and his book is a thoughtful, inquiring and
well-written book and commands a very necessary perspective.
It puts the light and shade on a complex character whom we
had seen only in black and white.

Professor Hemmings's first point is that Zola was a sensational
artist in a century which had turned to the novel for its emotions
and instruction very much in the way our own mass public
turns to the cinema, television and radio. The novel was the
medium. Like Dickens of an earlier generation, he went after
his public. He was an excellent storyteller with a strong sense of

fatality. The mills of Reason grind more dramatically than the mills of God: the fantasies of Zola depend on documentation and a deep concern for Truth and Justice. There *are* comic passages in Zola's novels, but our main impression is of the efficient pistons of the locomotive's seriousness. Yet, *L'Assommoir* (The Dram Shop), *La Terre* (The Land) and *Germinal* are probably great novels, the *Thérèse Raquin* is the work of an unflinching moralist. What can be held against him is that his subjects become vaguer as they become larger and larger at the end of his career.

Professor Hemmings is careful to see Zola's sensationalism against the background of his passionate liberal beliefs; Zola was no intellectual but he was the bitter enemy of authoritarianism, obscurantism and racial prejudice; he was the forceful man of reason who believed absolutely in the benefits of science; he can be called 'a true heir of the *encyclopédistes* of the eighteenth century. . . . He sought to consolidate the achievements of the Enlightenment.' Truth and Justice are his slogans.

But unlike the immensely marketable believer, the man is not all of a piece. Like Balzac, his exemplar, he was an almost perpetual worker, mostly seen grinding at his desk, a fat, sedentary, myopic figure. Unlike Balzac he lacks magnetism; he is even dull, respectable, shy and personally humourless. He certainly makes no attempt to live out his fantasies as Balzac so ruinously did, though he did keep a considerable tonnage of absurd bric-à-brac in the famous house at Médan. Late in middle age, when he broke his long fidelity to his childless wife and took a peasant girl as his mistress, we do indeed see a repressed Zola appear; even so, there is something dogged and planned about the passion. Overeating had made him (and his wife) gross and hypochondriacal; when he was considering the possibility of love for a young girl, he saw he must prepare for the contingency by going on a diet. As thorough here in self-documentation as he was in his career, he undertook this.

What had Zola repressed? When we turn to the account of Zola's remarkable and far more attractive father, we can see what haunted the novelist. Zola *père* was a Venetian of distinguished family, a brilliant, amorous and adventurous mining engineer and a pioneer among the builders of European railways. Heads of governments listened to him. He was far-seeing and practical, but, at the last moment, men more gifted in raising capital either diddled him or took over his work. In early middle age, he died poor in Aix, where he had married a working-class French woman and thereby established his son's kinship with the common people. The son's emotional capital and capacity for living, one would say, had been exhausted by his gifted father, who left him, however, his respect for work and the imaginative intelligence. (One curious connection with his father's life and career as an engineer can be seen in the peculiar dream of tunneling in *Germinal*.) Literature would be the young Zola's science and industry; his knowledge of working-class poverty and the desire to get out of it were the spur. His sexual temperature was low. His emotions would be absorbed by his simple mother first and then by the able and maternal mistress who became his wife. She also had had to make her own way as an illegitimate child and is thought to have been a florist.

It is a surprise to find that the vigorous, astute and apparently very masculine Zola was a frail and sickly, even rather feminine, young man shut in by anxieties. The violent interest in sex and the lusts of the flesh which give a carnal vividness to his novels was the fantasy of a shy man—it seems—of small performance. His continence in a free-living period was a popular joke among French cartoonists. His imagination was sensual to the point of being pornographic; his life was blameless. Men who have known hunger when they were young are likely to become gluttonous later on, and one can see why an imaginative greed and a dramatic sense of all human hungers appear in his novels:

a greed for sex, fame, money and success, for huge novels that are like enormous highly spiced meals. In one of his famous crowd scenes in *Germinal*, the people are described in terms of their hungry mouths. In *L'Assommoir* the mouth is the drinker's mouth. In these scenes there is gaudy poetry which is also visionary.

The visions have—when we turn to his life—a double source. One can trace this first to his early childhood in Aix where he was a happy and intelligent boy until his spirited Italian father died; secondly to the serious, dreaming, hopeful friendship with the young Cézanne when they talked about their genius as they went swimming. (Zola was at this time a better painter than Cézanne.) After the father's death and the family's move to Paris, the struggle against extreme poverty began. The young Zola slaving in a bookshop felt the iron sense of responsibility for the family. This experience and the haunting friendship with Cézanne—their common feeling of the dream of art—formed him. Cézanne was determined on solitude; Zola was cut out for action and publicity. About the latter he was shameless and pushing; when he was savagely attacked he collected the libels as a sort of treasury or capital. The greater feeder chewed them over: they added to his energies.

Professor Hemmings is especially suggestive on the subject of Zola and the Impressionists. One can see how important they were to him, of course, from *L'Oeuvre*, in which Cézanne is one of his models and in the end theatrically dramatized. One can see what the attraction was; the Impressionists too practised a scientific Naturalism in their manner. They were also in revolt against authority; and Zola was the man for a cause. He was fighting for his career and their careers. He knew what poverty and obloquy were. When in middle life he turned against Cézanne it was because Cézanne had not succeeded. At the height of his own career Zola could only pity failure—and perhaps feared failure himself. All this is evident from the correspondence between the two men.

Far more interesting is another suggestion: Mr Hemmings ponders the question of Zola's bad eyesight. A curious personal vanity made him refuse to wear glasses until late in life, and the suggestion is that his poor vision may have prevented him from really *seeing* the pictures of the Impressionists; their prismatic light was created by the accumulation of immense detail which, to Zola, would appear as a vague general mist, dreamlike at first, ultimately muddy. Is this the reason for the vagueness in Zola's crowd scenes, his large-scale images and his poster-like symbolism? On the other hand, vagueness in these painters would come to suggest weakness of purpose and lack of social direction to which Zola the storyteller and social moralist was emphatically hostile. Except for its brilliant account of the crowd at the Salon, *L'Oeuvre* is a naïvely divided book in which Sandoz-Zola presents himself as the truly great artist—successful, responsible, toiling, suffering the agonies of creation: Lantier-Cézanne is the *raté*, who in a preposterous scene which perhaps discloses the hysteria buried in Zola's life is raped by his own wife, renounces his art, destroys his last picture and hangs himself.

It is common for writers, indeed all artists, to sink into depression when they have finished a work, but it is strange that Zola's pessimism at this time took the form of a fantasy of violence and self-destruction. When the man who scarcely left his desk began his liaison with the gentle seamstress his wife had taken into the bourgeois mansion, his guilt once more led to fears of violence. He was convinced that his wife would murder the girl and the two children she bore. Perhaps the idea was, as we would say, very Italian; his imagination perhaps craved the operatic. In prosaic fact, after frightful scenes, the wife refused divorce for she did not want to throw away her status as the partner of a famous man, and was peaceably won over by the children. She had none of her own.

It is so much in character that Zola, the prophet of modernity and Naturalism, should have been taken by the craze for photography and, before the affair began, used the seamstress as his first model. His preparation via slimming now received the stimulus of a new form of documentation. Yet as Professor Hemmings says, the very nervousness and solicitude with which he approached the young girl were aspects of his solemn decency. His tenderness for human circumstance is the sign of a serious moral nature. If the theme of the guilty secret now appears in his later works, that simply shows that the great novelists have always used every bit of themselves. His guilt enhances his respectability and when we look between the excesses of his novels we see how moving and true he is about the consolations and responsibilities of everyday life in its work and its humble pleasures. When Madame Zola took an interest in his mistress's children, her husband wrote affectionate letters to her telling her what the children were doing and how once he had tested the little girl on her scripture lessons! Professor Hemmings writes:

> It is hard to decide which is stranger: that Zola should have kept his lawful wife informed about the activities of his children by another woman, or that this obdurate freethinker should have displayed such solicitude for their religious education. In a novel he would never have permitted himself such paradoxes. . . .

His melodramas came from another self.

Zola's intervention in the Dreyfus affair—he did not meet Dreyfus until it was all over and found him dim and disappointing—might seem to have a theatrical and even self-publicizing motive. In fact J'Accuse was the most disinterested act of Zola' life. It brought him great popular abuse and indeed exile. Stronger even than his hatred of anti-Semitism was his loathing of corrupt authority, the covering up by professional groups, the tricks of the High Command, the judges, the politicians and a self-serving bureaucracy. Zola was unbendable in his stand for truth-telling and the principles of the law. His tenacity is amazing. He acted as a citizen, not as a novelist, and stood firm against the considerable mass of people who were opposed to him. There is a story that when years later he died of asphyxiation caused by the fumes from the stove in his study, an anti-Semitic workman confessed to having closed the ventilator in the chimney as an act of revenge. The tale has never been confirmed; it sounds too Zola-esque to be true, but it is certainly possible.

George Sand

THE SPELL IMPOSED by George Sand on European and Russian readers and critics in the nineteenth century is understandable; her people and landscapes are silhouettes seen in streams of sheet lightning. For ourselves, what has been left is her notorious life story and the throbbing of her powerful temperament. Yet Balzac, Dostoevsky and—of all people—Matthew Arnold admired her as a novelist. Proust admired her sinuous and gliding prose and Flaubert her exotic imagination. There she was pouring out ink in her sixty novels, her enormous autobiography, her works of travel and her thousands of letters; a thinking bosom and one who overpowered her young lovers; all sybil, teacher, a Romantic, and, in the end, a respectable Victorian moralist.

There were hostile voices of course. As Curtis Cate reminds us in his exhaustive biography published four years ago, Baudelaire burst out with an attack on what had most allured her admirers:

> She has always been a moralist. Only, previously she had indulged in anti-morality. She has thus never been an artist. She has the famous flowing style dear to the bourgeois. She is stupid, she is ponderous, she is long-winded: she has in moral judgments the same depth of judgment and the same delicacy of feeling as concierges and kept women.

(These last two words are wildly wrong: one thing she certainly was not was a pampered courtesan. She spent the large sums of money she earned extravagantly and a large part in charity.)

Shuddering at her candour Henry James was closer to her in his judgement on her talents. Her novels, he said, had turned faint,

> as if the image projected, not intense, not absolutely concrete—failed to reach completely the mind's eye. . . . The wonderful change of expression is not really a remedy for the lack of intensity, but rather an aggravation of it through a sort of suffusion of the whole thing by the voice and speech of the author. . . . [There is] a little too much of the feeling of going up in a balloon. We are borne by a fresh cool current and the car delightfully dangles, but as we peep over the sides we see things—as we usually know them—at a dreadful drop beneath.

The woman who was known for her gifts as a silent listener took to the upper air when she shut herself up at night and became garrulous in ink.

Now, it is evident, an attempt to draw the general reader back to George Sand is underway. The most obvious reason for this is opportunism of the women's liberation kind, where she is bound to be a disappointment to those who look for a guru. A disconcerting sybil she may have been; as a priestess she hedged. The Saint-Simonians were discouraged when they tried to turn her into the Mrs Eddy of free love. A more interesting lure to contemporary taste is suggested by Diane Johnson in her introduction to the novelist's edifying Gothic romance, *Mauprat*, written in the 1830s. Mrs Johnson says that if George Sand's temperament was too strong for her writing, temperament was her subject as an artist:

> . . . readers have come to hold in new high regard the truths of the imagination, the romantic principle, the idea that the passionate artist had access to truths and secrets of human nature more interesting than mere dramas of social arrival.

Gothic melodrama is back with us, if in dank condition, 'for reasons best understood today in terms of psychology, but understood very well by George Sand in universal terms.' (The universal is the trouble.) It is true, at any rate, that the Romantics—especially those of the second wave, the *Hernani* generation—set the artist apart as the supreme seer in society; and that for all their extravagance of feeling and even because of it, they were excellent pre-Freudian psychologists. Their very violence is a prediction and their inflation of the ballooning self makes it dramatic and macroscopic. We have to add that she is shamelessly autobiographical. The love affair of the week, month or year, along with mysticism, socialism and The People was transposed into the novel that promptly followed; she spoke of herself as 'the consumer' of men and women too, and the men often turned out to be projections of herself. The passions of her characters, their powerful jealousies, their alternations of exaltation and gloom, were her own. She was half Literature.

Her finer powers emerged when her fame as a novelist declined, above all in her *Histoire de ma vie*, in her lively travel writing and her letters. In her letters there is no need of Gothic castles or dreadful ravines: her mundane experience was extraordinary enough in itself. As a traveller she had eyes, ears and verve. The short pastoral novels *La mare au diable* (*The Haunted Pool*) or *François le Champi* (*The Country Waif*) are serene masterpieces drawn from her childhood and her love of nature, which awakened her senses as they awakened Colette's. She was close to the peasants of Nohant. The self is in these tales, but it is recollected or transposed in tranquility—in her own early life she had known what it was to be a waif, albeit a very fortunate one. These works have never lost their quiet, simple, truth-telling power and we understand why Turgenev, Henry James, and, later, Malraux praised them.

George Sand was the child of one of Napoleon's well-born officers. He was a descendant of the great Maréchal de Saxe and therefore, on the wrong side of the blanket, of the King of Poland. Her mother was a plebeian woman, the hot-tempered daughter of a Paris innkeeper and bird fancier. The inner class conflict enriched both George Sand's exuberant imagination and those sympathies with the poor which took her into radical politics; strangely like Tolstoy—but without his guilt or torment—she turned to presenting the peasantry not as quaint folk or a gospel, but as sentient, expressive beings. She listened to the curious Berrichon dialect and translated it, without folkish affectations or condescensions, into a truthful expression of plain human feeling. She had the humility and concern to discard dramatic earnestness without losing her psychological acumen or her art as a story teller who keeps her people in focus as the tradition of Pastoral does: very often her best work is a gloss on traditional forms.

In the feminist foreground of the present revival is *Lélia*, the confessional novel which she wrote at the age of twenty-nine in 1833 after the rebellion against her marriage, the break with Jules Sandeau, and the disastrous attempts to obtain sexual pleasure from an expert like Mérimée, or from any other man as far as we know. Chopin said she loved extremely but was incapable of making love. Partly because of its attacks on the Church and the marriage system, the male hold on property and the double standard, partly because of its erotic revelation and the rumour of a lesbian attachment to the actress Marie Dorval, the book itself was attacked for outrageous and morbid candour. Lélia is intended to be a Romantic heroine, a doomed but indomitable soul, one pursuing a mystical quest for spiritual love. She is beautiful, intellectual, independent, yet tormented by a sensuality that is nevertheless incapable of sexual happiness. She cannot be a nun like Santa Teresa nor can she be a courtesan or married woman. The dreams of a poetically exalted adolescence have divorced the heart from the body. Literature has paralyzed her. She says of a lover:

When I was near him I felt a sort of strange and delirious greed which, taking its source from the keenest powers of my intelligence, could not be satisfied by any carnal embrace. I felt my bosom devoured by an inextinguishable fire, and his kisses shed no relief. I pressed him in my arms with a superhuman force, and fell next to him exhausted, discouraged at having no possible way to convey to him my passion. With me desire was an ardour of the soul that paralyzed the power of the senses before it awakened them. It was a savage fury that seized my brain and concentrated itself there exclusively. My blood froze, impotent and poor, before the immense soaring of my will . . .

When he was drowsy, satisfied, and at rest, I would lie motionless beside him. I passed many hours watching him sleep. He seemed so handsome to me! There was so much force and grandeur on his peaceful brow. Next to him my heart palpitated violently. Waves of blood mounted to my face. Then unbearable tremblings passed through my limbs. I seemed to experience again the excitation of physical love and the increasing turmoil of desire. I was violently tempted to awaken him, to hold him in my arms, and to ask for his caresses from which I hadn't yet known how to profit. But I resisted these deceiving entreaties of my suffering because I well knew it wasn't in his power to calm me.

The stone images of Catholic 'palaces of worship' give no comfort, for her imagination responds chiefly to the figurations of medieval nightmare: scaly serpents, hideous lizards, agonized chimeras and emblems of sin, illusion and suffering. Sublimation has two faces:

When the red rays of the setting sun played on their forms, I seemed to see their flanks swell, their spiny fins dilate, their faces contract into new tortures. . . . While I contemplated these bodies engulfed in masses of stone, which the hand of neither man nor time had been able to dislodge, I identified myself with these images of eternal struggle between suffering and necessity, between rage and impotence.

The nightmares of the unconscious haunt the aspirant. And

we are warned that when spring comes to stir the senses, all attempt to deny the calyx or the bud, by the study of botany, or to turn to science, will not annul the ferment of the imagination. As always in George Sand, poetic observation and imagery is rather fine: but the inevitable tutorial follows.

I take these passages from Maria Espinosa's translation. She has worked on the 1833 edition which George Sand toned down three years later. This early edition has not been done into English until now, and the version is remarkable for coming very close to the resonant vocabulary and its extraordinary physical images. If there is a loss it is because English easily droops into a near-evangelical tune; our language is not made for operatic precisions and we have a limited tradition of authorized hyperbole. Abstractions lose the intellectual formality that has an exact ring in French.

It is important to remember, also, that George Sand's prose feeds on a sensibility to music which dated from her childhood: she was alert to all sounds in nature and to all delicacies and sonorities of voice and instrument. (Her novels might be described as irresistible overtures to improbable operas which are —as they proceed—disordered by her didactic compulsion.) *Lélia*, I think, rises above this, because it is so personal and arbitrary in its succession of sounds and voices, and we are bounced into accepting the hyperbole as we would be if it were sung, though we may be secretly bored by the prolonging of the moans.

In *Lélia* we listen to five voices: there is the voice of Sténio, the young poet lover whom Lélia freezes with Platonic love: she is an exalted *allumeuse*; there is Trenmor, the elderly penitent gambler and stoic—her analysis of the gambler's temperament is the best thing in the book: George Sand was at heart a gambler—there is Magnus, the fanatic priest who is made mad by the suppression of his sexual desires and who sees Lélia as a she-devil; there is Pulchérie, Lélia's sister, a genial courtesan living for sexual pleasure; and Lélia herself, defeated by her sexual coldness, horrified by the marriage bed, the mocker of a stagnant society, religion and the flesh. She is sick with self-love and her desires approach the incestuous: she seeks weak men who cannot master her, to whom she can be either a dominating mother, sister or nurse.

In chorus these voices sing out the arguments for and against spiritual love. As in opera, the plot is preposterous and scenes are extravagant and end without warning. Pulchérie introduces a pagan and worldly note and also—it must be said—the relief of more than a touch of nature. She reminds the miserable Lélia of a charming incident in their childhood when the beauty of Lélia troubled her as they lay sleeping on the mossy bank dear to Romantic fiction. Pulchérie says:

Your thick, black hair clung to your face, and the close curls tightened as if a feeling of life had clenched them next to your neck, which was velvet with shadow and sweat. I passed my fingers through your hair. It seemed to squeeze and draw me toward you. . . . In all your features, in your position, in your appearance, which was more rigid than mine, in the deeper tint of your complexion, and especially in that fierce, cold expression on your face as you slept, there was something masculine and strong which nearly prevented me from recognizing you. I found that you resembled the handsome young man with the black hair of whom I had just dreamed. Trembling, I kissed your arm. Then you opened your eyes, and your gaze penetrated me with shame. . . . But, Lélia, no impure thought had even presented itself to me. How had it happened? I knew nothing. I received from nature and from God my first lesson in love, my first sensation of desire.

The scenes of Lélia's despair take place inevitably in an abandoned monastery, with its debris that suggest the horrors of death and the futility of existence. Lélia says:

At times I tried to find release by crying out my suffering and anger. The birds of the night flew away terrified or answered me with savage wailings.

(Nature always responds to George Sand.)

The noise echoed from vault to vault, breaking against those shaky ruins; and the gravel that slid from the rooftops seemed to presage the fall of the edifice on my head.

That gravel, it must be said, is excellent observation. Her comment is typically orchestral:

Oh, I would have wished it were so! I redoubled my cries, and those walls echoed my voice with a more terrible and heart-rending sound. They [the ruins] seemed inhabited by legions of the damned, eager to respond and unite with me in blasphemy.

These terrible nights were followed by days of bleak stupor.

A scene of Oriental luxury was indispensable to the Romantics: the looting of Egypt was Napoleon's great gift to literature. There is the fantastic ball given by Prince Bambuccj in which lovers can disappear into boudoirs and artificial caves as busily as bees. The trumpets, one must say, acclaim the triumphs of fornication; they are gorgeously brazen in the lascivious scene; the perfumes are insidious. Pulchérie and Lélia are masked and Lélia plots to pass off Pulchérie as herself so that Sténio is deceived into thinking his cold mistress has relented. He awakens and is shattered by the deceit. He stands at the window of the palace and hears the voice of Lélia mocking him—in a somewhat classy way—from a pretty boat that floats by in the Asiatic lagoon. This is an operatic scene of a high order. Calamity, of course. Having tasted flesh, Sténio becomes a drunken debauchee and eventually commits suicide. If he starts, in real life, as the innocent Jules Sandeau, he ends as the drunken

Musset. Magnus, the mad priest, is now sure that Lélia is possessed by a devil and strangles her. With a rosary, of course.
One recalls that Lélia has had fantasies of strangulation.

Lélia is one of those self-dramatizations that break off as
mood follows mood. She asks what God intended for men and
women: whether he intended them to meet briefly and leave
each other at once, for otherwise the sexes would destroy each
other; whether the hypocrisy of a bourgeois society is the
enemy; whether intellectual vision must be abnormal; whether
poetry and religion corrupt. All the voices are George Sand
herself—and very aware, as she frankly said, that she belonged
to a generation which, for the moment, was consciously out to
shock. What she did not expect was laughter. She had little
sense of humour.

One can see how much of the book comes out of Hoffmann
and even more precisely from Balzac's equally chaotic and
melodramatic *La Peau de chagrin*. Lélia, it has often been noted,
is the female Raphael de Valentin. Both writers feel the expanding energies of the new century; both have the confident impulse toward the Absolute and to Omniscience; but hers is the
kind of imagination and intellect that breaks off before
suggesting a whole. Balzac and Sand were both absorbed by an
imaginative greed; they worked themselves to the bone, partly
because they were like that, partly because they created debts and
openly sought a vast public. Their rhetoric was a nostalgia for
the lost Napoleonic glory.

How thoroughly she toiled in her social-problem novels!
The tedious *Compagnon du Tour de France* is a garrulous study of
the early trade unions, a politically pious book, enlivened by her
strong visual sense. In the far more sympathetic *Mauprat* she
goes to the heart of her life-long debt to Rousseau: the young
brutal Mauprat who belongs to the brigand and mafioso branch
of an aristocratic family rescues the aristocratic heroine from
his gang—but with the intention of raping her on the quiet. She

frustrates the attempt and is shown redeeming her brute: to love he must pass through a long psychological re-education. This is achieved but not entirely in a sentimental way; both he and the women are hot-tempered, sulky and sensitive to points of honour.

George Sand herself did not think we should be punished for our sins or our grave faults of character, but that we were called upon to learn from them: they were—*grace à* Rousseau—opportunities for interesting self-education and reform. She is not a doctrinaire like Gorki in his communist phase. Her advantage as a woman is that she is a psychologist who gives hostilities their emotional due: they are indications of the individual's right to his temperament. She may have been a domineering, ruthless woman and very cunning and double-minded with it, but there is scarcely a book that is not redeemed by her perceptions, small though they may be.

She understands the rich very well—'There are hours of impunity in château life'—and she thinks of the poor as individuals but flinches from them as a case. Two words recur continually in her works: 'delirium,' which may be ecstatic, bad, or, more interestingly, a psychological outlet; and 'boredom'—energy and desire had been exhausted. One can see that she is woman but not Woman. The little fable of *François de Champi* shows that she used every minute of her life; for not only was she in a fortunate sense a waif, as I have said, but an enlightened waif; and we note that when François grows up he marries the widow who has been a mother to him. Most of George Sand's men were waifs in one way or another; the Higher Incest was to be their salvation. Women were the real power figures, whereas men were consumable. She liked to pilfer their brains.

She certainly sought only gifted men who were usually sick and with whom she could assume the more powerful role of mother and nurse. Chopin was her 'child'. Sandeau was her 'little brother'. What about Michel de Bourges, her proletarian

lawyer and Christian Communist, who almost converted her
to the need for violent revolution and the guillotine? Here was
a virile man, and he could offer oratory, notoriety, and powerful embraces, but he was in bad health, too; she became frenzied
—but was it the frenzy she desired? It may have been. She
defiantly walked the streets of his native town in trousers and
smoking her pipe, enjoyed the scandal, and caused scenes between him, his wife and his fat mistress. He was a tyrant, and
one might think this was what she sought. Not at all. *She* could
not dominate *him*; despite her passion for him, which drove her
to ride for miles at night for a short, Chatterley-like tryst, he
could not subdue the strongest thing in her—her intellect.

Michel de Bourges was responsible for her wordy novels of
social revolt, but he could not break her opposition to the utilitarian view of art. Like all the Romantics, she believed in the
vision of the artist as the unique and decisive spiritual force in
society. He might dismiss all this as a self-regarding bourgeois
delusion, but she would not yield. All the same, she wrote propaganda for the republican cause in '48, and when the reaction
came she handed out money to the hunted proletarian poets and
took advantage of acquaintance with Louis Napoleon to get her
friends and fellow-writers out of jail. In Nohant, she was a
scandal because of her lovers. The villagers imagined orgies
when the young men came and went. After '48, she was a
political scandal. The obsequious villagers touched their caps
but sneered behind her back. This did not disturb her. She was
a country girl at heart and knew that revolution was an urban
industrial notion; in the countryside it meant nothing. And, in
fact, the country crowd, particularly the women, took her side
when the husband she had deserted made two savage and incompetent efforts in court to get Nohant from her.

This episode is thoroughly gone into by Mr Cate. It is important, for it brings out where she stood—or wobbled—on the
crucial question of marriage and free love. The two court actions

have the inevitable air of comedy: Michel de Bourges was her lover and her advocate, yet she had to appear respectable and demure. No trousers and no pipe now; she appeared in shawl and bonnet. An absurd but useful opportunity occurred for her to ascend astutely into the upper air when questions of adultery and free love were brought up. Those exalted ladies of the Saint-Simonian persuasion came to address her as a priestess. They invited her to become a 'mother' of the Saint-Simonian 'family', or phalanstery, and even sent a load of hand-made presents, which included shoes, trousers, waistcoats, collars, one watercolour and a riding crop. In reply, she recommended them to practice the ancient morality of faithful marriage for 'being the most difficult, [it] is certainly the finest', though she would not blame those who shook themselves free of tyranny, which was the product of a false society. The fact is that for her, as for her fellow-Romantics, the just society already existed metaphysically, and that in this sense she was chaste. And she was no fool. She *was* temporarily chaste with her lawyer, but at home, at Nohant, she kept another pretender, whom she was maddening with the kisses of platonic affection. This was Charles Didier, a Genevan, and Mr Cate differs from André Maurois' judgement in his opinion of his character. How far they went, no one knows; to judge by his tortured 'Journal', Didier himself seems unsure. All he could report was hugs that seem maternal. It is nearly impossible to translate the language of the Romantics, but in reply to one of his injured letters George Sands is masterly. She could easily squash rancour:

> You don't love, all I can do is love. Friendship for you is a contract with clauses for the well-combined advantage of both parties, for me it is sympathy, embrace, identity, it is the complete adoption of the qualities and faults of the person one feels to be one's friend. . . . You attribute to me . . . a calculated dryness, how shall I put it?—something worse, a kind of prostitution of the heart, full of baseness, egotism, falseness, you make

me out to be a kind of platonic slut. . . . My misfortune is to throw myself wholeheartedly at each fine soul I encounter. . . . What I took for a noble soul is a gloomy, sickly suspicious soul that has lost the ability to believe and thus to love.

Honesty or sophistry? Goodness knows. Better to call it incantation. Didier was soon forgotten. The loss of Michel de Bourges looked fatal to her reason, but she was quickly, so to say, back in the saddle. An amusing actor arrived, and there was soon a troupe of young men, all hoping to be the favourite.

And, distributing her kisses, back to her room she went for her nightly five- or six-hour stint on the next novel. The blood —her own and that of others—was turned into ink. We remember the cold words of Solange, the daughter who was no less wilful than herself: 'It would take a shrewd fellow to unravel the character of my mother.'

FLAUBERT

The Quotidian

ALTHOUGH MARRED BY affectations of style, Professor Brombert's study of the themes and techniques of Flaubert's novels is a full and very suggestive scrutiny of Flaubert's love-hate of realism, as it is woven into the texture of his narratives. Flaubert's own ambiguities on the subject are clear. 'I abhor what has been called realism, although they make me out to be one of its high priests,' he wrote to George Sand. He hated reality. (Or rather it disgusted him; that is also an attraction.) Art held priority over life. If so much of his work is minutely drawn from everyday life, he forced himself to depict it (in Professor Brombert's words):

> partly out of self-imposed therapy to cure himself of his chronic idealism, partly also out of a strange and almost morbid fascination. . . . Art for him was quite literally an escape . . . For hatred of reality . . . was intimately bound up with an inherent pessimism—and pessimism in turn was one of the prime conditions of his ceaseless quest for ideal forms.

In resilient moments he called himself an old '*romantique enragé*': even, a *troubadour*.

All this is well known; we know an enormous amount about Flaubert and Professor Brombert brings all the important critics into his net. But, a good deal owing to Marxist and Christian criticism, the quite gratuitous notion has got about that Flaubert was not what he ought to have been. He ought not to have been 'an alienated bourgeois'; yet, surely, a vast number of great artists have been 'alienated' from their dispensation and especially in the nineteenth century. Alienation is a cant term for a necessary condition. The 'hatred' of Balzac, Stendhal, Zola, Flaubert or Proust are the characteristic engines of a century bemused by its own chaotic energies. The force of criticism from an outside position of Marxist, Christian or psychoanalytical neo-conformity is now fading and one is at least heartened to see Professor Brombert applying himself to 'the unique temperament and vision that determine and characterize a novelist's work as we find them in the text'.

There can be two weaknesses in this kind of criticism; first it puritanically denies side glances at biography, social influences, etc., and rather hypocritically assumes that we have had these necessities privately at the back door. Professor Brombert is not too strict here; how could one leave out the effect of atheistic medical observation and the morgue on Flaubert's mind? Even Flaubert's obsession with style seems to have something of medical specialization in it. Secondly, the critic may find too much in the text and build top-heavy theories on images and symbols, as one finds, for example, when this kind of criticism deals with Dickens: all that talk of baptismal water! (I have only one doubt about Professor Brombert's attention to key words: this is when he catalogues the symbols of liquefaction.)

In Flaubert the danger is usually small for he was the most conscious of artists; a most ardent collector of echoes and symbols. His documentary interest in *things* is also a concern with what they tell of the imagination. Things are corrupted or corrupting. He is tortured by the fact that the century has turned mind into matter, the ideal converted into ludicrous or detestable paraphernalia.

Take the matter of the Algerian scarves in *Madame Bovary*. They were coming into fashion with the beginning of French colonisation of North Africa: that is a comment both on bourgeois enterprise and greed, and on the absurdities of provincial taste. It is nearly a comment on the economy of the textile city of Rouen. The nineteenth century will colonize; so, in its fantasies, did the nineteenth century soul. When Emma turns spendthrift and buys curtains, carpets and hangings from the draper, the information takes on something from the theme of the novel itself: the material is a symbol of the exotic, and the exotic feeds the Romantic appetite. It will lead to satiety, bankruptcy and eventually to nihilism and the final drive towards death and nothingness.

If anyone makes too much of his images, it will be Flaubert himself: for example, the snake, in the snake-like hiss of Madame Bovary's corset lace. It is a melodramatic excess, as one can tell by the eagerness with which the image was seized upon by the lurid and falsifying mind of the prosecuting lawyer when Flaubert was being charged with obscenity. The phrase could well have gone into the *Dictionnaire des idées reçues*. Flaubert's subject is the imagination and particularly of the orgiastic adolescent kind which he never outgrew and which received almost operatic support from an early reading of the Marquis de Sade and the early extremes of the Romantic movement.

How is it that—as it seems to us now—a whole century became adolescent? Is prolonged adolescence characteristic of a new class coming to power? This is not Professor Brombert's interest; but casting an eye on the ominous *Intimate Notebooks 1840–1841*—written when Flaubert was eighteen and already pretending to be twenty—and proceeding through the novels, Professor Brombert is able to show how, exhaustively and like an infected pathologist Flaubert presented the hunger for the future, the course of ardent longings and violent desires that rise from the sensual, the horrible, and the sadistic. They turn into the virginal and mystical, only to become numbed by satiety. At this point pathological boredom leads to a final desire for death and nothingness—the Romantic syndrome. The *Notebooks* contain eager cries on behalf of adolescent bi-sexuality;

moralize on the ecstatic yet soon-to-be ashy joys of narcissism; pass, without pause, into dreams of exotic travel:

> Often I am in India, in the shade of banana trees, sitting on mats: bayaderes are dancing, swans are fluffing out their feathers on blue lakes, nature throbs with love.

One is struck by the drunken accomplishment of the young diarist, particularly by the precision and clarity of his ingenious self-study at a time of life when one is most likely to be turgid and blind. The son of Dr Flaubert has made notes which a psychiatrist would find useful. How perceptive to write, at that age:

> Sensual pleasure is pleased with itself: it relishes itself, like melancholy—both of them solitary enjoyments. . . .

The style has already the élan and excessive conviction which are the startling qualities of his first novel *November*, unpublished in his lifetime. Luckily it has in Frank Jellinek a translator who responded to the youthful yet (again) accomplished puerilities of the writer. This book, above all, contains the emotional source of *Madame Bovary*; it states the imaginative condition of romantic love, underlines the onanism at the heart of the fantasy of the virgin whore. The very absurdities of this first novel are moving, not only because of the afflatus but because of the fidelity to the course of an emotion that may be extravagant but is precisely recognizable. What astonishes is Flaubert's understanding of his experience at that age. Here he begins his career as the doctor who proceeds to diagnosis by catching the patient's fever first.

We meet one or two of the famous Flaubert obsessions: 'There was one word which seemed to me the most beautiful of all human words: "adultery" '; his horror of begetting a child; and passages like:

Since I did not use existence, existence used me: my dreams
wearied me more than great labours. A whole creation, motionless, unrevealed to itself, lived mute below my life: I was a
sleeping chaos of a thousand fertile elements which knew not
how to manifest themselves nor what to be, still seeking their
form and awaiting their mould.

As Professor Brombert says, *November* is indispensable to an
understanding of *Madame Bovary*, where 'the thousand fertile
elements' manifested themselves in the facts of Normandy life.
Life is a dream, life is bad art; only Art, the supreme reverie can
redeem it: Flaubert's pessimism is clinical and absolute. Or is it?
Keeping close to the text, Professor Brombert tries to make a
path through Flaubert's ingenuities, duplicities and double
meanings; and taking a tip from Flaubert's own phrase that it is
stupid to come to conclusions, he points out that Flaubert's
pessimism is, at any rate, resilient. Style may not save us but it
is a force.

There are many good things in the discussion of *Madame
Bovary*. It is a novel as complex as the second part of *Don Quixote*: we shall never get to the bottom of it. For example, there is
the question of how Flaubert's lyrical intention was to consort
with the banal, especially in the matter of speech. In fact Flaubert's impersonality was a fraud: he contrived—since the book
was a work of self-discovery and confession—all kinds of intrusion. Often openly:

> . . . it is a grave mistake not to seek candour behind worn-out
> language, as though fullness of soul did not at times overflow in
> the emptiest metaphors.

And Professor Brombert comments:

> This feeling that human speech cannot possibly cope with our
> dreams and our grief goes a long way toward explaining why so
> often, in the work of Flaubert, the reader has the disconcerting

impression that the language of banality is caricatured and at the same time transmuted into poetry.

(Yes: the comic is poetry inverted. The effect of pure comedy is poetic.)

Flaubert has the power of transmuting the trivial. He wrote:

> My book will have the ability to walk straight on a hair, suspended between the double abyss of lyricism and vulgarity.

As Professor Brombert says, one misses the charity, the 'imperceptible human tremors' in Flaubert: there is a rift between the sophistication of the author and the confusion of the characters: but it is the test of a great writer that he can turn his dilemmas to effect. Flaubert disguises the rift by

> The telescoping of two unrelated perspectives which bestows upon the novel a unique beauty. A stereoscopic vision accounts in large part for the peculiar poetry and complexity of *Madame Bovary*.

On the subject of the death of Madame Bovary there have been wearying differences of opinion. To some she has been hounded. To others she is a silly and disreputable nonentity, her shame not worth the expense of spirit. To D. H. Lawrence she was crushed by the intellectual skill that had created her: to others no more than a cold exercise. Yet again, she has been used by Flaubert to cure himself of his own disease. In fact, as Professor Brombert shows, the theme and even something of the plot had been known to Flaubert since his youth. There are no exercises in literature. I was struck when I last read the novel —as Professor Brombert was—by the extent of the sympathy with which she is treated. She has, even when she is mocked, the honesty of an energy. Her periods of depravity do not single her out as an exceptionally deplorable being, but rather make her part of the general, glum strangeness of the people around her. She belongs to Rouen: she is what belonging to a place or a culture may mean. She is dignified by a real fate—not by the false word 'Fate', one of the clichés Flaubert derided. Delusion itself dignifies her. The comparison with *Don Quixote* imposes itself: we see

> ... her terrible isolation, her unquenchable aspiration for some unattainable ideal. Hers are dreams that destroy. But this destructive power is also their beauty, just as Emma's greatness (the word is inappropriate to literal-minded readers) is her ability to generate such dreams . . . at the moment of her complete defeat in the face of reality, she acquires dignity, and even majesty.

And despite the clinical attentions of Flaubert, her fellow adolescent, I can see no force in the criticism that, in drawing her, Flaubert tried to turn himself into a woman: it may be that in putting masculinity into her—as Baudelaire said—Flaubert made her perverse. But perversity is a normal sexual ingredient as well as an article in the Romantic canon. The Romantics were good psychologists.

Professor Brombert's final remarks are new. There is an apparent negation of tragic values in Flaubert! Does he suggest a new form of tragedy, the tragedy of the very absence of Tragedy, a condition familiar to contemporary writers? There is a link between him and ourselves.

> The oppressive heterogeneity of phenomena, the fragmented immediacy of experience, the constant fading or alteration of forms. . . .

These are twentieth-century assumptions. Equally important, Flaubert diagnoses the crisis of language.

> The breakdown of language under the degrading impact of

journalism, advertisement and political slogans parallels the breakdown of a culture over-inflated with unassimilable data.

It leads to the incoherence of *Waiting for Godot*, the triumph of the rigmarole.

My only serious criticism of Professor Brombert concerns his own use of language. It is depressing to find so good a critic of Flaubert—of all people—scattering academic jargon and archaisms in his prose. The effect is pretentious and may, one hopes, be simply the result of thinking in French and writing in English; but it does match the present academic habit of turning literary criticism into technology. One really cannot write of Flaubert's 'dilection for monstrous forms' or of 'vertiginous proliferation of forms and gestures'; 'dizzying dilation', or 'volitation'; 'lupanar'—when all one means is 'pertaining to a brothel'. Philosophers, psychologists and scientists may, I understand, write of 'fragmentations' that suggest 'a somnambulist and oneiric state'. But who uses the pretentious 'obnuvilate' when they mean 'dim' or 'darkened by cloud'? Imaginative writers know better than to put on this kind of learned dog. The duty of the critic is to literature, not to its surrogates. And if I were performing a textual criticism of this critic I would be tempted to build a whole theory on his compulsive repetition of the word 'velleities'. Words and phrases like these come from the ingenuous and fervent pens of *Bouvard and Pécuchet*.

Literary criticism does not add to its status by opening an intellectual hardware store.

STENDHAL

An Early Outsider

STENDHAL WAS ONE of those gamblers for whom the wheel of Fortune turned too late. Ignored by almost everyone except Mérimée and Balzac who considered that *La Chartreuse de Parme* was the most important French novel of their time, he declared, without a trace of self-pity, indeed confident in his blistering vanity, that the wheel would turn 100 years after his death. In fact in forty years the great egotist was justified by Zola. For Zola he was: 'a man composed of soul alone. . . . One always feels him there, coldly attentive to the working of his machine. Each of his characters is a psychologist's experiment which he ventures to try on man.' By the beginning of this century Henri Beyle—the figure hidden secretively behind more than 200 pseudonyms who had passed his life as a doubtfully combatant Napoleonic soldier in Italy and Russia, as a travelling and loitering journalist and plagiarizing high-class hack, as a dilettante, petty Consul, ugly and coarse in drawing rooms, as a misfiring, theorizing lover and a novelist poor in invention who left his great novels abruptly unfinished—had become a cosmopolitan cult.

One important reason for this is that he knew the lasting force of that clear, plain, dry and caustic prose style: and knew that something curt and preposterous in one's style as a person will have its hour. At certain periods of crises in history and manners an intelligent man is forced to see that a change of style is being born. As a youth growing up in the French Revolution and with youth's need of a persona, he found himself divided between the eighteenth century idea of 'the man of the world' and the first intimations of Romantic energy. One had to construct a new self. As an aspiring writer he was drawn to the art of his time: stage comedy—but he soon saw that this had become impossible. Stage comedy depended on a stable class system, fixed social values: these had gone with the Revolution and the post-Napoleonic world. He also saw that the novel was the new form to which the audience would respond but that it would impose a crude, impersonal omniscience and would be about 'other people' grouped in their acceptable categories: the novelist is drowned and effaced in other people, whereas he, Stendhal, secretive, addicted to masks and self-defence, was obsessed by his own intelligent private life, his need to begin constructing a Machiavellian and impervious self from the ground upwards. The egotist lay awake at night, tortured by the question: 'Who am I?' Even more important: 'What shall I make of myself? What is my role? What are the correct tactics?' It is easy to understand why he is the precursor of Romanticism in *La Chartreuse de Parme* and why in *Le Rouge et le Noir* Julien Sorel foreshadows the large population of outsiders and the disaffected formed by the revolutions, wars, social crises, prisons and police states that have revived something of the climate and complacencies of the Napoleonic period. In a recent biography Joanna Richardson says that he was 'a provincial born outside the Establishment, enjoying none of the privileges of birth, wealth or education. His sense of inequality and grievance led him bitterly to make amends. He despised authority, he professed to scorn the nobility and yet—like Julien Sorel—he wanted to conquer the nobility. He ridiculed the dignatories of the Tuileries, and yet, with monotonous persistence, he tried to ensure himself a barony . . . all his life he was conscious of status.' Yet, of course, the desire to be either Sorel or Fabrice was a deeply imaginative conspiracy that sailed far beyond social or political considerations. The egotist's pursuit of personal happiness—*la chasse du bonheur*—led him to the Romantic idealization of solitude and reverie, the brief sublime moment.

The biographer of Stendhal is in competition with a per-petual autobiography—Stendhal has no other subject, in his novels, his letters, his exhaustive *Journal*, in the *Souvenirs d'Egotisme* and *La Vie de Henri Brulard*. He saw himself as a con-spiracy. He was given to minute research into the moral history of his attitudes, so the biographer is left chiefly with the problem of deciding where, if ever, the candour ceased to be fantasy or petulance, where calculation in love was coxcombry, and where they were signs of a fatally split nature. There is no doubt that his celebrated hatred of his father and his sensual passion for his mother, who died when he was seven, reiterated the old Oedipus story, but it was political as well. Stendhal despised his father for being a bourgeois lawyer and a supporter of the Bourbons; very early the boy convinced himself that he was a putative aristocrat and yet at the same time a child of the French Revolution. He also despised his father for being a shrewd Dauphinois and a speculator in property, despised him even more for being unsuccessful in this, and resented the loss of a good deal of his inheritance. Stendhal was even jealous of his widowed father's grief, and went on to imagine that, on the mother's side, the family were of Italian origin and that they combined passionate Italian traits with the pride he oddly loved to call *espagnolisme*. Here, rather than in social snobbery, was the root of his aristocratic idea: he felt he belonged to the élite of another age and another country. Yet his truculence covered deep timidity. His temperament was lazy, but he read and worked like a diligent bourgeois. Only those who work, he said, were equipped for the true end of living—the study of the arts and the pursuit of pleasure.

For one who thought himself born into the wrong class, Stendhal was lucky in 'the bastard', 'the Jesuit' (his father) who gave him a decent allowance and sent him to Paris to study. He was lucky also in family friends—the Darus, who took the conceited youth into their house. He refused to go to the École Polytechnique, and they got him a job in the Ministry of War. Stendhal thrived on influence. In a few months, at the age of seventeen, he was commissioned an officer in Napoleon's reserve army in Italy. Italy transfigured him. Italy was freedom; hearing opera for the first time—'the Scala transformed me'. A lifelong dislike of France—indeed, the pretence that he was not really French—began. He fell in love with Angela Pietragrua, a married woman—older than himself—whom he was too timid to approach; she fulfilled his need for the remote goddess. There were untouched remote goddesses to follow; there was also syphilis, caught in the brothels of Milan, which affected his health for the rest of his life. The only woman he was really devoted to for many years was one of his sisters, and in his letters to her a tutorial figure appears and one begins to see that he is constructing his own system of self-education and behaviour. The outsider is studying and acting out a role, creating a self from scratch; it is defiant, touching and a good deal absurd. In his love affairs—he was determined on seduction—the tactics, the search for a style, the analysis of his amorous campaigns have the fidgetiness of artificial comedy; he spent half his youth putting obstacles in his own way, as Miss Richardson says. In the pursuit of these passions, he believed in the *coup de foudre*: when it occurred, he was paralyzed and in tears; if he was encouraged, he fell into long storms of melancholy; if he was victorious, boredom arrived sooner or later, generally sooner. The perpetual cry of this adolescent, whether he is with Napoleon's army in Germany or Russia, whether he is back in Italy, is that he is bored to death. He is one of those who exhaust an experience before the experience occurs—the Romantic malady that becomes a pose and second nature. But if he did not succeed in creating an impenetrable new self and in becoming the superior man of sensibility, he had fitted himself to become a master of comedy in which scornful epigram and abrupt observation go off like rifle shots and leave the dry smell of gunpowder. Each sentence of his plain prose is a separate shock.

The later Romantics were too young for the Napoleonic glory, but in his harsh, sardonic way Stendhal had known it on the battlefield, though not as a fighting officer. From Smolensk he wrote in 1812, when he was twenty-nine:

> How man changes! My former thirst for seeing things is completely quenched, after seeing Milan and Italy, everything repels me by its coarseness. . . . In this ocean of barbarity, there isn't a single sound that replies to my soul.

He was thinking of the music of Cimarosa and his love for Angela Pietragrua. When he watched Moscow burning, he had a toothache and read a few lines of *Virginie*, which revived him morally. He had taken the manuscript of his unfinished *Histoire de la Peinture en Italie* with him, read Mme du Deffand, pillaged a volume of Voltaire, whom he detested, and tried to think of the 'score of comedies' he would write 'between the ages of thirty-four and fifty-four' if only his father would die and leave him some money. He shows off to his correspondents, and rescues an early mistress who had married a Russian (she is very 'chilly'), but when the great fire starts he seems to keep his head and to display sang-froid—or so people reported. He was unconsciously collecting the material for the superb Waterloo chapter in *La Chartreuse de Parme*, and one catches its accent. (He was not at Waterloo.) Of the beginning of the retreat he wrote in his diary, as one seeing the scene *staged* for his benefit:

> We broke through the lines, arguing with some of the King of Naples' carters. I later noticed that we were following the Tverskoï, or Tver Street. We left the city, illuminated by the finest fire in the world, which formed an immense pyramid which, like the prayers of the faithful, had its base on earth and

its apex in heaven. [Very much like Stendhal's own nature.] The moon appeared above this atmosphere of flame and smoke. It was an imposing sight, but it would have been necessary to be alone or else surrounded by intelligent people in order to enjoy it. What has spoiled the Russian campaign for me is to have taken part in it with people who would have belittled the Colosseum or the Bay of Naples.

An aesthete's comment? Not entirely. It is an introspection we shall see transmuted when we find him examining the illusion of Napoleonic glory. Even before the grand scene the Stendhalian hero is a psychologist. History dished this outsider. He was the victim, he said, of the mediocrity that characterizes an age of transition.

There have been two revivals of interest in Stendhal in this century. In the twenties it was led by Francophiles who used it as a modish attack on the nineteenth century for its denigration of the eighteenth. Stendhal was useful, too, as a distant founder of the parricides' club which thrived after the 1914 war.

The hardness of his ego and his impudence were our admirations; and the 'enclosing reverie' no more than a charming Romantic nostalgia. Stendhal's curt, disabused and iconoclastic manner made the reader of Gide and Proust feel at home. But this movement fizzled out, though it persisted among Beylistes who had a delightful time taping Stendhal's mystifications, footnotes, vanishing tricks, love affairs and changes of address. In the thirties left-wingers and Catholics were frosty about Stendhal's politics and withering about his atheism: he gleamed like an arid Sahara. When the wheel turned, in a second revival, we could feel ourselves to be in something like a Stendhalian situation. Existentialists found the self-inventing man sympathetic; practitioners of *le nouveau roman* looked to the novel without a centre.

In his *Stendhal: Notes on a Novelist*, Mr Robert Adams says:

Perhaps the most enchanting yet terrifying thing about the heroes of Stendhal is the sense that they define their own beings only provisionally and temporarily, in conflicts of thought and action, in negations; without enemies, they are almost without natures and wither away, like Fabrizie, when deprived of danger. I think it is this vision of human nature which allies the novels of Stendhal with the great hollow, reverberant structures of Joyce, and the legerdemain card-houses of Gide; the fact that all systems of thought and feeling are tangential to the nature of their heroes is linked to the circumstances that their central natures are themselves a dark and hollow mystery. From this aspect there is no core or centre to the Stendhal fiction, as there is none to the fiction of Joyce: the more little anagrams and puzzles of correspondence one solves, the less one finds actually being asserted. What the novel means is its shape, its surface, its structure; the arcana of society, like those of thought, are simply emptiness which returns to the surface of life and the solitude of the cynical individual.

Another critic, Victor Brombert, writes in *Stendhal: Fiction and the Themes of Freedom*, that the self-inventing man is a life-long pursuer of freedom:

> Neither is it by coincidence that the greatest ecstasies of life take place behind austere and quasi-monastic walls. Ultimately it is freedom from all worldly ambitions, an almost spiritual elation, that Julien Sorel and Fabrice del Donga achieve. . . . Freedom remains a prisoner's dream, and man's vocation is solitude.

This conclusion certainly fits with Stendhal's view that our greatest happiness is in reverie. But it is important here to recall what he wrote about the purpose of *Lucien Leuwen*: it was to be 'exact chemistry: I describe with exactitude what others indicate with a vague and eloquent phrase'. The poetry is to be in the chemistry. Love is a consciously produced effervescence; it produces its transcendant, chemical moment of '*bonheur*'; then the beautiful experiment vanishes. One returns to contemplation until the next 'moment'. And it strikes one, especially when he abruptly creates his unbelievable and preposterous scenes—in this novel the affair of a faked childbirth before witnesses—that his model for the novel was opera, the failure to invent the plausible, or perhaps a success in rising above it.

Yet a political novel like *Lucien Leuwen* is saturated in the social material it offers. It is rich in people who have been 'placed' as astutely as any in Balzac, but with more militancy. The unpopular garrison at Nancy is superbly done, for the minor characters have their own malicious concern for style and role also. They distress the hero. There are portraits of people who are drying up in futile class hatred. Stendhal is as cool—perhaps in his coolness lies the contemporary appeal—about the crude new middle class: he is exact but without the heavy hatred that is sometimes too black and white in Balzac. The following portrait of Mlle Sylvanie, the shopkeeper's daughter, is full yet compressed, poetic yet also ironically of this world. Here the chemistry is indeed exact:

> A statue of June, copied from the antique by a modern artist; both subtlety and simplicity are lacking; the lines are massive, but it is a Germanic freshness. Big hands, big feet, very regular features and plenty of coyness, all of which conceals a too obvious pride. And these people are put off by the pride of ladies in good Society! Lucien was particularly struck by her backward tosses of the head, which were full of vulgar nobility, and were evidently meant to recall the dowry of a hundred thousand crowns.

His young women have tenderness and verve: their capacity for growing into their passions is extraordinary. He is always beginning again with his characters for they too are 'making themselves'. And abruptly too. This abruptness is excellent in his portraits of young men; here no novelist in any literature or period has surpassed him, not even Tolstoy. No one has so defined and botanized the fervour, uncertainty, conceit, timidity and single-mindedness of young men, their dash, their shames, their calculation for tactics and gesture. They shed self after self and a date is put to their manners. Stendhal's sense of human beings living now yet transfixed, for an affecting moment, by their future, gives the doctrine of self-invention an ironical perspective which is not often noticeable in its practitioners today.

EÇA DE QUEIROZ

A Portuguese Diplomat

EÇA DE QUEIROZ (1845–1900) is the Portuguese classic of the nineteenth century—not an Iberian Balzac, like Galdos but, rather, a moistened Stendhal, altogether more tender, and, despite his reformist opinions, without theories. He was a diplomat, something of a dandy and gourmet, whose career took him abroad in France, Britain, the Near East, Cuba and the United States, and he was responsive to the intellectual forces that were bringing the European novel to the height of its powers. The temptations of a light and elegant cosmopolitanism must have been strong, for he is above all a novelist of wit and style, and he was amused by the banalities of diplomatic conversation.

But the foreign experience usually serves to strengthen his roots in the Portuguese idiosyncrasy: under the lazy grace, there is the native bluntness and stoicism. A novel like *The Illustrious House of Ramires* is very rich, but it also contrives to be a positive and subtle unraveling of the Portuguese strand in the Iberian temperament. The soft, sensual yet violently alluring Atlantic light glides over his country and his writing, a light more variable and unpredictable than the Castillian; no one could be less 'Spanish' and more western European, yet strong in his native character.

The fear that one is going to be stuck in the quaint, exhaustive pieties of the *folklorico* and regional novel with its tedious local colour, its customs and costumes, soon goes at the sound of his misleadingly simple and sceptical voice. The Portuguese love to pretend to be diminutive in order to surprise by their toughness. Portuguese modesty and nostalgia are national—and devastating. In an introduction to an early short story, 'The Mandarin', he wrote a typically deceptive apology to its French publishers, in which he puts his case. 'Reality, analysis, experimentation or objective certainty,' he said, plague and baffle the Portuguese, who are either lyricists or satirists:

> We dearly love to paint everything blue; a fine sentence will always please me more than an exact notion; the fabled Melusine, who devours human hearts, will always charm our incorrigible imagination more than the very human Marneffe, and we will always consider fantasy and eloquence the only true signs of a superior man. Were we to read Stendhal in Portuguese, we should never be able to enjoy him; what is considered exactitude with him, we should consider sterility. Exact ideas, expressed soberly and in proper form, hardly interest us at all; what charms us is excessive emotion expressed with unabashed plasticity of language.

Eça de Queiroz, we can be certain, did not commit the folly of reading Stendhal in Portuguese. The most exact of novelists, he read him in French, and the comedy is that he was very much a romantic Stendhalian—he was even a Consul-General—and in exactitude a Naturalist. Under the irony and the grace, there are precision and sudden outbursts of ecstasy and of flamboyant pride in a prose that coils along and then suddenly vibrates furiously when emotion breaks through, or breaks into unashamed burlesque.

He was an incessant polisher of his style. The following passage, from *The City and the Mountains*, shows his extraordinary power of letting rip and yet keeping his militant sense of comedy in command. His hero has just been thrown over by a cocotte in Paris. His first reaction is to go and eat an expensive meal of lobster and duck washed down by champagne and Burgundy; the second is to rush back to the girl's house, punching the cushions of the cab as he goes, for in the cushions he sees, in his fury, 'the huge bush of yellow hair in which my soul was lost one evening, fluttered and struggled for two months, and soiled itself for ever'. He fights the driver and the servants at the house, and then he goes off home, drunk and maddened:

> Stretched out on the ancestral bed of Dom 'Galleon', with my boots on my pillow and my hat over my eyes, I laughed a sad laugh at this burlesque world. . . . Suddenly I felt a horrible anguish. It was She. It was Madame Colombe who appeared out of the flame of the candle, jumped on my bed, undid my waistcoat, sunk herself onto my breast, put her mouth to my heart, and began to suck my blood from it in long slow gulps. Certain of death now, I began to scream for my Aunt Vicencia; I hung from the bed to try to sink into my sepulchre which I dimly discerned beneath me on the carpet, through the final fog of death—a little round sepulchre, glazed and made of porcelain, with a handle. And over my own sepulchre, which so irreverently chose to resemble a chamberpot, I vomited the lobster, the duck, the pimientos and the Burgundy. Then after a super-human effort, with the roar of a lion, feeling that not only my innards but my very soul were emptying themselves in the process, I vomited up Madame Colombe herself. . . . I put my hat back over my eyes so as not to feel the rays of the sun. It was a new Sun, a spiritual Sun which was rising over my life. I slept like a child softly rocked in a cradle of wicker by my Guardian Angel.

This particular novel savages Paris as the height of city civilization, a wealthy Utopia; it argues for the return to nature in the Portuguese valleys. Eça de Queiroz can still astonish us in this satire with his catalogue of mechanical conveniences. They are remarkably topical. (His theatre-telephone, for example, is our television or radio.) The idea of a machine civilization that has drained off the value of human life recalls Forster's *The Machine Stops*. Maliciously Queiroz describes our childish delight in being ravished by a culture of affluence or surfeit. He was in at the birth of boredom and conspicuous waste. One brilliant fantasy of the hero is that he is living in a city where the men and women are simply made of newspaper, where the houses are made of books and pamphlets and the streets paved with them. Change printed-matter to the McLuhanite Muzak culture of today, and the satire is contemporary. The hero returns to the droll, bucolic kindness of life in Portugal, in chapters that have the absurd beauty of, say, Oblomov's dream.

The prose carries this novel along, but one has to admit there is a slightly faded *fin de siècle* air about it. *The Illustrious House of Ramires* is a much better rooted and more ambitious work. Obviously his suggestion that the Portuguese are not experimentalists is a Portuguese joke, for the book is a novel within a novel, a comedy of the relation of the unconscious with quotidian experience. One is tricked at first into thinking one is caught up in a rhetorical tale of chivalry *à la* Walter Scott; then one changes one's mind and treats its high-flown historical side as one of those Romances that addled the mind of Don Quixote; finally one recognizes this element as an important part of psychological insight. What looks like old hat reveals its originality.

Ramires is an ineffectual and almost ruined aristocrat who is rewriting the history of his Visigothic ancestors in order to raise his own morale. It is an act of personal and political therapy. He is all for liberal reform, but joins the party of Regenerators or traditionalists whose idea is to bring back the days of Portugal's greatness. Ramires revels in the battles, sieges and slaughterings of his famous family and—while he is writing this vivid and bloody stuff—he is taking his mind off the humiliations of his own life. The heir of the Ramires is a dreamer. He is a muddler and his word is never to be relied on. He shuffles until finally he gets himself in the wrong. This is because he is timid and without self-confidence: he deceives a decent peasant over a contract and then, losing his self-control when the peasant protests, has him sent to prison on the pretext that the man tried to assault him. Then rage abates and he hurriedly gets the man out of prison.

Ramires has a long feud with a local philandering politician of the opposite party, because this man has jilted his sister; yet, he makes it up with the politician in order to get elected as a deputy—only to see that the politician does this only to be sure of seducing the sister. The price of political triumph is his sister's honour and happiness. How can he live with himself after that? Trapped continually by his pusillanimity, he tries to recover by writing one more chapter of his novel of chivalry, fleeing to an ideal picture of himself. What saves him—and this is typical of the irony of Queiroz—is his liability to insensate physical rage, always misplaced. He half kills a couple of ruffians on the road by horsewhipping them and, incidentally, gives a fantastically exaggerated account of the incident; but the event and the lie give him self-confidence. He is a hero at last! He begins to behave with a comic mixture of cunning and dignity. He saves his sister, becomes famous as a novelist, long-headedly makes a rich marriage, and tells the King of Portugal that he is an upstart. Total triumph of luck, accident, pride, impulse in a helplessly devious but erratically generous character loved by everyone. Tortured by uncertainty, carried away by idealism and feeling, a curious mixture of the heroic and the shady, he has become welded into a man.

And who is this man? He is not simply Ramires, the aristocrat. He is—Portugal itself: practical, stoical, shifty, its pride in its great past, its pride in pride itself raging inside like an unquenchable sadness. There is iron in the cosiness of Queiroz. He has the disguised militancy of the important comedians. His comic scenes are very fine, for there is always a serious or symbolical body to them. His sensuality is frank. His immense detail in the evocation of Portuguese life is always on the move;

and the mixture of disingenuousness and genuine feeling in all his characters makes every incident piquant.

A match-making scene takes place in the boring yet macabre crypt where the ancestors of Ramires are buried. Ramires knows his ancestors would have killed his sister's lover; all *he* can do is to pray feverishly that her silly, jolly, cuckolded husband will never find out. Prudence and self-interest suggest caution; not mere caution but an anxious mixture of politeness, kindness, worldly-wisdom and a stern belief in dignity, if you can manage it, plus the reflection that even the most inexcusable adulteries may have a sad, precious core of feeling. Ramires is not a cynic; nor is Eça de Queiroz. He is saved from that by his lyrical love of life, his abandonment—for the moment—to the unpredictable sides of his nature; in other words, by his candour and innocence. His people live by their imagination from minute to minute. They are constantly impressionable; yet they never lose their grasp of the practical demands of their lives—the interests of land, money, illness, politics.

In the historical pages of Ramires's historical novel, there is a double note, romantic yet sardonic. The scenes are barbarous and bloody—they express the unconscious of Ramires, the dreams that obsess him and his nation—but the incidental commentary is as dry as anything in Stendhal. During a siege:

> The bailiff waddled down the blackened, spiral stairway to the steps outside the keep. Two liegemen, their lances at their shoulders, returning from a round, were talking to the armourer who was painting the handles of new javelins yellow and scarlet and lining them up against the wall to dry.

Yet a few lines farther down, we shall see a father choose to see his son murdered, rather than surrender his honour. The violence of history bursts out in Ramires's own life in the horse-whipping scene I have mentioned earlier. The sensation—he finds—is sublime. But when Ramires gets home his surprise at the sight of real blood on his whip and clothes shatters him. He does not want to be as murderous as the knights of old. He is all for humanity and charity. He was simply trying to solve his psychological difficulty: that he had never, in anything until then, imposed his own will, but had yielded to the will of others who were simply corrupting him and leaving him to wake up to one more humiliation. It is a very contemporary theme.

The making of this novel and indeed all the others, is the restless mingling of poetry, sharp realism and wit. Queiroz is untouched by the drastic hatred of life that underlies Naturalism: he is sad rather than indignant that every human being is compromised; indeed this enables him to present his characters from several points of view and to explore the unexpectedness of human nature. The elements of self-surprise and self-imagination are strong; and his excellent prose glides through real experience and private dream in a manner that is leading on toward the achievements of Proust. His translators have done their difficult task pretty well: Roy Campbell being outstanding.

GALDOS

A Spanish Balzac

Perez Galdos is the supreme Spanish novelist of the 19th century. His scores of novels are rightly compared with the work of Balzac and Dickens who were his masters, and even with Tolstoy's. Why then has he been almost totally neglected by foreigners? One reason is that wherever Spanish city life had anything in common with Western European societies, it appeared to be out of date and a provincial parody; and where there was no resemblance it was interpreted by foreign collectors of the outlandish and picturesque. One of the anglicized characters in his longest novel *Fortunata and Jacinta* returns to England saying, bitterly, that all the British want from Spain is tourist junk—and this in 1873! One could read the great Russians without needing to go to Russia; their voice carried across the frontiers. To grasp Galdos—it was felt—one had to go to Spain and submit to Spanish formality, pride and claustrophobia. Few readers outside of academic life did so.

These objections no longer have the same force and it is more likely that the great achievement of Galdos can be recognized here today. A few years ago, his short novel *The Spendthrifts* (*La de Bringas*) was translated by Gerald Brenan and Gamel Woolsey and now we have Lester Clark's complete translation of the 1,100 pages of his most ambitious novel. It takes its place among those Victorian masterpieces that have presented the full-length portrait of a city.

The originality of Galdos springs, in part, from the fact that he was a silent outsider—he was brought up in the Canaries under English influences. In time he learned how to drift to the Spanish pace and then, following Balzacian prescription and energy, set out to become 'the secretary of history'. He is reported to have been a quiet and self-effacing man and this novel gets its inspiration from the years he spent listening to the voices of Madrid. His intimacy with every social group is never the sociologist's; it is the personal intimacy of the artist, indeed it can be said he disappears as a person and *becomes* the people, streets and kitchens, cafés and churches. This total absorption has been held against him: the greatest novelists, in some way, impose—the inquirer does not. Yet this very passivity matches a quality in Spanish life; and anyway he is not the dry inquirer; his inquiry is directed by feeling and especially by tolerant worship of every motion of the heart, a tenderness for its contradictions and its dreams, for its everyday impulses and also for those that are vibrant, extreme—even insane. He is an excellent story-teller, he loves the inventiveness of life itself. Preaching nothing overtly, he is a delicate and patient psychologist. It is extraordinary to find a novel written in the 1880s that documents the changes in the cloth trade, the rise and fall of certain kinds of café, the habits of usurers, politicians and catholic charities but also probes the fantasies and dreams of the characters and follows their inner thoughts. Galdos is fascinated by the psychology of imitation and the primitive unconscious. He changes the 'point of view' without regard to the rules of the novelist's game. We are as sure of the likeness of each character as we are of the figures in a Dutch painting and yet they are never set or frozen, they are always moving in space in the Tolstoyan fashion. The secret of the gift of Galdos lies, I think, in his timing, his leisurely precision and above all in his ear for dialogue; his people live in speech, either to themselves or to each other. He was a born assimilator of speech of all kinds from the rich skirling dialect of the slums or the baby-language of lovers, to the even more difficult speech of people who are trying to express or evade more complex thoughts.

The dramatic thread that runs through the panorama of life in Madrid in 1873 is the story of the love and destructive jealousy of two women. Fortunata is a beautiful and ignorant slum girl who is seduced by the idle son of rich shopkeepers before his marriage and bears him a son who dies. Jacinta becomes the young man's beautiful but pathetic wife, tormented less by her husband's love affairs than by the fact that she cannot bear children. The deserted Fortunata takes up a life of promiscuity from which a feeble and idealistic young chemist sets about rescuing her. She longs to be a respectable wife and is bullied into going into a convent for a time so that she can be reformed. But she cannot get over her love of her seducer and although she comes out of the convent and marries the chemist, she feels no affection for him. He is indeed impotent, and going from one philosophical or religious mania to another, ends by becoming insane and murderous in his jealousy of her first lover who has resumed the pursuit. It becomes a battle, therefore, between the bourgeois wife and the loose woman. Fortunata is a tragic figure of the people, a victim of her own sensual impulses who, in the end, has a second child by her seducer and regards herself as his true respectable wife because the other is barren. But her child is taken over by the rich and legitimate wife and Fortunata dies raging. The scene is overwhelming. The last time I wept over a novel was in reading *Tess* when I was 18. Fifty years later Fortunata has made me weep again. Not simply because of her death but because Galdos had portrayed a woman whole in all her moods. In our own 19th-century novels this situation would be melodramatic and morally over-weighted—see George Eliot's treatment of Hetty Sorrel—but in Galdos there is no such excess. The bourgeois wife is in her limited way as attractive as Fortunata.

Among the large number of Fortunata's friends, enemies and neighbours, there are two or three portraits that are in their own way as powerful as hers. First there is Mauricia la Dura, an incorrigible, violent and drunken prostitute to whom Fortunata is drawn against her will in the convent. Mauricia attracts by the terror and melancholy of her face. She is a genuine Spanish primitive. There is a long and superb scene in which she manages to get hold of some brandy in the convent and passes from religious ecstasy to blasphemy, theft and violence. It is a mark of the great novelist that he can invent a fantastic scene like this and then, later on, take us into the mind of the violent girl after she has got over her mania. Galdos knows how to return to the norm:

'I was beside myself. I only remember I saw the Blessed Virgin and then I wanted to go into the church to get the Holy Sacrament. I dreamt I ate the Host—I've never had such a bad bout. . . . The things that go through your mind when the devil goes to your head. Believe me because I'm telling you. When I came to my senses I was so ashamed. . . . The only one I hated was that Chaplain. I'd have bitten chunks out of him. But not the nuns. I wanted to beg their forgiveness; but my dignity wouldn't let me. What upset me most was having thrown a bit of brick at Doña Guillermina, I'll never forget that—never —And I'm so afraid that when I see her coming along the street my face colours up and I go by on the other side so that she won't see me.'

Doña Guillermina, a rich woman who has given up everything for the rescue work, is another fine portrait of the practical good-humoured saint, a sort of Santa Teresa who— and this shows the acuteness of the novelist's observation—can be frightened, a shade automatic, and sometimes totally at a loss. Against her must be placed Doña Lupe, a lower-middle-class moneylender. She is a miser who shouts to her maid:

'Clean your feet on the next-door shoe-scraper . . . because the fewer people who use ours, the more we gain.'

But at the wedding of Fortunata to her nephew we recognise Doña Lupe as more than a grotesque. Galdos is superior to Balzac in not confining people to a single dominant passion:

> Once back in the house, Doña Lupe seemed to have burst from her skin for she grew and multiplied remarkably. . . . You would have thought there were three or four widow Jaurequis in the house, all functioning at the same time. Her mind was boiling at the possibility of the lunch not going well. But if it turned out well what a triumph! Her heart beat violently, pumping feverish heat all over her body, and even the ball of cottonwool at her breast [she had had one breast removed] seemed to be endowed with its share of life, being allowed to feel pain and worry.

The final large character is Max, the husband of Fortunata. She dislikes him, but he has 'saved' her. Puny and sexless, Max begins to seek relief in self-aggrandizement, first of all in prim and ingenuous idealism; when he realizes his marriage is null and that his 'cure' of Fortunata is a failure, he turns to experimenting with pills and hopes to find a commerical cure-all. His efforts are incompetent and dangerous. The next stage is paranoia caused by sexual jealousy. He moves on to religious mania: thinks of murder and then invites his wife to join him in a suicide pact, in order to rid the world of sin. For a while he is mad and then, suddenly, he recovers and 'sees his true situation'—but recovery turns him into a blank non-being. Here we see Galdos' belief in imitative neurosis, for in a terrible scene poor Fortunata is infected with her husband's discarded belief in violence. She declares she will love him utterly, if only he will go and murder her libertine lover. But Max has fallen into complete passivity: he enters a monastery where he will become a solitary mystic—and he does not realize that the monastery he has chosen is, in fact, an asylum.

It is surprising to find this Dostoevskian study in Galdos but, of course, Spanish life can offer dozens of such figures. They are examples of what Spanish writers have often noted: the tendency of the self to be obdurately as it is and yet to project itself into some universal extreme, to think of itself mystically as God or the universe. But usually—as Galdos showed in his portrait of the ivory-carving civil servant in *The Spendthrifts*—such characters are simply bizarre and finicking melancholics. Around them stand the crowd of self-dramatizers in the old cafés, the pious church-going ladies, the various types of priest, the shouters of the slums. What is more important is his ability to mount excellent scenes, and in doing so, to follow the feelings of his people with a tolerant and warm detachment. He is never sentimental. There is one fine example of his originality and total dissimilarity from other European novelists in his long account of Jacinta's honeymoon. The happy girl cannot resist acting unwisely: little by little she tries to find out about her husband's early love affair, mainly to increase the excitement of her own love. No harm comes of this dangerous love game, but we realize that here is a novelist who can describe early married life without reserves and hit upon the piquancy that is its spell. I can think of no honeymoon in literature to match this one. The fact is that Galdos accepts human nature without resentment.

MACHADO DE ASSIS

A Brazilian

FEW ENGLISH READERS had heard of Machado de Assis before 1953. His novel *Braz Cubas* was translated in that year by William Grossman, under the title of *Epitaph for a Small Winner*, forty-five years after his death. There was also a very good translation published in 1955, by E. Percy Ellis. Since then we have been able to read *Dom Casmurro*, a collection of stories called *The Psychiatrist*, and *Esau and Jacob*, which has awkward inflections of truck-driver's American in the dialogue. Assis is spoken of as Brazil's greatest novelist. He was born in 1839 and his work comes out of the period marked by the fall of the monarchy, the liberation of the slaves and the establishment of the Republic. He pre-dates the later European immigration which was to change the great cities of Brazil completely and introduce new Mediterranean and Teutonic strains into the Brazilian character.

Assis said that his simple novels were written 'in the ink of mirth and melancholy'. The simplicity is limpid and delightful, but it is a deceptive distillation. One is always doubtful about how to interpret the symbolism and allegory that underlie his strange love stories and his impressions of a wealthy society. The picture of Rio could not be more precise, yet people and city seem to be both physically there and not there. The actual life he evokes has gone, but it is reillumined or revived by his habit of seeing people as souls fluttering like leaves blown away by time. In this he is very modern: his individuals have the force of anonymities. His aim, in all his books, seems to be to rescue a present moment just before it sinks into the past or reaches into its future. He is a mixture of comedian, lyrical poet, psychological realist and utterly pessimistic philosopher. We abruptly fall into dust and that is the end. But it would be quite wrong to identify him with, the sated bankers, politicians, sentimental roués and bookish diplomats who appear in the novels. His tone is far removed from the bitter-sweet mockery and urbane scepticism of, say, Anatole France; and it is free of that addiction to rhetorical French romanticism which influenced all South American literature during the nineteenth century. He eventually became an Anglophile.

Epitaph for a Small Winner was a conscious break with France. It is a lover's account of an affair with a friend's wife. The affair is broken—perhaps luckily—by circumstance and the writer concludes that there was a small surplus of fortune in his life: 'I had no progeny, I transmitted to no one the legacy of our misery.' To get a closer idea of Assis, one must think chiefly of Sterne, Swift and Stendhal. He is an exact, original, economical writer, who pushes the machinery of plot into the background. His short chapters might be a moralist's notes. Like Sterne, he is obsessed with Time, eccentric, even whimsical; like Stendhal, accurate and yet passionate; like Swift, occasionally savage. But the substance is Brazilian. It is not a matter of background, though there is the pleasure of catching sight of corners of Rio and Petropolis—the little St Germain up in the mountains where Court society used to go to get out of the damp heat. Some of the spirit caught by Assis still survives in Rio: under the gaiety there is something grave; under the corruption something delicate; under the fever something passive and contemplative. The Portuguese *saudade* can be felt within the violence; and a preoccupation with evasive manoeuvre, as it occurs in games or elaborate artificial comedy, is a constant recourse and solace, in every department of life. Like the Portuguese before Salazar, the Brazilians attempted to circumvent their own violence by playing comedies.

Assis' career could be seen as a triumph of miscegenation. He was born in one of the *favelas* or shack slums that are dumped on the hills in the very centre of Rio, the son of a mulatto house-painter and a Portuguese woman. She died and he had no education beyond what he picked up in an aristocratic house where his stepmother worked as a cook. He learned French from the local baker, got a job as a typesetter and eventually turned journalist. It is not surprising that he was sickly, epileptic and industrious and that one of his interests was insanity. Like many other Latin American writers, he supported himself by working in the civil service; but in his spare time he wrote thirty miscellaneous volumes and became President of the Brazilian Academy.

It is said that he is even more admired in Brazil for his short stories than for his novels and from the small selection called *The Psychiatrist*, one can see why: here the dreamy monotone of his novels vanishes. From story to story the mood changes. He astonishes by passing from satire to artifice, from wit to the emotional weight of a tale like 'Midnight Mass' or to the terrible realism of 'Admiral's Night,' a story of slave-hunting which could have come out of Flaubert. In a way, all the novels, of Assis are constructed by a short-story-teller's mind, for he is a vertical, condensing writer who slices through the upholstery of the realist novel into what is essential. He is a collector of the essences of whole lives and does not labour with chronology, jumping back or forward confidently in time as it pleases him. A man will be described simply as handsome or coarse, a woman as beautiful or plain; but he will plunge his hand into them and pull out the vitalizing paradox of their inner lives, showing how they are themselves and the opposite of themselves and how they are in flux.

In *Esau and Jacob* there is a fine comic portrait of the pushing wife of a wobbly politician who has just lost his governorship. She is a woman who kisses her friends 'as if she wanted to eat them alive, to consume them, not with hate, to put them inside her, deep inside'. She revels in power and—a quality Assis admires in his women—is innocent of moral sense:

It was so good to arrive in the province, all announced, the visits aboard ship, the landing, the investitures, the officials' greetings. . . . Even the vilification by the opposition was agreeable. To hear her husband called tyrant, when she knew he had a pigeon's heart, did her soul good. The thirst for blood that they attributed to him, when he did not even drink wine, the mailed fist of a man that was a kid glove, his immorality, barefaced effrontery, lack of honour, all the unjust strong names, she loved to read as if they were eternal truths—where were they now?

The grotesque, Assis says in one of his epigrams, is simply ferocity in disguise: but here the beauty of the grotesque comes from tolerance. Sometimes people are absurd, sometimes wicked, sometimes good. Timidity may lead to virtue, deception to love; our virtues are married to our vices. The politician's wife gets to work on her husband and skilfully persuades him to change parties. He is morally ruined but this stimulates his self-esteem. The pair simply become absurd. This particular chapter of comedy is very Stendhalian—say, from *Lucien Leuwen*.

Esau and Jacob is, on the face of it, a political allegory, observed by an old diplomat. He has been the unsuccessful lover of Natividade, the wife of a rich banker, a lady given to a rather sadistic fidelity and to exaltation. She gives birth to identical twin boys and consults an old sorceress about their destiny. She is told they will become great men and will perpetually quarrel. And so they do. As they rise to greatness, one becomes a monarchist and defender of the old stable traditions, the other a republican and a believer in change and the future. They fall in love with the same girl, Flora, who can scarcely tell them apart and who, fatally unable to make up her mind about them, fades away and dies. (People die as inconsequently as they do in E. M. Forster.) The meaning of the allegory may be that Natividade is the old Brazil and that Flora is the girl of the new Brazil who cannot decide between the parties. But underlying this is another allegory. One young man looks to the Past, the other to the Future; the girl is the Present, puzzled by its own breathless evanescence, and doomed. All the people in Assis seem to be dissolving in time, directed by their Destiny—the old sorceress up in the *favela*.

The theme of *Esau and Jacob* is made for high-sounding dramatic treatment; but Assis disposes of that by his cool, almost disparaging tenderness as he watches reality and illusion change places. In *Dom Casmurro* we have another of his cheated lovers. A young seminarist has been vowed to the Church by his mother, but is released from his vow by a sophistry, so that he can marry a girl whom he adores and who patiently intrigues to get him. Their love affair and marriage are exquisitely de-scribed. But the shadow of the original sophistry is long. Dom Casmurro had made a friend at the seminary, and this friend becomes the father of the boy Dom Casmurro thinks his own. When the boy grows up, Dom Casmurro finds that he is haunted by this copy of his friend. All die, for the subject is illusion. The concern with exchanged identities and doubles—very much a theme of the Romantic movement—is not left on the level of irony or paradox: Assis follows it into our moral nature, into the double quality of our sensibility, and the uncer-tainty of what we are. We are the sport of nature, items in a game.

One sees how much Assis has in common with his contem-porary, Pirandello. With the growth of agnosticism at the end of the nineteenth century, people played intellectually with the occult—one of the Assis bankers consults a spiritualist—and amused themselves with conundrums about illusion and reality, sanity and insanity. In *The Psychiatrist* a doctor puts the whole town into his asylum. But there is something heartless and brittle in Pirandello. The Brazilian is warmer, gentler. One does not feel about him, as about Pirandello, that intellect and feeling are separate. At his most airily speculative and oblique, Assis still contrives to give us the sense of a whole person, all of a love affair, a marriage, an illness, a career and a society, by looking at their fragments. There is a curious moment in the *Epitaph for a Small Winner* when we are told that the poor, wronged, unhappy woman who is used by the clandestine lovers as a screen for their affair was perhaps born to have just that role and use in their lives: the reflection is good, for if it conveys the egoism of the lovers, it also conveys the sense of unconscious participation which is the chief intuition of Assis as an artist, and which makes his creatures momentarily solid.

MARQUEZ

The Myth Makers

IT HAS OFTEN been said of the Spanish nature and—by extension—of those who have inherited Iberian influences in South America, that the ego is apt to leap across middle ground and see itself as a universe. The leap is to an All. The generalization itself skips a great deal too, but it is a help towards beginning to understand the astonishing richness of the South American novelists of recent years. Their 'All'—and I think of Vargas Llosa and Garcia Márquez among others—is fundamentally 'the people', not in the clichés of political rhetoric, but in the sense of millions of separate lives, no longer anonymous but physically visible, awash in historical memory and with identities.

After reading *Leaf Storm*, the novella written by Gabriel Garcia Márquez when he was only nineteen, but not published until 1955, one sees what a distance lies between this effort and his masterpiece *One Hundred Years of Solitude*. The young author sows the seed of a concern with memory, myth and the nature of time which bursts into lovely shameless blossom in his later book. We get our first glimpse of the forgotten town of Macondo (obviously near Cartagena), a primitive place, once a naïve colonial Eden; then blasted by the 'leaf storm' of the invading foreign banana-companies, and finally a ghost town, its founders forgotten. Shut up in a room in one of its remaining family houses is an unpleasant doctor who 'lives on grass'— a vegetarian?—whom the town hates because he once refused to treat some men wounded after a civil rising. Now, secluded for goodness knows how many years, he has hanged himself, and the question is whether the town will riot and refuse to have him buried. The thing to notice is that, like so many South American novelists, Márquez was even then drawn to the inordinate character—not necessarily a giant or saga-like hero, but someone who has exercised a right to extreme conduct or aberration. Such people fulfil a new country's need for legends. A human being is required to be a myth, his spiritual value lies in the inflating of his tale.

Far better than *Leaf Storm* are some of the short stories in the new collection, and one above all. 'The Handsomest Drowned Man in the World'. The story is an exemplary guide to the art of Márquez, for it is a celebration of the myth-making process. Somewhere on the seashore children are found playing with the body of a drowned man, burying it, digging it up again, burying it. Fishermen take the corpse to the village, and while the men go off to inquire about missing people, the women are left to prepare the body for burial. They scrape off the crust of little shells and stones and weed and mess and coral in which the body is wrapped and then they see the man within:

> They noticed that he bore his death with pride for he did not have the lonely look of other drowned men who came out of the sea or that haggard needy look of men who drowned in rivers . . . he was the tallest, strongest, most virile and best built man they had ever seen . . . They thought if that magnificent man had lived in the village, his house would have had the widest doors, the highest ceiling, and the strongest floor, his bedstead would have been made from a midship frame held together by iron bolts and his wife would have been the happiest woman. They thought he would have had so much authority he could have drawn fish out of the sea simply by calling their names.

The women imagine him in their houses; they see that because he is tall, the doors and ceilings of their houses would have to be higher and they tell him affectionately to 'mind his head' and so on. The dead god has liberated so much fondness and wishing that when the body is at last formally buried at sea it is not weighed down by an anchor, for the women and the men too hope that the dead man will realize that he is welcome to come back at any time.

There is nothing arch or whimsical in the writing of this fable. The prose of Márquez is plain, exact, subtle and springy and easily leaps into the comical and the exuberant, as we find in *One Hundred Years of Solitude*. In that book the history of the Buendía families and their women in three or four generations is written as a hearsay report on the growth of the little Colombian town; it comes to life because it is continuously leaping out of fact into the mythical and the myth is comic. One obvious analogy is with Rabelais. It is suggested, for example, that Aureliano Segundo's sexual orgies with his concubine are so enjoyable that his own livestock catch the fever. Animals and birds are unable to stand by and do nothing. The rancher's life is a grandiose scandal; the 'bonecrusher' in bed is a heroic glutton who attracts 'fabulous eaters' from all over the country. There is an eating duel with a lady known as 'The Elephant'. The duel lasted from a Saturday to a Tuesday, but it had its elegance:

> While Aureliano ate with great bites, overcome by the anxiety of victory, The Elephant was slicing her meat with the art of a surgeon and eating it unhurriedly and even with a certain pleasure. She was gigantic and sturdy, but over her colossal form a tenderness of femininity prevailed ... later on when he saw her consume a side of veal without breaking a single rule of good table manners, he commented that this most delicate, fascinating and insatiable proboscidian was in a certain way the ideal woman.

The duel is beautifully described and with a dozen inventive touches, for once Márquez gets going there is no controlling his fancy. But note the sign of the master: the story is always brought back to ordinary experience in the end. Aureliano was ready to eat to the death and indeed passes out. The scene has taken place at his concubine's house. He gasps out a request to be taken to his wife's house because he had promised not to die in his concubine's bed; and she, who knows how to behave, goes and shines up his patent leather boots that he had always planned to wear in his coffin. Fortunately he survives. It is very important to this often ruthless, licentious and primitive epic that there is a deep concern for propriety and manners.

As a fable or phantasmagoria *One Hundred Years of Solitude* succeeds because of its comic animality and its huge exaggerations which somehow are never gross and indeed add a certain delicacy. Márquez seems to be sailing down the blood stream of his people as they innocently build their town in the swamp, lose it in civil wars, go mad in the wild days of the American banana company and finally end up abandoned. The story is a social history but not as it is found in books but as it muddles its way forward or backward among the sins of family life and the accidents of trade. For example, one of the many Aurelianos has had the luck and intelligence to introduce ice to Macondo. To extend the ice business was impossible without getting the railroad in. This is how Márquez introduces the railroad:

> Aureliano Centeno, overwhelmed by the abundance of the factory, had already begun to experiment in the production of ice with a base of fruit juices instead of water, and without knowing it or thinking about it, he conceived the essential fundamentals for the invention of sherbet. In that way he planned to diversify the production of an enterprise he considered his own, because his brother showed no signs of returning after the rains had passed and the whole summer had gone by with no news of him. At the start of another winter a woman who was washing clothes in the river during the hottest time of the day ran screaming down the main street in an alarming state of commotion.

'It's coming,' she finally explained. 'Something frightful like a kitchen dragging a village behind it.'

There are scores of rippling pages that catch the slippery comedies and tragedies of daily life, at the speed of life itself: the more entangled the subject the faster the pace. Márquez is always ready to jump to extremes; it is not enough for a girl to invite two school friends to her family's house, she invites seventy horrible girls and the town has to be ransacked for seventy chamber pots. Crude or delicate an incident may be, but it is singular in the way ordinary things are. Almost every sentence is a surprise and the surprise is, in general, really an extension of our knowledge or feeling about life, and not simply a trick. Ursula, the grandmother of the Buendía tribe, the one stable character, is a repository of superstitious wisdom, i.e., superstition, is a disguised psychological insight. In her old age, we see her revising her opinions, especially one about babies who 'weep in the womb'. She discusses this with her husband and he treats the idea as a joke. He says such children will become ventriloquists; she thinks that they will be prophets. But now, surveying the harsh career of her son who has grown up to be a proud and heartless fighter of civil wars, she says that 'only the unloving' weep in the womb. And those who cannot love are in need of more compassion than others. An insight? Yes, but also it brings back dozens of those talks one has had in Spain (and indeed in South America) where people kill the night by pursuing the bizarre or the extreme by-ways of human motive.

In no derogatory sense, one can regard this rapid manner of talk—non-stop, dry and yet fantastical—as characteristic of café culture: lives pouring away in long bouts of chatter. In North America its characteristic form is the droll monologue; in South America the fantasy is—in my limited reading—more agile and imaginative, richer in laughter and, of course, especially happy in its love of the outrageous antics of sexual life.

One Hundred Years of Solitude denies interpretation. One could say that a little Arcady was created but was ruined by the 'Promethian ideas' that came into the head of its daring founder. Or that little lost towns have their moment—as civilizations do —and are then obliterated. Perhaps the moral is, as Márquez says, that 'races condemned to one hundred years of solitude do not get a second chance on earth'. The notion of 'the wind passeth over it and it is gone' is rubbed in; so also is the notion Borges has used, of a hundred years or even infinite time being totally discernible in a single minute. But what Márquez retrieves from the history he has surveyed is an Homeric laughter.

Life is ephemeral but dignified by fatality: the word 'ephemeral' often crops up in *The Autumn of the Patriarch*, which has been well translated by Gregory Rabassa—the original would be beyond even those foreigners who read Spanish.

The Patriarch who gives the novel its moral theme is the elusive despot of a South American republic and we hear him in the scattered voices of his people and his own. As a young wild bull he is the traditional barefoot peasant leader; later he is the confident monster ruthlessly collecting the spoils of power, indifferent to murder and massacre, sustained by his simple peasant mother, surviving by cunning. Still later, in old age, he is a puppet manipulated by the succeeding juntas, who are selling off the country to exploiters, a Caliban cornered but tragic, with a terrifying primitive will to survive. His unnamed republic looks out on the Caribbean from a barren coast from which the sea has receded, so that he believes, as superstitiously as his people do, that foreigners have even stolen the sea.

By the time the novel opens he is a myth to his people. Those who think they have seen him have probably seen only his double, though they may have glimpsed his hand waving from a limousine. He himself lives among the remnants of his concubines and the lepers and beggars that infest the Presidential fort. His mother is dead. He stamps round on his huge feet and is mainly concerned with milking his cows in the dairy attached to his mansion. Power is in the hands of an untrusted Minister. The President no longer leaves the place but drowses as he reads of speeches he has never made, celebrations he has never attended, applause he has never heard, in the newspaper of which only one copy is printed and solely for himself. He is, in short, an untruth; a myth in the public mind, a dangerous animal decaying in 'the solitary vice' of despotic power, fearing one more attempt at assassination and, above all, the ultimate solitude of death.

At first sight the book is a capricious mosaic of multiple narrators. We slide from voice to voice in the narrative without warning, in the course of the long streaming sentences of consciousness. But the visual, animal realism is violent and forever changing: we are swept from still moments of domestic fact to vivid fantasy, back and forth in time from, say, the arrival of the first Dutch discoverers to the old man looking at television, in the drift of hearsay and memory.

The few settled characters are like unforgettable news flashes that disturb and disappear: the richness of the novel will not be grasped in a single reading. We can complain that it does not progress but returns upon itself in widening circles. The complaint is pointless: the spell lies in the immediate force of its language and the density of narrative. We can be lost in those interminable sentences and yet once one has got the hang of the transitions from one person to the next it is all as sharp as the passing moment is because Márquez is the master weaver of the real and the conjectured. His descriptive power astounds at once, in the first forty pages where the narrator is a naïve undefined 'we', i.e., the people. They break into the fortress of the tragic monster and find their Caliban dead among the cows that have long ago broken out of the dairy and graze off the carpets in the salons of the ruined Presidencia and even have

appeared, lowing like speakers, on the balconies. This is from
the opening scene:

> When the first vultures began to arrive, rising up from where
> they had dozed on the cornices of the charity hospital, they
> came from farther inland, they came in successive waves, out of
> the horizon of the sea of dust where the sea had been, for a
> whole day they flew in slow circles of the house of power until
> a king with bridal feathers and a crimson ruff gave a silent order
> and that breaking of glass began, that breeze of a great man
> dead, that in and out of vultures through the windows imagin-
> able only in a house which lacked authority, so we dared go in
> too and in the deserted sanctuary we found the rubble of gran-
> deur, the body that had been pecked at, the smooth maiden
> hands with the ring of power on the bone of the third finger,
> and his whole body was sprouting tiny lichens and parasitic
> animals from the depths of the sea, especially in the armpits and
> the groin, and he had the canvas truss of his herniated testicle
> which was the only thing that had escaped the vultures in spite
> of its being the size of an ox kidney; but even then we did not
> dare believe in his death because it was the second time he had
> been found in that office, alone and dressed and dead seemingly
> of natural causes during his sleep, as had been announced a long
> time ago in the prophetic waters of soothsayers' basins.

Only his double had been able to show him his 'untruth':
that useful ignoramus died of poison intended for his master.
There had been a period when the President really was of the
people, the easy joker who might easily get an upland bride-
groom murdered so that he himself could possess the bride. The
dictator's peasant mother who carried on in his mansion, sitting
at her sewing machine as if she were still in her hut, was the
only one aware of his tragedy. (Once when he was driving to a
ceremonial parade she rushed after him with a basket of empties
telling him to drop them at the shop when he passed. The
violent book has many homely touches.) His brutal sexual
assaults are not resented:—he fucks with his boots and uniform

on—but when very late he comes to feel love, he is at a loss. On a Beauty Queen of the slum called the Dog District, he pours gadgets and imported rubbish, even turns the neighbourhood into a smart suburb: she is immovable and he is almost mad.

He kidnaps a Jamaican novice nun and marries her, but two years pass before he dares go to bed with her. She spends her time bargaining for cheap toys in the market. She surrenders to him not out of love but out of pity and teaches him to read and sign his name. The market people hate her trading habits and her fox furs and set dogs on her and her children: they are torn to pieces and eaten. There is a frightful scene where his supposedly loyal Minister organizes an insurrection. The old man's animal instinct detects a plot in the conspiracy. The Minister warns him: 'So things are in no shape for licking your fingers, general Sir, now we really are fucked up.' The wily President won't budge but sends down a cartload of milk for the rebels and when the orderly uncorks the first barrel there is a roar and they see the man

floating on the ephemeral backwash of a dazzling explosion and they saw nothing else until the end of time in the volcanic heat of the mournful yellow mortar building in which no flower ever grew, whose ruins remained suspended in the air from the tremendous explosion of six barrels of dynamite. That's that, he sighed in the Presidential palace, shaken by the seismic wind that blew down four more houses around the barracks and broke the wedding crystal in cupboards all the way to the outskirts of the city.

The President turns to his dominoes and when he sees the double five turn up, he guesses that the traitor behind the rebellion is his old friend of a lifetime, the Minister. He is invited to a banquet and, at the stroke of twelve, 'the distinguished Mayor General Roderigo de Aguilar entered on a silver tray, stretched out, garnished with cauliflower and laurel, steeped with spices and oven brown—and, in all his medals, is served up roast.' The guests are forced to eat him.

Márquez is the master of a spoken prose that passes unmoved from scenes of animal disgust and horror to the lyrical evocation, opening up vistas of imagined or real sights which may be gentle or barbarous. The portrait of the mother who eventually dies of a terrible cancer is extraordinary. He has tried to get the Papal Nuncio to canonize her and, when Rome refuses, the President makes her a civil saint and has her embalmed body carried round the country. Avidly the people make up miracles for her. Once more, in his extreme old age and feeble, there is another insurrection, plotted by a smooth aristocratic adviser. The president survives. In his last night alive he wanders round the ruined house, counting his cows, searching for lost ones in rooms and closets; and he has learned that because of his incapacity for love he has tried to 'compensate for that infamous fate with the burning cultivation of the solitary vice of power' which is a fiction. 'We (the multiple narrator concludes less tritely) knew who we were while he was left never knowing it for ever . . .' The 'All' is not an extent, it is a depth.

Medallions

IN ONE OF his terse utterances about himself as an artist, Jorge Luis Borges says, 'I have always come to life after coming to books.' In a general sense this could be said by most storytellers and poets, but in Borges the words have a peculiar overtone. He appears to speak of something anomalous with the dignity of one who has been marked by an honourable wound received in an ambush between literature and life. Like Cervantes, he would have preferred to be a soldier who had pride in his wounded arm and had been forced by singularity into turning to the conceits of the *Exemplary Novels* and the *Romances* out of which he made *Don Quixote*.

Among South American writers Borges is a collection of anomalies, exceptional in the first place in having been brought up on English rather than French models; towards the Spaniards outside of *Don Quixote* (English translation preferred) and Quevedo, he is condescending. He had an English grandmother and an Anglophile father who was himself a writer and who brought up his son on *Tom Brown's Schooldays*, Kipling, Wells, Stevenson, Chesterton and Emerson. The poetry of Swinburne, Tennyson and Browning was important in the Argentine family who, on the Spanish side, had been violently concerned in earlier generations in the savage South American civil wars. The boy was frail and too near-sighted to follow a military career. Father and son, both slowly going blind, went to Europe for cure and education, mainly in Geneva, Germany and Spain. They detested Paris and thought Madrid trivial. One would guess that the erudition of Browning and the abrupt images of his dramatic narratives, made the deepest impression, though one sees no trace of this in Borges's own poetry. Returning to Buenos Aires where at first he could hardly leave his house, he eventually became a librarian in a small municipal library (from which he was dismissed for political reasons at the time of Perón), and later the Director of the National Library itself.

Borges has also spoken of how, after the age of thirty, when he began to go blind, he has lived physically in a growing twilight in which the distinctions between visible reality, conjecture and an immense reading are blurred. He had to remember, and a memory, in which he is rarely at a loss for the exact words of a long poem, has become literary, and the library a printed yet metaphysical domain. It is not surprising that Berkeley and Schopenhauer are his philosophers, and no more than natural, to one so attached to English literature, that he should have read William Morris and De Quincey. In conversation with Borges one hears life emerging out of phrases and scenes from literature and this, one understands at once from his writing, is not a merely browsing habit of mind. The emergence is dramatic, a creative act, as new landscapes are imagined and populated.

Such a reader is a full man, too full for the novelist. He has said:

I have read but few novels and, in most cases, only a sense of duty has enabled me to find my way to the last page. At the same time, I have always been a reader and re-reader of short stories—Stevenson, Kipling, Henry James, Conrad, Poe, Chesterton, the tales in Lane's translation of *The Arabian Nights*, and certain stories of Hawthorne have been a habit of mine since I can remember. The feeling that the great novels like *Don Quixote* and *Huckleberry Finn* are virtually shapeless, reinforced my taste for the short story form whose indispensable elements are economy and a clearly stated beginning, middle and end.

This sounds conventional enough. But in the writer of short stories as in the poet, a distinctive voice, unlike all others, must arrest us; in Borges the voice is laconic, precise yet rapt and unnerving; it is relieved by the speculations of the essayist and the disconnecting currents of memory. Even in a banal paragraph each word will create the sudden suspense made by a small move in chess. In the story of *Emma Zung*, a woman is shown getting a letter which tells her that her father whom she has not seen for years, has committed suicide: I give the English translation in which the dry exactitude of the Spanish is weakened—but still it catches the effect he desires:

> Her first impression was of a weak feeling in her stomach and in her knees: then of blind guilt, of unreality, of coldness, of fear; then she wished that it were already the *next* day. Immediately afterwards she realised that the wish was futile because the death of her father was the only thing that had happened in the world and it would go on happening endlessly.

Why did 'she wish it were the next day'? Why would the death 'go on happening endlessly' in real life? Because she is intent on revenge. These phrases ring in the imagination like an alarm bell, and this alarm is at the heart of all Borges's writing. The endlessness, the timelessness of a precise human experience, is his constant subject. How to convey the sense of endlessness curtly—with a vividness that is, on the face of it, perfunctory—will again and again be his dramatic task.

Nearly all the stories of Borges, except the earliest ones, are either constructed conundrums or propositions. The early ones are trial glosses on the American gangster tale transferred to the low life of Buenos Aires. He moved on to the stories of the gaucho: he heard many of these from his grandmother. They begin deceptively as short, historical reminiscences and then, at the crisis, they burst into actuality out of the past; he is recovering a moment:

Any life, no matter how long and complex it may be, is made up of *a single moment*—the moment in which a man finds out, once and for all, who he is.

In his stories of the gauchos, their violence will strike us as meaningless until Borges says:

> the gauchos, without realising it, forged a religion—the hard and blind religion of courage—and this faith (like all others) has its ethic, its mythology and its martyrs . . . they discovered in their own way the age-old cult of the gods of iron—no mere form of vanity, but an awareness that God may be found in any man.

The task of the writer in each story—it is usually a fight—is to find the testing crisis of *machismo*, as if he were chiselling it all out in hard, unfeeling stone. He is very careful to keep the tone of landscape or street low—he even refers to 'insipid streets' —in order to heighten the violence. The test may not be heroic, but will contain a dismissive irony. In *The Dead Man* a swaggering tough has been boasting to an able but ageing gang-leader. The gangs are expert cattle stealers. To the young man's surprise the old leader of the gang lets him get the better of him and even sends him up-country in charge of the next job. The gang obey the new young leader admiringly: the young man has even had the impudence to take the old leader's girl. They obey and love the young man. Why? Because he is the supplanter and winner? Because they are naturally treacherous time-serving cowards? Or simply recklessly indifferent? None of these things. An ancient knowledge comes to them. They *love* the young man because he is virtually dead already. He must be loved for his moment. They are really waiting, with interest, for the time when the old leader will come up-country, take his rightful revenge and kill him.

Or again, in a superb tale *The Intruder*, there are two brothers. A girl servant looks after them. She becomes the mistress of one brother, but when he goes off on his work the other brother sleeps with her. Both brothers fear their jealousy, so in the end they put the girl in a brothel. This does not solve their problem, for both secretly visit her. What is to be done? The test of their love for each other has arrived. They take her off at night and kill her. Lust is dead and now their love for each other is secure. Or there is the tale of Cruz, a soldier with a savage career behind him, who has been sent off to capture an outlawed murderer. The outlaw is cornered by Cruz and his soldiers and fights back desperately. Borges writes:

Cruz while he fought in the dark (while his body fought) began to understand. He understood that one destiny is no better than another, but that every man must obey what is within him. He understood that his shoulder braid and his uniform were now in his way. He understood that his real destiny was as a lone wolf, not a gregarious dog. He understood the other man was himself.

So he turns against his own men and fights beside the outlaw. This is the story of the semi-mythical hero of the gauchos, Martin Fierro.

Because of the influence of the cinema, most reports or stories of violence are so pictorial that they lack content or meaning. The camera brings them to our eyes, but does not settle them in our minds, nor in time. Borges avoided this trap by stratifying his tales in subtle layers of flat history, hearsay and metaphysical speculation: he is not afraid of trailing off into a short essay, ending with an appendix, for the more settled a violent subject looks, the more we can be misled, the more frightening the drama. It will not only be seen to be true, but will have the sadness and dignity of a truth that our memories have trodden away. History, in Borges, is never picturesque or romantic. It is the past event coming back like a blow in the face.

When we turn to the fantasies of the poet in Borges we find him first of all at play with spoof learning. In one of his best known works with the extraordinary title of *Tlön, Uqbar, Orbis Tertius*, the librarian puts on a learned, dry-as-dust air of research and slyly reveals how for generations a secret society of pedestrian scholars have slowly invented an imaginary planet, complete with civilization and language derived from a faked edition of the Encyclopaedia Britannica, so that the non-existent has become established. Or in another tale he pretends to have discovered how the Idea of Luck gradually became rooted in the thought of a Compañía—a religious Order—who since ancient times have been inventing luck, little by little, by trial and error, until it pervades life and may be life itself. What they were really documenting was the monotony of life.

A more serious preoccupation comes close to nightmare. Our imaginations may be housed in intellectual constructions. The labyrinth is one. Or we may be enacting feelings, scenes or events that simply belong to 'an endless series'—a favourite phrase—over which we have no control. A fatalistic symbol of time or memory is a corridor with two mirrors facing each other: the infinitely repeated reflections are symbols of our consciousness of people, sensations and even things. Indeed things—a knife, a room, for example, and facts of landscape, having a threatening existence of their own and the dead force of inventory. In the story called *The Aleph* which contains his characteristic changes of voice, the narrator talks flatly of the death of a shallow society woman whom he had vainly loved:

On the burning February morning Beatriz Viterbo died after an agony that never for one single moment gave way to self-pity or fear, I noticed that the billboards on the sidewalk round Constitution Plaza were advertising some new brand of American cigarette. The fact pained me for I realised that the wide, ceaseless universe was already slipping away from her and that this slight change was the first of an endless series.

The narrator who is a poet heightens his pain by going to visit another poet, a boring man called Carlos Argentino Daneri who was a cousin of Beatriz and probably her lover. Daneri is

> authoritarian and unimpressive. His mental activity was continuous, deeply felt, far-ranging and—all in all—meaningless.

Daneri is writing an enormous poem which will conscientiously describe 'modern man' and everything on modern man's earth. The attack on realism and fact fetishism is obvious:

> Daneri had in mind to set to verse the entire face of the planet, and by 1941, had already despatched a number of acres of the State Queensland, nearly a mile of the course run by the River Ob, a gasworks to the north of Vera Cruz, the leading shops in the Conception quarter of Buenos Aires, the villa of Mariana Cambaceres de Alvear in the Belgrano section of the Argentine capital, and a Turkish baths establishment not far from the well known Brighton Aquarium.

In this curtly sarcastic comedy of jealousy over the grave of Beatriz Viterbo, Borges is leading us by the nose. He is preparing us for one of his eloquent imaginative leaps out of the dead world of things into a rhapsody on the tragedy of human loss. Daneri is annoyed that the narrator does not praise his poem and, knowing his man, says that embedded in the stairs of his cellar he possesses a great wonder which has inspired him and which will vanish tomorrow because the house is going to be pulled down. The wonder is a magic stone called the Aleph. The Aleph is the microcosm of the alchemists and Kabbalists, 'our true proverbial friend' (he calls it) 'the multum in parvo':

> Go down into the cellar, you can babble with all Beatriz Viterbo's images.

The narrator is locked in the cellar. He sees the stone which is only an inch wide:

In that single gigantic instance I saw millions of acts both delightful and awful; not one of them amazed me more than the fact that all of them occupied the same point in space, without overlapping or transparency. . . . I saw, close up, unending eyes watching themselves in me as in a mirror; I saw all the mirrors on earth and none of them reflected me; I saw in a backyard of Soler Street the same titles that thirty years before I'd seen in the entrance of a house in Fray Bentos; I saw bunches of grapes, snow, tobacco, lodes of metal, steam; I saw convex equatorial deserts and each one of their grains of sand; I saw a woman in Inverness whom I shall never forget; I saw her tangled hair, her tall figure; I saw the cancer in her breast; I saw a ring of baked mud in a sidewalk, where before there had been a tree. . . . I saw in a closet in Alkmaar a terrestrial globe betweeen two mirrors that multiplied it endlessly. . . . I saw in the drawer of a writing table (and the handwriting made me tremble) unbelievable, obscene, detailed letters, which Beatriz had written to Carlos Argentino; I saw the circulation of my own dark blood; I saw the coupling of love and the modification of death. . . .

The story ends in what is a typical Borges manner. There is a short discussion of the metaphysical theories about the Aleph which contains the malicious phrase 'Incredible as it may seem, I believe that the Aleph of Garay Street was a false Aleph':

Our minds are porous and forgetfulness seaps in. I myself am distorting and losing, under the wearing away of the years, the face of Beatriz Viterbo.

In the story the shock of jealousy, grief and loss is transposed into a reel of mechanical effects.

In the elaborate fable of *The Circular Ruins*, a grey and silent teacher takes refuge in a ruined temple. 'His guiding purpose, though it was supernatural, was not impossible. He wanted to dream a man; he wanted to dream him down to the last detail and project him into the world of reality.' He 'creates' this phantom, thinks of him as his son; and then remembers that Fire is the only creature in the world who would know he was a phantom. In the end Fire destroys the dreamer. What is the meaning of the fable? Is it a fable of the act of creation in art? A solipsist conceit? A missing chapter from the Book of Genesis? An experience of panic caused by insomnia or reading Berkeley? Borges says,

> With relief, with humiliation, with terror, he understood that he too was a mere appearance dreamt by another.

One can argue that the later Borges is a learned pillager of metaphysical arguments: one who has made Chesterton rhapsodic, put blood into the diagrams of Euclid, or a knife into the hands of Schopenhauer, but the test of the artist is—Can he make his idea walk, can he place it in a street, a room, can he 'plant' the aftermath of the 'moment of truth'? Borges *does* pass this test. The poet is a master of the quotidian, of conveying a whole history in two or three lines that point to an exact past drama and intensify a future one.

To go back to the tale of Emma Zung. We see her preparing to avenge her father's death. To kill is a degrading act; first of all, therefore, she has to initiate herself into degradation by posing as a prostitute and sleeping with a sailor. She tears up the money he leaves her because to destroy money is impiety.

> Emma was able to leave without anyone seeing her; at the corner she got on a Lacroze streetcar heading west. She selected, in keeping with her plan, the seat farthest toward the front so that her face would not be seen. Perhaps it comforted her to verify in the insipid movement along the streets that what had happened had not contaminated things.

A small fact creates the impression of a link with some powerful surrounding emotion or some message from the imagination or myth. The very casualness of the sudden observation suggests the uncertainty by which our passions are surrounded.

Borges loves to borrow from other writers, either good or second-rate. He admires Poe who defined for all time what a short story intrinsically is. He certainly has been influenced by Kafka—he translated *The Castle* into Spanish—although he is far from being a social moralist. On the face of it he looks like one of the European cosmopolitans of the first thirty years of this century and, like them, very much a formalist. But on second thoughts one sees that his mind is not in the least European. The preoccupation with isolation, instant violence and the metaphysical journey of discovery or the quest for imagined treasure, marks him as belonging to the American continents. His sadness is the colonial sadness, not the European.

A bookish comment occurs to me. A few years ago when I was reading Borges for the first time I read two of the very late stories of Prosper Mérimée: *Lokis* and *La Vénus d'Ille*. There is a vast difference between the French Romantic and Borges, but they have one or two singular things in common. A short story writer cannot help being struck by the similarities that, in the course of more than 100 years, have diverged. Both writers have the English coolness and *humeur*, the background of the linguistic, historical, archaeological and mystical erudition. Mérimée was very much the wounded man, cold and detached, conservative and rational, but he had the civilized Romantic's fascination with the primitive and the unbelievable. In these two late stories—possibly because of a personal crisis—he is suddenly concerned with dream and the unconscious. It is true that the polished and formal Mérimée plays with his metaphysical anxieties, and has no interest in the self-creating man or woman, but he shares with Borges a love of hoaxing pedantry and the common approach of the misleading essay. The terrible story *Lokis* affects to arise in the course of a serious study of the Lithuanian language. (Mérimée was a philologist, so is Borges.)

Mérimée uses his learning to play down his subject for it will suddenly become a fantastic dream of the unconscious turned into gruesome reality. The same may be said of Mérimée's tale of Corsican vendetta and in the ghost story of *La Vénus d'Ille*.

A hundred and thirty years separate Mérimée and Borges. Where Mérimée's documentation is a closed study of folklore or custom, Borges takes a leap into space, into the uncertain, the mysterious and the cunning. The record has become memory feeding on memory, myth feeding on myth. Where Mérimée is the master of anecdote in which lives end when the artist decides, Borges has the poet's power to burst the anecdote open. He seems to say that the story must be open, because I, too, am like my characters, part of an endless series or repetitions of the same happenings. The risk is—and there are some signs of this already—that criticism of Borges will become an accretion that will force us to see his stories as conceits alone.

List of Books

List of Books

Books referred to

BORIS PASTERNAK

An Essay in Autobiography. Introduction by Edward Crankshaw. Translated by Manya Harari, 1959.
Prose and Poems. Edited by Stefan Schimanski. Introduction by J. M. Cohen. Translated by Beatrice Scott, Robert Payne, and J. M. Cohen, 1959.
Dr Zhivago. Translated by Max Hayward and Manya Harari, 1958.

ALEXANDER SOLZHENITSYN

August 1914. Translated by Michael Glenny, 1972.
Lenin in Zurich. Translated by H. T. Willetts, 1976.
First Circle. Translated by Thomas P. Whitney, 1968.
Cancer Ward. Translated by N. Bethell and D. Burg, 1968.
One Day in the Life of Ivan Denisovich. Translated by Max Hayward and Ronald Hingley, 1963.

ANTON CHEKHOV

The Letters of Anton Chekhov. Translated and edited by Avrahm Yarmolinsky with the assistance of Babette Deutsch, 1973.
The Letters of Anton Chekhov. Selected and edited by Simon Karlinsky. Translated by Michael Henry Heim in collaboration with Simon Karlinsky, 1973.
The Peasants. Translated by Ronald Hingley, 1965.
Eleven Stories. The Oxford Chekhov, 1950.
Life of Chekhov. By Ernest Simmons, 1950 and 1963.
Chekhov: The Evolution of his Art. By Donald Rayfield, 1975.
Anton Chekhov: A Life. By David Magarshack, 1953.

LIST OF BOOKS

LEO TOLSTOY

Tolstoy. By Henri Troyat, 1968.
Russian Thinkers. By Isaiah Berlin, 1978.

IVAN GONCHAROV

Oblomov and his Creator: The Life and Art of Ivan Goncharov. By Milton Ehre, 1974.

FYODOR DOSTOEVSKY

Dostoevsky: The Seeds of Revolt, 1821–1849. By Joseph Frank, 1977.
Problems of Dostoevsky's Poetics. By Mikhail Bakhtin. Translated by R. W. Rotsel, 1973.
Dostoevsky and his Devils. By Václav Černý. Translated by F. W. Galan, with an afterword by Josef Skvorecky, 1975.
A Self-Portrait. Edited by Jessie Coulson, 1976.
The Undiscovered Dostoevsky. By Ronald Hingley, 1975.
Dostoevsky. By Konstantin Mochulsky. Translated by Michae Minihan, 1968.

ALEXANDER PUSHKIN

The Letters of Alexander Pushkin. 3 vols. Translated by J. Thomas Shaw, 1963.
Pushkin on Literature. Translated and edited by Tatiana Wolff, 1971.
Pushkin: A Comparative Commentary. By John Bayley, 1971.
Eugene Onegin. Translated by Charles Johnston, 1977.

AUGUST STRINDBERG

Getting Married. Translated and edited with an introduction by Mary Sandbach, 1972.

FRANZ KAFKA

Letters to Friends, Family and Editors. Translated by Richard and Clara Winston, 1978.

JEAN GENET

Funeral Rites. Translated by Bernard Frechtman, 1973.
The Vision of Jean Genet. By Richard N. Coe, 1968.

EMILE ZOLA

The Life and Times of Emile Zola. By F. W. J. Hemmings, 1977.

GEORGE SAND

George Sand: A Biography. By Curtis Cate, 1975.
Mauprat. With an introduction by Diane Johnson, 1978.
Lélia. Translated and with an introduction by Maria Espinosa, 1978.
The Companion of the Tour of France. Translated by Francis George Shaw, 1976.
The Haunted Pool. Translated by Frank Hunter Potter, 1976.

GUSTAVE FLAUBERT

The Novels of Flaubert: A Study of Themes and Techniques. By Victor Brombert, 1967.
Intimate Notebook 1840–1841. Translated by Francis Steegmuller, 1967.
The Dictionary of Accepted Ideas. Translated by Jacques Barzun, 1968.
November. Translated by Frank Jellinek. Edited by Francis Steegmuller, 1967.

STENDHAL

Stendhal: Fiction and the Themes of Freedom. By Victor Brombert, 1968.
Stendhal: Notes on a Novelist. By Robert M. Adams, 1968.
The Novel of Worldliness. By Peter Brooke, 1970.
Stendhal. By Joanna Richardson, 1975.

EÇA DE QUEIROZ

The Mandarin and Other Stories. Translated by Richard Franko Goldman, 1966.